WEB BLOOPERS

60 Common Web Design Mistakes
and How to Avoid Them

The Morgan Kaufmann Series in Interactive Technologies

Series Editors:
- Stuart Card, Xerox PARC
- Jonathan Grudin, Microsoft
- Jakob Nielsen, Nielsen Norman Group

Web Bloopers: 60 Common Web Design Mistakes and How to Avoid Them
Jeff Johnson

Observing the User Experience: A Practitioner's Guide to User Research
Mike Kuniavsky

Paper Prototyping: Fast and Simple Techniques for Designing and Refining the User Interface
Carolyn Snyder

Persuasive Technology: Using Computers to Change What We Think and Do
B. J. Fogg

Coordinating User Interfaces for Consistency
Edited by Jakob Nielsen

Usability for the Web: Designing Web Sites that Work
Tom Brinck, Darren Gergle, and Scott D. Wood

Usability Engineering: Scenario-Based Development of Human-Computer Interaction
Mary Beth Rosson and John M. Carroll

Your Wish Is My Command: Programming by Example
Edited by Henry Lieberman

GUI Bloopers: Don'ts and Do's for Software Developers and Web Designers
Jeff Johnson

Information Visualization: Perception for Design
Colin Ware

Robots for Kids: Exploring New Technologies for Learning
Edited by Allison Druin and James Hendler

Information Appliances and Beyond: Interaction Design for Consumer Products
Edited by Eric Bergman

Readings in Information Visualization: Using Vision to Think
Written and edited by Stuart K. Card, Jock D. Mackinlay, and Ben Shneiderman

The Design of Children's Technology
Edited by Allison Druin

Web Site Usability: A Designer's Guide
Jared M. Spool, Tara Scanlon, Will Shroeder, Carolyn Snyder, and Terri DeAngelo

The Usability Engineering Lifecycle: A Practitioner's Handbook for User Interface Design
Deborah J. Mayhew

Contextual Design: Defining Customer-Centered Systems
Hugh Beyer and Karen Holtzblatt

Human-Computer Interface Design: Success Stories, Emerging Methods, and Real World Context
Edited by Marianne Rudisill, Clayton Lewis, Peter P. Polson, and Timothy D. McKay

WEB BLOOPERS

60 Common Web Design Mistakes
and How to Avoid Them

JEFF JOHNSON
UI WIZARDS, INC.

MORGAN KAUFMANN PUBLISHERS

AN IMPRINT OF ELSEVIER SCIENCE

AMSTERDAM   BOSTON   LONDON   NEW YORK
OXFORD   PARIS   SAN DIEGO   SAN FRANCISCO
SINGAPORE   SYDNEY   TOKYO

Senior Editor: Diane D. Cerra
Senior Developmental Editor: Belinda Breyer
Publishing Services Manager: Edward Wade, Simon Crump
Editorial Coordinator: Mona Buehler
Project Manager: Howard Severson, Kevin Sullivan
Cover Design: Ross Carron Design
Text Design: Chen Design Associates
Composition: Graphic World, Inc.
Copyeditor: Graphic World Publishing Services
Proofreader: Graphic World Publishing Services
Indexer: Richard Shrout
Interior Printer: Quebecor World
Cover Printer: Phoenix Color

Designations used by companies to distinguish their products are often claimed as trademarks or registered trademarks. In all instances in which Morgan Kaufmann Publishers is aware of a claim, the product names appear in initial capital or all capital letters. Readers, however, should contact the appropriate companies for more complete information regarding trademarks and registration.

Morgan Kaufmann Publishers
An Imprint of Elsevier Science
340 Pine Street, Sixth Floor
San Francisco, CA 94104-3205
http://www.mkp.com

Library of Congress Control Number: 2002115475
ISBN: 1-55860-840-0

This book is printed on acid-free paper.

CONTENTS

v

FOREWORD

When I wrote *Don't Make Me Think*, I told readers that I wasn't going to give them a checklist of Web design do's and don'ts because I thought it was more important that they really understood just a few key principles. The truth is, I knew that a checklist—the right kind of checklist—would be very useful. But I also knew just how much work it would be to compile the right kind (like the book you have in your hands), and I knew I'd never be able to muster the energy to do it justice.

Fortunately, all authors, like all Web users, are different people. Jeff Johnson has the three things it takes to write a book like this: He's a very smart fellow, he's been at this usability game for a long time, and he's determined and methodical by nature. (He also happens to be a very *nice* fellow, but that's just a bonus—I imagine you can probably write a useful book even if you're a louse.)

Oh, and a fourth thing: He knows how to write—which in this case means he knows how to make a complicated point without putting you to sleep. (While I was writing my own book, one of the happiest moments occurred when I opened Jeff's newly published *GUI Bloopers* and discovered that he only had one short chapter on Web bloopers. Whew!)

In this book, Jeff has compiled more than a checklist: It's a catalog of design lessons, each small enough to absorb, each telling a compelling little story that everyone working on a website should hear. Some are big ("Home Page Identity Crisis"), some small ("Compulsory Clicking: No Default Text Input Focus"), but they're all important and all very digestible—perfect train or bedtime reading. They're lessons every usability expert knows from experience, but I enjoyed reading them anyway because, as usual, the genius is in the details, and Jeff's details are consistently instructive and engaging.

Gathering all of these examples, thinking them through, and spelling them out is a huge job. I'm glad somebody else wanted to do it.

Steve Krug
Chestnut Hill, Massachusetts
February 2003

ACKNOWLEDGMENTS

First and foremost, I thank Belinda Breyer, Senior Developmental Editor at Morgan Kaufmann Publishers, who served both as my boss, setting the schedule and cracking the whip when necessary, and as my helper, chasing down references, finding suitable cartoons, devising clever names for bloopers, and numbering figures. The book would have been both much later and lower in quality without her oversight, advice, and help.

Others at Morgan Kaufmann who were instrumental in getting this book project started or finished were: Diane Cerra, Howard Severson, and Edward Wade. I thank them. I also thank Chen Design Associates, Graphic World Publishing Services, and Ross Carron Design for their parts in turning my manuscript into a high quality book.

This book benefited enormously from examples of bloopers contributed by people too numerous to list here. You know who you are. It also benefited from comments on *GUI Bloopers*—this book's predecessor—submitted by readers at *GUI-bloopers.com* and online bookstores. The book also was greatly improved by the comments and suggestions of several reviewers and usability testers: Richard Anderson, Jim Bartram, Cathy de Heer, Meghan Ede, Darren Gergle, Ryan Hanau, Austin Henderson, Ellen Isaacs, Carolyn Jarrett, Robin Kinkead, Steve Krug, Jim Miller, Stu Rohrer, Gitta Salomon, and Howard Tamler. Thanks are due to Jakob Nielsen for providing information on Web trends, to Kevin Mullet for advice on graphic design issues, and to Steve Krug for advice on designing the book's figures and for writing the Foreword.

I thank several dear friends for providing supportive friendship during this long project: Chuck Clanton, Robin Jeffries, Tom McCalmont, Jane Rice, and Kathy Thompson. Finally, I thank my wife and companion, Karen Ande, for being unconditionally supportive.

INTRODUCTION

The dot-com crash of 1999–2000 was a wake-up call. It told us the Web has far to go before achieving the level of acceptance predicted for it in 1995. A large part of what is missing is quality. A primary component of the missing quality is *usability*. The Web is not nearly as easy to use as it needs to be for the average person to rely on it for everyday information, communication, commerce, and entertainment.

A Few Choice Bloopers

As an example of poor quality and low usability, look at a Search results page from *WebAdTech.com,* an e-commerce site (Figure I.1). The results are for a search that found nothing. The page has several serious problems:

> *Where am I?* Neither the site we are in nor the page we are on is identified.

> *Where are my Search results?* The page is so full of ads, it is hard to spot the actual search results.

> *Huh?* The message shown for null search results is written in such abysmal English (not to mention inappropriate capitalization), it is hard to understand.

> *What now?* The remedy offered for not finding anything is a box for searching the entire Web.

Not surprisingly, *WebAdTech* was one of the casualties of the dot-com crash; it is gone. However, many sites with significant usability problems remain.

For example, searching for my name at the Yale Alumni website yields three Jeff Johnsons, with no other identifying information (Figure I.2). The only way to find the right one is by clicking on them.

There is also the site map at a Canadian government site that seems to have been designed based on the game of bingo (Figure I.3). Not very useful, eh?

Add the following to those:

> The auto company site that pops up "Method Not Allowed. An error has occurred." when visitors do things in the wrong order

2

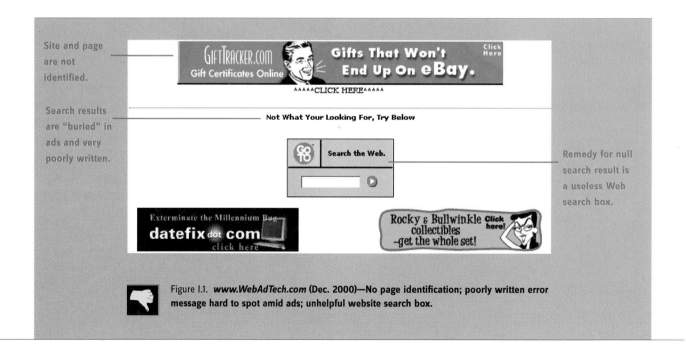

Site and page are not identified.

Search results are "buried" in ads and very poorly written.

Not What Your Looking For, Try Below

Remedy for null search result is a useless Web search box.

Figure I.1. ***www.WebAdTech.com*** (Dec. 2000)—No page identification; poorly written error message hard to spot amid ads; unhelpful website search box.

> The state unemployment form that won't accept former employer names like "AT&T" and "Excite@Home" because of "nonalphanumeric" characters

> The intranet Web-based application that displays large buttons but ignores clicks that aren't on the buttons' small text labels

> The computer equipment company site that contradicts itself about whether its products work with Macintoshes

> The airline website that can't remember from one page to the next the time of day you want to fly

> The bus company site that, failing to recognize a customer's departure or arrival city, substitutes the one in its list that is nearest—*alphabetically!*

Unfortunately, the examples are endless. The Web is *teeming* with bloopers.

Poor Usability Is Stifling the Web's Growth

Others agree that the Web is sorely lacking in usability. When I announced that I was collecting Web bloopers for a book, one fellow responded, "Man! You are going to spend the rest of your *life* collecting *Web* bloopers."

One author provides a blow-by-blow account of the frustrating experience he had trying to buy a wrench over the Web (Casaday 2001). Unfortunately, his experience elicits sympathetic grimaces from anyone who has shopped on the Web.

More systematic surveys have found the same sad truth. A recent survey of 2000 Web shoppers found that approximately half of the people surveyed were "neutral to very disappointed" with the websites they used (Rubin 2002). A Forrester report issued in April 2002 argued that the Web represents a large step *backward* in usability from desktop software (Souza 2002).

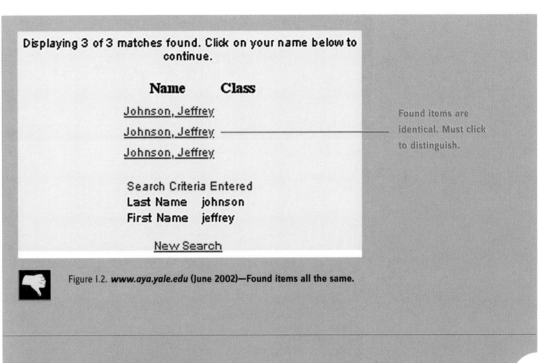

Displaying 3 of 3 matches found. Click on your name below to continue.

Name   **Class**

Johnson, Jeffrey

Johnson, Jeffrey

Johnson, Jeffrey

Search Criteria Entered
Last Name   johnson
First Name   jeffrey

New Search

Found items are identical. Must click to distinguish.

Figure I.2. ***www.aya.yale.edu*** **(June 2002)—Found items all the same.**

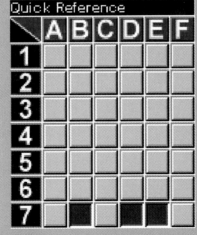

Quick Reference

	A	B	C	D	E	F
1						
2						
3						
4						
5						
6						
7						

Where would you like to go today? B6 or D3?

Figure I.3. ***www.cio-dpi.gc.ca*** **(Dec. 2000)—Cryptic site map.**

Most tellingly, a survey by Consumer's Union found that *two thirds* of Americans distrust and avoid e-commerce websites. This is higher than the percentage of Americans who distrust the federal government or—even in the wake of the Enron and WorldCom scandals—large corporations. A reporter summarizing the Consumer's Union survey suggested that the problem is mainly that e-commerce websites are not designed in a user-centered fashion:

> *These sites were often designed by computer programmers. . . . The designers frequently attempted to draw customers with technological bells and whistles while excluding the kind of practical information—return policies, for example—that's generally easy to find in a bricks-and-mortar retail setting. (Paul 2002)*

The bottom line is that for the general population, the Web is low in quality, confusing, aggravating, and insufficiently useful. Poor usability is a big part of the problem. To achieve its potential, the Web's usability must be improved.

Why Write about Bloopers?

Why did I write a book about Web design bloopers? Two reasons.

First, by pointing out common design blunders and showing how to avoid them, I hope to save Web designers the pain and cost of making those mistakes themselves. As a user-interface consultant, I review many websites for clients and find the same mistakes again and again in different sites. I'd like to help the Web industry get beyond endlessly repeating the same mistakes and move on to a point where other, higher level issues are the main concern.

Second, by showing example after example of mistakes in corporate and agency websites, I hope to demonstrate how poorly designed much of the Web is and how unacceptably

bad the experience of using it is for most people. I'm doing my part to help the Web industry realize that *poor usability* is holding back the Web's growth and success. The remedy is careful design focused on ensuring productive, enjoyable user experiences, supplemented by systematic usability testing of sites before deployment.

What Is a Web Blooper?

This book describes usability *bloopers*—mistakes—that Web designers and developers often make when designing and implementing websites and Web-based applications and explains how to avoid them. The focus is on bloopers that affect *usability*. How a website is designed also affects many other aspects of the user experience, such as brand recognition, organizational image, aesthetics, and trust. I am not an expert regarding such issues and defer to people who are (Flanders 2001; Flanders and Willis 1997; Mullet and Sano 1995).

Many of the bloopers discussed in this book are not the fault of poor design of the website itself, but of the *back* end: server-side applications, servers, and databases upon which the site depends. The point of presenting such bloopers is to convince developers and their management that successful websites and Web-based applications require user-centered, task-focused design of the *back*-end systems and the site itself. A good website cannot be slapped onto a poorly designed back end.

The bloopers in this book do not cover all of the mistakes Web designers make, or even all of the ones I have seen. To get into this book, a design mistake had to be not only embarrassingly bad but also common. There is little value in warning website developers away from rare or site-specific mistakes, no matter how horrible they may be. On the other hand, there is great value in warning developers away from common mistakes.

All Websites Have Bloopers

Every website I have ever seen has bloopers, including ones I have designed or helped design. On the other hand, every website I have seen also has *good* aspects: things its designers did well.

Committing a blooper doesn't make a site or Web-based application bad. Design requires trade-offs. Sometimes a designer must commit one blooper to avoid a worse one. Sometimes time pressure forces organizations to put sites on the Web with known bloopers. Some sites are cited in this book *both* as an example of one blooper and as an example of how to *avoid* another.

Who Should Read *Web Bloopers?*

The main intended audience for this book is *designers* and *developers* who create websites and Web-based applications. This group includes information architects, interaction designers, graphic designers, content writers and editors, and website programmers. For such people, this book is intended to serve both as a tool for self-education and as a reference. It is intended to supplement—not replace—Web design guidelines. Teachers and students of website and user-interface design may also find the book to be a useful supplement to textbooks on these topics.

A second audience for this book is *evaluators* of websites and Web-based applications: usability testers and quality-assurance engineers. People who serve these roles in a development organization can benefit from knowing in advance the problems most likely to arise in testing and watching for them.

A third target audience is *managers* of Web development teams. To provide proper oversight, managers need to be able to understand—at a functional rather than technical level—the common pitfalls in website design and how to avoid them. Managers also need to understand that successful, blooper-free websites require well-designed *back*-end systems. For managers' benefit, I provide, in Appendix 1, some advice on staffing for Web development.

A final audience is marketing and sales personnel at companies that market and sell on the Web. By understanding the negative impact of common, avoidable mistakes on usability—and by implication, sales—such readers may gain new appreciation for user-centered, task-focused design.

Origins of the Web

The World Wide Web was created in 1990 by Tim Berners-Lee to allow particle physicists to share information with each other over the Internet more easily. Before then, people shared information on the Internet using various programs and protocols: email, FTP, Gopher, and others. The Web standardized and unified data formats and file-transfer protocols, greatly simplifying the sharing of computer files. It defined HTML as the primary format for documents. Naturally, the first websites were created and hosted where Mr. Berners-Lee worked: the Centre European Research Nuclear (CERN) particle-accelerator facility in Geneva, Switzerland.

To access the Web, a Web browser is required. Tim Berners-Lee wrote the first browser and released it to the physics research community when he announced the World Wide Web. This first browser worked only on the NeXT computer.[1] Like today's browsers, it displayed "rich" text—bold, italics, fonts—formatted in HTML, and it displayed links as clickable underlined text. However, it displayed only text. Images, type-in fields, and other controls, if required by a website, had to be displayed in separate windows, using specialized browser plug-ins and protocols.

Because many early Web users did not have NeXT computers, other browsers were soon written. For example, many physicists in the early 1990s used a text-only "line-mode"

[1]NeXT computers were sold from the late 1980s through the mid-1990s.

5

browser that ran on most Unix computers. This "line-mode" browser was not at all graphical: It displayed only plain text and showed links as bracketed numbers next to the linked text (e.g., "black hole [2]"). To follow a link, you typed its number, as in many character-based library catalog systems.

The first U.S. website was put up in 1991 by Paul Kunz at the Stanford Linear Accelerator in northern California (Figure I.4). The main information available on the Web in those early days was physics experiment data, an index of physics papers, and address directories of physicists.

After 3 years of obscurity, the Web took off in 1994, when the National Center for Supercomputing Applications (NCSA) at the University of Illinois released Mosaic. Developed mainly by students, Mosaic was a graphical

"point-and-click" Web browser, available for free. Unlike the NeXT browser, Mosaic could display images. Immediately, people in technical professions began creating websites, for both work and pleasure. They were soon followed by a few pioneering online businesses. The Web began growing exponentially: 100 sites; 1000; 10,000; 100,000; 1,000,000; and so on. By the late 1990s, the number of websites was growing so rapidly that most attempts to plot it went essentially straight up.

Rise of the Web: Everybody Who Creates a Website Is a Designer

The meteoric rise in popularity of the Web immensely broadened access to information—and misinformation.

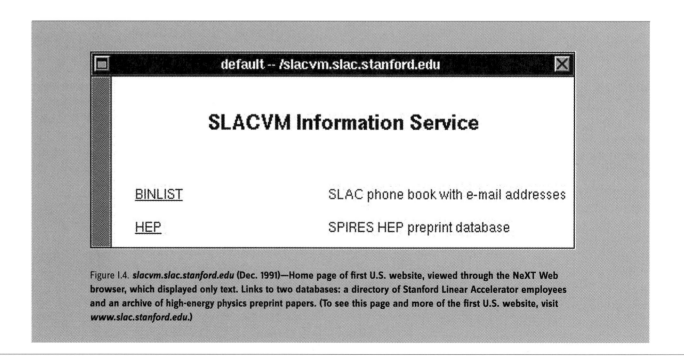

Figure I.4. *slacvm.slac.stanford.edu* (Dec. 1991)—Home page of first U.S. website, viewed through the NeXT Web browser, which displayed only text. Links to two databases: a directory of Stanford Linear Accelerator employees and an archive of high-energy physics preprint papers. (To see this page and more of the first U.S. website, visit *www.slac.stanford.edu*.)

DILBERT reprinted by permission of United Feature Syndicate, Inc.

Most relevant to this book, the rise of the Web has thrust many people into the role of user-interface designers . . . for better or worse. Furthermore, this trend will continue. Although the dot-com crash of 2001 slowed the growth of the Web, it did not stop it. At the time of this writing (mid-2002), credible estimates of the total number of websites vary tremendously—from about 10 million to 150 million—because of differences in how a "website" is defined.[2] Nonetheless, Web analysts agree that whatever the number of websites is, it is still growing.

Every one of those websites was designed by someone. As Nielsen has pointed out (Nielsen 1999a), there aren't enough trained user-interface designers on Earth to handle the number of websites that go online each year. Thus most sites are designed by people who lack training and experience in interaction and information design and usability. Put more bluntly: Everyone and his *dog* is a Web designer, and almost no one has any user-interface or interaction design training.

In addition to the explosion in the number of Web designers, we had the ascendancy of "Internet time"—extremely aggressive schedules—for Web development. Internet time usually meant no time for careful analysis of the intended users and their tasks, no time for usability testing before

The 5th Wave   By Rich Tennant

"Well, it's not quite done. I've animated the gurgling spit sink and the rotating Novocaine syringe, but I still have to add the high-speed whining drill audio track."

© The 5th Wave, www.the5thwave.com

taking the sites live, and no time for sanity checks on the soundness of the site's value proposition. From the late 1990s through about 2000, thousands of companies—many of them startups—developed websites and Web-based applications on "Internet time." Business plans were devised on Internet time, large sites were designed on Internet

7

[2]Depending on who is counting, a "website" is defined as a registered domain name, a home page, or a Web server that responds. Obviously, the number of sites counted depends on which criterion is used. Web analyst Jakob Nielsen suggests that the most credible estimate is the NetCraft survey: *www.netcraft.com/survey/*. In mid-2002, using a criterion based on responding Web servers, NetCraft estimated 37.5 million websites.

time, and back ends and front ends were implemented on Internet time. Not surprisingly, most of these efforts then crashed and burned . . . on Internet time. Lesson: Maybe "Internet time" is not such a great idea.

How Were the Bloopers Compiled?

I began collecting examples of Web usability bloopers shortly after *GUI Bloopers* (Johnson 2000) was published in early 2000 and continued collecting examples through October 2002. I found most of the examples through my own use of the Web. Some examples of bloopers were submitted by friends, colleagues, and *GUI Bloopers* readers who knew I was writing a book about the Web.

In early 2002, my publisher posted a notice on *GUI-Bloopers. com*—its website for that book—inviting submissions of examples of Web bloopers. The publisher also distributed flyers issuing the invitation. This resulted in many submissions, some of which are included.

In collecting examples of bloopers, I avoided personal websites and websites of very small businesses and organizations. Developing and maintaining a website can be expensive. Individuals and small organizations don't have much money to spend on Web development, so it isn't surprising when their sites contain bloopers. Furthermore, websites of individuals are often more for personal expression than anything else and so must be viewed with a large amount of tolerance.

Instead, I focused on larger organizations: companies, government agencies, and nonprofit organizations. All have—or at least should have—put significant effort and resources into designing and developing their sites.

All examples of bloopers in this book are dated to show when the example was collected. Many of the websites cited have been updated since the example was collected,

in some cases several times. At many cited websites, the bloopers have been corrected. Sadly, a few sites cited as examples of *avoiding* a blooper no longer avoid it. A 6-month publication lag guarantees that many more cited websites will have changed by the time the book appears. Nothing printed can keep up with the Web.

How Is the Book Organized?

The book has four main parts:

> *Part I,* Bloopers in the Content and Functionality of the Website, contains two chapters: Content Bloopers and Task-Support Bloopers.

> *Part II,* Bloopers in User Interface of the Website, contains three chapters: Navigation Bloopers, Form Bloopers, and Search Bloopers.

> *Part III,* Bloopers in Presentation of the Website, contains three chapters: Text and Writing Bloopers, Link Appearance Bloopers, and Graphic Design and Layout Bloopers.

> *Appendices:* Extra information some readers may find useful: Memo to Managers, Websites Cited, How This Book Was Usability Tested, and Related Books and Websites.

The overall sequence of parts and chapters starts with deep issues of website content, operation, and task flow and proceeds to more surface-level issues of presentation.

Throughout the book are Tech Talk sidebars presenting technical methods for avoiding certain bloopers. This is supplemental information intended primarily for Web implementers. Nonimplementors can skip these.

Web-Bloopers.com

Supplementing the book is a website, *Web-Bloopers.com*. There, readers will find:

> *Web Blooper checklist:* A terse list of all 60 bloopers discussed in the book, suitable for printing. Use it to check websites before releasing them onto the Web.

> *Discussion area:* A venue for issues and questions related to the book. Readers may use this to comment on the book, ask questions, answer others' questions, and submit blooper examples and new bloopers. The author will check this area periodically and participate in the discussion.

> *More Web Bloopers:* Additional bloopers not included in the book. This will be seeded with bloopers that didn't make the book's "final cut," but hopefully will be extended over time by suggestions from readers.

> *Sample chapters:* One or two chapters selected from the book, available for free download.

> *Purchase function:* A way to buy the book from the publisher.

> *More:* Additional content may be provided, depending on what readers request and the author and publisher decide makes sense to provide.

9

PART I   BLOOPERS IN THE CONTENT AND FUNCTIONALITY OF THE WEBSITE

CONTENT BLOOPERS

CHAPTER 1

The Web is about content, first and foremost. Web analyst Jakob Nielsen writes:

> *Ultimately, users visit your website for its content. Everything else is just the backdrop. The design is there to allow people to access the content. (Nielsen 1999)*

It doesn't matter whether a website is easy or difficult to use if it provides nothing useful, entertaining, up-to-date, or trustworthy. Few people will go there, and the few that do won't return.

To reflect the primacy of content on the Web, I begin with a chapter about bloopers in Web content. These are bloopers in the information a site provides—about products, services, or the organization itself. They are therefore more concerned with information design or information architecture (Rosenfeld and Morville 2002) than they are with Web design *per se.* Nevertheless, content is so important on the Web that any book about Web design mistakes must discuss problems of content.

© Hilary B. Price. Reprinted with Special Permission of King Features Syndicate.

14

Blooper 1: Home Page Identity Crisis

Home pages should allow website visitors to determine the site's purpose in a quick scan of the page. People want to quickly determine whether the site has something of interest to them. Home pages that don't let users easily do this commit not only a content blooper, but also a navigation blooper.

Look at the home page of PriceWaterhouseCoopers' website (Figure 1.1) and try to figure out what the company does. The home page offers few clues, so if you don't already know, looking at the home page probably won't help.

The navigation links and menus around the margins of the page could be for any business. The list of headlines in the middle suggests that it might be a business news service. The main thing suggesting the company's identity is the Who We Are section at the bottom middle of the page. What it suggests is that PriceWaterhouseCoopers is a foundation sponsoring international events.

In fact, PriceWaterhouseCoopers is a large accounting, auditing, and management consulting company. Where does it say that on its home page? On the bottom right, buried under a golf logo in hard-to-read white text, are the words . . . *Official Professional Services Firm of the PGA Tour.* Not very helpful. First, *professional services* is an

insider industry term that to outsiders means anything from lawyers to prostitutes. Second, even if you know what *professional services* means in this context, this tiny clue on the home page gives you no reason to believe that PriceWaterhouseCoopers provides services for anyone besides sports organizations.

PriceWaterhouseCoopers' vague home page is made worse by another problem not entirely its fault: The Web address most people would try in attempting to reach the site, *PWC.com,* is owned by a *different* company and takes you to that other company's website. PriceWaterhouseCoopers' site is at the much harder-to-guess address *PWCGlobal.com* (although *PriceWaterhouseCoopers.com* also works). Worse, the home page at *PWC.com* is even *less* well identified than PriceWaterhouseCoopers' home page (Figure 1.2). One can't even tell what the full name of that company is, much less its business. It looks as if it could be an e-commerce company (see later discussion), but that's not clear.

The combination of these two poorly identified websites puts PriceWaterhouseCoopers in a very bad situation. People who look for the company under *PWC.com* can't immediately tell that they are in the wrong place. And if people seeking an accounting or auditing firm happen to find *PWCGlobal.com,* they might not realize that they are in the *right* place.

Next, see the home page of Acer Corporation (Figure 1.3). What business is it in? It makes and sells computer equipment, but you couldn't tell that from its home page. To figure out what this website (and the company) is about, you have to go a few pages into the site.

Acer's home page asks, "Which word best describes Acer?" I'll guess that many visitors leave it set to *Don't know.*

Figure 1.1. *www.PWCGlobal.com* (Jan. 2002)—Home page is vague about what this company does.

Figure 1.2. **www.PWC.com** (Jan. 2002)—Home page doesn't fully identify the company, much less its business. Also has a Web address that many would expect to point to PriceWaterhouseCoopers.

Figure 1.3. **www.Acer.com** (Feb. 2002)—Home page provides few clues about what Acer does.

AVOIDING THE BLOOPER

As an example of a website that explains its identity and purpose very well, check out the home page of Earthwatch (Figure 1.4). I don't have to explain what Earthwatch is; you can tell from its home page.

Before and After: A Company Improves Its Home Page

37 Signals is a Web design firm. In early 2002, its website was clearly meant to show how unconventional and "bleeding edge" the firm was. The problem was, the home page was so unconventional that it provided no clues about what the company does (Figure 1.5). To find out what it does, visitors had to follow the link to the Start page. Not a good quality for the website of a Web design firm to have.

Predictably, the company soon realized this home page wasn't working and radically redesigned it; which is to say, the company redesigned it to be less radical. By June 2002, 37 Signals had a new home page (Figure 1.6).

Some people might say the new home page is too conventional. Okay, maybe an image or two might jazz it up a bit, but the purpose of this site is not to entertain; it is to inform. The main question to ask is, therefore, can people tell where they are, and can they find what they are looking for? Without a doubt, the answer is yes.

Essential Ingredients of a Home Page

What makes Earthwatch's home page and 37 Signals' revised home page so successful at summarizing the purpose of their respective organizations and the content of the site? These sites have most or all of the following characteristics:

> Organization name is placed prominently.

> Organization name is fairly self-explanatory.

Featured Expedition of the Week: New Zealand Dolphins

Earthwatch Institute promotes sustainable conservation of our natural resources and cultural heritage by creating partnerships between scientists, educators, and the general public.

Search

- About Earthwatch
- Select an Expedition
- Membership
- Scientific Field Grants
- News and Events
- Sign Our Guestbook
- Order an Expedition Guide
- Copyright Notice
- Contact Us
- Merchandise
- Site Map
- Earthwatch Australia
- Earthwatch Japan
- Earthwatch Europe

- EARTHWATCH: BRINGING PEOPLE TOGETHER
- NEWEST EXPEDITIONS
- SCUBA/SNORKEL EXPEDITIONS
- DISCOVERY WEEKENDS
- TEACHER FELLOWSHIPS AVAILABLE
- SPECIAL OFFERS

Earthwatch Institute operates on a very simple but radical notion: that if you fully involve the general public in the process of science, you not only give them understanding, you give the world a future. Join us. The next discovery may be yours.

Our website has been named as Best of the Web by Forbes/Best of the Web

- About Earthwatch - Select an Expedition - Membership - News and Events -
- Merchandise - Sign our Guestbook - Order an Expedition Guide -
- Copyright Notice - Contact Us - Japanese Site - Site Map -
- Newest Expeditions - Scientific Field Grants -
- Special Offers - One Week Expeditions - Discovery Weekends -

Figure 1.4. *www.Earthwatch.org* (Jan. 2002)—Home page clearly and succinctly describes what Earthwatch does.

37signals simple for sale

Signals

00 Start Here	**19** Suits Who?
01 We See People	**20** Sloganeering
02 Manager of External Reporting?	**21** A not "Q"
03 <blink>12:00</blink>	**22** B2whatever
04 Not Full Service	**23** Sightings
05 Size Does Matter	**24** My Cousin's Buddy...
06 $6,000,000,000	**25** Just Because You Can...
07 Are They Experienced?	**26** Make it Useful
08 Experience	**27** Simplicity by Design
09 And I Quote	**28** Tulipomania
10 Refugees	**29** Linkin' Logs
11 Copy Righting	**30** ASAP
12 Occam's Razor	**31** Reference
13 Eight Seconds	**32** Highest
14 Breadcrumbs	**33** What's in a Name?
15 83%?!	**34** Our Team
16 Short Story	**35** We Come in Peace
17 No Awards Please	**36** Signal vs. Noise
18 eNormicom.com	**37** SETI

Work (new 11/19/01)

Case studies for some of our latest client projects:

- Transportation.com
- Advertise with Dex
- Kicksology
- MissileLock
- Zen Hospice Project
- More...

Other

Internal projects, press clips, appearances, and other goodies:

- Design Not Found
- Signal vs. Noise
- eNormicom.com
- ShirtSignals
- NYT article
- 37Fakebank
- More...

Figure 1.5. *www.37Signals.com* (Jan. 2002)—Home page was purposely unconventional but in doing so provided no clue what the company does. Hint: It designs websites. The company's revised home page is shown in Figure 1.6.

Figure 1.6. *www.37Signals.com* (June 2002)—Revised home page clearly describes what 37 Signals does.

📄 **Why Should I Hire 37signals?** (PDF, 46K): World-class experience, real results, straight talk, and more.

design | usability reviews | workshop | our work | resources | news | contact | home

37signals simple for sale

We design web sites, conduct usability reviews, and educate people about the real-world advantages of simplicity and clarity online.

Interface Design

We offer a range of visual interface design services for web sites, intra/extranets, and web-based applications. Our focus on simplicity, usability, and clarity will make your customers happy.

Learn more

Usability Reviews

Our unique scenario-based Contingency Plan and Reality Check usability reviews provide an honest, unbiased take on your site's usability and customer experience issues.

Learn more

Workshop [NEW!]

Sign up for 37signals' "Making Mistakes Well" contingency design workshop on August 9, 2002. If you care about usabilty, don't miss this workshop taught by the industry experts.

Learn more & register now

About 37signals Q&A

How is 37signals different than other web firms?
We're a small, honest, agile team of experts with tons of experience (we've all been working on the web since 1995). We give all of our clients personal attention and are proud that 100% of our clients are references. Our obsession with simplicity and clarity in interface design is why we're called "the masters par excellence of HTMinimaLism" by the author of Fresh Styles for Web Designers, and the sites we've designed prove that usability can be elegant.

37signals highlights

Recent client projects
- Kicksology: Shoe fetish
- Tenzing: In-flight email interface
- MissileLock: Contact management interface
- FastWeb: #1 scholarship finder
- More in work...

37signals' projects and writing

> Brief textual summary of the organization's purpose is presented.

> Picture(s) illustrate the organization's product or service.

> Labels of links to other pages provide good overview of site contents.

Although all of these features act in concert to clarify the site's purpose, the most important one is the brief textual summary; it is mainly this that the sites shown as blooper examples lack.

Both the textual summary and the pictures need to make sense to organizational outsiders (assuming the site is intended for outsiders). In particular, the textual summary should not rely on industry jargon or company organization names or abbreviations.

Blooper 2: Confusing Classifications

One of the most important aspects of Web content is how it is organized. The schemes used to categorize and classify products, services, and information on a website can make or break the site, because they affect how difficult it is for site visitors to find what they are looking for. Thus content organization strongly affects navigation.

Mermaids, Suckling Pigs, Stray Dogs, and Others

The novelist and essayist Jorge Luis Borges wrote of an ancient Chinese encyclopedia containing a system for classifying animals (Weinberger 1999). The encyclopedia, probably fictional, was supposedly entitled *Celestial Emporium of Benevolent Knowledge*. According to Borges, it divided all animals into the following categories:

> Belong to the Emperor

> Embalmed

> Trained

> Suckling pigs

> Mermaids

> Fabulous

> Stray dogs

> Included in this classification

> Tremble as if they were mad

> Innumerable

> Drawn with a very fine camel's hair brush

> Others

> Have just broken a flower vase

> From a great distance, resemble flies

It is not a classification scheme that today would be considered very logical. The categories are arbitrary, overlapping, nonexhaustive, and subjective—skewed by the perceptions of the scheme's supposed author. It is these characteristics that make the scheme seem humorous to us.

Many Web designers seem to be trying to amuse us by mimicking, in their own way, Borges' "ancient Chinese" classification scheme. The problem is, Web users aren't laughing. Well, maybe you will laugh when you see some of the examples I've found of weird categorization schemes from websites, but Web users who are trying to find something aren't laughing. They're wasting time. They're getting frustrated. They're cursing at their computers. And they're hitting the Back button.

For example, check out the categories on the Binoculars page of *ZBuyer.com*, an e-commerce site (Figure 1.7[A]). The categories include Camera and Photo, Products, See more Education & How-To software, Really Cool Stuff, and Michael Lewis, among others. I'll discuss the inconsistent wording and capitalization later (see Chapter 6, Blooper 46: Inconsistent Style). For now, I am concerned about a

19

A

- Camera & Photo
- Products
- See all our Canon binoculars
- See all Night Owl gear

- astronomy and birding titles
- See more Education & How-To software
- Really Cool Stuff
- Michael Lewis

- Binocular glossary
- Telescope glossary
- Binocular buying guide
- Telescope buying guide

B

Really Cool Stuff

With our Really Cool Stuff collections, you too can adopt the lifestyle of the hip and trendy. From the Zen simplicity of making coffee to the transcendent chic of digital imaging, each collection below addresses its own funky audience.

 New Cool

 Affordable Low Tech

 Affordable High Tech

 Spy

 Always Cool

 Extravagant Low Tech

 Extravagant High Tech

 Excessive Power

Figure 1.7. *www.ZBuyer.com* (Feb. 2002)—**A** and **B**: Arbitrary, subjective categories.

deeper, more important problem: The arbitrariness and subjectiveness of the categories. It is almost as if ZBuyer's Web designers had Borges' "ancient Chinese" classification scheme in mind.

What's in Really Cool Stuff? Products to help you lead a lifestyle somewhere between Zen and extravagant (Figure 1.7[B]). That's a pretty broad category: almost anything could be in it. The subcategories of Really Cool Stuff are almost as arbitrary. The category Michael Lewis isn't a product category at all; it's about the people—two people, not just Michael Lewis—who edit this section of the site. People who really want to use this site have to browse through a lot of categories to find where things are.

The U.S. Postal Service's website employs a category scheme that is only a little more sensible than that of *ZBuyer.com*. The categories overlap considerably and it seems, at least to a postal service outsider, that what is in them is arbitrary (Figure 1.8). Here is a brief analysis of the major categories listed on the left side of the page:

> ***Online Services.*** Everything on the site is in some sense an online service and so could be in this category. However, only some of the site's functions are in this category. Are the other services—such as Business Rate Calculator—supposed to be offline?

> ***Mailing.*** Again, nearly everything you do at a postal service website could be considered to be about mailing. As long as the categories overlap so much, why aren't buying stamps and looking up postage rates considered to be about mailing?

> ***Shipping.*** To the postal layperson, mailing and shipping are the same, but to the postal service, *shipping* seems to refer only to mailing by businesses. However, notice that in the gray horizontal navigation bar near the top of the page, Mail/Ship is treated as one functional category.

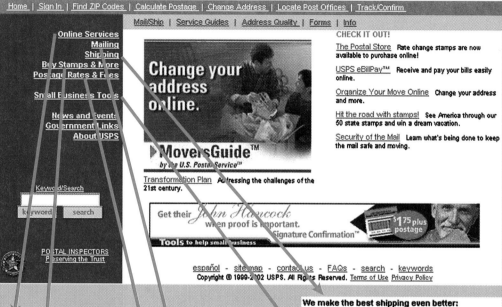

Figure 1.8. *www.usps.gov* (June 2002)—**A:** On the USPS home page, the top-level categories seem arbitrary. **B:** The pages for each category show that the categories overlap.

21

There is a separate category for small businesses, so maybe the Shipping category is only for *large* businesses.

> **Buy Stamps and More.** This might at first seem to be the category for buying things, but it isn't the only one containing functions involving purchasing from the postal service. In fact, it seems to be a miscellaneous category, not unlike Jorge Luis Borges' Other category.

> **Postage Rates and Fees.** This is one of the more sensible categories in the set. However, the categories overlap. *Rates* also appears in the Shipping category.

> **Small Business Tools.** This is more of a collection of functions—from all around the site—that are useful to small businesses than it is a true category. That may be why it is set apart from the foregoing items in the list.

Because computer-based systems make it easy and fairly natural for items to be in several categories simultaneously, it is common for categories in computer information systems—including websites—to overlap. Unfortunately, this gives site designers an excuse for haphazard design. Ideally, Web designers should carefully analyze, design, test, and revise a category scheme until it makes sense to prospective users. In practice, many Web designers concoct their site's categories quickly, then try to cover inadequacies by putting items in all the categories where they think people might look for them. Taken to an extreme, this approach leads to "categories" that each contain everything, which is not very useful. This is the primary problem with the postal service's categories.

A secondary problem is that the content of each category seems to depend on the page-designer's subjective whim.

Why Is This Here?

At some websites, the categories initially seem reasonable, until you look at what is in them. At Northwest Airlines' website, *NWA.com*, a "More Specials" category supposedly

offers special airfares (Figure 1.9). However, someone at *NWA.com* thought More Specials would be a convenient place to put two announcements about new airplanes the airline is using. Hey, it had to go *somewhere!*

Walmart.com, the website of a retail chain, makes the opposite mistake: items that should be in a category are not. On its home page is a Digital Cameras category linking to a Digital Camera Collection page. Visitors to this site probably assume that the 11 cameras listed on the Digital Camera Collection page (Figure 1.10[A]) are all the digital cameras Wal-Mart sells. Bad assumption! Clicking "See similar items" under most of the cameras displays a page showing a few similar cameras, but clicking that link under the S300 Digital Elph camera[3] displays an All Digital Cameras page that lists 17 cameras (Figure 1.10[B]). It is unclear why the Digital Camera Collection page doesn't list all the cameras. Customers could easily not happen across those extra six cameras.

AVOIDING THE BLOOPER

The eighteenth century Swedish botanist Karl von Linne—better known by his Latin name *Carolus Linnaeus*—devised a logical and objective biological taxonomic system. The categories in it are organized hierarchically and are independent, mutually exclusive, and exhaustive. Most competing biological classification systems of that day were almost as subjective and arbitrary as Borges' "ancient Chinese" animal taxonomy and thus had little scientific utility. The Linnaean system—as it came to be called—soon replaced all the others and today remains the basis for all biological classification *(anthro.palomar.edu/animal/animal_1.htm)*.

Classifying Goods and Services

Wouldn't it be wonderful if we had a Linnaean system for classifying goods and services? Assuming it became widely accepted and used in e-commerce websites, imagine how

[3]This item is missing a brand name; to see what company makes the Digital Elph, customers have to click on the link.

More Specials

| Northwest Fare Sales | WorldPerks Bonus Miles | New Routes | More Specials |

More Specials

- The Ultimate Lift Ticket Resort Listings
- Northwest WorldVacations CyberDeals
- Elite. Elated. Fly Higher with WorldPerks® Elite
- Planning a wedding? Let Northwest Airlines help you bring home friends and family to celebrate!
- Northwest Airlines Offers New A319 Aircraft
- Northwest Airlines Offers New CRJ Aircraft
- NorthBest Senior Travel Program

Figure 1.9. *www.NWA.com* (Feb. 2002)—Two items on this list are not travel specials; they are announcements about new planes.

A

WAL★MART®

Home Page | Help | Your Account | 🛒 Cart & Checkout

Electronics | Photo | Video Games | Toys | Gifts | Jewelry | Home & Garden | Sports | Movies | Books | Music

Search [Photo] for: [ ] [Find]

Digital Camera Collection

Zoom in on our Every Day Low Prices

Whether you're new to digital photography or a pro, our selection of cameras makes finding the right one a snap. From point-and-shoot pocket pals to the newest digital sensation, we have a camera you'll click with -- at a price that'll make you smile. **Learn more about digital cameras. Click here!**

This model offers point-and-shoot ease and interfaces with both PCs and Macs.
HP PhotoSmart 318 Digital Camera
NEW Item!
$198.76
▸ Add to Cart
See similar items

S300 Digital ELPH
$459.47
▸ Add to Cart
See similar items

Sony Mavica MVC-FD87 Digital Camera
NEW Item!
$397.78
Was: $498.46
▸ Add to Cart
See similar items

Sony Cyber-shot Digital Camera DSC-P30
$298.97
▸ Add to Cart
See similar items

Brio D-150 Digital Camera
$267.00
▸ Add to Cart
See similar items

B

WAL★MART®

Home Page | Help | Your Account | 🛒 Cart & Checkout

Electronics | Photo | Video Games | Toys | Gifts | Jewelry | Home & Garden | Sports | Movies | Books | Music

Search [Photo] for: [ ] [Find]

You are here: Home Page › Photo › Digital Camera Collection

All Digital Cameras

Visit our digital camera buying guide. **Click here.**

Sort this list by: [Top Sellers]

Items 1-17 of 17 Total

Samsung Digimax 210 SE Digital Camera 2.1 Megapixel
$229.00
▸ Add to Cart

HP PhotoSmart 318 Digital Camera
NEW Item!
$198.76
▸ Add to Cart

Sony Mavica MVC-FD87 Digital Camera
NEW Item!
$397.78
Was: $498.46
▸ Add to Cart

Toshiba PDR-M25 Digital Camera with BONUS 16 MB Memory Card
NEW Item!
$279.86
▸ Add to Cart

Polaroid PhotoMAX PDC 640 Plus Digital Camera
$99.88
Out of Stock

Sony Mavica MVC-FD75 Digital Camera
NEW Item!
$348.67

Canon PowerShot S110 Digital ELPH Camera
$398.86
Out of Stock

Sony Cyber-shot Digital Camera DSC-P30
$298.97
▸ Add to Cart

Figure 1.10. *www.Walmart.com* (Jan. 2002)—Main page for category doesn't list all products in category. **A:** Digital Cameras category page lists 11 cameras. **B:** All Digital Cameras page lists 17 cameras.

Relatively inaccessible
All Digital Cameras page lists more cameras.

Digital Camera main category page omits several cameras.

Most "similar items" links go to sub-category pages, but this camera's goes to All Digital Cameras.

much it would improve Web surfers' ability to find what they are looking for.

Until then, Web designers need to design their site's categories carefully. In so doing, they should try to avoid the arbitrariness and subjectivity that make Borges' "ancient Chinese" animal categories humorous and useless. Detailed guidelines and best practices for information architecture are beyond the scope of this book, but entire books have been devoted to the subject (Rosenfeld and Morville 2002). I'll simply suggest a few methods that can help designers organize a site's content usefully for its users:

> *Literature search.* Do your homework. Someone has probably thought and written about your site's topic before. Don't be afraid of research literature; it could save you reinventing the wheel.

> *Competitive analysis.* Examine sites of competitor businesses or similar organizations. What categories do they use? What's in them? How is their site structured? What did they do well? If they are a weak competitor, look for obvious flaws in how they've organized their content, and avoid those.

> *Testing.* After devising a category scheme for a site, Web designers should test it on typical users. This can be done *long* before the website is implemented, using paper and pencil or rough static on-screen prototypes. This allows designers to improve and reevaluate the category scheme several times before the site architecture and the development team become too resistant to changes.

Though innovative, unique categorization schemes may pay off for particular websites, experience shows that it is hard to go wrong if your content categories are

> Organized hierarchically

> Independent

> Mutually exclusive

> Exhaustive

> Nonarbitrary

A Site with Well-Organized Content

An example of a website with an excellent set of categories is *Yale.edu*, the site of Yale University. The top-level categories and the subcategories under them are clear, nonarbitrary, exhaustive, and sensible (Figure 1.11). This is not surprising, for two reasons. First, Yale is not an Internet startup. It had no need to rush its site to market on "Internet time." Its designers could carefully design the site. And so they did. Second, Yale's Web designers have demonstrated their commitment to good Web design by writing the authoritative and widely-used Yale style guide (Lynch and Horton 2002), and then actually *following* their own guidelines.

Maybe more Internet startups should follow Yale's example. By rushing to put sites on the Web, often with little or no usability testing before release, perhaps they are inadvertently dooming themselves to arbitrary, subjective, "ancient Chinese" schemes for categorizing whatever it is they offer.

Blooper 3: Unhelpful Descriptions

Websites often display a choice of products or services, each one with a name, a brief description, and (for products) perhaps a picture. Two things to keep in mind:

> The information about the items should allow people to determine whether any are what they want.

> In case multiple items seem relevant, the information should help choose between them.

These guidelines apply not only to descriptions of products and services, but also to descriptions of sections of the site itself.

At many websites, item names and descriptions do not help site visitors with either of these two decisions. Often, it seems as if they were written at different times, by different people, with no coordination, no consideration of how the items might best be contrasted, and no thought to how item descriptions will be interpreted in the context of the array in which they appear.

A good example comes from the website of Pitsco-LEGO Dacta, a maker of construction toys. The company has two catalogs customers can order. Unfortunately, the names and descriptions of the two catalogs appear to have been written without regard for each other (Figure 1.12). Both the catalog names and the descriptions are just noise words carrying no information in this context: "new, bigger, better," "brand-new, full-color." There is nothing here to help site visitors choose between the two catalogs. I'll bet many people simply order both and decide when they get them which one is relevant to them.

For an example of a poorly written set of product descriptions, let's look at a software download page from *Netscape.com*. The descriptions on the page aren't just unhelpful for distinguishing the items, they are actually *misleading* (Figure 1.13).

Assume that you want Netscape Communicator—the whole works: Web browser, email reader, instant messenger, calendar, and other tools. Which item would you click? The header "Netscape Communicator" naturally grabs your attention; it exactly matches what you want. However, a closer look reveals that this item is for Communicator 4.79, which at this point is almost two major releases old. What you actually want is the first item. Why is it labeled "Netscape 6" instead of "Netscape Communicator 6?"

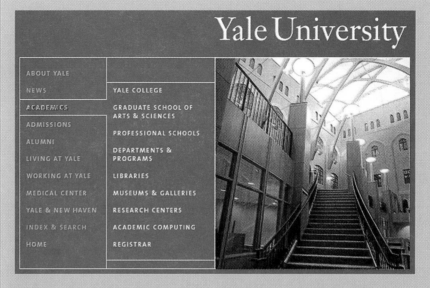

 Figure 1.11. ***www.Yale.edu*** (June 2002)—Categories at Yale University's site are clear, nonarbitrary, and sensible.

25

 Figure 1.12. ***www.pitsco-legodacta.com*** (Feb. 2002)—The names and descriptions of two product catalogs were apparently written in isolation and don't help site visitors choose between them.

Because that's what the person who added it to the page called it.

Now assume you don't want the whole Communicator package. You just want the latest browser, in this case Netscape Navigator 6. Which item would you click? The third one, perhaps? Sorry, that's an old link for downloading Netscape Navigator 4.76. To get the latest browser, you must choose the first item and perform a custom, rather than a normal, installation.

It seems that Netscape never updates a link name or description once it goes up, even if that name or description no longer is current. In fact, the list of items is not really a catalog of choices at all, but an archive of past downloads. Interesting for Netscape's developers, perhaps, but useless to Netscape customers.

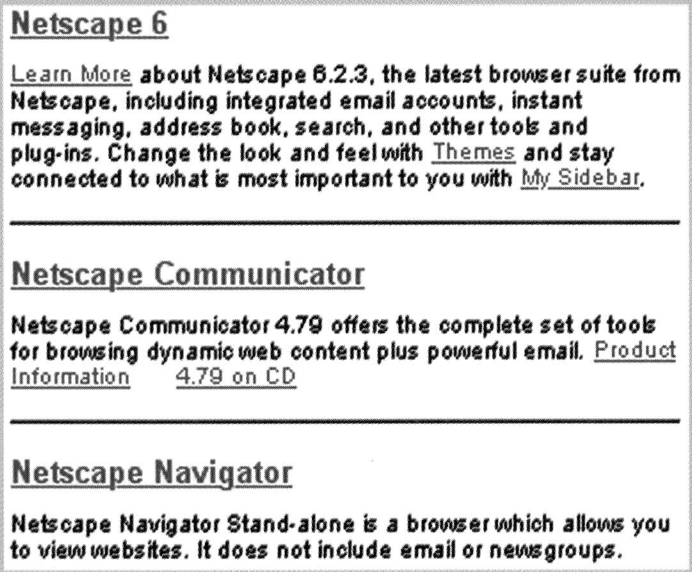

AVOIDING THE BLOOPER

When a website or Web-based application displays a set of items, information about the items must help users answer two questions:

1. Do *any* of these items match what I want?

2. *Which* of these matching items best suits my purpose?

To do that, the item names and descriptions should not consist of marketing noise words, such as new, bigger, awesome, and fully functioned! They should consist of honest descriptions of what the item does and does not do, perhaps with reference to other items that have something a given item lacks.

Also, item descriptions cannot each be written in isolation, each by its own product manager. You can't list 10 products all claiming "Does everything you need!" You also don't want items to inadvertently detract from other items. Item descriptions must be written *together,* with consideration for how they will be interpreted in context and how they contrast with each other.

The electronic products page of *SharperImage.com* provides an example of excellent descriptions of stereo systems (Figure 1.14). Visitors to this page will have no trouble understanding how products differ.

Similarly, the home page of Macromedia, a software company known for its Director and Flash products, provides good descriptions of the various sections of the site. The labels and brief descriptions of the sections of the website allow a clear choice between them (Figure 1.15).

When new items are added, old items, if they are retained, should be revisited and possibly revised to ensure that they contrast properly. Alternatively, old items can be deleted or removed to an Archive category.

Netscape 6

Learn More about Netscape 6.2.3, the latest browser suite from Netscape, including integrated email accounts, instant messaging, address book, search, and other tools and plug-ins. Change the look and feel with Themes and stay connected to what is most important to you with My Sidebar.

Netscape Communicator

Netscape Communicator 4.79 offers the complete set of tools for browsing dynamic web content plus powerful email. Product Information   4.79 on CD

Netscape Navigator

Netscape Navigator Stand-alone is a browser which allows you to view websites. It does not include email or newsgroups.

Figure 1.13.
www.Netscape.com
(June 2002)—The names and descriptions of three software download packages are not only unhelpful for distinguishing between them but also misleading.

Futuro 3-CD
Stereo with
AM/FM Digital PLL
Tuner

Slim 3-CD
Stereo

Modern Design
2-CD Stereo

Sleek Solo CD
Stereo with
AM/FM Digital
Tuner

Vertical 4-CD
Stereo with
AM/FM Digital PLL
Tuner

Figure 1.14. ***www.SharperImage.com*** **(Sept. 2002)—Products in a family are easy to distinguish from each other by their pictures and descriptions.**

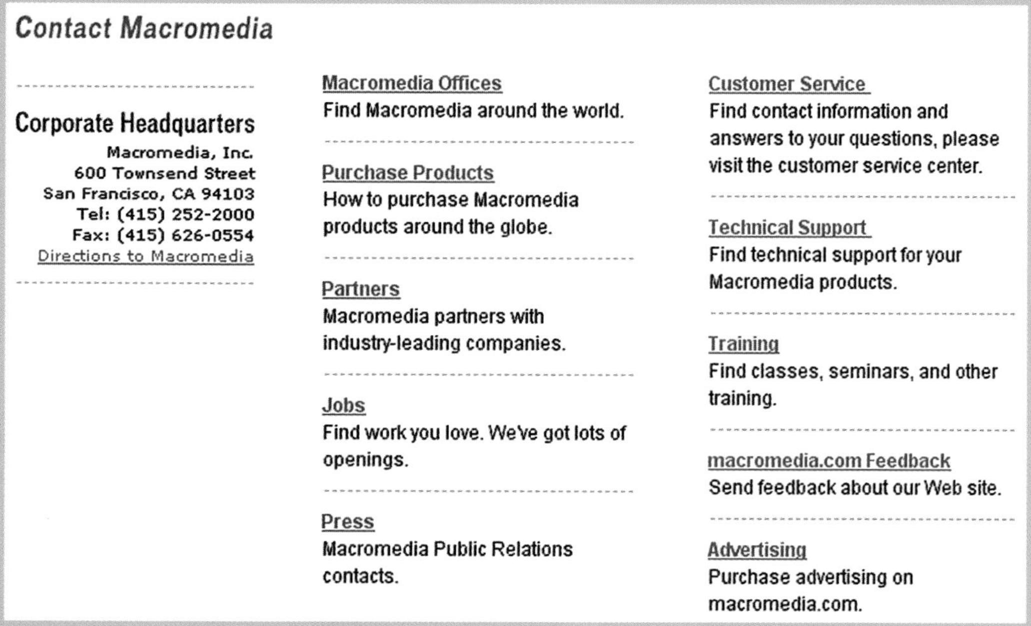

Contact Macromedia

Corporate Headquarters

Macromedia, Inc.
600 Townsend Street
San Francisco, CA 94103
Tel: (415) 252-2000
Fax: (415) 626-0554
Directions to Macromedia

Macromedia Offices
Find Macromedia around the world.

Purchase Products
How to purchase Macromedia products around the globe.

Partners
Macromedia partners with industry-leading companies.

Jobs
Find work you love. We've got lots of openings.

Press
Macromedia Public Relations contacts.

Customer Service
Find contact information and answers to your questions, please visit the customer service center.

Technical Support
Find technical support for your Macromedia products.

Training
Find classes, seminars, and other training.

macromedia.com Feedback
Send feedback about our Web site.

Advertising
Purchase advertising on macromedia.com.

Figure 1.15. ***www.Macromedia.com*** **(June 2002)—Site sections are well described and easy to distinguish.**

Finally, a website's category names should be tested on representative users, to see whether they actually mean to users what the site designers intended them to mean. If users misinterpret the category names, the users aren't wrong, the designers are, and the names need to be changed.

Blooper 4: Conflicting Content

If information about something—a product, service, coming event, news story, person, policy—appears on your website in more than one place, you'd better make sure it is consistent. Otherwise, your site will give visitors a very strong impression that your organization is not very organized.

But conflicting information on a website does far more damage than just conveying an impression of disorganization. It creates uncertainty in the minds of site visitors. How much does that product really cost? When is that event really occurring? What actually happened? What is this company's privacy policy?

When people are uncertain what the outcome of an online transaction will be, they are extremely unlikely to proceed with the transaction. This includes purchases, registrations, downloads, or anything else involving providing information to a website. When Web users feel the least bit unsure about the information they are receiving over the Web, they hit that Back button in a New York microsecond. Then, they either give up on that organization and go to another site or call the company to talk to a live person to try to clear up their uncertainty. The latter possibility means that conflicting information on a website greatly increases the volume of telephone calls to the company or organization. Management often hopes that their website will decrease the volume of telephone calls to sales, support, and information lines, but they can kiss that hope goodbye if the site contains contradictory information.

How Much?

In early 2002, United Airline's website had a clear example of conflicting information. The discrepancy was between its home page and another page. The home page offered vacation flights to London and Paris. Flights to London supposedly started at $499, and those to Paris supposedly started at $594 (Figure 1.16[A]). However, if a customer followed the link to learn more about these fares, the fares shown on the resulting page differed from those shown on the home page: London fares started at $369, and fares to Paris started at $429—in both cases more than $100 less (Figure 1.16[B]). Differences in this direction are less bothersome than ones in which the price goes *up* when one checks the details, but the discrepancy still raises uncertainty in customers' minds about what the fares really are.

Conflicting Privacy Policy

Many websites encourage visitors to register to receive certain benefits: discounts, news, announcements, customized service, or even simply access to the site. Registration con-

28

FOXTROT © 2002 Bill Amend. Reprinted with permission of UNIVERSAL PRESS SYNDICATE. All rights reserved.

sists of providing contact information and sometimes also preference and demographic information.

Wary of opening themselves to consumer fraud, identity theft, or unwanted commercial email, Web users are becoming more concerned with how, exactly, their data will be used. Companies and organizations, aware of this growing sensitivity among consumers, often provide links to their privacy policy. Many also state on their registration form how the data will and will not be used. Some provide ways for registrants to opt in or out of (1) receiving announcements or (2) having their information shared with other organizations.

When an organization's website contains statements about how it will treat registrant or customer data, it is important that the statements be consistent with each other. When privacy statements in different places on a website contra-

dict each other or even can be interpreted as doing so, site visitors will be wary of submitting personal information to the site.

That is precisely the problem on the Guestbook page at *Earthwatch.org* (Figure 1.17). Creating doubt in visitors' minds about how their data will be used certainly will not encourage them to register.

A more serious case of conflicting content was at the website of computer equipment company Acer Inc. Potential customers trying to learn whether Acer sells Macintosh-compatible film scanners would find conflicting information in different parts of the site.

First, product pages at *Acer.com* disagree about which film scanners Acer sells. The main product catalog lists one, the ScanWit 2720S (Figure 1.18[A]). In contrast, the Acer

29

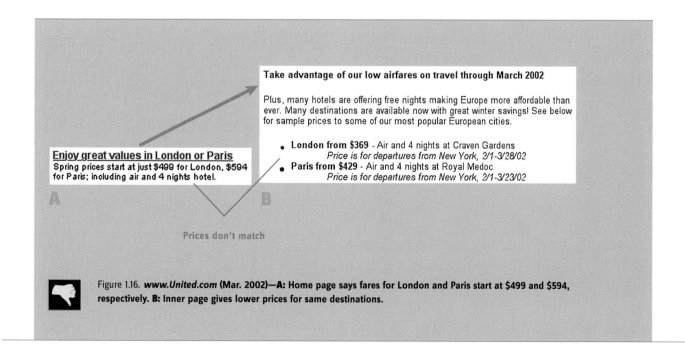

Take advantage of our low airfares on travel through March 2002

Plus, many hotels are offering free nights making Europe more affordable than ever. Many destinations are available now with great winter savings! See below for sample prices to some of our most popular European cities.

- **London from $369** - Air and 4 nights at Craven Gardens
  Price is for departures from New York, 2/1-3/28/02
- **Paris from $429** - Air and 4 nights at Royal Medoc
  Price is for departures from New York, 2/1-3/23/02

Enjoy great values in London or Paris
Spring prices start at just $499 for London, $594 for Paris; including air and 4 nights hotel.

A   B

Prices don't match

Figure 1.16. *www.United.com* (Mar. 2002)—A: Home page says fares for London and Paris start at $499 and $594, respectively. B: Inner page gives lower prices for same destinations.

America area of the site has its own product catalog, which lists two film scanners: 2720S and 2740S (Figure 1.18[B]).

Second, the main catalog's spec sheet for the 2720S doesn't mention Macintosh (Figure 1.19[A]), but Acer America's 2720S product page lists "Mac" as one of the drivers available for it (Figure 1.19[B]).

Finally, Acer America's spec sheet for the *second* scanner, the 2740S, lists "Macintosh" as a supported platform but then gives operating system requirements that exclude Macs (Figure 1.20).

With all this conflicting information, people with Macintoshes might hesitate to order an Acer scanner.

AVOIDING THE BLOOPER

If Information Isn't Copied, Copies Can't Differ

The best way to make sure information about an item—product, service, or topic—doesn't differ from one place to another on a website or family of sites is simply not to have it in more than one place. That isn't as limiting as it sounds. Instead of duplicating information in different places, link from different places to a single presentation of the information. After all, the Web is mainly *about* linking. For example,

> All pictures of a particular item should be image links to a single image file.

> All listings of an item in an online catalog should be links to a single item page.

> All descriptions and other attributes of the item should come from a single source.

This "single source" approach need not be restricted to simple static HTML links. Many websites and Web applications extract information dynamically from databases and

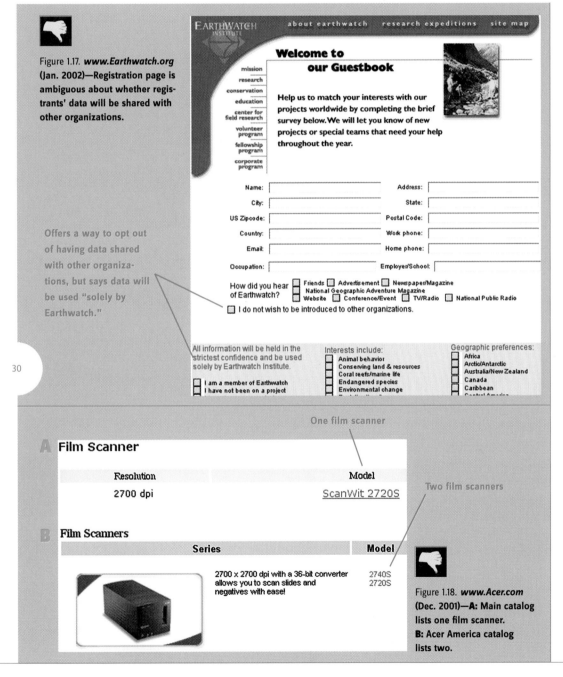

Figure 1.17. *www.Earthwatch.org* (Jan. 2002)—Registration page is ambiguous about whether registrants' data will be shared with other organizations.

Offers a way to opt out of having data shared with other organizations, but says data will be used "solely by Earthwatch."

One film scanner

Two film scanners

Figure 1.18. *www.Acer.com* (Dec. 2001)—A: Main catalog lists one film scanner. B: Acer America catalog lists two.

ScanWit 2720S

Features | Specification | **Bundle software**

Scanner Type	1 pass, film scanner
Optical Resolution	2700 x 2700 dpi
Scanning Mode Color Gray Scale	36 bit (over 68.7 billion colors) 12 bit (4096 levels of gray)
Scanning Area Positive Slide: Negative Filmstrip:	35mm mounted size (Max. batch scan 4 units) 35mm size (Max. batch scan 6 units)
Interface	SCSI II
System Requirement	• IBM PC Compatible • Pentium CPU • 16MB RAM • CD-ROM drive • Windows98/Win95/WinNT 4.0

Main catalog's
spec-sheet
doesn't
mention Mac.

Acer ScanWit 2720S

The **Acer Scanner ScanWit 2720S** enables you to scan slides and negative film with one-touch of a button. The auto-loading mechanism can preview or scan up to six frames at one time.

User's rants and raves
An enthusiastic professional user has created a website dedicated to the ScanWit 2720S. Click to read his review and tips and tricks.

BUY NOW   eacer

Key Features:

- 36-bit, over 68.7 billion colors for true-to-life accuracy
- 2700 x 2700 dpi optical resolution, 2700 x 2700 optical resolution
- 3.2D Dynamic Range
- Fast scan speed; Complete 2700 dpi scan within 40 sec.

Manual
English / French / Spanish

Driver
Win9x/NT/2000 / Mac / Help

Acer America's
product page
says Mac driver
available.

Figure 1.19. ***www.Acer.com*** (Dec. 2001)—**A:** Main catalog's spec sheet for 2720S doesn't mention Mac. **B:** Acer America's 2720S product page lists "Mac" as an available driver.

Figure 1.20. ***www.Acer.com*** (Dec. 2001)—Acer America's 2740S spec sheet disagrees with itself about the scanner's Macintosh compatibility.

Interface	SCSI II
Platform	Windows / Macintosh
System Requirements	Pentium CPU with 32MB RAM, Power PC with 32MB RAM, CD-ROM drive, PCI SCSI slot
Operating System	Win98/Win95/WinNT 4.0
Dynamic Range	3.2D

Mentions Mac under Platform but not under
Operating System

31

"content management" systems. Duplication is avoided if wherever a particular item is mentioned, the data has come from a single source for that item. When information is not duplicated, updating and maintaining it is simplified and divergent copies are impossible.

If Information Must Be Copied, Do Whatever It Takes to Keep It Consistent

If duplication of information in different places on a website or family of sites cannot be avoided, the organization that owns the site must "bite the bullet," budgeting the resources required to ensure that there are no contradictions. Otherwise, the organization will be disappointed in the success of its website.

Blooper 5: Outdated Content

Almost as bad as contradictory information on a website is information that is clearly out-of-date. Sites that have outdated information are basically telling the world, "We are disorganized and unreliable." Although out-of-date information on someone's personal website is perhaps not surprising, it is amazing how common it is on websites of large corporations and organizations.

Russell Stover, a candy company, felt it needed a Web presence to keep up with competitors like See's Candy, which has for several years had a website that allows customers to order candy online—even customized selections of candy. So Russell Stover created *RussellStover.com.*

Or at least, it announced plans to create the site. In the late 1990s, the company put up a placeholder site promising that the real site would be up in "Fall 2000." Unfortunately, the company then failed to meet its own deadline. Until recently, people who visited Russell Stover's Web address saw what appeared to be a home page but was really just a *picture* of the company's *planned* home page, which supposedly was "Coming Soon . . . Fall 2000." The entire placeholder page was a single image, with almost no actual working links (Figure 1.21). A friend told me he tried to use the site to buy candy in December 2000, well after the stated "Fall 2000" deadline. He wasted several minutes clicking on parts of the image before he noticed the Coming Soon sign and realized that the only way to order candy was to call the 800 number at the bottom of the page.

After my friend told me about *RussellStover.com,* I checked it every few months. As of January 2002, the new site was still "Coming Soon . . . Fall 2000." In February 2002—a year and a half after the promised deadline—Russell Stover's promised new site finally went online.

A more recent example comes from the California Shakespeare Festival website. Its home page lists the season's plays and marks the one currently playing. Or at least, that's the plan; the execution sometimes lags a little. On September 16, 2002, the home page still marked *The Seagull* as "now playing," even though that play ended on September 1 and *The Winter's Tale* started on September 11 (Figure 1.22).

© Zits Partnership. Reprinted with Special Permission of King Features Syndicate.

A website in severe need of updating is that of Enron Corporation, an energy company that in late 2001 declared bankruptcy. Although Enron's corporate website was partially updated to reflect its new circumstances (see the next section, Avoiding the Blooper), much out-of-date information remained. In March 2002—several months after its stock had crashed to zero and it had laid off most of its employees, Enron Energy Services' home page continued to describe Enron as "one of the world's leading electricity, natural gas, and communications companies . . . " (Figure 1.23). "Leading in what?" one might ask.

A somewhat specialized example of outdated content comes from the publisher of this book, Morgan Kaufmann Publishers. Its website, *MKP.com*, provides secure e-commerce functions to allow people to buy books using a credit card number. Providers of secure

Figure 1.21. **www.RussellStover.com (Jan. 2002)—Home page says site will be ready "Fall 2000."**

Figure 1.22. **www.CalShakes.org (Sept. 2002)—On September 16, The Seagull is still marked as "now playing" even though it ended on September 1 and another play started 5 days previously.**

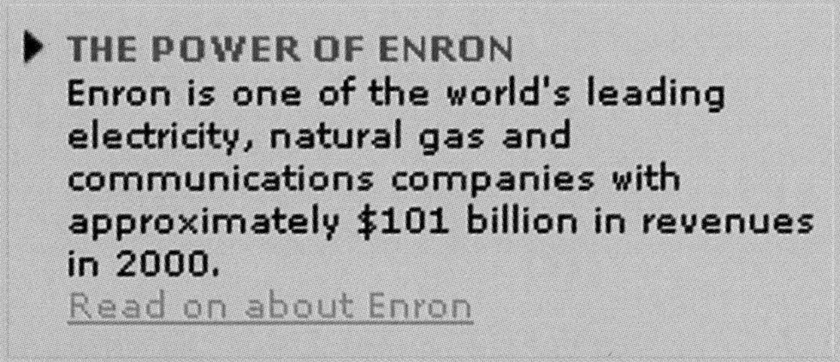

▶ **THE POWER OF ENRON**
Enron is one of the world's leading electricity, natural gas and communications companies with approximately $101 billion in revenues in 2000.
Read on about Enron

Figure 1.23. **www.Enron.com (Mar. 2002)—Months after the Enron scandal became public and Enron filed bankruptcy and laid off most of its employees, its Enron Energy Services page continued to describe it as "one of the world's leading" power companies.**

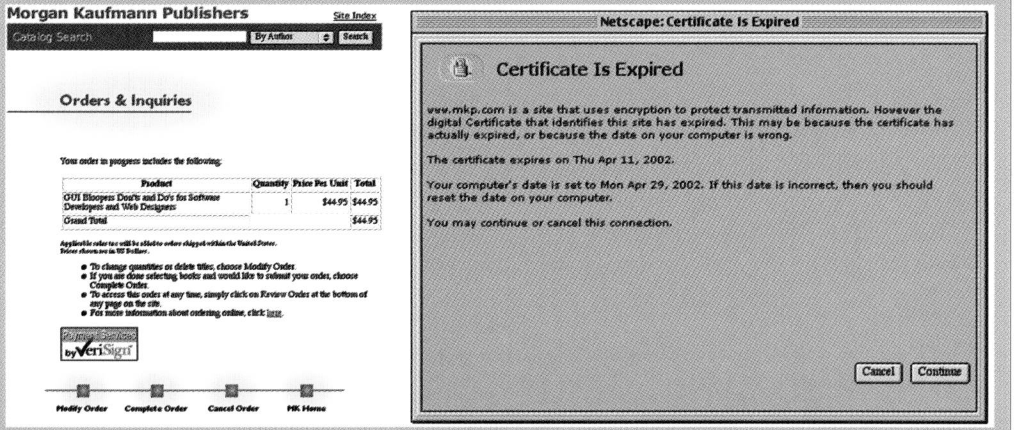

Morgan Kaufmann Publishers			Site Index

Orders & Inquiries

Your order in progress includes the following:

Product	Quantity	Price Per Unit	Total
GUI Bloopers Don'ts and Do's for Software Developers and Web Designers	1	$44.95	$44.95
Grand Total			$44.95

Applicable sales tax will be added to orders shipped within the United States.
Prices shown are in US Dollars.

- To change quantities or delete titles, choose Modify Order.
- If you are done selecting books and would like to submit your order, choose Complete Order.
- To access this order at any time, simply click on Review Order at the bottom of any page on the site.
- For more information about ordering online, click here.

Payment Services by **VeriSign**

Modify Order   Complete Order   Cancel Order   MK Home

Netscape: Certificate Is Expired

🔒 **Certificate Is Expired**

www.mkp.com is a site that uses encryption to protect transmitted information. However the digital Certificate that identifies this site has expired. This may be because the certificate has actually expired, or because the date on your computer is wrong.

The certificate expires on Thu Apr 11, 2002.

Your computer's date is set to Mon Apr 29, 2002. If this date is incorrect, then you should reset the date on your computer.

You may continue or cancel this connection.

[Cancel] [Continue]

Figure 1.24. **www.MKP.com (Apr. 2002)—Attempts to purchase a book warned that the site's digital certificate for secure transactions had expired.**

transactions are supposed to provide a user's browser with a digital certificate—issued by a trusted authority such as VeriSign—to ensure the customer that the transaction is secure. Unfortunately, Morgan Kaufmann allowed its certificate to expire. Anyone trying to buy a book from *MKP.com* in late April 2002 received a warning that the certificate had expired, implying that the transaction might not be secure (Figure 1.24). Needless to say, the company quickly renewed its certificate when told of the problem.

AVOIDING THE BLOOPER

Many organizations want a Web presence. Too often, however, management has no idea how much of a commitment that requires. Websites have to be kept up-to-date. That takes time, effort, staffing, and money.

Stuff Happens: There Is No Such Thing as Permanent Content

Even websites that are only brochures for a company or organization have to be updated. People mentioned in the site leave or change roles. Companies move to new offices. Contact information changes. Organizations change their names and logos. Company circumstances change.

Consider Enron. Although, as described earlier, it overlooked items on its site that it would have been wise to update or remove, it at least did a good job of updating its home page (Figure 1.25).

Variable Content Requires Extraordinary Effort

If a site includes content that is *supposed* to change over time—product availability and prices, special offers and sales, press releases, articles, event calendars, facts and figures, sports scores, weather, and downloads—the commitment required to keep it up-to-date skyrockets.

Meet Your Own Stated Deadlines, or Don't State Them

Don't embarrass your organization by posting dates for revisions and additions to your website and then failing to meet those dates. If you post an announcement of an update and the announcement promises the update by a certain date, you should meet that deadline. If, for unforeseen reasons, you miss the deadline, at least yank the announcement down so it doesn't serve as a giant indicator of your company's unreliability.

Websites Must Be Maintained!

The bottom line: If company managers think they want a Web presence for the organization but plan their budget and staffing only for the initial site development, ignoring maintenance, they should think again.

Blooper 6: Missing or Useless Content

I talked about poorly described content, conflicting content, and out-of-date content—what's left? How about content that is missing or useless? Since content is primary on the Web, pages or sites that are missing important content are just using up space and domain names.

You Just Have to Know

In late 2001, Slims, a nightclub in San Francisco, hosted a bluegrass music festival in Golden Gate Park. Its website, *Slims-SF.com,* publicized the event (Figure 1.26[A]). It announced that the festival would take place in "Speedway Meadows." For people who know where Speedway Meadows is, that's sufficient, but for people who don't, it isn't. I didn't know. I browsed around the site trying to find out where in the park the festival would be. I eventually found a link to Shuttle Details (Figure 1.26[B]). After clicking there, I was transported to a generic shuttle bus page provided by the Golden Gate Park Concourse Authority

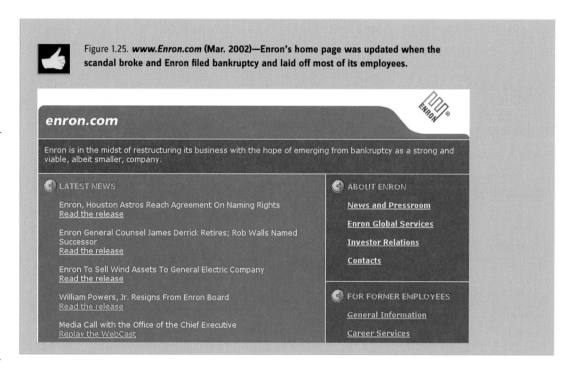

Figure 1.25. *www.Enron.com* (Mar. 2002)—Enron's home page was updated when the scandal broke and Enron filed bankruptcy and laid off most of its employees.

(Figure 1.26[C]). It had almost no information, but it did have a link to a map of Golden Gate Park (Figure 1.26[D]). Unfortunately, the map did not mark where Speedway Meadows is. So much for the power of the Web.

Hey, Buddy! Want to Buy an LGW40?

The previous examples were strictly informational websites. For an example of missing important content at an e-commerce site, take a look at a catalog page at online electronics store *ValcoElectronics.com.* The excerpt shown lists two products (Figure 1.27[A]). The first one has a product code and a name, but the second has only a product code. If you don't know what an LGW40 is, you can just click on the link to go to the detailed product page, right? Right, but you won't find much more information there

Figure 1.26. ***www.Slims-SF.com*** **(Oct. 2001)—Festival site doesn't indicate the festival's location in Golden Gate park.**

Festival home page doesn't say where in GG Park Speedway Meadows is.

Subsequent pages, including a park map, don't either.

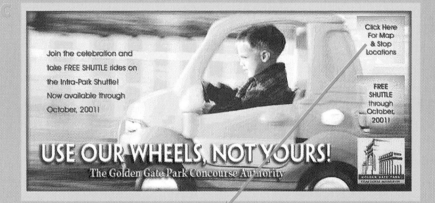

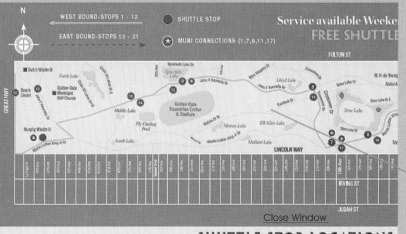

Speedway Meadows is here, but the map doesn't mark it.

(Figure 1.27[B]). Sure, whatever an LGW40 is, I'll take a dozen! At least they don't weigh much.

If the LGW40 were the only product on ValcoElectronics' site that exhibited this lack of information, it could be dismissed as an isolated slipup. However, other products for sale on the site also exhibit the problem. Therefore, it is either a systematic data-extraction bug or a design flaw.

Thank You So Much for Such Useful Information!

My final example of useless content comes from *United.com*. While customers are trying to book a flight, the site distracts them with enticing links to useless marketing statements. Two examples are shown in Figure 1.28.

AVOIDING THE BLOOPER

To avoid building sites that lack important content or supply useless content, Web designers should follow these guidelines:

> *Learn what site visitors will need and then include it.* During site design, conduct interviews and focus groups with people who are like your intended users to determine what people will use the site for (Brinck, Gergle, and Wood 2001), and then design in the content they need to accomplish their goals.

> *Don't distract users from their goals.* Help people do what they came to your site to do. In particular, once customers have started down the path of making a purchase, you are harming your own sales if you distract them from completing the transaction (van Duyne, Landay, and Hong 2001). Enticing links that lead to nothing useful not only annoy users and waste their time but also increase the transaction dropout rate.

> *Test to find what's missing.* Test the site for usability before it goes live to make sure nothing important is missing, and if it is, add it. After the site is released, continue observing and interviewing users to discover if anything is still missing.

Obviously, following these guidelines takes time, effort, and money.

Blooper 7: Unfinished Content

An important special case of websites missing content is sites with pages that obviously have not been finished. In some cases, sites were knowingly put online while still

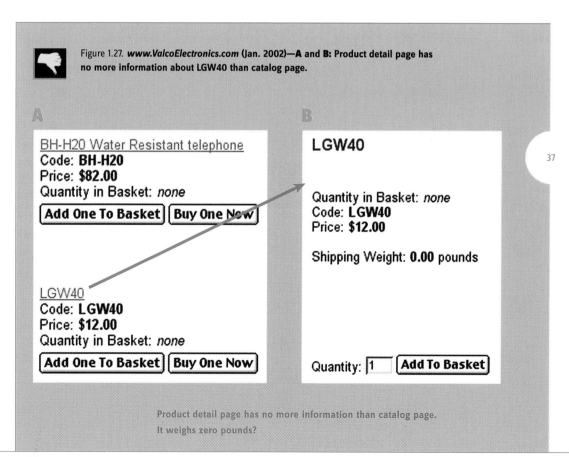

Figure 1.27. *www.ValcoElectronics.com* (Jan. 2002)—**A** and **B**: Product detail page has no more information about LGW40 than catalog page.

A

BH-H20 Water Resistant telephone
Code: **BH-H20**
Price: **$82.00**
Quantity in Basket: *none*

[**Add One To Basket**] [**Buy One Now**]

LGW40
Code: **LGW40**
Price: **$12.00**
Quantity in Basket: *none*

[**Add One To Basket**] [**Buy One Now**]

B

LGW40

Quantity in Basket: *none*
Code: **LGW40**
Price: **$12.00**

Shipping Weight: **0.00** pounds

Quantity: [1] [**Add To Basket**]

Product detail page has no more information than catalog page. It weighs zero pounds?

37

Figure 1.28. *www.United.com* (Mar. 2002)—While you are trying to book a flight, the site distracts you with enticing links to useless marketing statements.

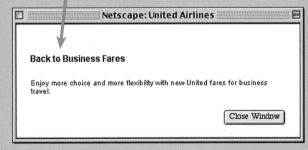

Distracting links to pop-up windows that have no useful information.

under construction. In other cases, content is missing because of an oversight: Developers failed to check all the pages before taking the site live. Sites that are obviously incomplete make a poor impression on prospective customers.

Lorem Ipsum Dolor Sit Amet

Call up any Web search engine and search for "Lorem ipsum dolor sit amet" (including the quotation marks). Depending on the search engine, the search will return at least hundreds of hits, if not thousands. For example, conducting this search on *Google.com* yielded more than 10 pages of hits.

What does this mean? Many website designers initially mock up their sites with pseudo-Latin text so they can determine and evaluate the layout before the actual content is written.[4] Some Web development tools help by providing the Latin filler. The most common Latin filler begins "Lorem ipsum dolor sit amet, consectetuer adipiscing elit. . . . " When this text appears in a live website, it means that the designer neglected to replace the filler text with real content text before putting the site on the Web. Vincent Flanders first called attention to this common problem in 1998 in his website *WebPagesThatSuck.com*.

Following the links returned by such a search reveals a surprising fact: Most of the sites with leftover filler Latin are commercial and organizational sites presumably created by professional Web designers. If, instead, most were personal sites created by individuals, the commonness of leftover filler Latin text would not be so surprising.

For example, International Wafer Service, a supplier of silicon wafers, has a What's New page on its website that includes an announcement of improved chip-lithography methods (Figure 1.29). The announcement begins normally but degenerates into filler text, including fake Latin.

An example of filler text with potential legal implications comes from *ThePattySite.com*, a website offering resources for Dreamweaver Web developers. The site's Legal Disclaimer consists entirely of fake Latin filler (Figure 1.30). This could be either a joke or a political statement, but it more likely is an oversight. Some people consider legal language to be gibberish. At this site, it *is* gibberish. The irony is that the site's home page states, "Featuring original content not available anywhere else."

 Figure 1.29. ***www.siwafer.com*** (Mar. 2002)—Announcement contains filler text.

BETTER LITHOGRAPHY -CD Lithography-0.25/0.35 micron CD Lithography and etch oxides and metal films now available. Stand line/space and VIAs patterns available pages. Resize, move, add or delete this and other page elements to accommodate your information needs. Lorem ipsum, Dolor sit amet, consectetuer adipiscing elit, sed diam nonummy nibh euismod tincidunt ut laoreet dolore magna aliquam erat volutpat. Ut wisi enim ad minim veniam, quis nostrud exerci tation ullamcorper suscipit lobortis nisl ut aliquip ex ea commodo consequat.

[4]The practice of filling text areas with fake text is called "greeking," but the fake text most often used is Latin, not Greek.

Face to Face with the Void

Finding oneself staring at pseudo-Latin is not the only clue that a website is unfinished. Sometimes the clue is more of a Zen experience: pages of nothing.

An excellent example of nothing is provided by the website of the New Hampshire Association of School Principals (NHASP). On its home page, *NHASP.org* has a link to Administrative Job Vacancies (Figure 1.31[A]). Clicked on in early 2002, it displayed a blank page (Figure 1.31[B]). A notice that "no jobs are available at this time" would be nicer. The blank page's title—shown in the title bar of the browser—may be familiar.

Web surfers can also encounter The Void elsewhere on the Web, such as the site map at *siwafer.com* (Figure 1.32[A]) and the About Continuing Studies page at *Stanford.edu* (Figure 1.32[B]).

Heed my words, grasshopper: Blank Web pages do not bring us closer to oneness with the universe. They bring us closer to "zeroness."

40

Used by permission of Jennifer Berman.

Figure 1.30. *www.ThePattySite.com* (Jan. 2002)—Legal disclaimer is fake Latin filler.

Back

LEGAL DISCLAIMER

Lorem ipsum dolor sit amet, consectetur adipscing elit, sed diam nonnumy eiusmod tempor incidunt ut labore et dolore magna aliquam erat volupat. Et harumd dereud facilis est er expedit distinct. Nam liber a tempor cum soluta nobis eligend optio comque nihil quod a impedit anim id quod maxim placeat facer possim omnis es voluptas assumenda est, omnis dolor repellend. When I'm drivin' in my car and a man comes on the radio, and he's tellin' me more and more about some useless information, trying to fire my imagination, I can't get no, no, no, no. Temporem autem quinsud et aur office debit aut tum rerum necesit.

Atib saepe eveniet ut er repudiand sint et molestia non este recusand. Lorem ipsum dolor sit amet, consectetur adipscing elit. Sed diam nonnumy eiusmod tempor incidunt ut labore et dolore magna aliquam erat volupat. Temporem autem quinsud et aur office debit aut tum rerum necesit atib saepe eveniet ut er repudiand sint et molestia non este recusand. Ooh, I bet you wonder how I knew of your plans to make me blue with some other girl you knew before. Between the two of us girls, you know I love you more.

Lorem ipsum dolor sit amet, consectetur adipscing elit, sed diam nonnumy eiusmod tempor incidunt ut labore et dolore magna aliquam erat volupat. Et harumd dereud facilis est er expedit distinct. What you want, baby, I've got. What you need, don't you know, I've got it. All I'm askin' is for a little respect when you get home, baby. When you get home, Mister. Nam liber a tempor cum soluta nobis eligend optio comque nihil quod a impedit anim id quod maxim placeat facer possim omnis es voluptas assumenda est, omnis dolor repellend.

Temporem autem quinsud et aur office debit aut tum rerum necesit atib saepe eveniet ut er repudiand sint et molestia non este recusand. La plume de ma tante est sur la table. It's been three weeks since you've been lookin' for your friend - the one you let hit it and never called you again. Remember when he told you he was 'bout the Benjamins? You act like you ain't hear him, then give him a little trim. Lorem ipsum dolor sit amet, consectetur adipscing elit, sed diam nonnumy eiusmod tempor incidunt ut labore et dolore magna aliquam erat volupat. Et harumd dereud facilis est er expedit distinct.

Figure 1.31. *www.NHASP.org* (Jan. 2002)—Job Vacancies link yields blank page.

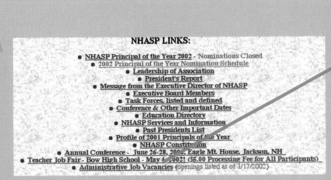

Figure 1.32. **A:** *siwafer.com* (Mar. 2002); **B:** *Stanford.edu* About Continuing Studies
Program page (Sep. 2001)—Pages of nothing.

41

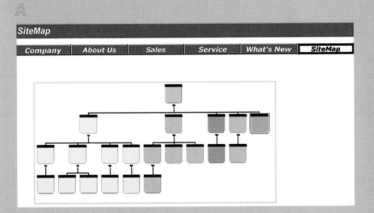

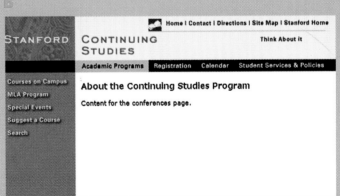

AVOIDING THE BLOOPER

It's a bad idea to put a site online with clearly unfinished content. It makes your organization look amateurish and disorganized. Instead, do the following:

> *Don't go live until ready.* If you currently have no Web presence, don't rush it. Wait until your site is complete before exposing it to the world. Reserve your desired domain name as soon as you know what it will be, but you can do that without putting up a website. If absolutely necessary, put up a placeholder page providing contact information, a brief description of the site's or your organization's mission, and the information that the new site is coming.

> *Don't miss your own deadline.* If you publicly post a completion date, you really have committed yourself to making that date. If you posted a date and aren't going to make it, yank it down as soon as possible. Leaving a date for a new site posted after the date is passed *really* makes your organization look bad (see Blooper 5: Outdated Content, in this chapter).

> *Keep the old site up.* If a previous—presumably complete—version of your site is already on the Web, leave it up a little longer, until you have the new one ready.

> *Omit unfinished pages.* If you anticipate adding content to your site later, after it is up, don't leave blank pages or filler content where it will be. Leave the unfinished pages, sections, or paragraphs completely out of the site, with no links or references to them.

> *Check it!* Review your site thoroughly before putting it online. Check it on your intranet before putting it on the Internet. It is good to begin this checking by having members of the design and development organization systematically walk through the site. However, before taking the site live, it is also important—for various reasons, not only for checking completeness—to test the site on people from outside the organization or even outside the company.

TASK-SUPPORT BLOOPERS

If a website is more than just an online brochure—that is, if it supports tasks requiring significant inter-action and manipulation—one can ask how *well* it supports those tasks. Is completing a task easy and pleasant, allowing users to think mainly about their own goals and not much about operating the web-site? Or is getting anything done agonizing and frustrating, with the website constantly tripping users up and making them think about how to operate it or work around its deficiencies?

A website's support—or lack thereof—for its intended tasks depends on more than just its surface details. Issues such as graphic design, layout, labeling, error messages, navigation, and form fields are of course important aspects of Web design, but they are not the whole story. In fact, as I said in Chapter 1, surface details aren't even *most* of the story.

In this chapter, I examine bloopers that hurt a site's business logic and task flow, hindering users in ac-complishing their tasks. These issues fall somewhere between the content issues covered in Chapter 1 and the surface-level issues covered in subsequent chapters.

Task-support bloopers are the most difficult ones to correct. They aren't simply problems in the design of the *front* end, that is, the website itself. They are often caused by poorly designed *back* ends—services and databases on which the website depends—or by faulty interaction and communication between the back end and the front end. Because in large organizations, the front and back ends of websites are developed by separate teams, task-support bloopers cross organizational boundaries. Therefore, no single development team owns them: Preventing and fixing them is a shared responsibility of multiple organizations.

Poor support for task flow in a website often is the result of combinations of smaller problems. To provide the proper perspective, this chapter first presents very specific task-fit bloopers, then finishes with more general bloopers of poor task flow that arise from combinations of more specific bloopers.

Blooper 8: Redundant Requests

Few things annoy people more than having to give an organization the same information twice. It doesn't matter whether the information is requested by a website, a desktop software application, a paper form, a telephone operator, or a receptionist.

When an organization asks you for information you already gave it, the message is that they didn't care enough about you to implement procedures for using already-provided information wherever they need it. They offloaded that work onto you. In some cases, different organizations involved in the processing of your information failed to cooperate or communicate well enough.

Due to the fundamental nature of the Web, avoiding this blooper can be difficult. As a result, it is common for websites and Web applications to require users to reenter data they already entered. This blooper comes in several forms, which are discussed in turn, with examples. The examples are followed by a discussion of why this is a difficult blooper to avoid and ways of avoiding it.

Not Using Already-Provided Information

Some sites ask for the same information twice because they ignored what the user already told them.

An example comes from *Microsoft.com*. If you want to ask their customer-support department a question, you set a menu to the product you are asking about (Figure 2.1[A]) and click Go. That takes you to a Personal Support Incident Submission page, with another menu for specifying the product. Annoyingly, it is not set to the product you just indicated on the previous page (Figure 2.1[B]). You have to set it *again*.

Figure 2.1. *www.Microsoft.com* (Feb. 2001)—Asks for same information twice. **A:** User specifies PowerPoint as subject of question. **B:** Menu on next page doesn't reflect choice from previous page.

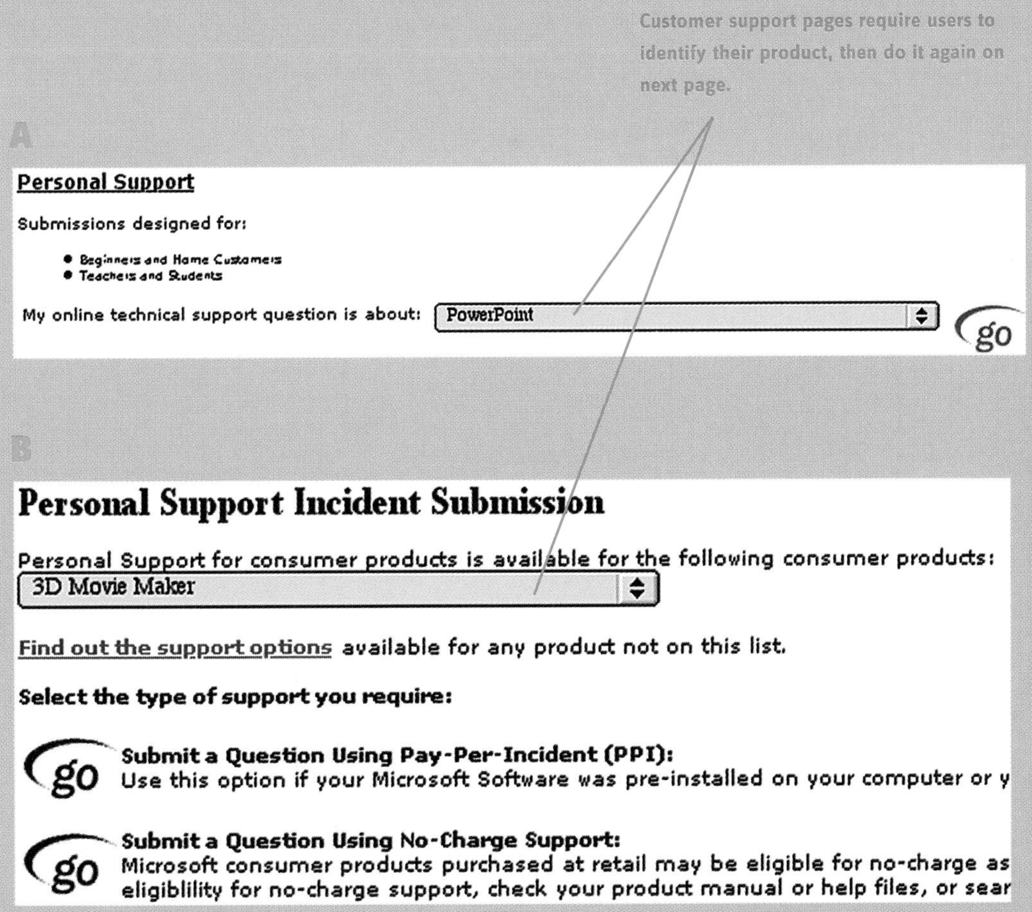

Customer support pages require users to identify their product, then do it again on next page.

A

Personal Support

Submissions designed for:

- Beginners and Home Customers
- Teachers and Students

My online technical support question is about: PowerPoint ▾   *go*

B

Personal Support Incident Submission

Personal Support for consumer products is available for the following consumer products:

3D Movie Maker ▾

Find out the support options available for any product not on this list.

Select the type of support you require:

 Submit a Question Using Pay-Per-Incident (PPI):
Use this option if your Microsoft Software was pre-installed on your computer or y

 Submit a Question Using No-Charge Support:
Microsoft consumer products purchased at retail may be eligible for no-charge as
eligiblility for no-charge support, check your product manual or help files, or sear

45

Figure 2.2. **www.ProxyVote.com (Oct. 2001)—Asks for same information twice. A: User provides 12-digit control number. B: New user registration form (InvestorDelivery.com) asks for same 12-digit control number.**

A

PROXY Vote

You can submit your proxy voting instructions right over the Internet

It's fast, convenient, and your voting instructions are immediately posted.

If you received notification by postal mail:

1. Read the Proxy Statement. The accompanying Voting Instruction Form or Proxy Card contains your Control Number.
2. Enter the 12 digit Control Number to access an electronic ballot.
3. Complete the electronic ballot and submit your voting instructions.
4. Provide your E-Mail address if you want confirmation of your voting instructions.

If you received notification by E-Mail:

1. To access an electronic ballot, enter the 12 digit Control Number contained in your E-Mail message and the PERSONAL IDENTIFICATIO... when you enrolled for electronic delivery.
2. The ballot displayed contains Internet Links to the Proxy Statement and the Annual Report; read them carefully.
3. Complete the ballot and submit your voting instructions.

Enter your CONTROL NUMBER: `09890132255`   (Please skip any spaces)

Enter your PERSONAL IDENTIFICATION NUMBER (PIN): `☐`   (Required for the E-Mail option only)

`Click to Continue`

Voter control number must be given twice.

B

InvestorDelivery.com

New Enrollment-Create

Listed below are the fields you must enter to create your new InvestorDelivery enrollment.

After entering the information, click on the "Submit" button.

Enrollment Number (or Proxyvote.com Control Number): `☐` (Example: M123456789012)

Internet E-Mail Address: `☐` (Example: yourID@providerID.com)

Confirm your E-Mail Address: `☐`

PIN: `☐`
(Choose 4 numeric digits)

Confirm your PIN: `☐`

`Submit`

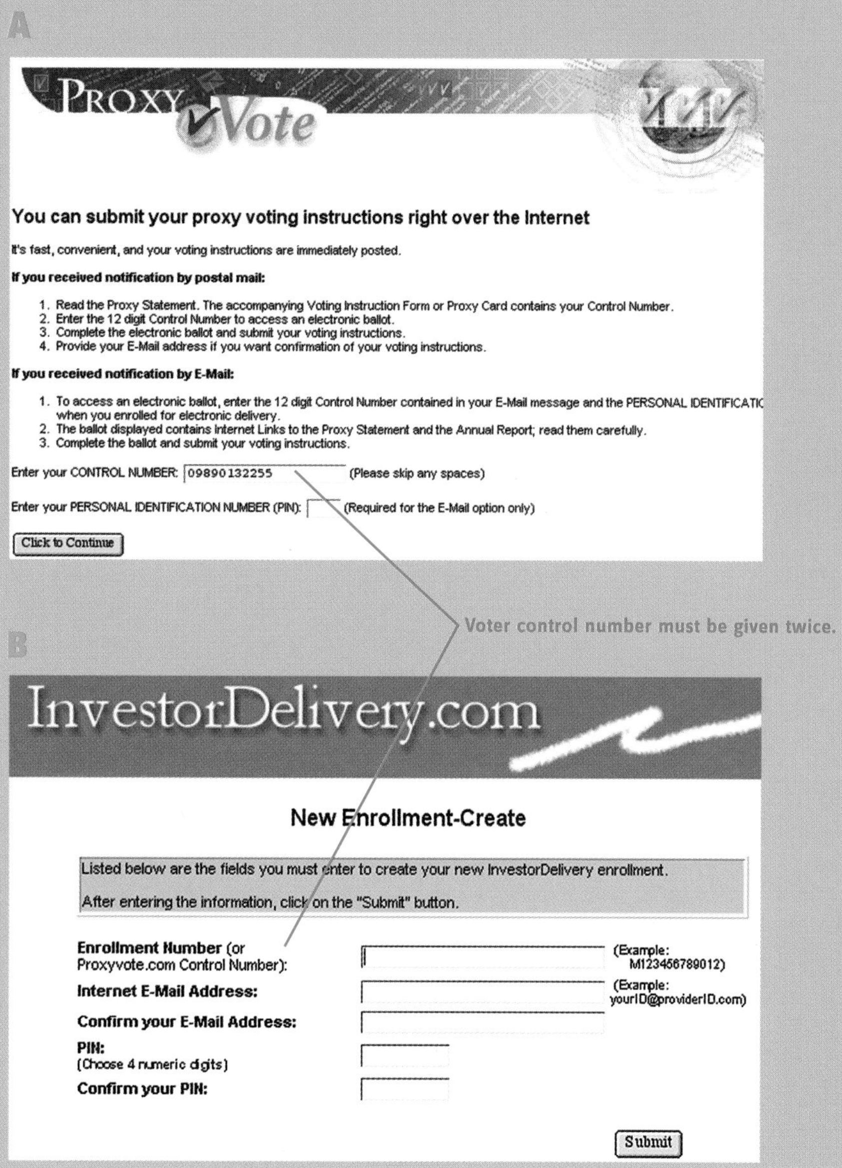

A related blooper—requiring users to indicate more than once where they want to go on a site—is discussed in Chapter 3 (see Blooper 18: Not Linking Directly).

Poor Coordination between Systems

A similar annoyance can be found at the website of *ProxyVote.com*, a site for voting online in stockholder elections. However, here the cause isn't a simple lack of transfer between forms. It's a lack of communication between *organizations* (Figure 2.2).

The process starts with a letter announcing an election. The letter provides ProxyVote's Web address. At *ProxyVote.com*, you are asked to prove you're a stockholder by providing the 12-digit control number from the letter (Figure 2.2[A]). The first time you vote through *ProxyVote.com*, it temporarily hands you off to a different website—*InvestorDelivery.com*—to register you as a ProxyVote user. The annoyance is that *InvestorDelivery.com* asks you for the same 12-digit control number you just gave to *ProxyVote.com!* Even though the second request comes from a different organization, users see it as a repeated request because from their standpoint it is all part of the same task.

Forgetting User's Stated Preferences

Airline reservation websites seem to have trouble remembering from one screen to the next what time of day you want to fly.

Southwest Airlines' website provides an example. Suppose you tell it you want to depart on a day sometime between *noon* and *6:00 PM* and return on another day *after 6:00 PM* (Figure 2.3[A]). At least the flights it finds reflect those departure and return times; some websites don't even manage to do that. However, on the Search results page, the "Edit your Search?" control panel shows both departure and return times as *Anytime* (Figure 2.3[B]). Someone could easily overlook those settings, change the date, search again, and get a list of flights leaving at unsuitable times.

Southwest.com isn't the only airline site that commits this blooper. *Continental.com* and *United.com* also sometimes "forget" your preferred travel times as you proceed through the ticket-ordering process.

Losing Data on Return to Page

A special case of asking for data twice is when you return to a previous page—intentionally, or because the website sends you back because of an error, or even just because the page is refreshed—and information you had put on that page is gone.

For example, the website of the California Shakespeare Festival, *CalShakes.org*, has a ticket-ordering form but resets it if you back up to change your order (Figure 2.4[A–C]). The date menu is reset to the default date, and the text fields are cleared. If you retype the number of tickets but don't notice that you need to reselect your desired date, you end up ordering tickets for the wrong date. Or if you reselect your date and proceed without retyping the other fields, the site shows you an order for *no* tickets, for which it still wants to charge you a $4 service charge (Figure 2.4[D]). This is almost funny.

The *CalShakes* blooper is annoying but pales in comparison to a data-deletion blooper at *UBid.com*. The site provides a form to send email to UBid. If the email form page needs to be refreshed while you are filling it out—for example, you change the browser window size—all fields except the First Name field are cleared (Figure 2.5). Now you get to type it all again. Or hit Back and go somewhere else.

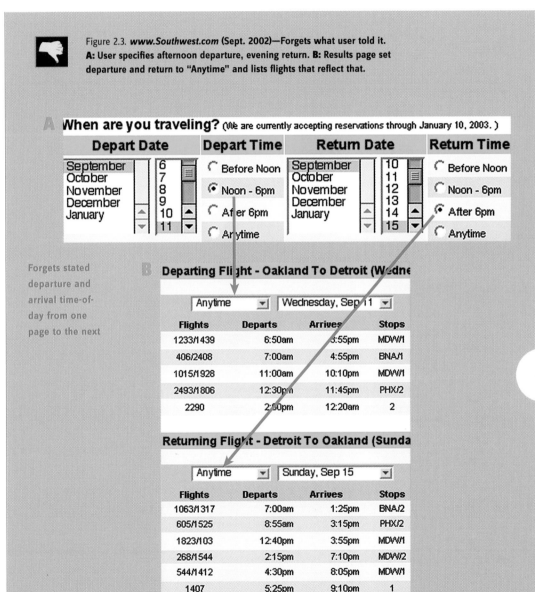

Figure 2.3. *www.Southwest.com* (Sept. 2002)—Forgets what user told it.
A: User specifies afternoon departure, evening return. **B:** Results page set departure and return to "Anytime" and lists flights that reflect that.

Forgets stated departure and arrival time-of-day from one page to the next

47

Figure 2.4. ***www.CalShakes.org*** (July 2002)—Ticket order form is reset when revisited to change the order.

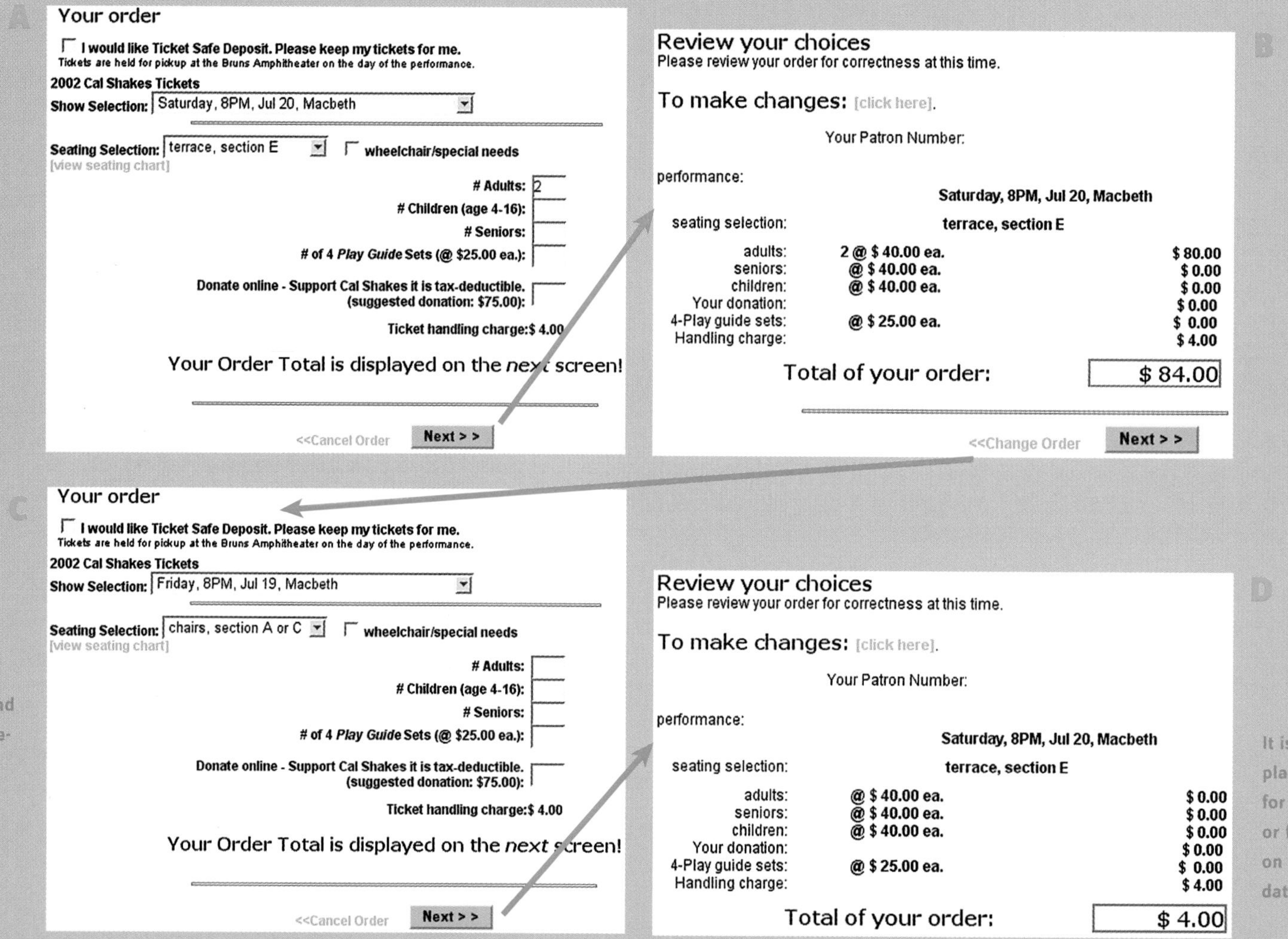

A

Your order

☐ **I would like Ticket Safe Deposit. Please keep my tickets for me.**
Tickets are held for pickup at the Bruns Amphitheater on the day of the performance.

2002 Cal Shakes Tickets

Show Selection: Saturday, 8PM, Jul 20, Macbeth ▾

Seating Selection: terrace, section E ▾ ☐ **wheelchair/special needs**
[view seating chart]

Adults: 2
Children (age 4-16):
Seniors:
of 4 *Play Guide* Sets (@ $25.00 ea.):

Donate online - Support Cal Shakes it is tax-deductible.
(suggested donation: $75.00):

Ticket handling charge: $ 4.00

Your Order Total is displayed on the *next* screen!

<<Cancel Order   **Next > >**

B

Review your choices
Please review your order for correctness at this time.

To make changes: [click here].

Your Patron Number:

performance:
Saturday, 8PM, Jul 20, Macbeth

seating selection: terrace, section E

adults:	2 @ $ 40.00 ea.	$ 80.00
seniors:	@ $ 40.00 ea.	$ 0.00
children:	@ $ 40.00 ea.	$ 0.00
Your donation:		$ 0.00
4-Play guide sets:	@ $ 25.00 ea.	$ 0.00
Handling charge:		$ 4.00

Total of your order: $ 84.00

<<Change Order   **Next > >**

C

Your order

☐ **I would like Ticket Safe Deposit. Please keep my tickets for me.**
Tickets are held for pickup at the Bruns Amphitheater on the day of the performance.

2002 Cal Shakes Tickets

Show Selection: Friday, 8PM, Jul 19, Macbeth ▾

Seating Selection: chairs, section A or C ▾ ☐ **wheelchair/special needs**
[view seating chart]

Adults:
Children (age 4-16):
Seniors:
of 4 *Play Guide* Sets (@ $25.00 ea.):

Donate online - Support Cal Shakes it is tax-deductible.
(suggested donation: $75.00):

Ticket handling charge: $ 4.00

Your Order Total is displayed on the *next* screen!

<<Cancel Order   **Next > >**

D

Review your choices
Please review your order for correctness at this time.

To make changes: [click here].

Your Patron Number:

performance:
Saturday, 8PM, Jul 20, Macbeth

seating selection: terrace, section E

adults:	@ $ 40.00 ea.	$ 0.00
seniors:	@ $ 40.00 ea.	$ 0.00
children:	@ $ 40.00 ea.	$ 0.00
Your donation:		$ 0.00
4-Play guide sets:	@ $ 25.00 ea.	$ 0.00
Handling charge:		$ 4.00

Total of your order: $ 4.00

Date menu and other fields re-set on return for changes.

It is easy to place an order for *no* tickets, or for tickets on the wrong date.

Requiring User to Log In Repeatedly

A second special case of asking for information twice is asking people to log in repeatedly. When you log in, you are telling the site who you are. Depending on the site, it might be done using your actual name, a login name, a frequent-flier number, a credit-card number, or a student ID number. Often, sites require you to *prove* your identity by supplying a password. Once you have identified yourself to a website, it should not ask you to identify yourself again, at least not with the same identifying information you already gave it. But many sites do.

Internet provider *EarthLink.net* requires customers to log in *three* times, always with the same email address and password, to activate or deactivate an auto-reply "vacation" message. The first login is to access one's Personal Support Center page (Figure 2.6[A] and [B]). Clicking "Manage Your Mailboxes" displays the "Dial-up Account Maintenance Login" page (Figure 2.6[C]), requiring users to log in again to get to the "Mailbox Maintenance" page (Figure 2.6[D]). Finally, clicking "Vacation Message" displays a page that asks users to log in a third time, with the same "email ad-

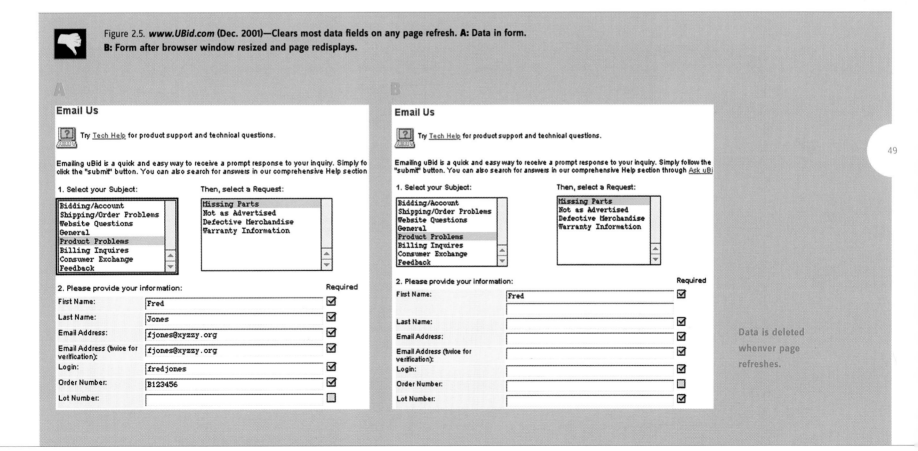

Figure 2.5. *www.UBid.com* (Dec. 2001)—Clears most data fields on any page refresh. **A: Data in form.**
B: Form after browser window resized and page redisplays.

49

Data is deleted whenver page refreshes.

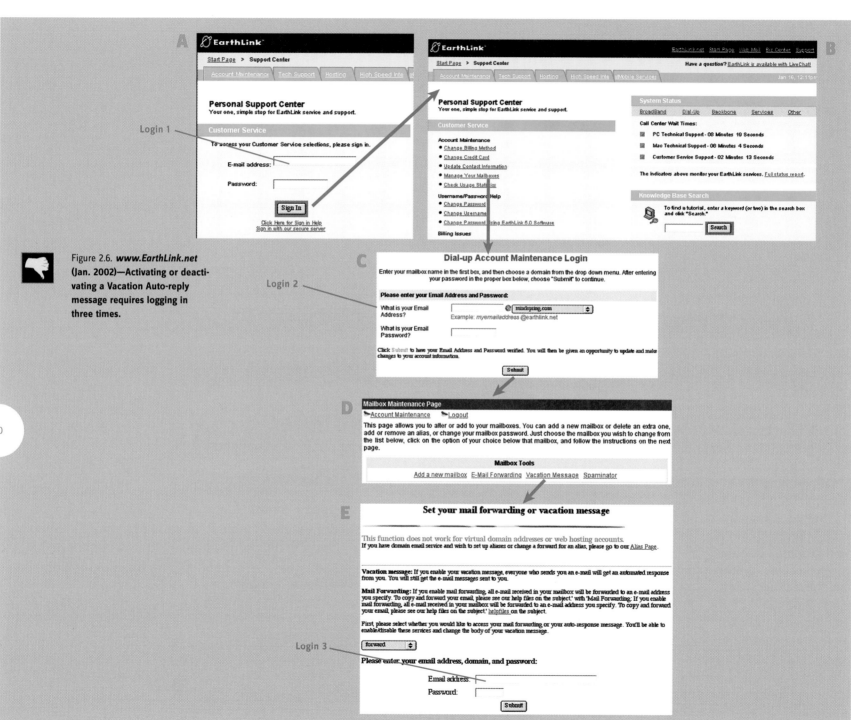

Figure 2.6. *www.EarthLink.net*
(Jan. 2002)—Activating or deacti-
vating a Vacation Auto-reply
message requires logging in
three times.

dress, domain, and password" (Figure 2.6[e]). Only after this third login is the page for setting Vacation messages displayed.

United.com is another site that often makes people log in repeatedly during a session.

One reason many sites require users to log in repeatedly is that there may be multiple ways to arrive at certain sections of the site. If a section requires login but can't tell whether the user already is, it will require a login of its own. If the user has already logged in, this will be a second—or third—request.

It's a Difficult Problem

One should not be too hard on sites that repeatedly ask users to log in or enter data. Avoiding it is difficult. The "stateless" nature of the Web—page accesses are treated as independent—makes it awkward at best to follow users through a site, bringing their data along. This contrasts with desktop software and non-Web online information systems, in which all windows displayed to a user are part of a single session.

Avoiding the blooper gets even more difficult when completing a task involves *multiple* websites, as in the *ProxyVote* example. To avoid asking for data twice, it must be transferred between sites. This is difficult or impossible for two reasons:

> *Statelessness:* Transferring data between pages is at *least* as difficult when pages are from different sites as when they are from the same site.

> *Legal restrictions:* In addition to technical obstacles, data transfer across organization boundaries may face legal obstacles: privacy policies, rules, and laws.

Not only is avoiding the blooper difficult from a technical standpoint, the "repeated-login" form of it is sometimes *intentional.* For all a site knows, the user walked away from the computer without logging out or quitting the browser, and now a second person is using it and is about to access information or buy something in the first person's name. Such scenarios are unlikely in private homes but are more likely in schools, libraries, and Internet cafes.

However, most Web users, and an even greater majority of *potential* Web users, don't know or care how hard the problem is. They don't know or care that the Web is stateless. And they don't know or care that repeated logins may be for their own protection. They just know that having to give the same data again is a bother and is something "good" organizations and desktop software don't require. And since they are the customers, they are right.

AVOIDING THE BLOOPER

Not making Web users enter data more than once should be a high-priority goal. Yes, it's difficult, but website designers, architects, and developers can do better than they have. We know this because some sites are better than others at remembering what users told them. Development teams that downplay the importance of this issue to save development time or costs are making an important business decision for their company. They are creating a website that will have lower customer loyalty than it would have if it preserved user data and propagated it to wherever it was needed.

Let's consider some things Web developers can do to avoid the blooper. Here, the focus is on high-level goals, not implementation details. The sidebar (Tech Talk: Methods for Avoiding Asking Twice) describes technical methods for achieving these goals.

51

Don't Lose Data on Return to Page

Losing data when a page refreshes or a user backs up should be considered a showstopper bug. Do whatever it takes to avoid it.

Don't Force Users through Multiple Sites

Websites should avoid architectures that route essential tasks through other sites (see Chapter 3, Blooper 18: Not Linking Directly), especially when completing the task requires getting information from the user. If one site needs a service from another site, fine, but it should do it "behind the users' back" rather than by explicitly handing the user off to the other site. For example, one website can act as a user interface to another site, feeding data to it and retrieving data from it, filtering and reformatting the data from the other site for presentation to users.

Design Site with a Single Universal Login

To avoid requiring multiple redundant logins, websites should keep track of the user's login status in a way that is accessible to all parts of the site. A particular page's designer should not assume that a user who arrives at the page either is already logged in or needs to be logged in. Instead, any page that needs the user to be logged in should check the user's login status, and if the user is not logged in, display a login page or dialog box before proceeding.

One website that avoids multiple logins is the American Cancer Society's Cancer Survivor Network site, *ACSCSN.org.* Certain functions on the site are restricted to logged in members, but no matter where members go on the site, they are never asked to log in more than once.

Some websites require multiple levels of security. A user may log in to access a low-security area of the site, then log in again to access a higher security area. However, the higher security login should require *different* identifying information than the lower security one; otherwise, it's not really higher security.

Push for Better Support from Browsers and the Web

Website developers and designers are limited to makeshift methods of bringing user data from page to page. Better, universal solutions will require help from browser developers and even the architects of the World Wide Web. The sidebar (Tech Talk: Methods for Avoiding Asking Twice) describes the methods Web developers use to avoid this blooper—Web "cookies" and "stuffed" URLs—and explains how better browser support and Web protocols can help even more.

Blooper 9: Requiring Unneeded Data

Almost as annoying as websites that ask for the same data more than once are sites that ask for data they don't really need. All Web users have encountered sites that

> Require a company name when registering a purchase even though you didn't buy the product for any company

> Ask for both a unique ID number (such as an account number) *and* a name

> Treat all data fields as "required" even though some aren't really necessary and should be optional

Your Zip Code Isn't Enough; We Need Your State Too

House.gov, the website of the U.S. House of Representatives, provides a page for sending email to your representative. That page requires site users to specify both a postal zip code and a state to locate their congressional representative (Figure 2.7[A]). Providing only a zip code is treated as an error (Figure 2.7[B]). Although a state is not usually enough to determine one's representative, a zip code is enough, since the zip code fully determines the state. Obviously, the

TECH TALK

TECH TALK: METHODS FOR AVOIDING ASKING TWICE

The Web was originally designed with no notion of an extended session—a connected series of requests. Web servers receive requests for individual pages from around the Internet and respond by sending each page to its requester. Each request is treated independent of others. As a result, Web servers—and therefore websites—initially had no way to know that two successive page requests came from the same user.

Why was the Web designed this way? Because it was designed for sharing information, not for processing transactions. When people were just looking at archived documents and each other's Web pages, there was no problem.

When forms, scripts, and e-commerce were added to the Web, the problems of propagating data through a stateless system arose. Web implementers had to devise ways to let Web servers determine that a series of requests is from the same user, and ways to propagate data between pages.

It isn't so much of a problem when data is to be shared between forms on two successive Web pages. In that special case, the script processing the first form's data can load the next form with any data that carries over. The problem arises when there are intervening pages without data on them: Data collected on page 1 isn't needed on page 2 but is needed on page 3. Compounding the problem is that Web users can—and do—navigate unpredictably around a site, rather than in predefined paths.

To allow sites to propagate users' data throughout a site to avoid asking for it again, three quite different methods were devised: "hidden forms," "cookies,"

and "stuffed" URLs. A fourth, very different approach involving browsers is described afterward.

HIDDEN FORMS

In this approach, every page has a form on it, but most pages hide them. All links from the page trigger a Submit script, which (among other things) passes the data to the next page. This is cumbersome and slow, because

> The form pages must be generated dynamically to be filled in automatically by the scripts. The hidden forms method doesn't work for static HTML forms.

> A site's pages contain extra, invisible baggage, inflating their size and download times.

> All the data is sent back and forth between the browser and the server every time a link or button is clicked.

The "hidden forms" approach is now regarded as "old fashioned"; the next two methods are preferred.

COOKIES

Website developers and browser makers devised a way for a website to send a small token—known as a *cookie*—to a Web user's browser and later retrieve it. The cookie identifies the site that issues it and assigns a unique ID to the user. It can also store other data. The browser saves the cookie and, whenever the site asks for it, sends it back. When a user accesses a page on a site, the site asks the user's browser if it has the site's cookie. If the browser has the cookie, it sends it back to the site. The site uses the cookie's user ID to retrieve the user's data from its database for use on the current page.

There are two types of cookies:

> *Session cookies:* Browsers store these in memory and delete them when the user navigates to a new Web domain (e.g., from *Amazon.com* to *Powells.com*). Session cookies allow sites to track a user through a session.

> *Persistent cookies:* Browsers store these in disk files and don't delete them until asked to by the issuing domain or the user. Persistent cookies allow sites to recognize returning users and relieve them of the need to log in every time they revisit a site.

Cookies are the primary way websites avoid asking users twice for the same data. For example, *ACSCSN.org* achieves a single site-wide login by setting a login cookie on the user's computer and having all restricted functions check for the cookie. If the cookie is absent, the user is asked to log in before he or she can access the function.

However, cookies are controversial, especially persistent ones. They can be abused to track individuals around the Web, violating their privacy. Although a given Web domain can check only for its own cookies, banner ads can issue and check for their own cookies from all the sites on which the ad appears. Web advertisers sometimes do this. Some Web users dislike the idea of being tracked. Another problem is that persistent cookies consume space on users' computers. Although the amount of space cookies require is usually miniscule, some people don't like the thought that any website they visit can put cookies on their computer. Based on these concerns, some Web users set their browsers to refuse some or all cookies. Sites that rely on cookies may not work properly for such users.

53

TECH TALK: METHODS FOR AVOIDING ASKING TWICE–cont'd

Browser makers such as Netscape and Microsoft have tried to address concerns about cookies. Newer browsers give Web users more control over what cookies their browser accepts and allow users to examine and delete persistent cookies. However, the tracking problem remains. Browser makers and architects of the Web could help alleviate concerns about cookies by making it harder to abuse them.

Stuffed URLs

Another way to follow users from page to page in a site involves "stuffing" the URL of a destination page with data from the current Web session (visit), such as a unique session ID. For example,

```
<a href="checkout.html">Checkout</a>
```

would be sent as either

```
<a href="checkout.html?id=543XYZZY">
Checkout</a>
```

or

```
<a href="checkout.html?email=
FredFlinstone@bedrock.net">Checkout</a>
```

The site receives the URL and sends the page, either augmenting it directly with the user's data or using the session ID to fetch the user's data and then augmenting the page.

Of course, this method results in long, complex URLs most users can't decipher. Such URLs also make poor bookmarks. If the appended data is more than just site-generated unique session IDs, such as an email address or telephone number, there are more serious disadvantages: (1) The data is transmitted unencrypted over the Internet, where it can be intercepted, and (2) the data becomes part of the site's permanent Web log, where many people can access it.

Designers of Web protocols and browser companies could improve this situation by devising a way for browsers and websites to pass session data–preferably encrypted–without appending it to URLs.

Browser-Based Solution: Automatic Form Fill-in

Browser makers recently began offering their own solution to the "repeated request" blooper. Newer browsers can detect forms on displayed pages and offer to fill in data automatically. The browser either remembers the data from previous website forms the user filled out or gets it from a special user-profile form the user filled out.

This approach assumes–probably correctly–that Web users don't care *how* the "repeated request" problem is solved; they just don't want to have to reenter data. It shifts the responsibility for remembering data from websites to the browser.

The problems of browser-based form fill in are as follows:

> Not all browsers provide it yet.

> Few Web users use it, even if their browser provides it.

> Browsers sometimes miss data fields for which they have data.

> Browsers sometimes fill in data fields incorrectly.

Web developers can foster browser-based automatic form fill-in by using semantic page-description languages such as XML instead of HTML and by tagging data fields in standard ways. For example, if email address fields in all forms were tagged "<email_addr>," browsers could recognize them reliably.

Browser-based automatic form fill-in may eventually be the dominant way the "repeated request" problem is solved. Until then, the burden is on *site* developers, who have to do whatever they can to avoid asking their users for data repeatedly.

implementation is too simplistic, probably to save development costs. I'll bet that many people who use this page initially give only their zip code, get the error message, emit a sigh (or curse), and then give both state and zip code.

This site also commits Blooper 8, Redundant Requests. When a user reads "You must select a State" and clicks the link to return to the "Write Your Representative" page, the zip code field has been blanked, requiring the user to type it again.

EarthLink.net provides a function for looking up EarthLink's dial-up access phone numbers in cities around the world. For example, if an EarthLink customer were traveling to New York City and wanted to connect from there, he or she could use the function to find the local access number. However, the number lookup function is too demanding: To determine where the user will be, it requires that you give it a complete phone number (Figure 2.8) even though an area code would, in principle, be enough. Customers who don't yet know where they will be staying might not have a complete phone number. All they would know is the area code. In such situations, customers have to make up a phone number. Even when customers know a phone number where they will be, why should they have to type it, when an area code will do?

EarthLink's developers might argue that some area codes have more than one access number. Fine, but when a user gives a complete number, *EarthLink.net* displays not one, but a *list* of access numbers in and *around* the specified area—the same list that would presumably be displayed for just an area code. Therefore, requiring a specific phone number as input is pointless.

Figure 2.7. **www.*House.gov* (Nov 2001)—A:** "Write Your Representative" page requires state and zip code. **B:** Error message indicating that state is required.

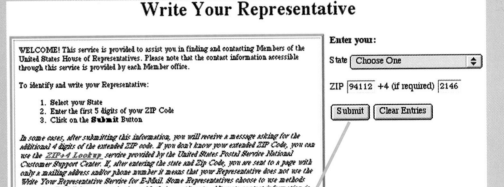

Write Your Representative

WELCOME! This service is provided to assist you in finding and contacting Members of the United States House of Representatives. Please note that the contact information accessible through this service is provided by each Member office.

To identify and write your Representative:

1. Select your State
2. Enter the first 5 digits of your ZIP Code
3. Click on the **Submit** Button

In some cases, after submitting this information, you will receive a message asking for the additional 4 digits of the extended ZIP code. If you don't know your extended ZIP Code, you can use the *ZIP+4 Lookup* service provided by the United States Postal Service National Customer Support Center. If, after entering the state and Zip Code, you are sent to a page with only a mailing address and/or phone number it means that your Representative does not use the Write Your Representative Service for E-Mail. Some Representatives choose to use methods other than E-Mail for communicating with their constituents. Alternate contact information is given.

Enter your:

State [Choose One ⬍]

ZIP [94112] +4 (if required) [2146]

[Submit] [Clear Entries]

The U.S. House Of Representatives

Determining Your Representative From Your ZIP Code

You must select a **State**.

Write Your Representative Home Page
House of Representatives Home Page

Figure 2.8. **www.*Earthlink.net* (May 2002)—Asking for more data than needed. A:** Form requires full phone number. **B:** Error message when only area code given. Area code should be enough.

Access Numbers

Dialup Access Numbers

To find the best numbers to use to connect to EarthLink from another location (work, travel, etc.), enter the local area code/phone number in the boxes below and click the Search button.

[212] - [ ] - [ ] [Search]

support.earthlink.net – [JavaScript Application]

⚠ Please check the length of your phone number

[OK]

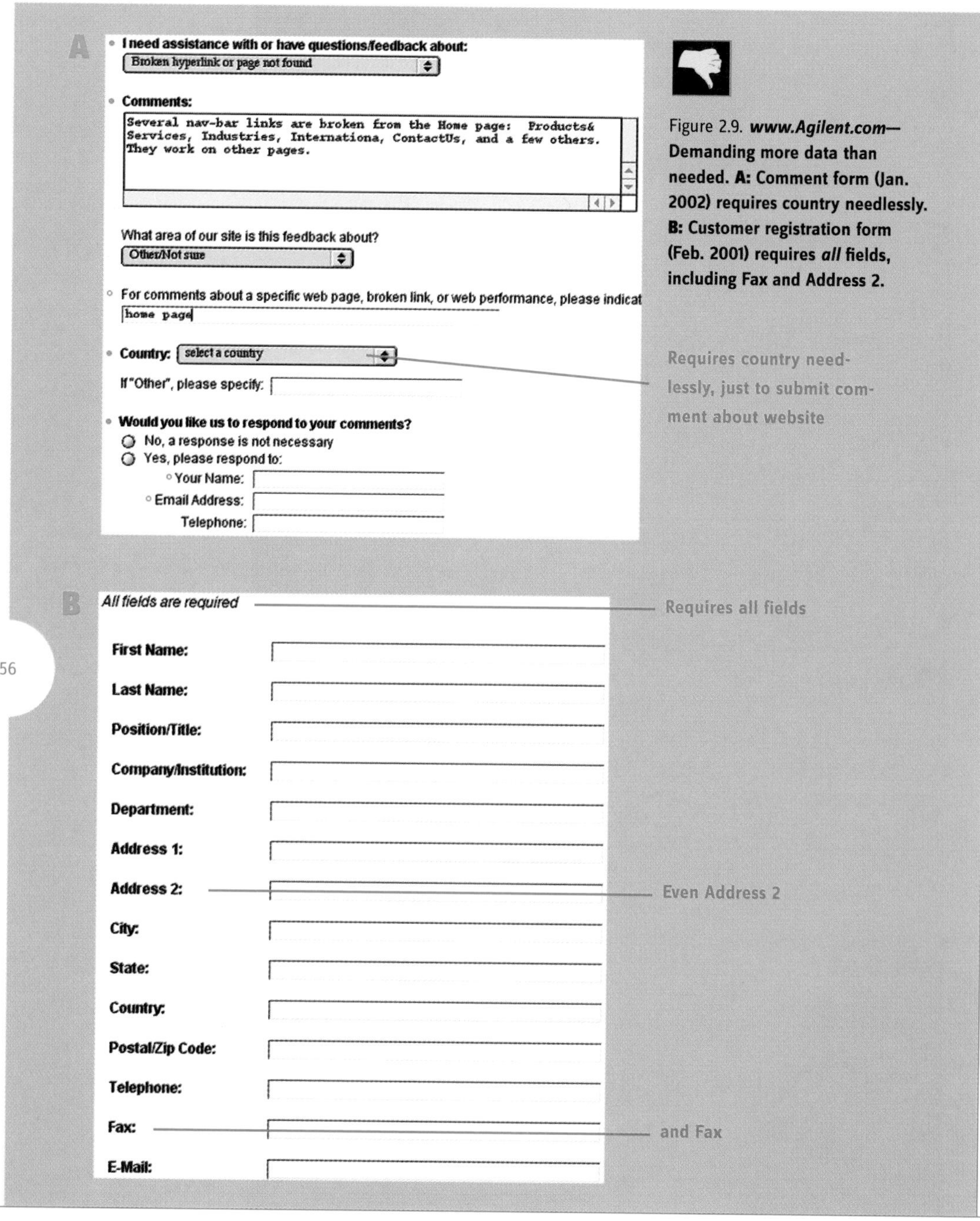

Figure 2.9. **www.Agilent.com—
Demanding more data than
needed. A: Comment form (Jan.
2002) requires country needlessly.
B: Customer registration form
(Feb. 2001) requires all fields,
including Fax and Address 2.**

Requires country need-
lessly, just to submit comment about website

Requires all fields

Even Address 2

and Fax

56

You Must Tell Us; It's Required

Some sites designate certain data fields as "required" for no
good reason. Two examples of this come from *Agilent.com*.
The form for submitting questions or comments about the
site includes a Country setting and treats it as required
(Figure 2.9[A]). What country? The user's? Agilent's? Why
must users specify a country to comment on the website?
A customer registration form asks for a *lot* of data and
states at the top "All fields are required" (Figure 2.9[B]). All
fields? What if a customer doesn't *have* a department, fax,
or address 2? Answer: They have to make one up to register.

AVOIDING THE BLOOPER

The way to avoid this blooper is not to be overzealous
about collecting data:

> Ask for as little data as you can—only what you really
need. If you aren't sure what you will do with a certain
piece of information, you don't need it, so don't ask for it.

> Stick to the current transaction. Data you would like to
obtain for other purposes, such as marketing or estab-
lishing a relationship with the user, should be requested
in separate and optional areas of the site, such as registration pages, membership applications, and email announcement subscription forms.

> Don't make any data "required" unless you really cannot
proceed without it.

> Don't require data some customers won't have: You
would just force them to make it up or take their business elsewhere.

> When someone gives you information, deduce as much
as you can from it. Use what you know to fill in other
data fields if possible. For example, it would be very un-
friendly for a website to ask visitors for both date of birth
and age, because age can be deduced from date of birth.

Asking for data you don't really need scares privacy-minded people away, hampers customers from achieving their goals, frustrates those who don't *have* the information you require, and slows throughput at your site, thereby hindering its success.

Blooper 10: Pointless Choice

Related to redundant requests and asking for data you don't need is the blooper of offering needless or meaningless choices.

Some Web developers might protest, "Hey, but choice is good, isn't it? Offering users more choice makes the site more functional for them, no? How could more choice be bad?" Let's enumerate four ways choice can be unnecessary, meaningless, useless, or otherwise undesirable:

> *No significant difference:* The options are not different enough to make a difference.

> *Users don't know:* The options are meaningless to users.

> *Obvious answer:* There is an obvious choice, but the site ignores it.

> *Site could figure it out:* There is no need to ask this; it could be figured out automatically.

I will discuss these in turn.

No Significant Difference

Some websites confront their users with a choice in which the available options to choose from are all the same or at least seem that way from users' point of view. Therefore, choosing between them is pointless—it is just an annoying waste of time.

Continental Airlines' website commits an example of this blooper (Figure 2.10). If you tell it you want to fly to

Detroit, it tells you "More than one airport matches your request. Please select an airport from the list below." Listed are "All airports" and "DTW." It is asking you to choose whether you want to consider flights into the DTW airport or into "all airports," where "all" is exactly one airport: DTW. You get the same flights no matter which of these you choose!

A different sort of pointless choice can be seen at *ZBuyer.com.* The site provides two Search functions from which site users can choose (Figure 2.11). However, the lower Search function is functionally equivalent to the upper one when its menu is set to "all products." Furthermore, "all products" is the menu's default value. Therefore, there is no reason to make users choose between these two Search functions. The lower one is all that is needed.

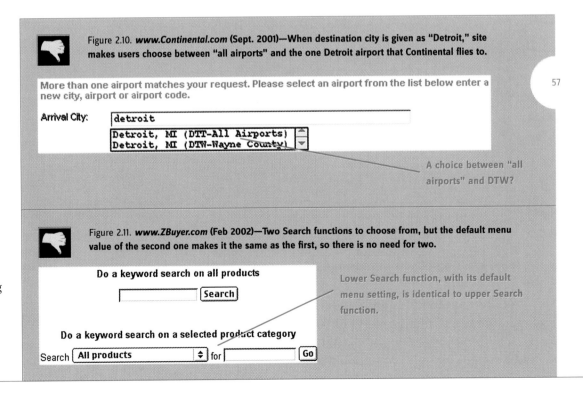

Figure 2.10. *www.Continental.com* (Sept. 2001)—When destination city is given as "Detroit," site makes users choose between "all airports" and the one Detroit airport that Continental flies to.

More than one airport matches your request. Please select an airport from the list below enter a new city, airport or airport code.

Arrival City: detroit

Detroit, MI (DTT-All Airports)
Detroit, MI (DTW-Wayne County)

A choice between "all airports" and DTW?

57

Figure 2.11. *www.ZBuyer.com* (Feb 2002)—Two Search functions to choose from, but the default menu value of the second one makes it the same as the first, so there is no need for two.

Do a keyword search on all products

[ ] [Search]

Do a keyword search on a selected product category

Search [All products ▼] for [ ] [Go]

Lower Search function, with its default menu setting, is identical to upper Search function.

Figure 2.12. *www.Sibelius.com* (Jan. 2002)—Cryptic download locations, such as "UK 1" and "UK 2" make choosing between them impossible.

Step 2 of 3: Choose your download location

Now choose the location nearest to you and click **Download**. Installation instructions will appear when the download begins.

- ⊙ USA 2   ○ UK 2
- ○ UK 1   ○ UK 3 (FTP)

[Download]

Users don't know where UK1, UK2, and UK3 servers are, so they have no basis for rational choice.

Figure 2.13. *www.ProxyVote.com* (Oct. 2001)—Choice is incomprehensible to most ProxyVote users.

PROXY ✓Vote

Most users don't have the knowledge required to make this choice.

WELCOME TO PROXYVOTE.COM

Please select one of the links below...

If you received your proxy material in the mail, please have your material and your control number ready.

If you received a notification via e-mail, please have your control number and Personal Identification Number ready.

To submit your voting instructions over our secure site, click HERE.

If your browser cannot support secure transactions via SSL encryption, click HERE.

Need to update to a security enabled browser? Click HERE.

Users Don't Know

When the available options are meaningless to users, they have no basis for choosing among them. If the site won't let users ignore the choice, they have to guess.

For example, *Sibelius.com* allows customers to download software. To expedite downloading, the site lets customers choose from four download locations (Figure 2.12). The trouble is some of the download locations are labeled so cryptically—UK 1, UK 2, UK 3—that customers from the United Kingdom will have no idea which one to choose. These options probably make sense only to Sibelius employees who manage the download servers.

Asking users whether a transaction should use "secure" versus "insecure" protocols is a common way to ask users to choose between options they don't understand. *ProxyVote.com* makes this mistake (Figure 2.13). *ProxyVote* instructs its users as follows: "To submit your voting instructions over our secure site, click HERE. If your browser cannot support secure transactions via SSL encryption, click HERE" (see also Chapter 7, Blooper 52: "Click Here": Burying Links in Text). ProxyVote's users are average people who own stock in companies. Few of them are engineers. Many are seniors. Most will have no idea whether their browser can support secure transactions or what SSL encryption is. Forcing nontechnical Web users to make such a choice is ridiculous (see also Chapter 6, Blooper 42: Speaking Geek).

Obvious Answer

Some sites make their users choose even though it is obvious which option is most likely the right one. The obvious choice can be based on knowing how people use the site, common sense, or previous user input. Unfortunately, many sites ignore the obvious, making users choose needlessly.

A good example of this comes from the website of a company for which I have consulted (Figure 2.14). The site used to have a splash screen offering a choice of three language-specific sites: English, Spanish, and Portuguese. Offering language options is good, but the way this choice is offered is not. An overwhelming majority of people who use this site speak English. Furthermore, the other language sites were not even *available* when I collected this example; they were both labeled "under construction." The obvious choice is to default to the English site, providing links from there to the Spanish and Portuguese sites. Fortunately, a recent site update fixed this blooper.

As explained in Blooper 8: Redundant Requests, a Web user's previous input can make what the user wants obvious, eliminating the need for further questions. However, many sites seem to ignore what their users have already told them.

An example of this problem can be found at American Airlines' website, *AA.com*. Imagine you are planning a flight to New York City and don't care which of New York City's several airports you arrive at. You give "NYC" as your destination and click Go. A message appears: "We are unable to determine your desired airport(s) from your entry. Please select the . . . arrival airports(s) from the list below and click on the Go button to continue your flight search." With the message is a menu of airports, with Newark International as the default (Figure 2.15[B]).

Remember, we are assuming you don't *care* which airport you arrive at. You want it to show flights into *all* New York City airports. You might notice that one of the options in the menu is not a specific airport, but "NYC, New York—All Airports," exactly what you said you wanted. But now you have to say it again. Worse, it isn't even the default! (See Chapter 4, Blooper 24: No Defaults and Blooper 25: Faulty Defaults.)

Figure 2.14. **Client website (Nov. 2000)—Users must select a language to proceed, even though more than 90% of users will choose English, and even though the Spanish and Portuguese sites are "under construction." The site should just go to the English pages, with links from there to the Spanish and Portuguese sites.**

English   Españoles   Portuguêses
Está bajo construcción.   Está vindo logo.

Must choose language, even though most users want English, and the Spanish and Portuguese pages aren't yet available.

Site Could Figure It Out

Finally, some websites and Web-based applications ask users to make choices that the software could figure out on its own. Usually, this occurs when the site needs to know the user's location, browser, plug-ins, computer, or operating system to deliver the correct goods or optimize service, but the developers didn't want to write the code to determine that, so they ask users to tell the site.

The classic form of this is asking Web users to identify their browser. An example can be found at *eDesignCorp.com,* the website of a design firm. The site has a splash screen that asks visitors "Which browser are you using?," with choices America Online, Netscape, Internet Explorer, and Other (Figure 2.16). This is presumably to allow the site to optimize its presentation for the visitor's browser. We will ignore the fact that the three most popular browsers—the ones listed in the choice—are not different enough to warrant optimizing the site for each. With a little work, websites can be coded so they work in all three of these browsers with no browser-specific optimization. We will also ignore the problem that the "Other" category lumps together Web browsers as disparate as Mosaic, Opera, WebTV, Mozilla, and Lynx. For now, the point is that the site does not need to ask this question because it can

59

Figure 2.15. **www.AA.com** (May 2002)—**A: Reservation form, specifying "NYC" as destination. B: User is told the destination is ambiguous and is asked to choose a destination but is offered one option that is the same as already given.**

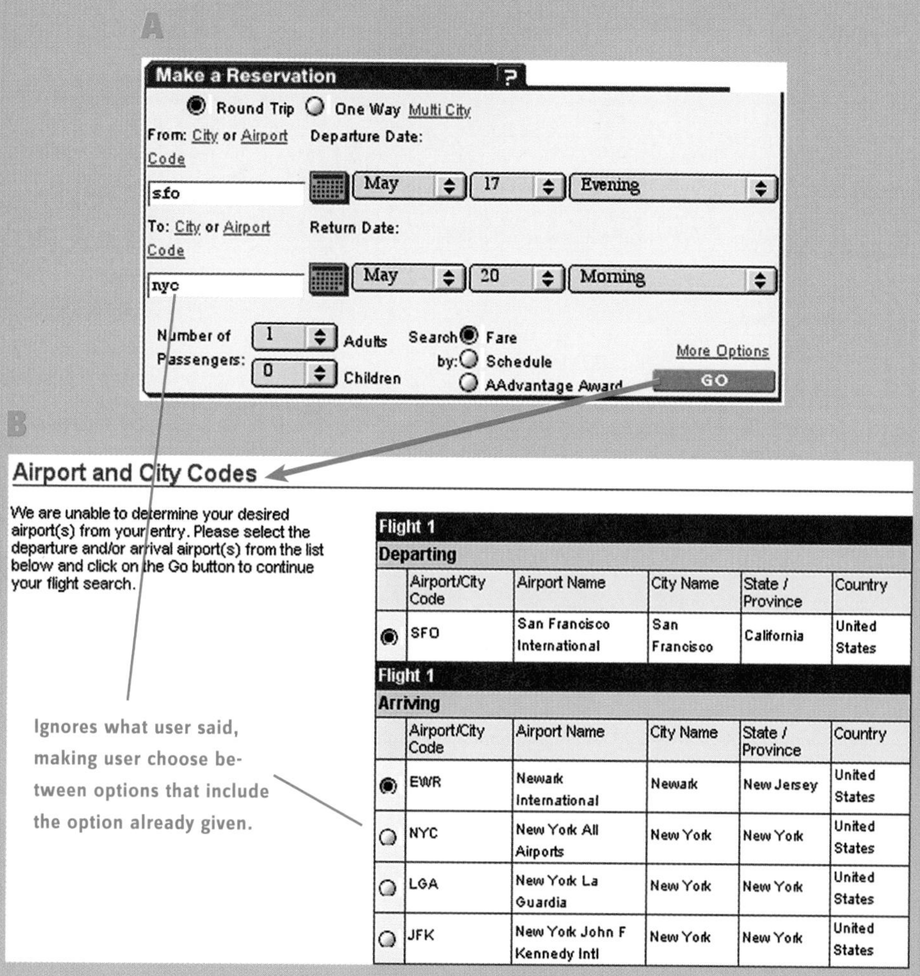

Ignores what user said, making user choose between options that include the option already given.

identify the users' browser itself. Most Web browsers, if asked by a site, identify themselves and the operating system on which they are running (for details, see the sidebar Tech Talk: "Sniffing" the User's Browser).

The bottom line: If it is important for your site to know which browser a visitor is using, it should be important enough to spend the small amount of extra development time it takes to have the site figure it out without bothering visitors.

AVOIDING THE BLOOPER

How to avoid presenting unnecessary choices depends on why the choice is unnecessary.

If the Choice Makes No Difference, Don't Offer It

A website that asks users to choose between options that make no significant difference in what they get is just wasting users' valuable time. Don't do it.

How do you discover that your site presents absurd identical choices? By testing it before it is released. To find this sort of problem, you may be able to get away with using members of your own team as test subjects. Keep in mind, however, that members of a development team, when testing their own software, tend to overlook many annoyances. It is better to observe people who are like the site's intended users. Even if they don't explicitly complain about being required to choose between identical options, you'll be more likely to spot the problem than if you just test on yourself.

If Users Won't Understand the Question or Know the Answer, Don't Ask

Consider whether the choice your site asks visitors to make is understandable to them. Site visitors may seem like the only people you *can* ask, but that doesn't make them the *right* people to ask. If they have no idea what you're asking, you won't get useful responses. If you haven't provided a default, you're forcing users to guess. If you *have* provided a default, as *Sibelius.com* does, users will probably just leave it as is, whether or not it's right for their situation.

How do you determine whether a choice presented by your website is meaningful to users? The only reliable way is by usability testing. Such tests need not—and should not— wait until the site is about to go live. They can be conducted early, cheaply, using paper or simple HTML prototypes, before anything real has been implemented.

Even if you know your site's users will understand a choice, they may not know the answer. Perhaps you're asking the wrong people. To avoid delaying, frustrating, and annoying your site's users, consider whether there is another way to get the answer.

If There Is an Obvious Likely Choice, Choose It

As illustrated already by the unnamed and American Airlines websites, sometimes the correct option is obvious based on common sense, normal usage patterns, or previous user input. Sites that don't use such "knowledge" waste users' valuable time and effort. They are annoying.

Don't annoy your visitors and customers with questions that have obvious answers. Assume the answer, with a way for people to change it if they want to. They usually won't.

If the Site Can Figure It Out, Don't Bother Users

Finally, don't ask users to tell you things that the system can figure out on its own. Appliance makers figured this out: They finally stopped asking consumers to set cameras for film ASA and cassette players for cassette type (Johnson 1990). People couldn't set them correctly, and even if they could, why should they have to? Nowadays, consumer

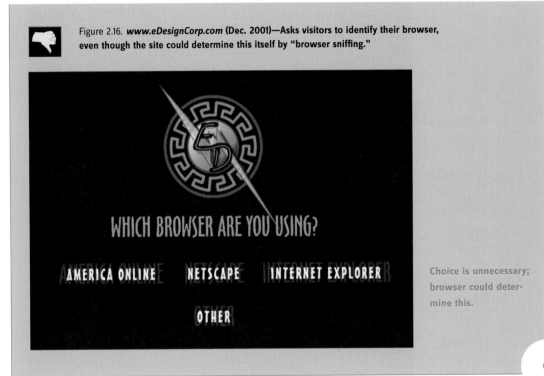

Figure 2.16. ***www.eDesignCorp.com*** **(Dec. 2001)—Asks visitors to identify their browser, even though the site could determine this itself by "browser sniffing."**

Choice is unnecessary; browser could determine this.

61

cameras set themselves to the film's ASA, and cassette players set themselves for the type of cassette being used.

The Web needs to be more like consumer appliances: simple, focused in functionality, and as automatic as possible. If a website needs to know something but can figure it out by itself, it should not ask its users for the information.

Although *Sibelius.com* commits a form of the blooper when it asks users to choose a server to download from (see Figure 2.12), it avoids the blooper in another situation. When a customer downloads software, the site determines which version of the software the user probably wants to download—Windows versus Mac—by using information supplied by the user's browser. The appropriate version of the software is presented as the default (Figure 2.17).

Figure 2.17. ***www.Sibelius.com*** **(Jan 2002)—Site "knows" what computer and operating system visitor is using. A: When accessed from a Mac, default platform is correct. B: The same when accessed from a Windows PC.**

A

Step 1 of 3: Choose your platform

Please type your email address into the b

Platform	Language
◉ Mac	English
○ Windows	

B

Step 1 of 3: Choose your platform

Please type your email address into the b

Platform	Language
○ Mac	English
◉ Windows	

Figure 2.18. ***www.Netscape.com*** **(June 2002)—Netscape's download page "sniffs" users' browsers.**

Detects what browser is being used ————

You are currently using:
Netscape Communicator 4.76
English language, Macintosh PPC

Upgrade Now!* Netscape 6.2.3
English language, Macintosh PPC

[Download]   [Order CD!]

MacOS X users · <u>Click Here</u>

Figure 2.19. ***www.NetWorldMap.com*** **(June 2002)—Can usually correctly guess a Web visitor's approximate location from the IP address.**

Don't tell me, let me guess!

You wouldn't by chance be viewing this page from **United States** would you? Somewhere around the **San Francisco** area? (I mean, like within 3 or 4 hours drive.)

☑ Yes, or ☒ No.

Netscape.com's download page shows that a site can determine what browser is being used to view the site (Figure 2.18). The sidebar gives technical details on how to tell what browser a site visitor is using.

Finally, *NetWorldMap.com* shows that sites that need to know a visitor's approximate location can make a good guess based on the visitor's IP address (Figure 2.19). *NetWorldMap* has a database of IP addresses mapped to locations. The mapping is not perfect, but it is good enough to be useful.

Blooper 11: Omitting Important Options

Another way many websites and Web-based applications fail to support users' tasks is by omitting crucial options when users are asked to make choices. Although this blooper has roots in a site's front-end Web design, its roots also extend into the content and business logic embodied in a site's back-end services.

Often, choices are presented explicitly as controls such as menus or radiobuttons. On the Web, choices are also frequently presented simply as arrays of links on Web pages. However the choices are presented, all plausible options must be present; otherwise, site visitors will feel trapped—"I have to choose, but the option I need isn't here! What now?"—and frustrated—"This %@&# website won't let me do what I want to do!" Providing all plausible options requires that designers understand and consider all the different goals that users could have at each choice point. Sadly, many Web designers don't do their homework and end up presenting choices that trap and frustrate users.

Classic . . . Just Classic!

A classic example of this blooper comes from the website of the University of California at Los Angeles, *UCLA.edu*. The UCLA extension program's section of the site,

TECH TALK

TECH TALK: "SNIFFING" THE USER'S BROWSER

Detecting which browser a site visitor is using is called "browser sniffing." It requires that the server be running a script, such as CGI or Java script.

When a browser hits a website, it automatically sends a bunch of information to the Web server. Included in that information is a text-string labeled HTTP_USER_AGENT. An example of this type of data, for a person using Microsoft Internet Explorer 5.14 on a Macintosh, is

```
HTTP_USER_AGENT="Mozilla/4.0
(compatible; MSIE 5.14; Mac_PowerPC)"
```

A Web server that needs to know which browser a visitor is using would have a script to examine the USER AGENT string and act accordingly; for example, send pages optimized for the visitors' browser.

Here are two websites about browser sniffing:

> *www.eit.ihk-edu.dk/instruct/browsersniffing.php*–
Explains browser sniffing, with sample scripts. Provided by the Engineering College of Copenhagen, Department of Electronics and Information Technology.

> *gemal.dk/browserspy/*–Shows what your browser sends to sites you visit. Provided by Henrik Gemal.

unex.UCLA.edu, begins with a splash page that asks visitors to choose between two options: "Connecting with 28.8 or slower? Click here" *and* "Flash Enhanced Site Click here" (Figure 2.20). Um, where do I click if I have a 28.8-kbaud modem *and* the Flash browser plug-in? What if I have a fast Internet connection such as DSL but don't have or want Flash? The site asks users to choose between options that (1) are not mutually exclusive and (2) don't cover all the possibilities. Many visitors to this site will feel stymied by this choice. Perhaps the designers of this site assumed no one with a 28.8-kbaud modem would have Flash and no one with a faster connection wouldn't, but if that's what they assumed, they are simply wrong.

You Want to Fly WHEN?

In websites for booking air travel, the controls for specifying flight details are all pretty similar to each other.

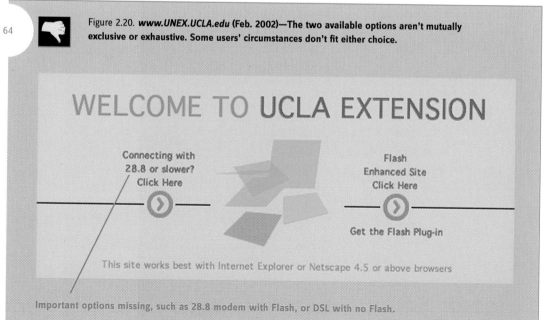

Figure 2.20. **www.UNEX.UCLA.edu (Feb. 2002)—The two available options aren't mutually exclusive or exhaustive. Some users' circumstances don't fit either choice.**

WELCOME TO UCLA EXTENSION

Connecting with
28.8 or slower?
Click Here

Flash
Enhanced Site
Click Here

Get the Flash Plug-in

This site works best with Internet Explorer or Netscape 4.5 or above browsers

Important options missing, such as 28.8 modem with Flash, or DSL with no Flash.

Customers specify a departure airport, a destination, dates, preferred departure times, and maybe some other optional settings such as the number of passengers, and then click a "Find Flights" button.

One way flight-search controls differ is in the menu options for desired flight times. Although one could imagine this becoming standardized across the air-travel industry, that hasn't happened—at least not yet. Whether this is for competitive reasons or is due to each company's implementation constraints is unclear. What is clear, however, is that some travel-time menus on the Web are better than others. The travel-time menus of some airlines and travel agencies lack important options.

Table 2.1 shows travel-time menus from five air-travel websites. The first three menus in Table 2.1 (columns 1 through 3) show one common flaw: providing only specific times. This makes it impossible for travelers to specify that *any* time of day is okay, that any time of *morning* is okay, or that they want a red-eye (late evening) flight. The hourly times listed by NWA, Cheap Tickets, and Travelocity also give users the false impression that the site's search for flights will be restricted to the indicated hour. The last two menus (columns 4 and 5), from *AA.com* and *United.com,* list both specific times and general time periods. Although this is an improvement over the previous three menus, one problem is that it makes little difference to the Search results whether a user chooses a general time like "morning" or a specific one like "8:00 AM." None of the menus in Table 2.1 provide an "any time" or "all day" option.

In the Avoiding the Blooper section, we examine travel-time menus that provide the time-of-day options travelers need and don't provide ones they don't need.

Only Specific Times of Day			Specific Times + General Time-Periods	
Northwest Airlines *www.NWA.com* (Feb. 2002)	*CheapTickets.com* (Feb. 2002)	*Travelocity.com* (June 2002)	**American Airlines** *www.AA.com* (June 2002)	**United Airlines** *www.United.com* (June 2002)
12:00 midnight	1:00 am	12:00am	Early Morning	Morning
1:00 AM	2:00 am	1:00am	✓ Morning	Afternoon
2:00 AM	3:00 am	2:00am	Noon	Evening
3:00 AM	4:00 am	3:00am	Afternoon	12 am
4:00 AM	5:00 am	4:00am	Early Evening	1 am
5:00 AM	6:00 am	5:00am	Evening	✓ 2 am
6:00 AM	7:00 am	6:00am	1 am	3 am
7:00 AM	8:00 am	7:00am	2 am	4 am
8:00 AM	✓ 9:00 am	8:00am	3 am	5 am
9:00 AM	10:00 am	9:00am	4 am	6 am
10:00 AM	11:00 am	10:00am	5 am	7 am
11:00 AM	Noon	11:00am	6 am	8 am
12:00 noon	1:00 pm	12:00pm	7 am	9 am
1:00 PM	2:00 pm	1:00pm	8 am	10 am
2:00 PM	3:00 pm	2:00pm	9 am	11 am
3:00 PM	4:00 pm	3:00pm	10 am	12 pm
4:00 PM	5:00 pm	4:00pm	11 am	1 pm
5:00 PM	6:00 pm	✓ 5:00pm	12 pm	2 pm
6:00 PM	7:00 pm	6:00pm	1 pm	3 pm
7:00 PM	8:00 pm	7:00pm	2 pm	4 pm
8:00 PM	9:00 pm	8:00pm	3 pm	5 pm
9:00 PM	10:00 pm	9:00pm	4 pm	6 pm
10:00 PM	11:00 pm	10:00pm	5 pm	7 pm
11:00 PM	Midnight	11:00pm	6 pm	8 pm
Morning			7 pm	9 pm
✓ Noon			8 pm	10 pm
Evening			9 pm	11 pm
			10 pm	
			11 pm	
			12 am	

Table 2.1 **Air-travel reservation menus that provide no way to specify "any time."**

If You're from D.C., You're Nowhere, Man!

It's astounding how many websites provide menus for specifying a U.S. state but fail to include the District of Columbia—also known as Washington, D.C.—as a choice. If that is where you live, you have no straightforward way of ordering a product or registering with the site. You can give the address of a relative in another state, but why bother, when you can go to other sites that know D.C. exists.

Pitsco-legodacta.com's catalog order form has a menu for specifying one's state. The District of Columbia is missing. The menu's label also falsely suggests that it includes provinces in Canada or elsewhere, but it doesn't (Figure 2.21).

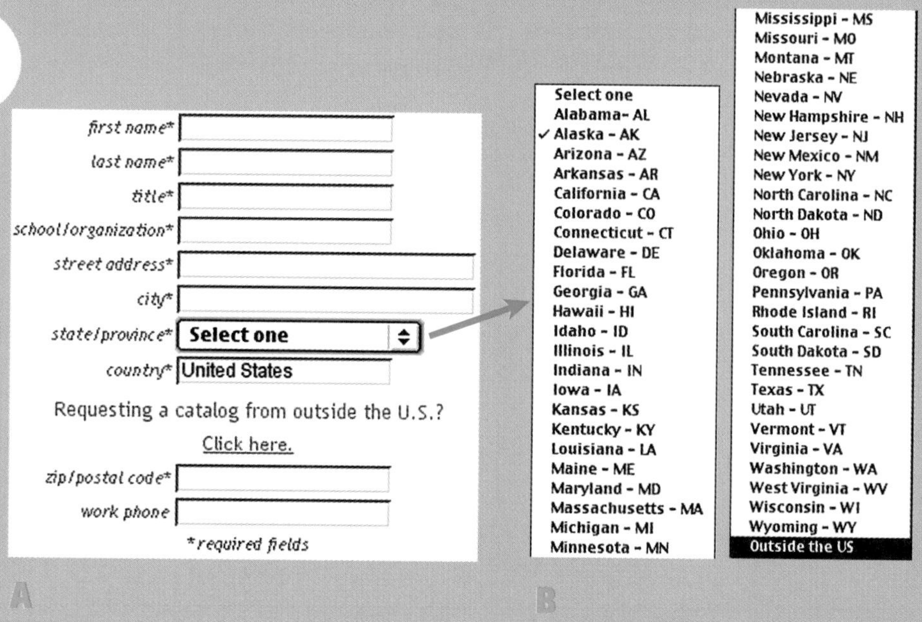

AVOIDING THE BLOOPER

The way Web designers and developers can avoid this blooper is to do their homework: Analyze fully the requirements of the intended users and then design the site or Web application to provide options that match those requirements. For the UCLA Extension splash page, a full analysis would have exposed the need for more options or combinations of options. Analysis, design, and development should be followed up with usability testing, beta-testing, and customer focus groups to check whether the site provides all the options users need. Costly? Yes, but not as costly as a website no one visits.

Table 2.2 shows travel-time menus from the websites of Continental Airlines and Greyhound Bus Company that avoid the blooper of omitting important options. The first menu (column 1) is from *Continental.com*'s Ticket Purchase page. It has every departure-time option anyone could possibly need, including "all day." As explained already, the specific hourly times are misleading because the search is never restricted to a specific hour anyway. For this reason, the much simpler menu on the site's home page (column 2 of Table 2.2) is better: It gives travelers a choice of morning, afternoon, evening, or all day, without facing them with a huge menu. *Greyhound.com*'s departure-time menu (column 3, Table 2.2) provides slightly more specific options than Continental's, plus a "Show All" option. I consider it just about perfect for specifying departure times and think all airlines and online travel agencies should simply adopt it.

Pitsco-LEGO Dacta's developers could have avoided their blooper—omitting Washington, D.C.—simply by copying code from other pages on another site of theirs. The site with the blooper is the main company site. Their online store is at a different site, *PLDstore.com*. The customer-registration form at *PLDstore.com* includes the District of Columbia in its State menu. No doubt, the store site was

Figure 2.21. *www.pitsco-legodacta.com* (June 2002)—**A: Catalog order form, with State/Province menu. B: Menu omits District of Columbia (Washington, D.C.).**

Continental Airlines
www.Continental.com
(June 2002)

✓ All Day
12:00 midnight
1:00 AM
2:00 AM
3:00 AM
4:00 AM
5:00 AM
6:00 AM
7:00 AM
8:00 AM
9:00 AM
10:00 AM
11:00 AM
12:00 noon
1:00 PM
2:00 PM
3:00 PM
4:00 PM
5:00 PM
6:00 PM
7:00 PM
8:00 PM
9:00 PM
10:00 PM
11:00 PM
Early Morning
Morning
Late Morning
Noon
Afternoon
Evening
Late Evening

Continental Airlines
www.Continental.com
(June 2002)

✓ all day
morning
afternoon
evening

Greyhound Bus Company
www.greyhound.com
(Jan. 2002)

Early Morning
Mid-Morning
Noon
Afternoon
Evening
Late Evening
Over Night
✓ Show All

Table 2.2 **Air-travel reservation menus that provide all necessary options. The latter two provide a simpler set of choices well suited for searching.**

Figure 2.22. **www.pldstore.com** (June 2002)—The customer registration form at the PLD Store site has a state menu that includes the District of Columbia.

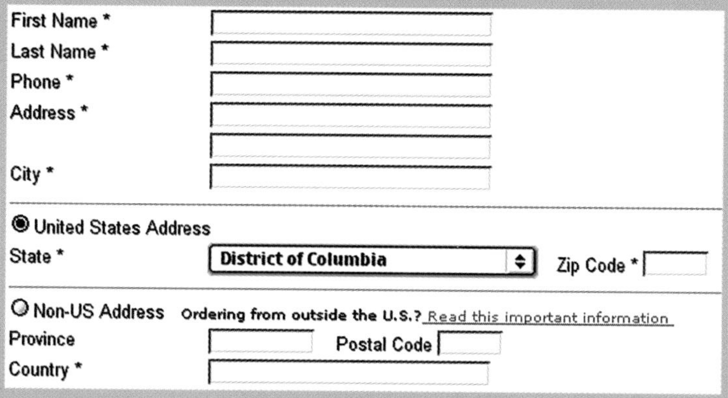

First Name *

Last Name *

Phone *

Address *

City *

⦿ United States Address

State * `District of Columbia` Zip Code *

◯ Non-US Address   Ordering from outside the U.S.? _Read this important information_

Province   Postal Code

Country *

A

Flight Search

From
s £o

Depart (MM/DD/YY)
10/18/2001

Time
morning

To
ann arbor

Return (MM/DD/YY)
10/21/2001

Time
evening

Figure 2.23. **A: www.Continental.com** (Sept. 2001); **B: www.NWA.com** (Sept. 2001)—Airline websites that don't know Detroit DTW is Ann Arbor's nearest major airport.

Search   Review   Review
Flights Itinerary Traveler Info   Book   Confirm

Search Flights (Roundtrip)

Travel Cities

Departure
City: San Francisco, CA (SFO-San Francisco Intl.)

ann arbor is not currently served by Continental or its partners. You may modify your search criteria, or call 1-888-308-1547 for assistance.

Arrival City: ann arbor

Sites don't know Detroit DTW is Ann Arbor's nearest major airport.

B

Fast Trip Finder

Search by: ⦿ Best Price ◯ Schedule
           Enter Departure Date
           (MM/DD/YY)
From
sfo   4/20/2002   Evening
           Enter Return Date
           (MM/DD/YY)
To
ann arbor 4/24/2002   Afternoon
Number
of Adults 1   More
               Options   SEARCH FLIGHTS

No Matching Flights Found

No Northwest Airlines and KLM Royal Dutch Airlines, or our codeshare partner, flights were found between San Francisco, CA (SFO-San Francisco Intl.) and Ann Arbor, MI (ARB) that matched your request.

You chose an airline that may have limited service dates or destinations. Click the **Change Search** button below to go back and change options to perform a new search on nwa.com Reservations, or click the **Cancel** button below to go back to Overview.

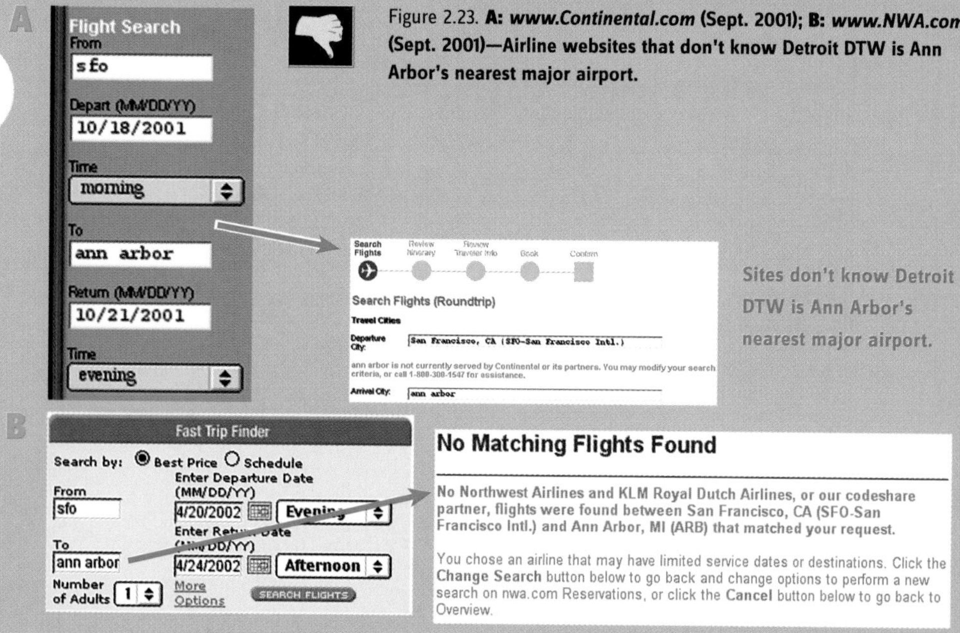

developed independently of the main site, with no oversight to ensure consistency between them (Figure 2.22).

Blooper 12: Clueless Back-end

Many e-commerce websites and Web information services exhibit an astounding lack of "common sense" about the domain they are supposed to cover. You ask them to do something, and they respond in a way that no person, no matter how uneducated or new to the job, would respond. In such cases, the problem is usually that the databases composing the "back end" of the service are missing important, "task-focused" data. Bluntly, the back end wasn't designed to support user tasks. If a Web service has this problem, it doesn't matter how "easy to use" the front end is; the overall user experience will still frustrate users and limit their productivity.

You Can't Get There from Here

Online reservation systems of major airlines allow customers to book flights over the Web, but many lack information about cities and towns that don't have commercial air service. I'm talking about towns like New Haven, Connecticut (U.S.A.); Paderborn (Germany); or Sienna (Italy). If you try to book a flight to such a place, many airline websites simply say they don't fly there and can't help you. In contrast, a human reservation agent would immediately—without even asking you—assume you want to fly to the nearest major airport and take ground transportation from there to your destination.

For instance, I had to travel recently to Ann Arbor, Michigan. I knew that major airlines don't fly into Ann Arbor but wasn't sure what major airport is nearest. Any human ticket agent knows that Detroit (DTW) serves as Ann Arbor's airport, but I didn't know it. I gave "Ann Arbor" as my destination. Some airline websites (e.g., United) automatically assume Detroit, but many do not. Continental Airlines' website told me, "Ann Arbor is not currently served by Continental or its partners"

(Figure 2.23[A]). Northwest Airlines' site said, "No Northwest . . . flights were found . . . between San Francisco (SFO-San Francisco Intl.) . . . and Ann Arbor, MI (ARB) that matched your request" (Figure 2.23[B]), even though Detroit is one of Northwest's hubs.

American Airlines' website exhibited even less common sense. When giving it my travel data, I had to choose whether I was more concerned about "price" or "schedule"

(Figure 2.24[A]). I chose "price." It responded essentially that Ann Arbor is not serviced by American Airlines, so I can't "choose by price" (Figure 2.24[B]). I have to "choose by schedule" instead. Huh? I went back to the home page and clicked "Choose by schedule." Now it listed several possible itineraries, some involving flights on other airlines, all using Detroit as the destination (Figure 2.24[C]). For some reason, *AA.com* can't figure out that Ann Arbor is served by Detroit DTW if you "choose by price," but it can if you

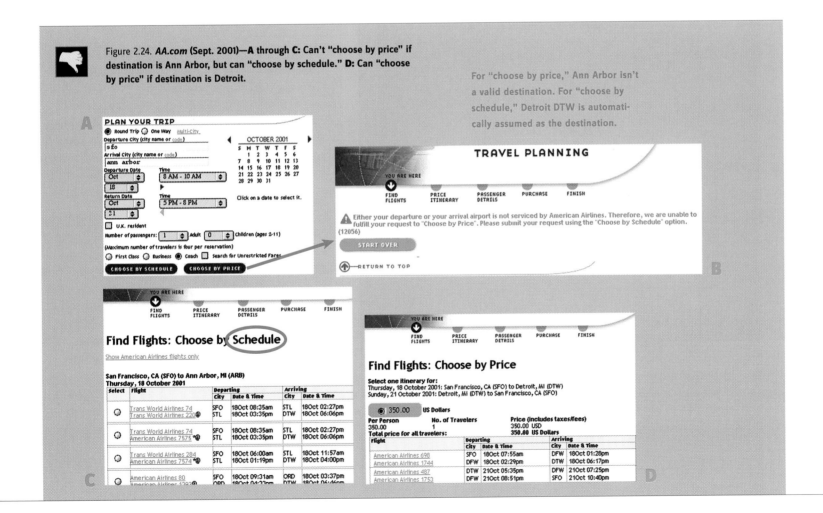

Figure 2.24. *AA.com* (Sept. 2001)—A through C: Can't "choose by price" if destination is Ann Arbor, but can "choose by schedule." D: Can "choose by price" if destination is Detroit.

For "choose by price," Ann Arbor isn't a valid destination. For "choose by schedule," Detroit DTW is automatically assumed as the destination.

Figure 2.25. *www.Greyhound.com* (Jan. 2002)—**A:** Ask to travel from Fremont to Torrance (both in California). **B:** Greyhound has no stations in those towns, so site substitutes alphabetically by nearest towns that have bus stations.

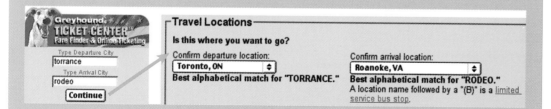

Figure 2.26. *www.Greyhound.com* (Jan. 2002)—Ticket Center on home page results in even more ridiculous substitutions.

"choose by schedule." Do the two options use different databases, perhaps?

However, the "choose by schedule" list showed no prices and I was concerned about price, so I backed up to the home page and tried a third time; this time giving Detroit as my destination and clicking "choose by price." Finally, flights with prices (Figure 2.24[D]). So if you give your destination as Detroit rather than Ann Arbor, "choose by price" works. But it can't figure out that Ann Arbor really means Detroit. Major back-end blooper!

The Web Goes to the Dogs

Airlines aren't the only companies with frustratingly ignorant websites. Greyhound Bus Company's site shows clearly that an easy-to-use front end cannot make up for a back end designed without regard to actual user tasks. The site accepts only the locations of Greyhound bus stations as departure and arrival points. Furthermore, it provides no help in figuring out what stations are nearest to your starting and ending locations. You have to know where the bus stations are. You do know, don't you?

However, it's even worse than that. Let's say you go to *Greyhound.com*'s ticket-center page and type in that you wish to travel from Fremont, California, to Torrance, California (Figure 2.25[A]). Greyhound has no stations in those towns, so it substitutes the closest towns that have stations. The problem is "closest" means *alphabetically*. Fresno is substituted for Fremont, and Tehachapi for Torrance. In fact, Fresno is nowhere near Fremont, and Tehachapi is about 90 miles from Torrance. It is hard to imagine anything less useful.

If instead of using the site's Ticket Center page, you type your departure and arrival cities into the mini-Ticket Center on the home page, the substituted cities may not even be in the same *state* as those you type. If you give the California towns Torrance and Rodeo as your Departure and Arrival cities, respectively, it asks you if you meant Toronto, Ontario (Canada), and Roanoke, Virginia (Figure 2.26)!

Airline and bus-line websites may not recognize many small towns and villages, but they at least know the names of major cities. Not all Web services do. The weather-reporting services *Weather.com* and Yahoo Weather don't seem to know about New York City, for example. Ask them for the weather in New York City, and one responds blankly while the other offers several irrelevant New York towns (Figure 2.27). Clearly, the back ends of these two sites are missing important keywords.

AVOIDING THE BLOOPER

Artificial intelligence researchers are working to endow computer-based systems with the sort of reasoning abilities that in people are called "common sense," but at the present time (2002), they seem far from that goal. Until they get closer (if they ever do), Web developers should work to ensure that their sites and services don't exhibit failures of common sense so blatant that people avoid the site.

It's the Back End Too!

This means that developers can't just slap a front end—no matter how easy it is to use—onto a non–task-focused back end and expect to have a usable and useful Web service. They have to design the entire system—back end and front end—to support users and their tasks. Furthermore, they have to test the service on representative users early and often during development to check that it really supports user tasks and doesn't exhibit any blatant common sense bloopers.

If United Can Do It, You Can Too

It can be done. As mentioned earlier, in contrast to several other airlines, United Airlines' online booking service accepts towns that lack major commercial airports.

71

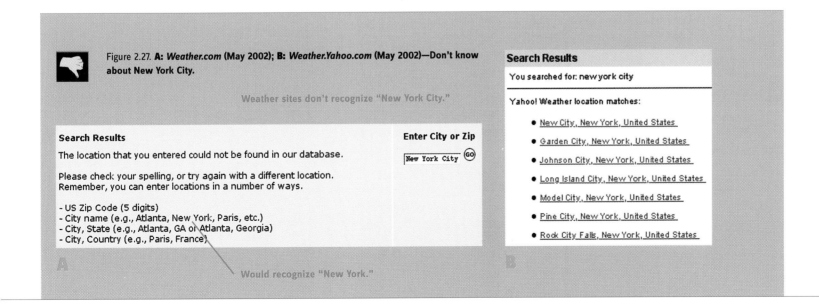

Figure 2.27. **A:** *Weather.com* (May 2002); **B:** *Weather.Yahoo.com* (May 2002)—Don't know about New York City.

Weather sites don't recognize "New York City."

Search Results

The location that you entered could not be found in our database.

Please check your spelling, or try again with a different location. Remember, you can enter locations in a number of ways.

- US Zip Code (5 digits)
- City name (e.g., Atlanta, New York, Paris, etc.)
- City, State (e.g., Atlanta, GA or Atlanta, Georgia)
- City, Country (e.g., Paris, France)

Enter City or Zip

New York City GO

Would recognize "New York."

A

Search Results

You searched for: new york city

Yahoo! Weather location matches:

- New City, New York, United States
- Garden City, New York, United States
- Johnson City, New York, United States
- Long Island City, New York, United States
- Model City, New York, United States
- Pine City, New York, United States
- Rock City Falls, New York, United States

B

Figure 2.28. **www.United.com** (June 2002)—Knows that Detroit DTW serves as Ann Arbor's airport.

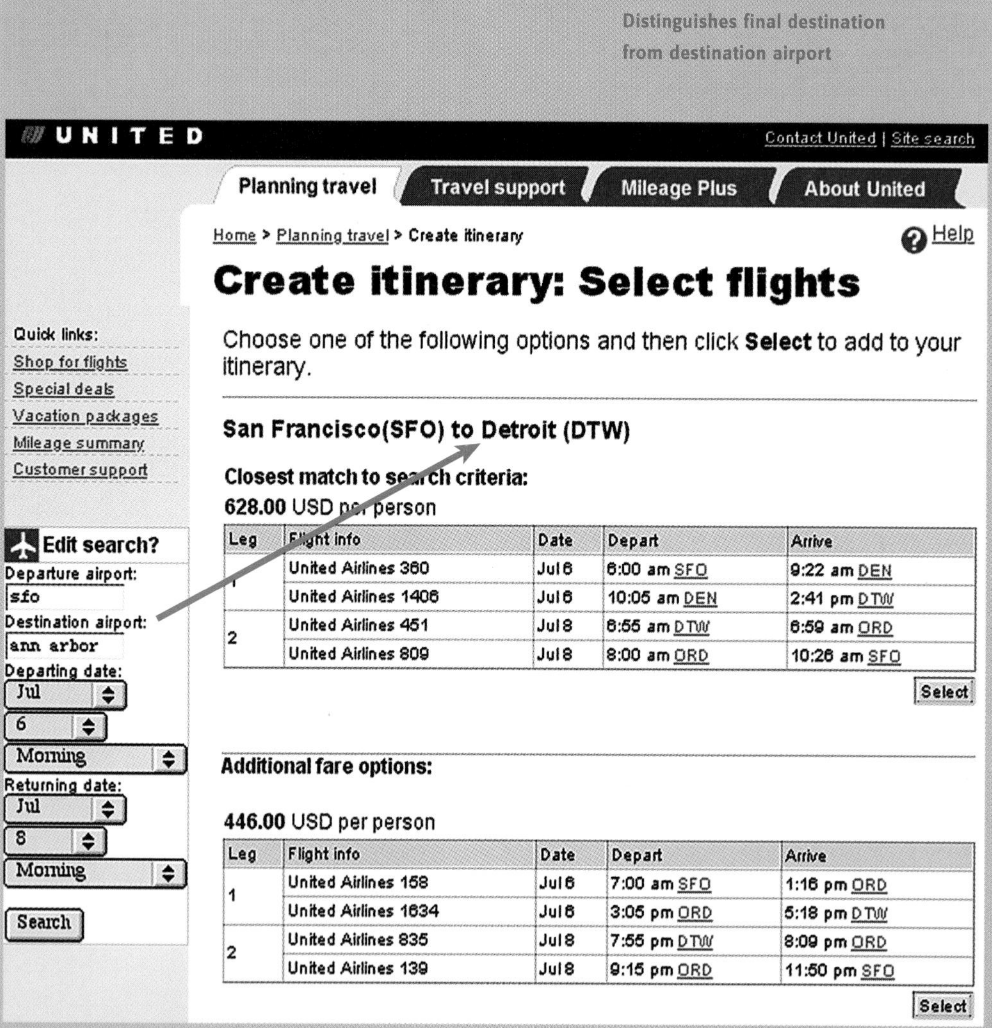

Like human travel agents, *United.com* distinguishes between a customer's final destination and the destination *airport*. When given Ann Arbor, Michigan, as a destination, it simply assumes Detroit DTW as the destination airport (Figure 2.28). The difference here is in *United.com*'s back-end servers, not its front-end site.

Blooper 13: Dead-end Paths: *Now* You Tell Me!

An excellent way to disrupt task flow and annoy your site's users in the process is to let them get several steps down a path toward their goal and then tell them, after they've invested time and effort, that what they told you they wanted several steps ago isn't available.

For example, someone I know recently used *TicketMaster.com* to try to order tickets for a performance. He indicated the number of tickets he wanted and the section of the theater he wanted to sit in, among other information. The site responded "Sorry. No tickets available in this section." He repeated the process several times, specifying different sections of the theater. Each time it said the section was full. A phone call to TicketMaster revealed that the entire show was sold out. Instead of telling its customers that the concert was completely sold out, *TicketMaster.com* lets them waste valuable time on dead-end paths.

People who order Internet service from EarthLink may find themselves hitting a dead end when they attempt to use its customer-service website. When customers try to check the status of their DSL order, the site dutifully displays its Order-Status checking form and allows them to fill it out (Figure 2.29[A]). Only after users have taken the time to read the form, look up their new DSL phone number and EarthLink work-order number, type them into the form, and submit it does the site bother to check whether the work-order status back end is available. If not, it displays, "The DSL Work Order Status page is temporarily unavailable at this time" (Figure 2.29[B]). We will ignore the redundant wording of this message and focus on the problem that it simply comes one step too late. The *previous* page is where the message should have appeared so users wouldn't have to waste time filling out the form.

AVOIDING THE BLOOPER

At both *TicketMaster.com* and *EarthLink.net,* how to avoid the blooper is obvious. Users should have been notified of the unavailability—of any concert seats in one case; of order status checking in the other—as soon as they indicated what they wanted to do. An example of how the EarthLink DSL Order Status page *should* have appeared is shown in Figure 2.30.

Blooper 14: Agonizing Task Flow

Having discussed specific bloopers that affect the degree of task fit of websites, let's now examine a site that provides almost intolerable support for certain tasks: Citibank's Direct Access home-banking service. The problems arise from a combination of non–user-centered design of the back-end services, specific task-fit bloopers already mentioned in this chapter, and bloopers covered elsewhere in this book.

Following the discussion of Citibank's site is a section presenting a user's complaints about another Web application that provides agonizingly bad support for its intended task.

Citibank.com's Direct Access service allows people to bank from home over the Web. One of its features is that it lets customers create and manage a list of "payees"—companies to which the customer expects to write checks or transfer funds. Unfortunately, accomplishing what should be a simple common task with the site can be an exercise in frustration. Here is a blow-by-blow account of what a customer

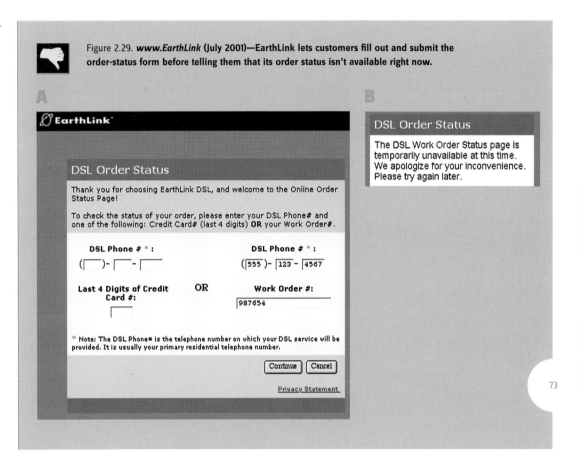

Figure 2.29. ***www.EarthLink*** **(July 2001)—EarthLink lets customers fill out and submit the order-status form before telling them that its order status isn't available right now.**

A

B

DSL Order Status

The DSL Work Order Status page is temporarily unavailable at this time. We apologize for your inconvenience. Please try again later.

73

Reprinted with Special Permission of King Features Syndicate.

Figure 2.30. **Correction of blooper at *EarthLink.net*—First DSL Order Status page immediately tells users that order status is unavailable.**

would have to go through to add a payee (First USA Bank) to his or her payee list:

1. Find "Payments and Transfers" section, then find "Payee List" page (Figure 2.31). Examine options. Click "Add a Payee."

2. Site offers a choice of typing the payee name or choosing it from a bank-supplied directory of merchants (Figure 2.32). One problem is that this and most of the subsequent pages have the same title as the last page (see Chapter 3, Blooper 19: Lost in Space: Current Page Not Indicated), which could cause confusion about one's location in the process. Decide to choose from the list. Click "Merchant Directory."

3. Instead of showing a list of merchants (since it is long), the site requires users to specify which part of the list to display. Users can specify either "by beginning letter(s)" or "by alphabetic range" (Blooper 10: Pointless Choice). Decide to use "by beginning letters," since it's the default method. Type "first" into text box. Click "View Merchants" (Figure 2.33). (The page title is still the same as the previous page.)

4. Site displays merchants whose names begin with "first." The user wants to add "First USA," but there are three. Two have numbers after them. There is no way to tell which one is the right one (Blooper 10: Pointless Choice, and Blooper 33: Hits Look Alike). Pick one at random and hope its details will clarify whether it's the right one (Figure 2.34).

5. Site displays details for chosen item. It looks promising, but there is a warning that "the address may be different due to a special delivery arrangement with the payee." Decide to add the payee anyway in hopes that it either is the right one or it can be changed later; click "Yes" (Figure 2.35).

Figure 2.31. ***www.Citibank.com*** **(July 2002)—Start at Payee List maintenance page.**

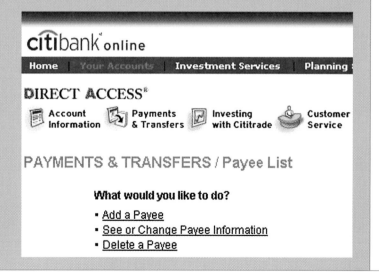

Figure 2.32. *www.Citibank.com* (July 2002)—Can either type payee name or select from list. (Page has same title as previous page.)

PAYMENTS & TRANSFERS / Payee List

Please enter the full name of the payee you want to add.

Full name: [   ]

or select the **Merchant Directory** to view the current list of merchants.

◀ **Back**　　　　**Merchant Directory**　　**Next** ▶

Figure 2.33. *www.Citibank.com* (July 2002)—To select from Merchant Directory, have to indicate which part of list to show. (Page still has same title.)

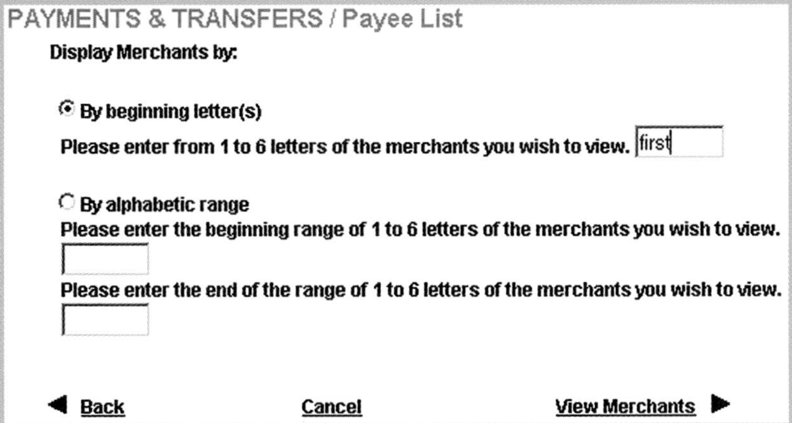

PAYMENTS & TRANSFERS / Payee List

Display Merchants by:

⦿ **By beginning letter(s)**

Please enter from 1 to 6 letters of the merchants you wish to view. [first]

○ **By alphabetic range**

Please enter the beginning range of 1 to 6 letters of the merchants you wish to view.

[   ]

Please enter the end of the range of 1 to 6 letters of the merchants you wish to view.

[   ]

◀ **Back**　　　　　**Cancel**　　　　　**View Merchants** ▶

Figure 2.34. *www.Citibank.com* (July 2002)—Choose Merchant. Three merchants have the same name.

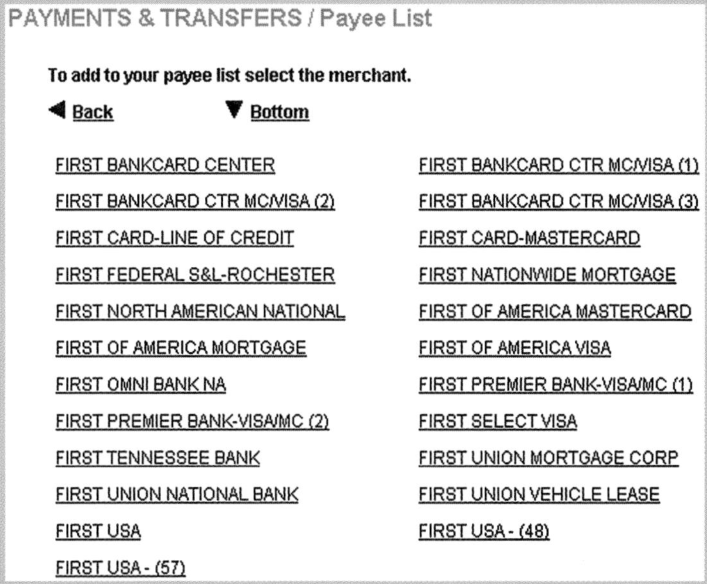

PAYMENTS & TRANSFERS / Payee List

To add to your payee list select the merchant.

◀ **Back**　　　　　▼ **Bottom**

FIRST BANKCARD CENTER	FIRST BANKCARD CTR MC/VISA (1)
FIRST BANKCARD CTR MC/VISA (2)	FIRST BANKCARD CTR MC/VISA (3)
FIRST CARD-LINE OF CREDIT	FIRST CARD-MASTERCARD
FIRST FEDERAL S&L-ROCHESTER	FIRST NATIONWIDE MORTGAGE
FIRST NORTH AMERICAN NATIONAL	FIRST OF AMERICA MASTERCARD
FIRST OF AMERICA MORTGAGE	FIRST OF AMERICA VISA
FIRST OMNI BANK NA	FIRST PREMIER BANK-VISA/MC (1)
FIRST PREMIER BANK-VISA/MC (2)	FIRST SELECT VISA
FIRST TENNESSEE BANK	FIRST UNION MORTGAGE CORP
FIRST UNION NATIONAL BANK	FIRST UNION VEHICLE LEASE
FIRST USA	FIRST USA - (48)
FIRST USA - (57)	

Figure 2.35. *www.Citibank.com* (July 2002)—Merchant details. Still can't be sure this is the right one.

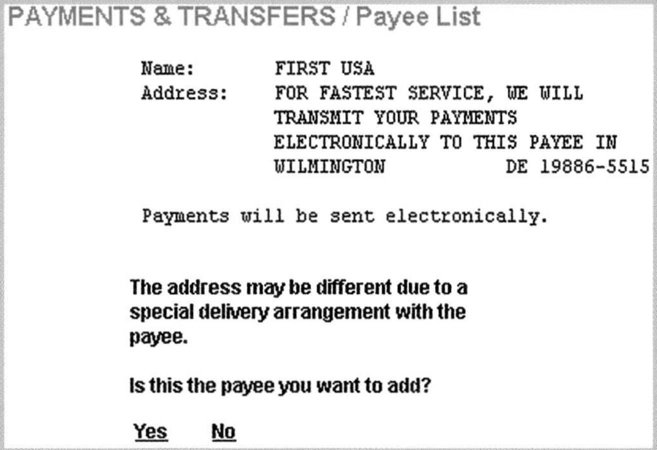

PAYMENTS & TRANSFERS / Payee List

```
Name:      FIRST USA
Address:   FOR FASTEST SERVICE, WE WILL
           TRANSMIT YOUR PAYMENTS
           ELECTRONICALLY TO THIS PAYEE IN
           WILMINGTON        DE 19886-5515

   Payments will be sent electronically.
```

The address may be different due to a special delivery arrangement with the payee.

Is this the payee you want to add?

Yes　　**No**

Figure 2.36. *www.Citibank.com* (July 2002)—Merchant details again, with mysteriously editable name. Requires customer account number at merchant.

PAYMENTS & TRANSFERS / Payee List

Please enter the following information and select **Add Payee** when finished.

List Name: FIRST USA

Full Name: **FIRST USA**
Address Line1: **FOR FASTEST SERVICE, WE WILL**
Address Line2: **TRANSMIT YOUR PAYMENTS**
Address Line3: **ELECTRONICALLY TO THIS PAYEE IN**
City: **WILMINGTON**
State: **Delaware**   Zip: **19886- 5515**
**XXXXXXXXXXXXXXXX ACCOUNT BEGINS
40,41,42,43,44,46,51,52,54,55**
Account #:

◀ **Back**   **Add Payee** ▶

Figure 2.38. *www.Citibank.com* (July 2002)—Clicking "Yes" in the previous screen takes user back to get a new account number.

PAYMENTS & TRANSFERS / Payee List

Please enter your changes and select **Add Payee** when finished.

List Name: FIRST USA

Full Name: **FIRST USA**
Address Line1: **FOR FASTEST SERVICE, WE WILL**
Address Line2: **TRANSMIT YOUR PAYMENTS**
Address Line3: **ELECTRONICALLY TO THIS PAYEE IN**
City: **WILMINGTON**
State: **Delaware**   Zip: **19886- 5515**
**XXXXXXXXXXXXXXXX ACCOUNT BEGINS
40,41,42,43,44,46,51,52,54,55**
Account #:

◀ **Back**   **Add Payee** ▶

Figure 2.37. *www.Citibank.com* (July 2002)—
Error message: invalid account number
(erroneous as it turns out).

PAYMENTS & TRANSFERS / Payee List

I'm sorry. The payee account number
you entered is invalid. Please check
your payment coupon.

Would you like to try again?

Yes   No

Figure 2.39. *www.Citibank.com* (July 2002)—Clicking on Back from account number form takes user back several steps, to first payee specification page.

PAYMENTS & TRANSFERS / Payee List

Please enter the full name of the payee you want to add.

Full name:

or select the **Merchant Directory** to view the current list of merchants.

◀ **Back**   **Merchant Directory**   **Next** ▶

6. Site doesn't add payee; instead, it shows the details again, this time with an editable name, although it seems unlikely that a user would want to edit the merchant name at this point. It also wants the customer's account number at the merchant. Type account number and click "Add Payee" (Figure 2.36).

7. Site displays error message saying the account number is invalid. User is sure account number is correct and valid, so calls Citibank. Citibank agent says the error message is inaccurate; the real problem is that First USA is one of a few merchants that cannot be added to a payee list using the online system (Blooper 13: Dead-end Paths: *Now* You Tell Me!). User asks why First USA is on the Merchant list if it can't be added as a payee from there. Citibank agent doesn't know why. (NOTE: Why First USA has three listings and how users choose between them was not explained.) User hangs up and returns to computer. Site asks if user wants to try again. User wants to add other payees, so clicks "yes" (Figure 2.37).

8. Site returns to page where account number was entered, since it thinks the user entered an invalid number. User clicks "Back" link, wanting to return to list of Merchants (step 3) to select another one from the list of merchants starting with "first" (Figure 2.38).

9. Site takes user back all the way to step 2, where user must again select the Merchant Directory and respecify which part of it to list (Figure 2.39).

The many bloopers and other obstacles *Citibank.com's* Direct Access service places in users' way add up to absolutely abysmal support for a task that is fairly common and so should be very easy to do.

Email from an Irate User

A professor at the University of California got fed up with the internal website he is required to use to approve administrative requests. He sent an email to the university system administrators describing his frustrations with the site and suggesting improvements. He sent me a copy of his message. Because it illustrates how poorly designed Web applications can frustrate users, I include it here. Names and minor details have been changed.

From: Prof. Lawrence Smith

To: University Administration

Re: Website for Approving Requests is Horrible!

This Request Approval system is incredibly confusing. Your email says to go to a web page to approve a request. Fine, I'm happy to do it.

First I go to the Request Approval web page where I am asked to enter the request number.

I am taken to a login page where I have to login—good, we need to ensure that it is me making the request.

After logging in, I am again asked to enter the request number even though I already did that. OK, usual stupid UI through the web.

But now, I'm trying to figure out how to approve the request. There is no command that says "approve request." There are four commands:

> Cancel request
> Review request
> Edit request
> Logout

Where is Approve? I look at Review since approval implies reviewing and your email said: "Please review/approve the request . . . ," but no that isn't correct.

So I grope around until I try Edit and sure enough, if I happen to scroll to the bottom of the page, I see the "Approve" button. Great, I'm done.

No, not really. Now you present me with a business procedure I have no clue about: I have to route the request somewhere. Fine, where? You give me 3-4 options, but no instructions on where or to whom it needs to go next.

How can you fix the problem? First and foremost, put more documentation on the screens about what to do. Second, after I'm logged in, take me directly to the pending request. It must be possible since other apps on campus do it. Third, put an Approve command right out there where no one can miss it. Finally, rather than presenting me with a choice for the routing procedure, just send the request wherever it needs to go next, automatically.

AVOIDING THE BLOOPER

Because other more specific bloopers often contribute to poor task flow, one way to avoid it is to avoid the more specific bloopers. Because they are especially likely to degrade task flow, the following bloopers are important to avoid:

> All previous bloopers in this chapter

> Unhelpful descriptions (Blooper 3, Chapter 1)

> Missing or useless content (Blooper 6, Chapter 1)

> Not linking directly (Blooper 18, Chapter 3)

> Making people type (Blooper 22, Chapter 4)

> Intolerant data fields (Blooper 23, Chapter 4)

> No defaults or faulty defaults (Bloopers 24 and 25, Chapter 4)

> No default text input focus (Blooper 26, Chapter 4)

> Unclear how to operate controls (Bloopers 27 through 30, Chapter 4)

> Hits look alike (Blooper 33, Chapter 5)

> Missing relevant items (Blooper 35, Chapter 5)

> Speaking geek (Blooper 42, Chapter 6)

> Insider jargon (Blooper 44, Chapter 6)

> Different words for the same thing (Blooper 45, Chapter 6)

Perform Task Analysis and Conceptual Design before Designing Web Pages

Ultimately, however, providing good support for tasks requires more than just avoiding certain specific bloopers. It requires having a good understanding of the tasks for which the website or Web application is being designed. Such an understanding should be developed before anyone starts sketching or coding Web pages. To do this, the following steps are recommended:

1. Analyze the target tasks by interviewing representative users, both individually and in focus groups. Discover the steps users expect tasks to require and the data they expect to provide. (For details, see Johnson [2000].)

2. Write a document that specifies what users can do with the website or application—what data they can manipulate and how they can manipulate it. This document should not discuss user interfaces—how users operate the site. It should only mention functionality and the concepts users need to know about. Such a document is called a "conceptual model." The goal is to design a conceptual model that is simple and completely focused on the intended tasks before jumping into designing pages. (For details, see Johnson [2000] or Johnson and Henderson [2002].)

Task Performed	By Many	By Few
Frequently	Make "task start" highly visible. Minimize steps. Provide shortcuts for experienced users.	"Task start" can be suggested. Try to minimize steps.
Occasionally	"Task start" can be suggested. Can allow more steps. Shortcuts not necessary.	"Task start" can be hidden. Can allow more steps.

Table 2.3 **Categorizing a website's supported tasks according to how many people will use them, how often. The category a task is in determines how important it is to minimize the number of steps it takes.**

3. Create a 2×2 matrix categorizing the site's target tasks two different ways (Table 2.3). One axis is whether a task is performed by many users or only a few users. The other axis is whether the average user performs a task frequently or occasionally. Tasks in the "frequently by many" cell should be designed to minimize the number of steps. All other tasks can take more steps. (For details, see Isaacs and Walendowski [2001].) This analysis is independent of the usual priority analysis categorizing features into "core," "important," and "nice to have" to determine which ones are in, in later, or out.

4. After the website or Web application is designed, but before it is implemented, write scenarios describing in detail how a user would perform each of the important supported tasks. (For details, see Rosson and Carroll [2001].) If any scenarios seem too complicated, performing the task in the actual website would most likely be awkward and frustrating if implemented as designed. In that case, redesign it and try again.

These four steps may seem too time consuming and expensive. However, by skipping them and jumping straight into hacking out code, Web developers put themselves at high risk of ending up with task support similar to that in the Citibank home-banking site.

PART II | BLOOPERS IN THE USER INTERFACE OF THE WEBSITE

CHAPTER 3

NAVIGATION BLOOPERS

People encounter many problems and obstacles when trying to use the Web. The most pervasive problem is navigating: finding your way to what you are seeking. The main reason for this is inadequate cues.

According to Web design analyst Jakob Nielsen (1999), successful navigation cues let people know

> Where they are
> Where they've been
> Where they can go

To those I'll add another:

> Whether their goal is near or far

Copyright Mark Parisi.

As any Web user knows, the Web does *not* always let users know where they are, where they've been, where they can go, and whether their goal is near or far. As a result, people often don't find what they seek. Sometimes they even lose their way, becoming lost or disoriented.

This chapter describes the most common methods Web designers use—unintentionally of course—to hinder, divert, and block Web users from navigating to the content they seek. It also explains how to avoid using those methods.

Blooper 15: Site Reflects Organizational Chart

According to Nielsen (1999), websites that reflect a company or agency's organizational chart are "a common mistake." I would strengthen that to "very common." Not only is it common, it is a *disaster* for a site's navigability and usability.

When a business or agency's organizational structure or history influence the design of its website, it is difficult for people to find what they are seeking or do what they want to do. It makes the site seem arbitrary, ad hoc, and nonsensical. It impedes learning, retention, navigation, you name it. In fact, this blooper is a significant cause of the chaotic categorization schemes discussed in Chapter 1 (see Blooper 2: Confusing Classifications).

Visitors to a website don't care how your company is structured or which division, department, development team, or developer was responsible for each part of the site. They bring their own goals to a website and don't care about your organization's goals and history.

Let's look at some websites where the company's organization seems to have intruded into the site, detracting from users' ability to accomplish their goals.

Am I Still at the Same Company?

In Chapter 1, I showed that different parts of *Acer.com* disagree on what scanners Acer sells (see Blooper 4: Conflicting Content). That blooper is related to the "organizational chart" blooper: Different suborganizations are responsible for the different parts of Acer's site. Acer also commits the "organizational chart" blooper in another way: Its site shows that some of its product "divisions" are distinct corporate entities, with distinct names, logos, and site designs.

For example, the part of Acer that makes scanners recently reorganized as a subsidiary company called Benq. Clicking on "scanners" from Acer's main product page drops would-

be customers onto Benq's scanner page, making them wonder whether (1) they are still at Acer and (2) these are Acer products (Figure 3.1).

I Just Want a Camera!

Imagine that you go to *zBuyer.com*, shopping for a cheap camera. You look at zBuyer's product categories (Figure 3.2[A]), and see "photo." Good. But wait . . . what's this "outlet" just above it? "Outlet" usually means discount prices, so maybe you should look there. And what's this "Target" link below it? You were just in a Target store yesterday, looking at cameras. Is this a link to their website, or what? Clicking around, you learn that zBuyer has a special outlet store, whose product categories are virtually identical to zBuyer's (Figure 3.2[B]). After more clicking, you discover that zBuyer apparently has a deal with Target stores to sell products for them, and that Target's product categories overlap with zBuyer's (Figure 3.2[C]). So now you know zBuyer has an outlet subsidiary and is partnered with Target, but you don't yet know where on this site to get the best price on a camera. And it looks as if it's going to take time and work to find out. You've just been hit by the "organizational chart" blooper.

Use *Our* Support! No, Use *Ours!*

An example from Silicon Graphics' customer service home page shows how offerings from different internal organizations can appear to compete for customers' attention and business, thereby confusing customers. The page formerly had three links for customer support: Support Services, Online Support, and SupportFolio Online (Figure 3.3). Two of those offered "online" support. Furthermore, SupportFolio Online offered "patches," whereas Online Support offered "security patches." If someone wanted customer support, what should they choose? (See Chapter 1, Blooper 3: Unhelpful Descriptions.) It seems clear—to an outsider anyway—that different organizations were behind

Figure 3.1. *www.Acer.com* (Dec. 2001)—Site reflects that Acer's scanner maker is Benq. **A:** Acer's Product page. **B:** Benq's Scanner page.

Site shows that Acer scanners are made by a subsidiary with a different name. Customers don't care.

85

Some product "categories" link to sub-stores that sell similar products.

Figure 3.2. *www.zBuyer.com* (Feb. 2002)—Site shows organization chart. **A:** zBuyer's product categories include "Outlet" and "Target." **B:** Outlet categories are very similar to zBuyer's. **C:** Target's categories overlap with zBuyer's.

these competing offerings. The site was recently upgraded, reducing—but not eliminating—evidence of Silicon Graphics' organizational chart.

AVOIDING THE BLOOPER

Websites and Web applications should be organized according to the needs of their intended *users*. What do *users* want to do at the site? This means:

> Devoting resources up-front, before coding, to interviewing prospective users (Brinck, Gergle, and Wood, 2001)

> Watching them use previous versions of the planned site or competitor sites

> Getting their reactions to paper or online mock-ups of the site

> Designing the site to reflect user tasks, not organizational fiefdoms

Unfortunately, unlike many of the other bloopers discussed in this book, this one is hard to avoid. Organizations do have structure; they do have suborganizations. Each suborganization has its own responsibilities. Nonetheless, it is very important to avoid this blooper. As Nielsen (1999) points out:

> *Admittedly, it is easiest to distribute responsibility for the site to divisions and departments . . . but doing so results in an internally centered site rather than a customer-focused site.*

Put the Web Team at the Corporate or Agency Level

Giving responsibility for developing different parts of your external website to different suborganizations is a recipe for a site that commits this blooper. Instead, create a Web team that serves at a corporate- or agency-wide level. This team would gather requirements, information, and content

Competing support offerings, probably from different organizations.

Both are "online," both offer "patches."

SGI
global services offers comprehensive, high quality services that enhance and support SGI products. We design, implement, support, and help you get the most from the SGI solution that's perfect for your business.

World Class Service

Fast, Expert, Online Help

⊘ **Professional Services**
SGI consultants help Global 1000 companies solve complex problems related to media commerce, data visualization, Linux migration, and more.

⊘ **Online Support**
Troubleshooting a bug? Need warranty information? From security patches to software licensing, find technical resources here.

⊘ **Productivity Services**
Managed Services
Accelerate your productivity with expert implementation and system managed services.

⊘ **Supportfolio™ Online**
Supportfolio, the premier online customer support, features patches, technical support, service-call logging and tracking.

⊘ **Support Services**
Choose the SGI support offering that works the way you do--from 7x24 Mission-Critical support to HardwareCare and SoftwareCare.

⊘ **Education Services**
Expand your skills with SGI training, geared to all levels--from novice to advanced graphics programmers.

⊘ **List of Services**
SGI offers a range of service solutions.

 Figure 3.3. ***www.SGI.com*** **(Jan. 2002)—Customer service page has offerings that seem to compete with each other.**

87

from various suborganizations and integrate these to produce a coherent, unified website.

Furthermore, the Web team should be given responsibility for the *entire* external site. The product sales, customer support, and company information sections should not be "balkanized" into separate organizations; otherwise, the site will reflect that balkanization.

Intranets are an exception. It probably makes sense for a company's internal website and collection of Web-based applications to be designed and managed by a *different* group than that responsible for the external site. On the other hand, it also makes sense for the intranet to be a company- or agency-wide function so employees won't have to struggle with the negative effects of intranet-Web balkanization.

Links to Other Sites

The whole point of the Web is to link to information that might be useful, wherever it might be. Indeed, the distinction between pages that are "in" and "not in" a particular site is fuzzy: Isn't anything a site links to "in" that site? Not exactly.

All pages within a site should have a consistent appearance. Users should be able to tell instantly whether they've left a site by whether the appearance of the pages has changed or whether the new page appears in a new browser window.[5] Pages in a site should provide any information or functionality that users must have to use the site successfully. External links should be strictly for auxiliary information and functionality. If information necessary to operate a site successfully is provided on another site, it should be incorporated into the first site . . . with permission, of course.

[5] A convention is emerging that offsite links bring up a new browser window, but it is not yet widely followed.

Test Your Site against These Criteria

As a site is developed or upgraded, its managers and architects should beware of organizational artifacts sneaking in. Such artifacts should be eradicated before becoming entrenched. Site architects, managers, and even top executives should ask these questions (with the right answers in parentheses):

> Does the site organization make sense to people who don't know the company's organizational chart? (Yes)

> Can users deduce significant aspects of your organizational structure by examining the site? (No)

> Have all traces of "dirty laundry"—such as the fact that different divisions developed similar products—been eradicated? (Yes)

> Are there subsites that exist only because there is— or was—an internal organization corresponding to them? (No)

> Have pages or sections inherited from legacy sites been updated to fit seamlessly into the new site? (Yes)

> Is content consistent throughout the site? (Yes)

> Is there conflicting information resulting from cross-organizational miscommunication or conflicting sub-organization goals? (No)

> Can users tell clearly which linked pages are internal or external to the site? (Yes)

> Do all internal pages follow the same conventions and guidelines? (Yes)

By continually asking these questions and working to make the answers the right ones, those responsible for the success of a website can help fend off creeping balkanization.

Applying the Criteria to the Examples

If the three websites given as examples of the "organizational chart" blooper were evaluated against the criteria and then improved so as to give the right answers, the following changes would result:

> *Acer.* Visitors to Acer's website would see all products offered by Acer presented as Acer products, on pages designed to fit into Acer's website. Visitors to subsidiary sites such as Benq would see that subsidiary's products presented as its own.

> *zBuyer.* The "Outlet" and "Target" pseudo-categories would be eliminated. Clicking on a category such as "camera" would provide access to all products in that category, regardless of which store offers it. If the store matters from a customer's point of view, it could be indicated either by subcategories on product category pages or by marking individual products.

> *Silicon Graphics Incorporated.* There would be one offering for customer support services. Going to its page might display various options, with clear explanations to allow customers to choose what they need. All patches—security or not—would be available from one place.

Blooper 16: Numerous Navigation Schemes

Another very common high-level navigation blooper is for a website to have multiple competing navigation schemes. Multiple navigation schemes can delay, distract, and divert site visitors: "So many different ways to get around! How do I choose one? Where do I start?" They compete with each other for users' attention.

Competing Navigation Schemes with Duplication

The jury duty website of the Superior Court of San Francisco is a subsite of San Francisco's city government website. When citizens of San Francisco are notified to report for jury duty, they are advised to visit the site for further information. The jury duty home page displays three navigation bars (Figure 3.4). Two are the same except in their position and orientation—needless duplication.

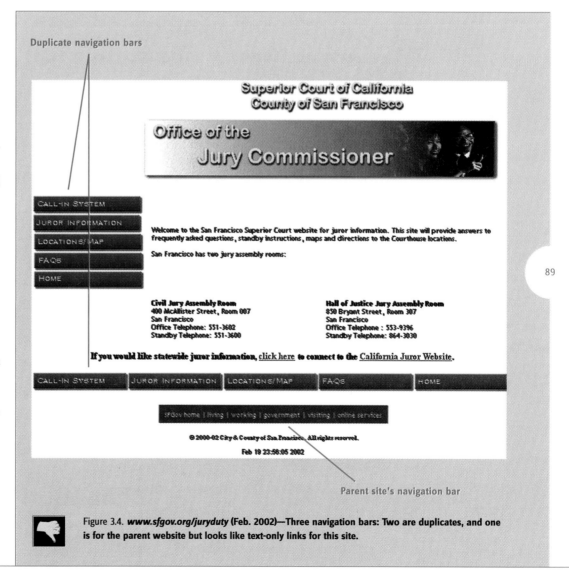

Figure 3.4. **www.sfgov.org/juryduty (Feb. 2002)—Three navigation bars: Two are duplicates, and one is for the parent website but looks like text-only links for this site.**

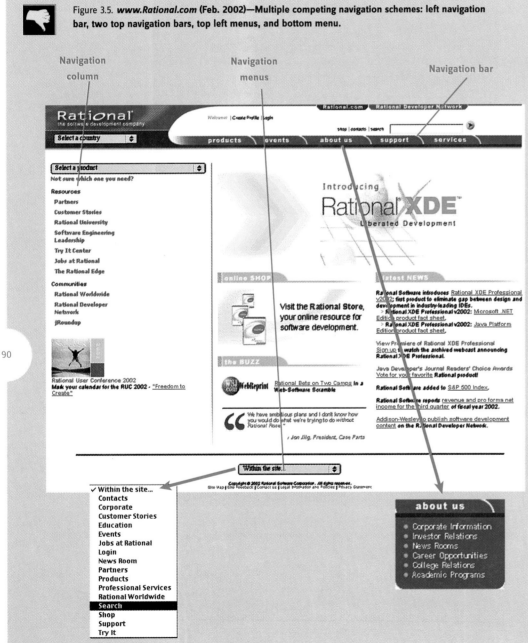

Figure 3.5. **www.Rational.com (Feb. 2002)—Multiple competing navigation schemes: left navigation bar, two top navigation bars, top left menus, and bottom menu.**

Navigation column

Navigation menus

Navigation bar

The third navigation bar—the blue one at the bottom of the page—is for the city government website. It is not well identified as being for the parent site: It looks like text-only links for *this* Superior Court site, especially since there are no other text-only links on this page. In fact, many people arrive here directly, without coming through the main city site, because they use the URL given in their jury duty notice. Therefore, many users of this Superior Court site probably do not understand what the blue navigation bar is.

Thus visitors to this site—especially newcomers—are faced with three navigation bars to choose from, two of which are duplicates and one of which is mysterious. Which one should they use?

Competing Navigation without Duplication

Competing navigation schemes need not contain obvious duplication to cause confusion and distraction. This can be seen at the home page of Rational, a software company (Figure 3.5). The page has at least five competing navigation schemes: a left navigation column, a top navigation bar (or perhaps two), two top left menus, and a bottom menu. How is a user to choose?

Furthermore, the bottom menu is labeled "Within the site. . . ." Does that mean the "Select a product" and "Select a country" menus take us to *other* sites?

Perhaps the clearest example of how multiple competing navigation schemes can confuse Web users is provided by *iFilm.com,* an online movie guide. This site has so many different navigation schemes that it is difficult to even *count* them all, much less know which one to use.

While looking at the information for a particular movie, users are faced with three navigation bars (Figure 3.6[A]). Two of the navigation bars appear as rows of tabs, although the tabs are depicted differently. Clicking on one of the top tabs—such as Short Films—replaces the bottom set of tab panels with a single tab panel (Figure 3.6[B]).

At this site, even though I was looking for information about a specific movie, I found myself clicking aimlessly for a while, trying to decide which navigation scheme was the right one to find the movie. I soon gave up and used the site's Search facility. Thank goodness for that Search box on every page.

AVOIDING THE BLOOPER

Unless your goal is for visitors to your site to wander aimlessly, which *is* the goal for some sites, you should minimize the number of navigation schemes the site presents. It is okay to have multiple navigation schemes, such as navigation bars both down the left side and across the top of the page, but each scheme should have a clear, unique purpose.

For example, the navigation bar on the left lists the content areas of the site, and the one across the top lists standard company or organization topics such as About Us, FAQ, Contact Us, and Privacy Policy. Or vice versa. A very succinct statement of this guideline is in the book *Homepage Usability* (Nielsen and Tahir 2001). They say,

> It's critical that users be able to find the appropriate navigation area effortlessly, differentiate between the choices, and have a good sense of what lies beneath the links . . .
> Locate the primary navigation area in a highly noticeable place . . .
> Group items in the navigation area so that similar items are next to each other . . .
> Don't provide multiple navigation areas for the same type of links. . . . (p. 19)

Classic examples of sites that follow these guidelines are *Monterey.com* and *Yale.edu*. These home pages have only

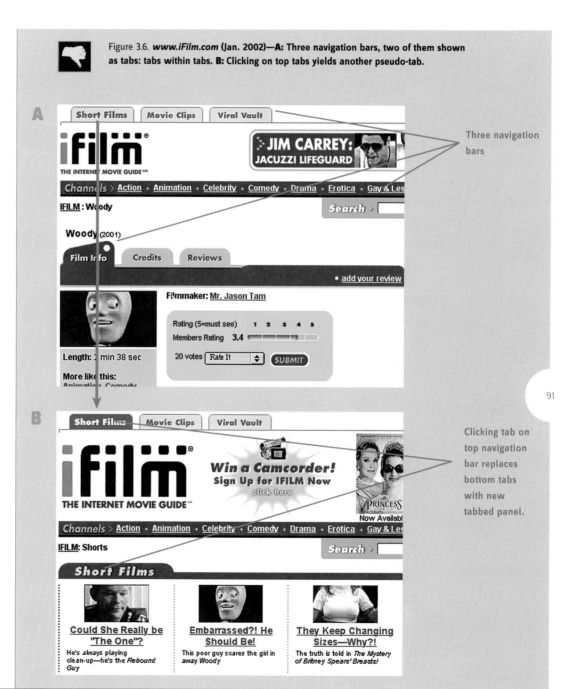

Figure 3.6. *www.iFilm.com* (Jan. 2002)—**A:** Three navigation bars, two of them shown as tabs: tabs within tabs. **B:** Clicking on top tabs yields another pseudo-tab.

Three navigation bars

Clicking tab on top navigation bar replaces bottom tabs with new tabbed panel.

91

● ● ○ ● ● ● ●

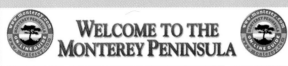

Figure 3.7. **A:** *Monterey.com* (Sept 2002); **B:** *Yale.edu* (Sept 2002)—
Single main navigation scheme separated from site logistics.

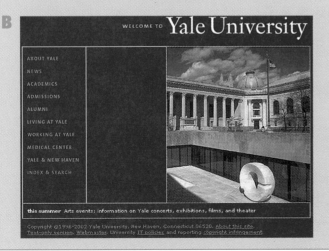

one set of main content links in the middle: down both sides for Monterey (Figure 3.7[A]) and down the left side for Yale (Figure 3.7[B]). At both sites, standard site logistical links are across the bottom.

Exception: Text-Only Links

The exception to the rule against multiple navigation schemes containing the same links is text-only links. If a website provides the standard—and recommended—text-only links to its important sections, it will have at least two navigation schemes. This is okay, because Web users are familiar with the convention, so the text-only navigation bar doesn't really compete with the main one.

What About Very Large Sites?

One could argue that the *Monterey.com* and *Yale.edu* sites don't have much content—at least not in comparison to the Web's largest sites—and so don't need many links and multiple ways to navigate. Okay, let's look at how two very large websites avoid multiple competing navigation schemes. Each solves the problem differently.

Sun.com (Figure 3.8) avoids a large number of links and multiple navigation bars by presenting only a few very high level content categories on its home page. Organizing the site's content in this way required careful, costly information architecture but paid off well by simplifying the home page.

In contrast, United's home page (Figure 3.9) presents three task-oriented tools and many very specific links. Despite all the links, there aren't several navigation schemes competing for users' attention; there is only one. Their home page may look cluttered, but functionally it's very simple.

Blooper 17: Deceptive Duplicate Links

Having multiple competing navigation schemes is only one way for a site to have needless duplication. Many websites suffer from too much or misleading duplication of links. Although certain duplicates are okay or even desirable, gratuitous duplication inflates the perceived complexity of sites, wastes time, and can send users astray.

If two links look different and go to different places, they aren't duplicates; they are *distinct.* There are three types of duplicate links:

> *Stealth duplicates* look different but go to the same place.
> *False duplicates* look alike (or very similar) but go to different places.
> *True duplicates* look alike (or very similar) and go to the same place.

Stealth and false duplicates are potentially misleading. Except in certain standard cases (discussed later), even true duplicate links can raise questions in users' minds about whether they *really* go to the same place. Duplicate links of any type also make a site seem bigger and more complex than it really is.

Let's first look at examples of each type of link duplication. These are followed by an exercise to let you experience firsthand the confusion duplicate links can cause.

Stealth Duplicate Links: Look Different, Go to the Same Place

The primary problem of stealth duplicate links is that they imply the existence of additional pages or options that don't exist. Users can waste time exploring them, only to discover that their destinations are the same.

 Figure 3.8. *www.Sun.com* (Sept. 2002)—A lot of content behind a simple navigation scheme.

Figure 3.9. *www.United.com* (Sept. 2002)—Many links, all organized in a single navigation scheme.

93

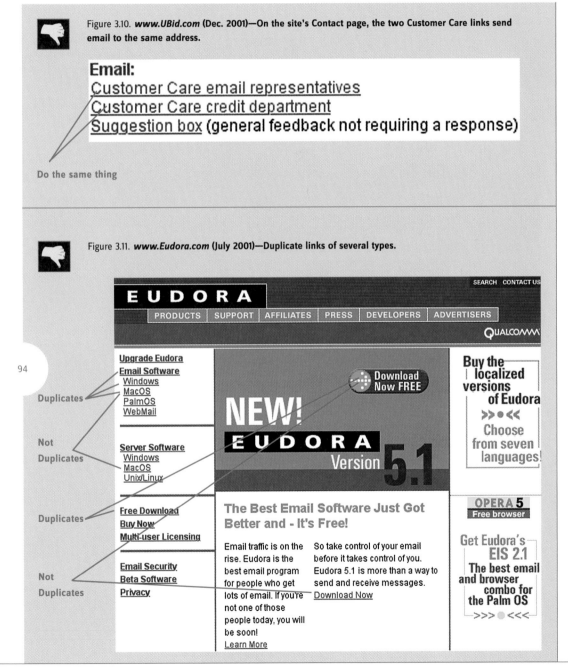

Figure 3.10. ***www.UBid.com*** (Dec. 2001)—On the site's Contact page, the two Customer Care links send email to the same address.

Email:
Customer Care email representatives
Customer Care credit department
Suggestion box (general feedback not requiring a response)

Do the same thing

Figure 3.11. ***www.Eudora.com*** (July 2001)—Duplicate links of several types.

Duplicates

Not Duplicates

Duplicates

Not Duplicates

94

This can be seen in an example of stealth duplicate links from *UBid.com* (Figure 3.10). Clicking either of the first two links starts an email message addressed to the same place: UBid's Customer Care department.

Perhaps the two links are intended to be distinct someday, but for now they aren't and so are misleading. At the least, users may be confused that following one of these links causes both of them to change to the "already followed" color.

Stealth duplicates and other types can be found at *Eudora.com,* a website hosted by software and telecommunications company Qualcomm for its Eudora email software. The Eudora 5.0 download page has duplicates of several types (Figure 3.11):

> *True:* "Free Download" on the left and "Download Now Free" at top middle both go to *www.eudora.com/ products/eudora/download.*

> *False:* "Download Now" at bottom middle goes to *www.eudora.com/download,* a different page than "Download Now Free" goes to.

> *Almost false:* "Upgrade Eudora" at top left, which might be expected to be the same as the download links, is not; it goes to *www.eudora.com/email/upgrade.*

> *Stealth:* The three links just under "Upgrade Eudora"— "Email Software," "MacOS," and "Windows"—all go to the same place: *www.eudora.com/email.*

Stealth duplicates are not always bad. Sometimes they serve a useful purpose: increasing the chance that visitors will find something the designer wants them to find. For example, Qualcomm obviously wants to guide visitors to its Eudora email page whether they use a Mac or a Windows PC.

However, stealth duplicate links can be misused: A cynic might rephrase their purpose as "tricking visitors into viewing certain pages." More importantly, there are trade-offs to consider even when stealth duplicates are used in good faith: They raise questions in users' minds—"Are these the same?"—and add complexity without adding functionality.

False Duplicate Links: Look Alike, Go to Different Places

Connectix.com provides an example of false duplicate links (Figure 3.12). The two links labeled "Home" go to different pages. The one at the top left goes to the Support home. The one at the lower left goes to the Answer Path home.

One might argue that it makes sense that the "Home" link under Answer Path goes to the Answer Path home. However, some people scanning this might not assume that the lower "Home" link is for the Answer Path because the link and heading are in visually distinct areas.

True Duplicate Links: Look Alike, Go to the Same Place

Even true duplicate links can be problematic. Figure 3.13 shows the home page of *WisconSUN.org*. It's a relatively simple site, with six content areas: About, Learn, News, Fund, Connect, and Contact.

The repetition on this page is excessive. Some of the repetition is not links, as the yellow paragraph headings are just headings. But most of the repetition is duplication of links: Three copies of each link to the site's six content areas.

It's good to provide text-only versions of graphical links on Web pages, but the links in the middle of the page are not graphical. They are already text and as such don't need text-only equivalents elsewhere on the page. Even if they did, two text-only copies of each link is overkill.

A common way for links to be truly duplicated is to display them in *both* a navigation bar and the page's central content area. This form of the blooper can be seen on the Contact page of *Rational.com*, a developer of software-

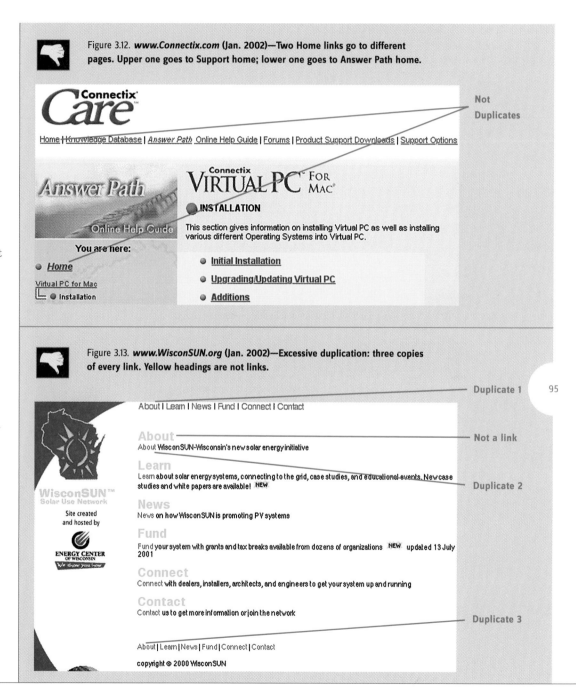

Figure 3.12. *www.Connectix.com* (Jan. 2002)—Two Home links go to different pages. Upper one goes to Support home; lower one goes to Answer Path home.

Not Duplicates

Figure 3.13. *www.WisconSUN.org* (Jan. 2002)—Excessive duplication: three copies of every link. Yellow headings are not links.

Duplicate 1

Not a link

Duplicate 2

Duplicate 3

95

Figure 3.14. ***www.Rational.com*** **(Feb. 2002)—Needless link duplication: If links are on a navigation bar, they should not be duplicated in the content area.**

Home > Contact

Rational Headquarters	**Contact**
Product Information	Want to reach a specific group at Rational? Whether you need directions, general information or technical support, you'll find the information below. Need more information about our products, tools and best practices? Submit this form.
General Information	
Technical Support	
Investor Relations Contact	• Rational Headquarters
	Find the addresses, directions, and maps to the corporate headquarters in Cupertino, CA, and Lexington, MA.
Press Contact	• Product Information
	Request additional information about our products.
Documentation Feedback	• General Information
	General request about Rational
Worldwide Sales Offices	• Technical Support
	Request help for your technical problems.
Rational Training Locations	• Investor Relations Contact
	Request investor-related information.
Website Feedback	• Press Contact
	Submit your press requests or questions.
	• Documentation Feedback
	Send us your comments or suggestions about our product documentation.
	• Worldwide Sales Offices
	Find the Rational sales office serving you.
	• Rational Training Locations
	Find the Rational training center near you.
	• Website Feedback
	Let us know if you have questions or comments about our website.

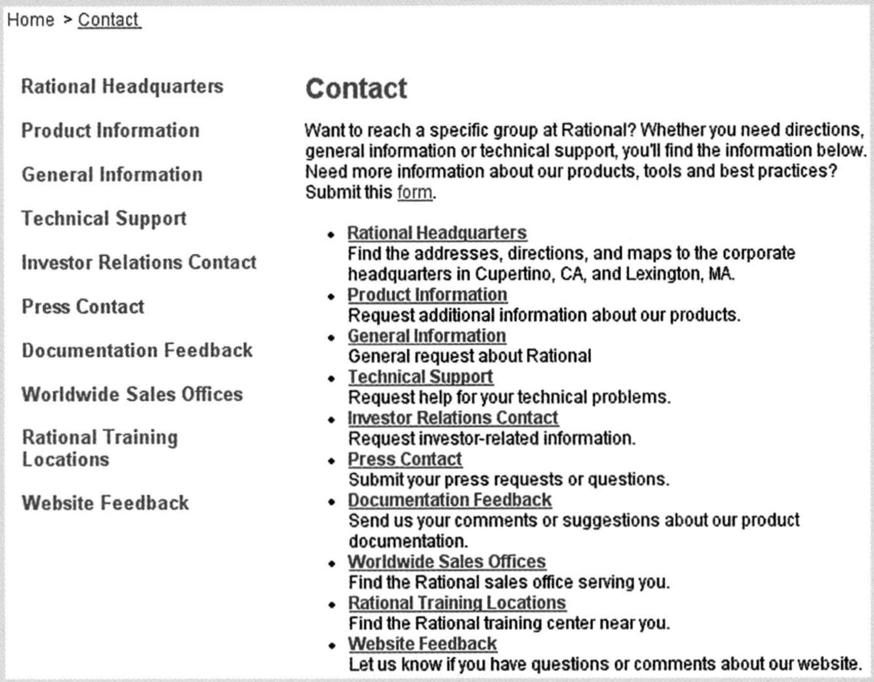

development tools (Figure 3.14). If links are on a navigation bar, they need not be—and *should* not be—duplicated in the content area. The next section describes a case of needless link duplication in an intranet web-application, and describes how the duplication was eliminated.

Needless Link Duplication in an Intranet Web Application

A company was developing an intranet Web application for managing networks of Web servers. On the left of every page was a navigation hierarchy of all the components managed by the system: servers, network switches, Web service software, operator consoles, and user accounts, among others. Users could expand and contract the hierarchy to see more or less of it. Some items in the hierarchy were *categories* of components; some were individual components.

The bulk of the browser window was devoted to the content area, positioned to the right of the navigation hierarchy. The content area displayed information about the currently selected item in the hierarchy. Selecting an individual component in the hierarchy displayed its status and settings in the content area, as expected. However, when a *category* in the hierarchy was selected, the content area listed links to the category's content elements, duplicating the links under the category in the navigation hierarchy (Figure 3.15).

The developers justified the duplication this way: "We weren't sure what to put on category pages and didn't want to leave them blank. And we thought some users might prefer to use those links anyway."

We redesigned category pages in the Web application to summarize the status of all components in the category, eliminating the duplicate links (Figure 3.16).

This "navigation hierarchy on the left and item details on right" design is a common design pattern for Web

Figure 3.15. **Intranet Web application—Original design showing Directory (i.e., home) page. Links in navigation column are duplicated in content area of display.**

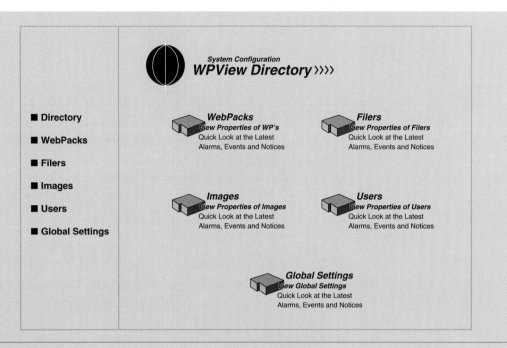

Figure 3.16. **Intranet Web application—Redesigned Directory (i.e., home) page. Content area summarizes system status.**

97

Content area summarizes selected navigation hierarchy item.

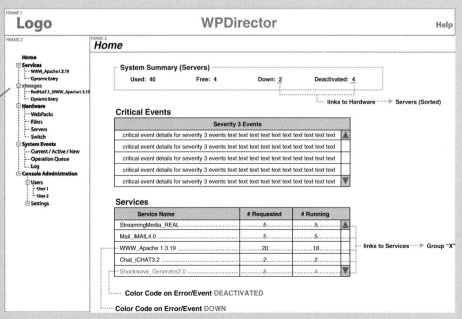

applications. When using it, a design rule to follow is: Category pages in the hierarchy summarize the *category's* state. Pages for individual components show the component's details.

Duplicate Links Make Users Stop to Think

An example of duplicate links not involving navigation bars comes from *Microsoft.com* (Figure 3.17). The link labels "FAQs & Highlights for Office 98 Macintosh Edition" and "FAQ for Office 98 Macintosh Edition" are almost the same. Visitors have to stop to think about whether these go to the same place. The default assumption is that they don't; oth-

erwise, why have both? Even more similar are the two links labeled "Online Support Requests"—one in the middle of the page and one near the bottom under "Other Microsoft Support Resources." If it's already in the upper list, why have it also in "Other . . . Resources"?

Why are true duplicate links bad? They aren't misleading. They are bad because, except in certain special cases, most people assume that separate links on a page go to different places. Duplicate links therefore needlessly inflate the perceived complexity of a website. At best, duplicate links force users to *think about* which of the duplicate links to click, distracting them from their task and taking time (Krug 2000).

Figure 3.17. *www.Microsoft.com* (Jan. 2001)—Duplicate and similar links in center of yellow area and bulleted list below.

Microsoft Office 2001 for Mac

- FAQs & Highlights for Microsoft Office 2001 for Mac

Microsoft Office 98 Macintosh Edition

- FAQs & Highlights for Office 98 Macintosh Edition
- Online Support Requests Submit a question to a Microsoft Support Professional using Online Incident Submission
- FAQ for Office 98 Macintosh Edition
- Office for Macintosh Information (current and previous version)
- FAQ for Office 4.2.1 Macintosh Edition

❗ Support Tip

Join a Newsgroup to share your questions and answers with other users.

Office 2001 for Mac

Office 98

Other Microsoft Support Resources

- Microsoft Knowledge Base **Search by subject or question**
- Online Support Requests **Submit a question to a Microsoft Support Professional using Online Incident Submission**
- Phone Numbers and Support Options
- How to contact Microsoft Product Support Services
- For replacement software (CD and floppy disks), call the Order Desk (800) 360-7561.

Duplicates?   Duplicates?

THE GUY WHO TOOK A WRONG TURN OFF THE ELECTRONIC SUPERHIGHWAY AND WOUND UP IN A MICROWAVE OVEN IN DAVENPORT, IOWA

Exercise: Find the Duplicates

To see for yourself how confusing duplicate links can be to Web users, try to spot duplicate links at *Monterey.com*, a website of the Monterey, California, Chamber of Commerce (Figure 3.18). It has all three types of duplicate links: true, stealth, and false.

Of course, this is a book, not a website—you can't follow the links to check your answers. However, that is part of the point: Web users, faced with a page of links, have to decide based on *looking* which links go where. Once they click on a link, they are taken to another page, which takes time and may distract them from their task. They should be able to predict where links will take them *without* clicking.

Answers are provided on the following page.

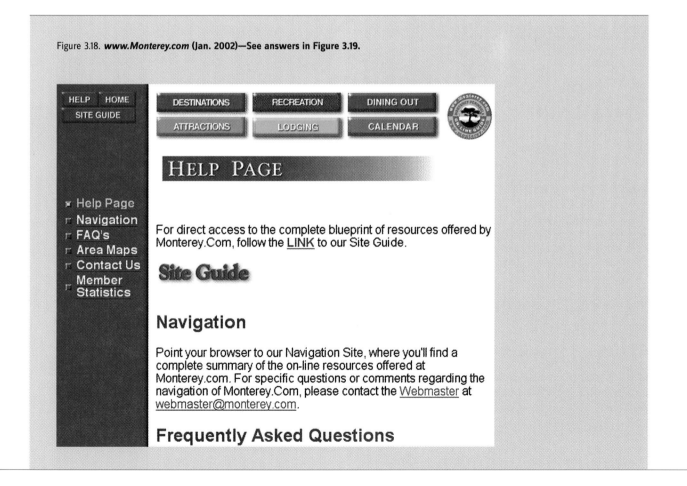

Figure 3.18. ***www.Monterey.com*** **(Jan. 2002)—See answers in Figure 3.19.**

99

Figure 3.19. *www.Monterey.com* (Jan. 2002)—Answers to exercise.

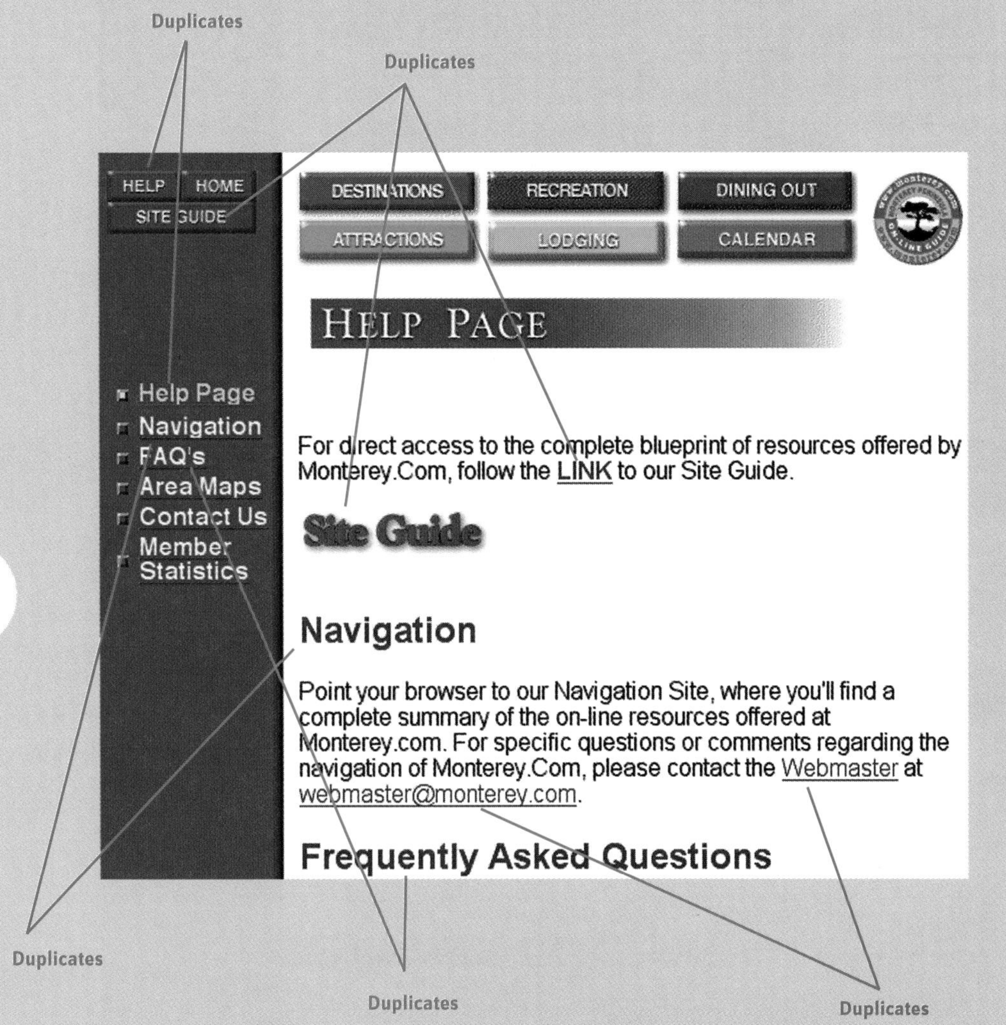

Answers to the Exercise

Monterey.com—Several links on the site's Help page (and other pages) are true or stealth duplicates (Figure 3.19):

> Two links to Help page (this page): button at top left and yellow link in left navigation column.

> Three links to Site Guide: button at top left, underlined word "LINK" in middle of page, and graphical text "Site Guide" near middle of page.

> Two links to Navigation page: one in the left navigation column and one that looks like a blue heading in the middle of the page.

> Two links to send email to the site's Webmaster: underlined word "Webmaster" and underlined email address following it.

> Two links to FAQ's page: one in the left navigation column and one a blue heading at the bottom of this view of the page.

AVOIDING THE BLOOPER

As the designer, you are trying to *simplify* things as much as possible. Duplicate links inflate the perceived size and complexity of a website or Web application. Don't duplicate links just because you can't decide which link design or location is best. Take responsibility for your design. Decide. If in doubt, prototype alternative link schemes and test them on your intended users.

Even though the *WisconSUN* home page has little on it, its triple duplication and highlighted non-link headings make it look much more complex that it is. See how much simpler it looks when the unnecessary upper text-only links are gone? The main links are on the *headings* instead of the first word of the explanations, and the headings look a lot like links (Figure 3.20).

On Category Pages, Don't Duplicate Navigation Bar Links

In websites or Web applications that have an ever-present navigation bar, you should avoid duplicating navigation bar links in the main body of pages. Category pages lacking content or controls of their own can summarize the category (see the previous section Needless Link Duplication in an Intranet Web Application), perhaps highlighting important events, products, or information.

If navigation bar links are duplicated in the content area, they should be accompanied by more information, such as a brief description or picture.

Text-Only Duplicate Links Are Okay

One specific type of link duplication is allowed or even *required:* text-only equivalents for graphical links. Put them at the top or bottom of the page in a horizontal row. An example of text-only duplicate links can be found at the University of Florida website (Figure 3.21).

Home Pages May Have a Few True Duplicates

Most Web-usability experts agree that home pages serve special functions requiring special design rules (Krug 2000; Nielsen 1999; Nielsen and Tahir 2002). A home page may need to highlight or explain certain site content, even though the site's ever-present navigation bar provides links to it.

When duplicating links on the home page, remember the following:

> *Use true duplicates only.* Make sure that the link labels in the navigation bar and content area match exactly. You don't want users to be misled or distracted by wondering whether links are the same.

> *Avoid duplicates on different navigation bars.* The duplication that is okay on home pages is between one navigation bar and the central content area. Duplicate links in

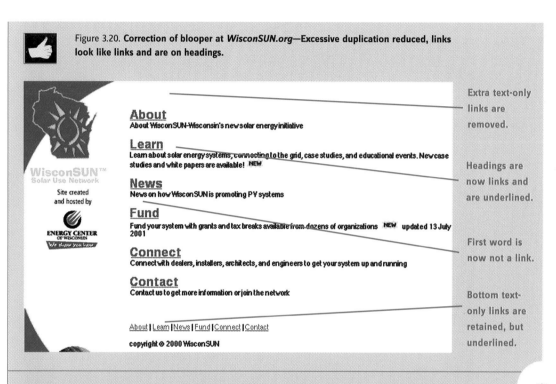

Figure 3.20. **Correction of blooper at *WisconSUN.org*—Excessive duplication reduced, links look like links and are on headings.**

Extra text-only links are removed.

Headings are now links and are underlined.

First word is now not a link.

Bottom text-only links are retained, but underlined.

Figure 3.21. ***eng.ufl.edu* (May 2002)—Textual duplicate links at top of all pages on the site.** Supports visitors who use text-only browsers or have graphics disabled on their browser.

101

Figure 3.22. **Link duplication on home page. A:** *www.Safeway.com* **(Sept. 2002)—Minimal duplication. B:** *www.CalPerfs.Berkeley.edu* **(Mar. 2002—Highlighting everything.**

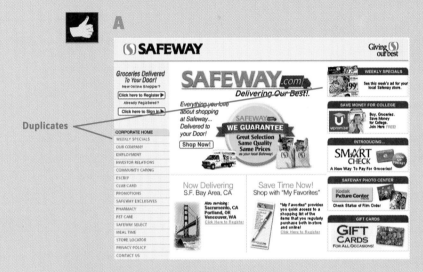

A 👍

Duplicates

B 👎

Most navigation bar
links are duplicated in
main content area.

different navigation bars on the same page are not okay, with the exception of text-only navigation bars. If a page has more than one navigation bar, the different bars should present different types of links (see Blooper 16: Numerous Navigation Schemes).

> *Duplicate sparingly.* As discussed already, even true duplicate links have disadvantages and thus should be used in moderation.

Grocer *Safeway.com's* home page has a sensible amount of duplication (Figure 3.22[A]): one pair of true duplicates. Contrast this with the University of California's Cal Performances home page, in which most of the links in the navigation bar are duplicated in the content area (Figure 3.22[B]). Even though all the duplications are exact, this seems excessive. If everything is highlighted, nothing is.

Blooper 18: Not Linking Directly

Imagine that you're looking on the Web for something specific—a product, service, or piece of information. After browsing and searching for a while, you spot a link that promises to be exactly what you're looking for. You triumphantly say "Yes!" and click on the link . . . only to find yourself looking at the home page of some website that *might* have what you're seeking, assuming you care to look for it there.

Whatever it is called—not linking directly, misleading links, links that lie, bait-and-switch—it is so common and so unpleasant that I'm surprised it isn't more widely denounced. Nielsen and Tahir (2001, p. 16) warn against having links on home pages from specific examples to general category pages, but this blooper is really more general than that. That is indeed one form of the blooper, but it has other forms as well.

Dumping Users at Another Site's Home Page

The primary form of the blooper is exemplified by *Monterey.com*. The site's home page includes a button promising weather information (Figure 3.23[A]). Visitors probably expect it to display weather forecasts for the Monterey peninsula. Instead, it displays the home page of *News46.com*, a news site that includes weather reports (Figure 3.23[B]). Users would have to go to that site's Weather section and look for Monterey weather. Or not. On the Web, users don't "have to" do anything. For example,

when I found myself unexpectedly at News46, I immediately hit Back.

Dumping your site's visitors at another site's home page can hurt your organization, as is made clear by the website of the Institute for Global Communication (IGC). *IGC.org's* home page includes a "Donate" link to encourage visitors to help support the organization (Figure 3.24[A]). Such links usually go to a page with instructions for donating, an address, maybe a donation form, and the tax status of the organization. At *IGC.org*, the "Donate" link goes to the home

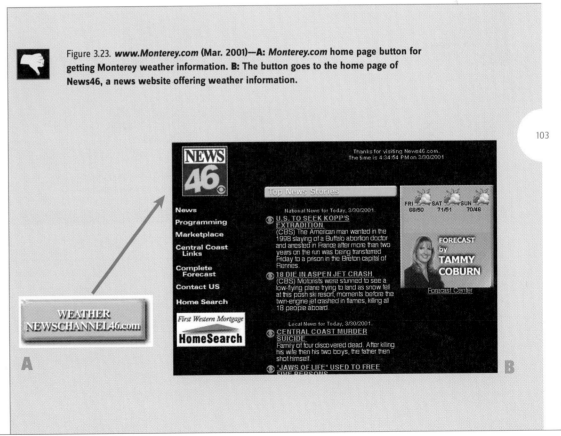

Figure 3.23. ***www.Monterey.com*** (Mar. 2001)—**A:** *Monterey.com* home page button for getting Monterey weather information. **B:** The button goes to the home page of News46, a news website offering weather information.

103

Figure 3.24. **www.IGC.org** (May 2002)—**A:** *IGC.org's* home page has a "Donate" link. **B:** Clicking the "Donate" link displays the home page of *GiveForChange.org*, a separate organization.

A

B

page of *GiveForChange.org*, a donation clearinghouse for nonprofit organizations (Figure 3.24[B]). Once there, it isn't clear how to donate to IGC. One has to find IGC in GiveForChange's listings of organizations. Or not.

Dumping Users at a Generic Page of Your Site

Another form of the blooper is specific-looking links that dump users at a generic page. It occurred at *BarnesAndNoble.com.* In December 2001, their Computer Books page listed popular computer books and provided links to "More Computer Books." One link under that heading was "Best of 2001" (Figure 3.25[A]). Most people would expect that link to go to Barnes&Noble's list of the best *computer* books of 2001, but it actually went to a list of the best books of 2001, in *all* subject areas (Figure 3.25[B]). Users had to scan that list for computer books.

But I Already Told You!

Our final variation of the "not linking directly" blooper is making users indicate repeatedly where they want to go. This is related to the blooper Redundant Requests (see Chapter 2, Blooper 8), but here the focus is on navigation.

As an example, the Institute for Electrical and Electronics Engineers (IEEE) provides a Web page for renewing one's membership. On it is a link labeled "I need to register for a Web account" (Figure 3.26[A]). Members probably expect it to take them to a registration form. Instead, it goes to a general page of membership-related links, one of which is "Register for an IEEE Web account" (Figure 3.26[B]). Thus a person indicates a desire to register, but the site ignores that and goes to a generic page, forcing the user to indicate the desire *again*.

Figure 3.25. **www.BarnesAndNoble.com** (Dec. 2001)—**A:** Computer Books page has "Best of 2001" link. **B:** That link displays best books in all topics, not just computer books.

Figure 3.26. **www.IEEE.org** (Dec. 2001)—**A:** IEEE's renewal page offers option to register for online account. **B:** That link goes to generic Web Account page offering same option.

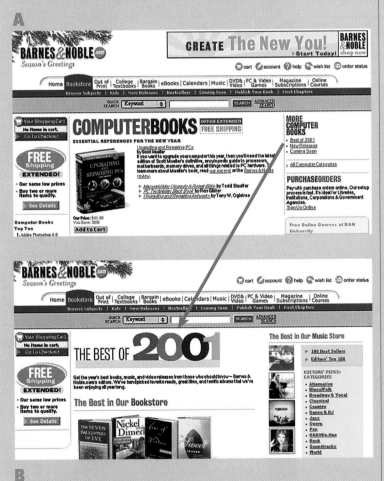

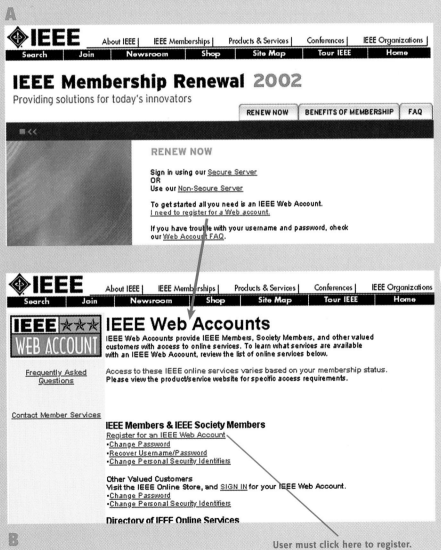

User must click here to register.

105

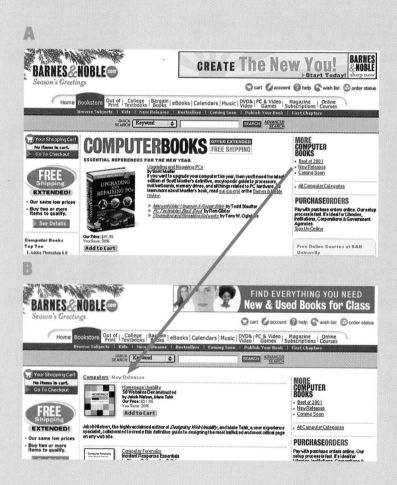

Figure 3.27. ***www.BarnesAndNoble.com*** (Dec. 2001)—**A: Computer Books page has "New Releases" link. B: That link correctly displays newly released computer books.**

106

AVOIDING THE BLOOPER

The guidelines for avoiding this blooper are as follows:

> *Links should fulfill their promise.* A link that names or shows a specific product should go to that product's page. It should not go to the home page of a site that sells that product, or to the front page of a category containing that product, or to a site map listing that product.

> *Stay on track to goal.* If users have navigated down into the content hierarchy or along a sequence of steps, links to proceed should preserve the level of specificity already achieved. It is poor design to unexpectedly pop a user out of the track they were on into a more generic area of the site, forcing them to find the track again.

Except for the aforementioned example of the blooper, Barnes&Noble's site follows these guidelines fairly well. For example, in the same page and list of links as the one exhibiting the blooper is a "New Releases" link (Figure 3.27[A]). It goes to a page of newly released *computer* books, as expected (Figure 3.27[B]). Likewise, the "Coming Soon" link does not forget the level of specificity the user had reached.

Like the website of IGC (see Figure 3.24), CharityFocus is a nonprofit organization that receives donations through a donation clearinghouse, rather than accepting them directly. Therefore, like IGC, clicking "Donate Now" on CharityFocus' donations page (Figure 3.28[A]) goes to another website, in this case *NetworkForGood.org*. Unlike IGC, CharityFocus donors are taken directly to CharityFocus' *own page* at *NetworkForGood.org* (Figure 3.28[B]), rather than to the donation clearinghouse's *home* page.

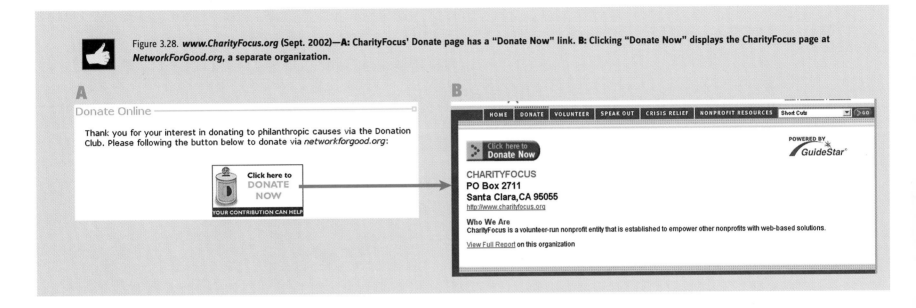

Figure 3.28. *www.CharityFocus.org* (Sept. 2002)—**A:** CharityFocus' Donate page has a "Donate Now" link. **B:** Clicking "Donate Now" displays the CharityFocus page at *NetworkForGood.org*, a separate organization.

Blooper 19: Lost in Space: Current Page Not Indicated

Have you ever tried to get around in an unfamiliar town or neighborhood but found yourself stymied by a lack of street signs? When it's difficult to tell where you are, it's easy to get lost. Even if you don't actually get lost, you *feel* lost. That's how Web users feel when they visit websites that don't show clearly what page they are on.

The current page can be indicated by either marking its item in the navigation bar or by putting a page title prominently on the page. Well-designed sites do one or both of these. Many websites either don't do either or try to do one or both but don't make the markers or titles prominent enough. Let's look at some examples.

Navigation Bar Not Marked, No Page Title

ValcoElectronics.com doesn't mark the current page on the navigation bar or provide page titles (Figure 3.29). The page

shown is the Catalog page, but there is no way to know that from what's on the page. For example, this page could easily be a home page.

Sometimes Web pages lack identification because of poor enforcement of sitewide policies. For example, most pages at *RealEstate.com* are identified, but the site's "Find an Agent" page has a banner ad in the page title's position (Figure 3.30). If temporarily distracted from your computer after arriving here, you might not remember if you were at "Find an Agent," "Find an Appraiser," or "Find a Broker."

Navigation Bar Not Marked, Page Title Not Prominent Enough

Like Valco, the California Department of Motor Vehicles' website does not mark the current page on its navigation bar (Figure 3.31). It does show a page title (such as "Driver License Information"), but its color and small size make it

Figure 3.29. *www.ValcoElectronics.com* (Jan. 2002)—Catalog page. Current page not indicated on navigation bar or with page title. Users can't see where they are.

Current page not marked

No page title

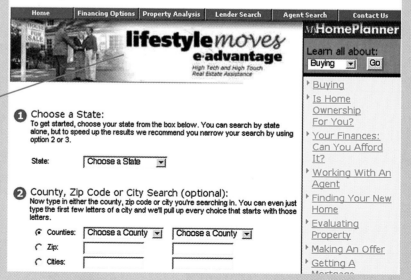

Figure 3.30. *www.RealEstate.com* (Sept. 2002)—Agent Search page has banner ad instead of title.

Banner ad instead of page title

hard to see. The page title's wording also doesn't exactly match any of the items in the navigation bar. The total effect is that it is hard to recognize which page you are on.

The California DMV could do some or all of the following to improve navigation at its website:

1. Make the page title, "Driver License Information," larger than the section title, "Department of Motor Vehicles."

2. Move the page title up higher.

3. Change the page title so that it is dark text on a white background. The text could be in any of several prominent colors, excluding blue, the link color.

4. Make page titles match their navigation bar item, by changing either the title or the navigation bar item.

Alternative "Solutions" that Don't Work

Some may argue that there are other ways to indicate the current page besides marking it on the navigation bar and displaying a prominent page title. They're right; there are other ways, but they don't work. Here are two of the more popular alternatives:

> *Page title in browser title bar:* Use the HTML <TITLE> tag to put a page title into the browser's title bar. This by itself isn't enough. People rarely notice what's in the browser title bar. If you do only this, site visitors will think you don't identify your pages. There are reasons site *should* set titles for the browser, but keeping users informed of their location is not one of them.

> *Watermark title in page background:* Give each page a distinctive background pattern, with the page title appearing as a faint watermark, perhaps in fake 3D. People don't notice watermark backgrounds; they focus on the foreground: the page's content.

Figure 3.31. *www.DMV.ca.gov* (Jan. 2002)—Catalog page. Current page not indicated on navigation bar or with page title. Users can't see where they are.

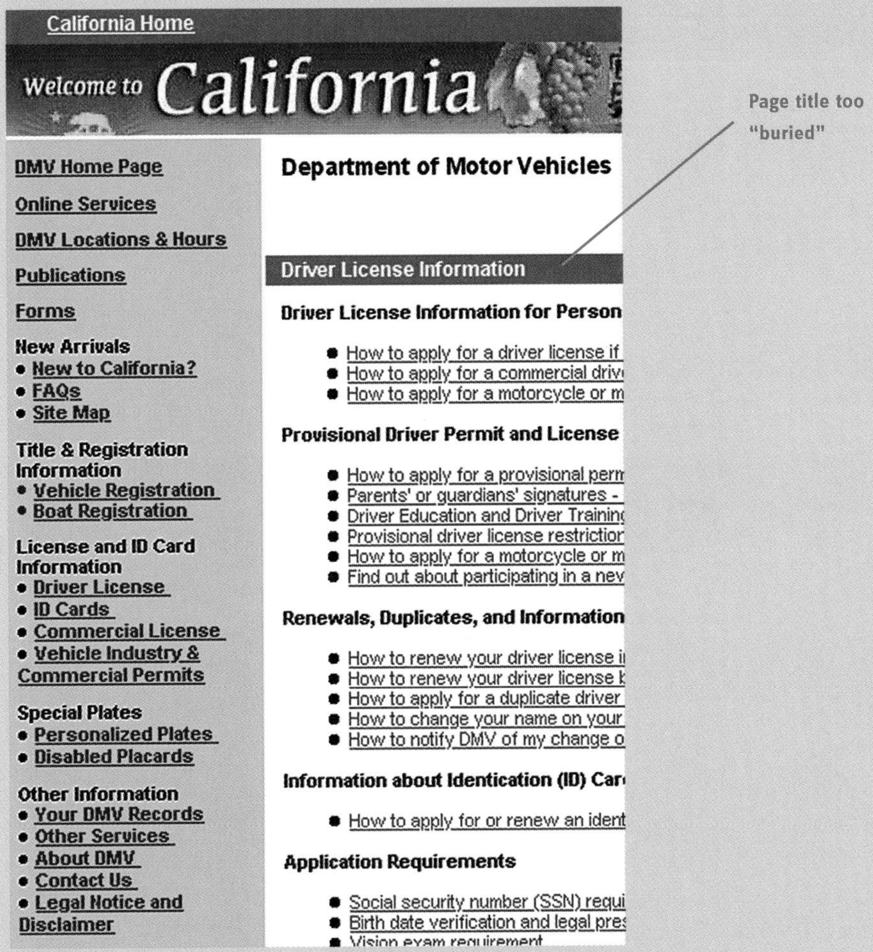

Page title too "buried"

California Home

Welcome to California

DMV Home Page

Online Services

DMV Locations & Hours

Publications

Forms

New Arrivals
- **New to California?**
- **FAQs**
- **Site Map**

Title & Registration Information
- **Vehicle Registration**
- **Boat Registration**

License and ID Card Information
- **Driver License**
- **ID Cards**
- **Commercial License**
- **Vehicle Industry & Commercial Permits**

Special Plates
- **Personalized Plates**
- **Disabled Placards**

Other Information
- **Your DMV Records**
- **Other Services**
- **About DMV**
- **Contact Us**
- **Legal Notice and Disclaimer**

Department of Motor Vehicles

Driver License Information

Driver License Information for Person
- How to apply for a driver license if
- How to apply for a commercial driv
- How to apply for a motorcycle or m

Provisional Driver Permit and License
- How to apply for a provisional perm
- Parents' or guardians' signatures -
- Driver Education and Driver Training
- Provisional driver license restriction
- How to apply for a motorcycle or m
- Find out about participating in a nev

Renewals, Duplicates, and Information
- How to renew your driver license i
- How to renew your driver license k
- How to apply for a duplicate driver
- How to change your name on your
- How to notify DMV of my change o

Information about Identication (ID) Car
- How to apply for or renew an ident

Application Requirements
- Social security number (SSN) requi
- Birth date verification and legal pres
- Vision exam requirement

109

Figure 3.32.
www.RealEstate.com
**(Sept. 2002)—Appraiser
Search page has title.**

Unmarked
navigation
bar

Page title

Figure 3.33. ***www.Pentagram.com*** (Oct. 2002)—Current page is marked on
navigation bar. No separate page title.

Navigation
bar marked

AVOIDING THE BLOOPER

As I said in introducing this blooper, the current page can
be indicated in one of two ways:

> *Navigation bar.* Marking the current page's item in the
site's navigation bar.

> *Page title.* Placing a page title prominently near the top of
the page content.

Well-designed sites use one or both of these on every page.
Here are some examples.

Prominent Page Title

A few pages at *RealEstate.com* lack titles (see Figure 3.30),
but most have them. The site doesn't mark its navigation
bar to indicate the current page, but its page titles are
prominent enough that few users would be confused about
where they are (Figure 3.32).

Navigation Bar Marked

Pentagram.com is a site that indicates the current page on
the navigation bar only (Figure 3.33). Even without separate
page titles, the marked navigation bar clearly indicates the
current page.

Navigation Bar Marked Plus Prominent Page Title

Obviously, if indicating the current page by marking the
navigation bar is helpful and showing page titles prominently is helpful, doing both would be absolutely clear.

As an example, examine a page from the 2002 ACM
Conference on Computer-Human Interaction,
ACM.org/CHI2002 (Figure 3.34). This site actually has
two page titles on each page: one in the navigation trail[6]
("<u>home</u> > location") at the top of the page content area
and one just below that.

Use Alternative Indicators Together with the Standard Ones

The two alternative page-indication methods that users don't notice—page titles in the browser's title bar and watermark backgrounds—should always be supplemented by one or both of the successful methods. However, even though few users notice, all Web pages *should* always set a title for the browser's title bar. Otherwise, the page will be nameless when bookmarked. Watermark backgrounds can enhance the visual appeal of a site as long as the background is very subtle and doesn't interfere with the legibility of foreground text (see Chapter 8, Blooper 55: Camouflaged Text).

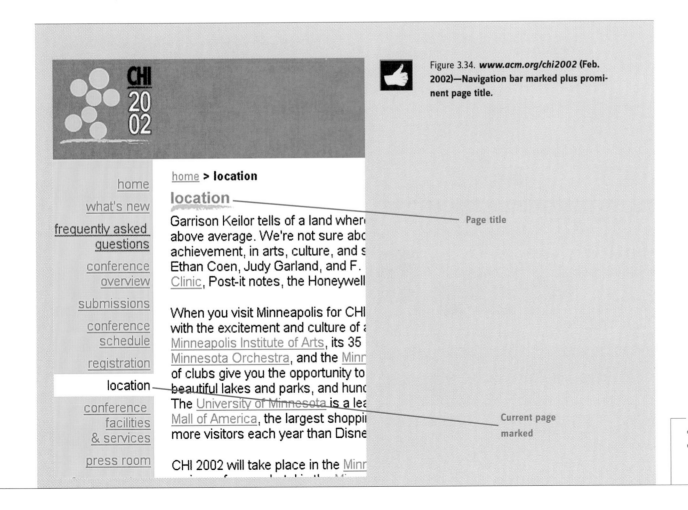

Figure 3.34. *www.acm.org/chi2002* **(Feb. 2002)—Navigation bar marked plus prominent page title.**

Page title

Current page
marked

[6]Often called a "bread-crumb path."

111

Blooper 20: The Circle Game: Active Link to Here

We can't return; we can only look behind from where
we came
And go 'round and 'round and 'round in the circle
game

—*Joni Mitchell, "The Circle Game"*

An extremely common navigation blooper is for a Web page to include an active link to itself. Clicking on such a link merely reloads the page. At best, this wastes people's time as the page reloads. At worst, it can be very disorienting, because users may not recognize the redisplayed page

as the same one they were on. How can they not notice that? Consider the following situations:

> The user clicks a self-link while scrolled down the page, but it redisplays at the top. The user may never have even *seen* the top of the page due to arriving from elsewhere via a direct link to an anchor point far down the page.

> The page has images that change each time it is displayed.

> The page contains animations, applets, or other dynamic content that takes so long to start up that the user temporarily can't see what page this is.

In addition to these problems, disguised self-links can cause unintended loss of data, because any data that had been entered into forms on the page will be lost.

This blooper has several variations, depending on where the active self-links are positioned on the page.

Self-links in Navigation Bar

The most common form of this blooper is for all the links in a site's ever-present navigation bar to be active on all pages. Examples can be seen at *ComputerWorld.com,* an online computer magazine, and *MSDN.Microsoft.com,* the Microsoft Developers' Network website (Figure 3.35).

The main cause of this form of the blooper is that the HTML code for the navigation bar is often simply copied onto every page of the site. Every navigation bar link is therefore active on every page. It takes more work to alter the code for each page so a page's own navigation bar item is not active.

How harmful is this? It depends on how clear it is to site users that the link is a self-link. If the current page is strongly identified, either at the top of the page content or on the navigation bar itself, users probably realize that the link is a self-link. If the current page is not clearly identi-

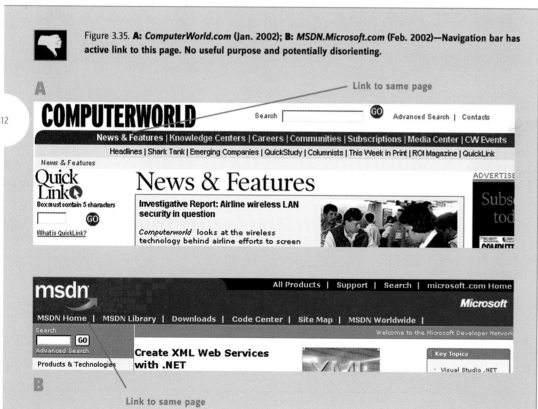

Figure 3.35. **A:** *ComputerWorld.com* (Jan. 2002); **B:** *MSDN.Microsoft.com* (Feb. 2002)—Navigation bar has active link to this page. No useful purpose and potentially disorienting.

fied, users may well not realize that the link is a self-link and click it.

For example, health and safety organization NSF International's home page could easily be mistaken for a splash page (Figure 3.36). It doesn't indicate that this *is* the home page, so visitors might think the home page is a *different* page and click Home to get there.

Which Home Page?

A related form of linking to the current page concerns large websites segmented into several subsites, each with its own home page. Often, such sites provide an auxiliary navigation bar to allow users to navigate *between* subsites in addition to the normal navigation *within* the current subsite. In such sites, if the home page link is active on its own home page, it is a blooper. *Enron.com* provides an example (Figure 3.37).

Self-Links *Not* in Navigation Bar

Self-links that are *not* in the navigation bar tend to be more trouble than those that are in the navigation bar. Site users

"All you had to do was press the 'Home' key."
Copyright 2002 Casey Shaw/USA Weekend magazine, used with permission.

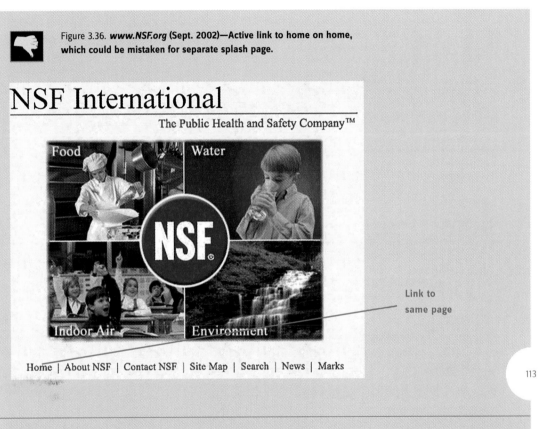

Figure 3.36. *www.NSF.org* (Sept. 2002)—Active link to home on home, which could be mistaken for separate splash page.

Link to same page

113

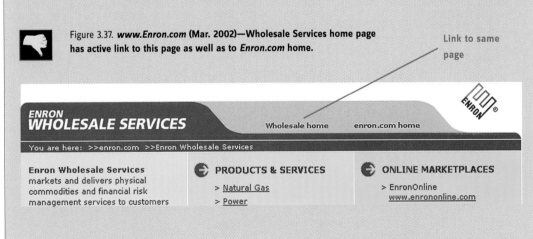

Figure 3.37. *www.Enron.com* (Mar. 2002)—Wholesale Services home page has active link to this page as well as to *Enron.com* home.

Link to same page

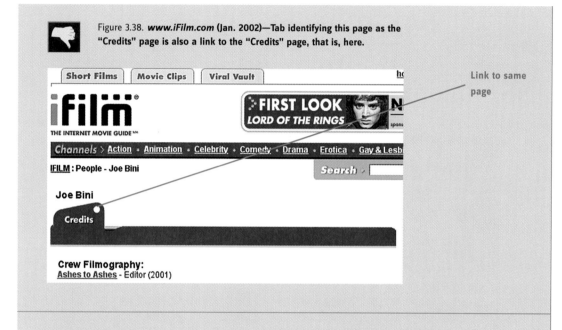

Figure 3.38. ***www.iFilm.com*** (Jan. 2002)—Tab identifying this page as the "Credits" page is also a link to the "Credits" page, that is, here.

Link to same page

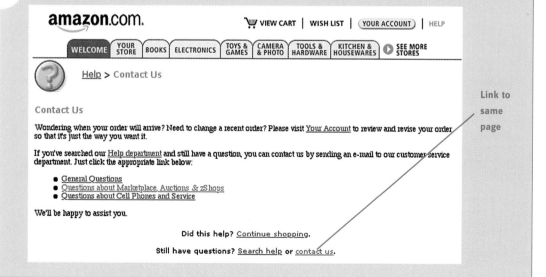

Figure 3.39. ***www.Amazon.com*** (Feb. 2002)—"Contact Us" link at the bottom of page returns to this page.

Link to same page

often can't easily tell whether such links come back to this page or not. Users who click on such a link may not initially realize that the same page has been redisplayed, especially if they were scrolled down the page or the content changes with time. As we shall see, that's only one of several potential problems.

At *iFilm.com*, the tab that labels the film-credits page as the "Credits" page is also a link to . . . the Credits page (Figure 3.38). It is not apparent that the link is to this page.

Amazon.com provides an excellent example of how non–navigation bar self-links can disorient users. In the Help section of the site is a Contact Us page for emailing questions to the company. At the bottom of the page is this instruction: "Still have questions? Search help or contact us" (Figure 3.39). The "contact us" link goes to the Help>Contact Us page, which is *this* page. Some customers may go around this loop a few times before realizing they aren't going to get their questions answered.

When self-links on web pages are combined with poorly managed frames, the results can be downright hilarious. *RCN.com*, a site providing position papers on technology policy, employs a common two-frame design for displaying papers: a table of contents in one frame and the paper content in the other frame (Figure 3.40[A]). The first page of some papers includes a link to the paper. Clicking on those links displays the paper—table of contents *and* page content—in the right frame (Figure 3.40[B]). If users don't realize what is happening (e.g., because they didn't realize that the link was a self-link), they can get into an infinite sequence, with the paper displayed in ever-shrinking frames (Figure 3.40[C] and [D]).

Self-links sometimes appear *both* in the navigation bar and elsewhere on a page; we saw this at *Monterey.com*'s Help page (see Figure 3.19). In such cases, the likelihood for user confusion about which links are self-links and which are not is very high.

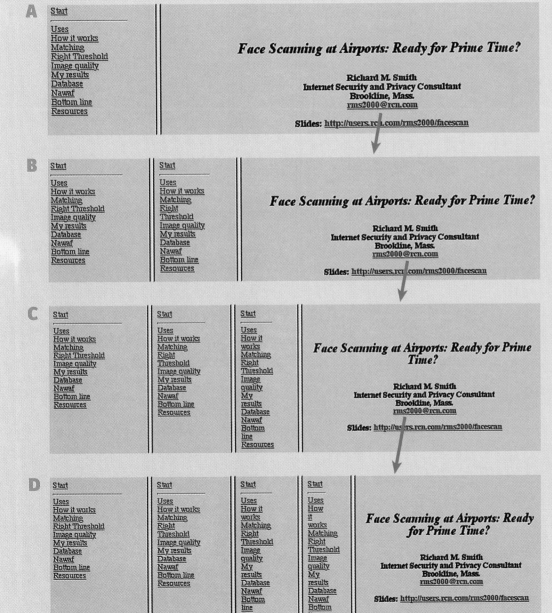

Figure 3.40. *www.RCN.com* (Nov. 2001)—**A:** Papers shown in two frames: table of contents in left frame, document content in right frame.
B: Clicking on a document link in the right frame redisplays the document in the right frame, splitting the right frame into two frames.
C and D: Continuing to click on a document link in the rightmost frame causes an infinite sequence.

115

Figure 3.41. *www.Google.com* (Sept. 2002)—Navigation bar item for current page (marked) is not a link.

Not a link

AVOIDING THE BLOOPER

Nielsen and Tahir (2001, p. 19) give the following design rule:

Don't include an active link to the homepage on the homepage.

This rule can be generalized to any page:

Don't include an active link to the current page.

Some Web developers "justify" active navigation bar links to the current page by arguing that Web users occasionally need a way to refresh the page. Sorry, that's a poor excuse. Most browsers have a "Reload" button, allowing users to refresh the page in the rare cases when they must. The main reason this blooper is so common is that it's easier to use the exact same navigation bar code on every page than it is to alter the code for each page.

[7]Browsers can be displayed in "kiosk" mode, meaning that display of browser controls is suppressed. Also, some software applications incorporate specialized Web browsers, which may or may not have the normal browser controls.

But hey, it's not *that* much more work, after copying the navigation bar code, to edit out the link to the current page. The Search site *Google.com* does this (Figure 3.41).

Blooper 21: Missing Links: It's *Back* or Nothing

Some Web pages lack *not only* an indication of the current page, but *any* navigation links at all. This is a serious blooper that is unfortunately fairly common. It forces Web users to use the Back button or other browser controls to navigate away from the page. That may not sound too bad, but consider that

> If the page was displayed in a new browser window, the Back button won't work.

> Sometimes pages are displayed in browser windows lacking a Back button and other controls.[7]

Error Messages with No Way Out

Pages that display error messages are a common place to find this blooper. Apparently, when Web developers write code to display error messages, they often think of the message as if it were appearing in a dialog box, as in a desktop software application. When error messages appear in small pop-up dialog boxes, navigation controls aren't necessary because users need only close the window to resume what they were doing. But when error messages are just another Web page the browser displays, a lack of navigation links is a problem.

As an example, the website of the Feldenkrais Guild displays an error page with no navigation controls when a Search fails to find anything (Figure 3.42). A lack of navigation links is of course only one of many problems with this page (see Chapter 6, Blooper 42: Speaking Geek).

Sibelius.com displays a pretty unhelpful error message if a visitor's attempt to download software fails: "sql error."

However, for the present discussion, the *text* of the message is less important than the lack of *any* other information or links on the page (Figure 3.43).

"Task Completed" Pages with No Way Out

Web pages displayed when a task is completed or canceled are a second type of page that often lacks navigation controls. *RussellStover.com* used to display a Thank You message when a visitor successfully registered for email notification of site updates (Figure 3.44). The message appeared in the middle of an otherwise blank page, leaving users wondering what to do next. Fortunately, the company eliminated this problem when it upgraded its website.

An example of the same blooper for a *canceled*—rather than completed—task occurs in the website of Morgan-Kaufmann Publishers. If you start to order a book, but click "Cancel Order" before getting to the end of the ordering sequence, you find yourself staring at a nearly blank page, with only a Search button and a barely noticeable Site Index link (Figure 3.45). It doesn't even acknowledge that the order has been canceled. The navigation controls at the bottom of most *MKP.com* pages are absent on this page.

Of course, most *MKP.com* users don't *know* the page is blank. When it appears, most will assume that the page simply hasn't finished downloading into the browser. They will waste many seconds waiting for it to download and then eventually notice that it *has* downloaded and is simply blank. Thus besides providing no obvious way out, this blank page delays users significantly even though it appears quickly.

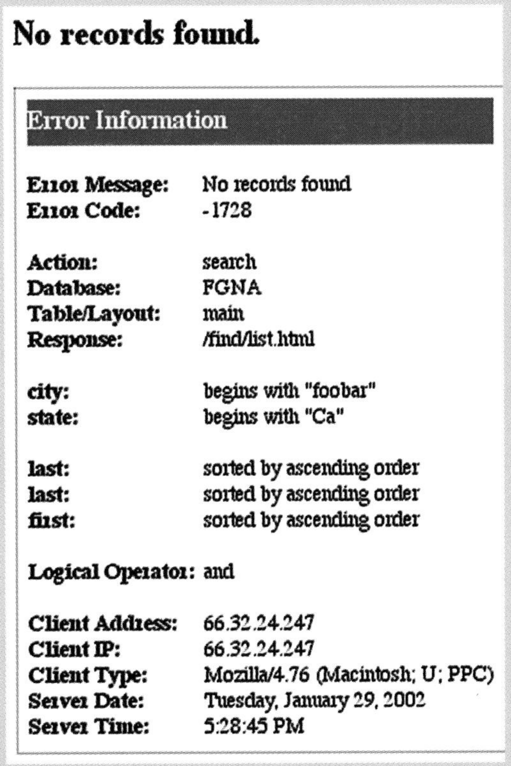

Figure 3.42. ***www.FeldenkraisGuild.com*** **(Jan. 2002)—No navigation links provided when search finds nothing.**

No records found.

Error Information

Error Message:	No records found
Error Code:	-1728
Action:	search
Database:	FGNA
Table/Layout:	main
Response:	/find/list.html
city:	begins with "foobar"
state:	begins with "Ca"
last:	sorted by ascending order
last:	sorted by ascending order
first:	sorted by ascending order
Logical Operator:	and
Client Address:	66.32.24.247
Client IP:	66.32.24.247
Client Type:	Mozilla/4.76 (Macintosh; U; PPC)
Server Date:	Tuesday, January 29, 2002
Server Time:	5:28:45 PM

Figure 3.43. ***www.Sibelius.com*** **(Jan. 2002)—Error message displayed when software download fails. No navigation links on page; just a cryptic message.**

sql error

Figure 3.44. *www.RussellStover.com* (Feb. 2001)—Thank You message displayed after a user signed up for email updates. No navigation links on page.

Thank you. We will email you the announcement of Russell Stover's new site.

118

Figure 3.45. *www.MKP.com* (Apr. 2002)—Blank page displayed after an order is canceled. What now?

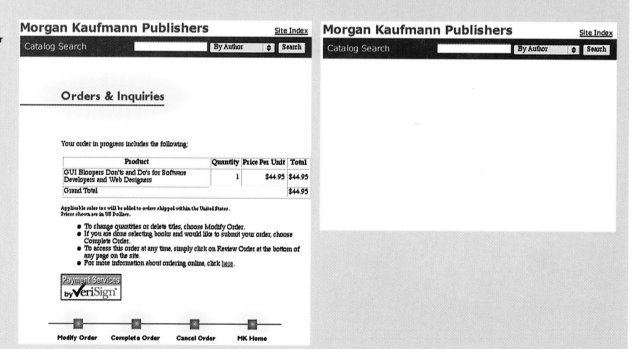

404–Page Not Found

Every Web user has experienced the infamous "404—page not found" error. It often appears on an otherwise blank page, with no navigation controls or site identification. This is one of the most common causes of the "no navigation links" blooper.

AVOIDING THE BLOOPER

To avoid the blooper, all of the aforementioned example pages should include the standard navigation bar that appears on the site's "normal" pages. An example of how *MKP.com's* nearly blank cancellation page could avoid the blooper is shown in Figure 3.46.

At the very least, "task-completion" messages and confirmations should include a simple "Return to XYZ" button or link that displays whatever page is the appropriate restart point. Another way to put it is that there is no reason message pages should be considered any different from other pages, unless they will be displayed in pop-up windows.

To prevent the "404—page not found" variation of this blooper, sites can define pages to be displayed when that error occurs. Such pages should provide links back into the site or, better, the site's standard navigation bar and text-only links.

Don't leave visitors hanging. Always give them a way out.

119

Figure 3.46. **Correction of blooper at *www.MKP.com*—Cancellation acknowledgment page is no longer mostly blank and includes variant of MKP's navigation bar at bottom.**

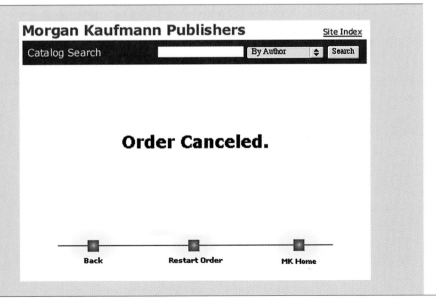

FORM BLOOPERS

The Web, originally devised as a global medium for sharing and browsing static information, has evolved into an interactive medium. The most common method of interaction today is the data-entry form.

Forms consist of data fields, controls, labels, and action buttons. A form can be as brief as a single Search box or as long as a multipage survey or insurance application. Data fields and controls in Web forms consist mainly of standard controls inherited from pre-Web graphical user interfaces (GUIs): text and number fields, radiobuttons, checkboxes, menus, and so on. However, the Web is a new and rapidly evolving medium in which designers are exercising their creativity to devise new interaction techniques and controls, for better or worse.

Unfortunately, many forms and control panels on the Web have been designed—"hacked together" is often a more accurate term—with little or no support from user-interface designers. Other forms suffer from too much creativity and not enough common sense.

This chapter describes the most common bloopers Web designers and developers make when devising forms and control panels.

Blooper 22: Making People Type

The text field is the most heavily used component in Web forms. In fact, it is heavily *overused*. The Web is full of sites that use text fields for specifying structured or constrained data values such as times of day, volume levels, dates, money amounts, and numbers of dependent children. For such data, text fields are too free-form. Unless an example or pattern is provided as part of the field label, they give little or no guidance about what values are valid, so it is easy to type an invalid value. They usually check what you type only when you submit the form. If something you typed is invalid, you get an error message like the following:

`! Invalid entry. Try again.`

Error messages wouldn't be needed if the form allowed you to *choose* data values rather than typing them. Entering invalid values wouldn't be possible. Unfortunately, many websites don't reflect this philosophy.

Figure 4.1 is a data field from a client company's internal Web application for reporting time and expenses. This field has only two valid values: Time (*T*) and Expense (*E*). Users must type one of the two. Lower case *t* and *e* are not allowed. There is simply no excuse in this case for not providing a way to choose.

Radiobuttons are the best way to present this choice, because (1) with only two values, they wouldn't take much space; (2) they show the possible values, so the label wouldn't have to; and (3) they require only one click to set. A menu would also be possible, but (1) it wouldn't show what the possible values are, so the label would still need to show that; (2) it wouldn't save much space compared with radiobuttons; and (3) it requires two clicks to set—one to open and one to choose.

For a more public example of forcing users to type, try the U.S. Postal Service's Web page for looking up postal zip codes (Figure 4.2). To look up a zip code, you type in the location and click the Process button.

A crucial piece of information for determining the zip code is the state. Notice that you can't *choose* a state, you must type it. Worse, you have to type its standard two-letter abbreviation. Do you know the abbreviation for, say, Arkansas? Luckily, the U.S. Postal Service is here to help you: Next to the State text field is a link that pops up a win-

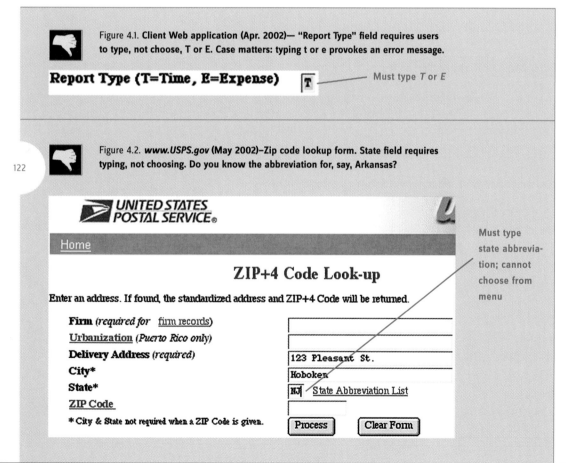

Figure 4.1. **Client Web application (Apr. 2002)— "Report Type" field requires users to type, not choose, T or E. Case matters: typing t or e provokes an error message.**

Report Type (T=Time, E=Expense) `T` —— Must type *T* or *E*

Figure 4.2. ***www.USPS.gov* (May 2002)–Zip code lookup form. State field requires typing, not choosing. Do you know the abbreviation for, say, Arkansas?**

Must type state abbreviation; cannot choose from menu

dow with a state abbreviation list, part of which is shown in Figure 4.3.

On this list, we see that AK, most people's first guess for Arkansas, is actually the abbreviation for Alaska. The correct abbreviation for Arkansas is AR. However, once you've found the correct abbreviation for the state you want, you'd better memorize it, because you can't *choose* it from this list. You have to close the list, then *type* the abbreviation you just looked up into the text field in the form. How helpful!

AVOIDING THE BLOOPER

How can you let people choose rather than making them type? The prime directive is this: Spend development effort to save users work.

Help Users Enter Data

Design forms and controls to help users as much as possible to enter their data. Consider whether it is possible to list all possible values in advance. Even when there are too many possible values for that, there is often a structured way to *construct* values. Here are more concrete guidelines, with examples:

> *Devise data-type–specific controls.* Where possible, controls for entering data into a Web service should be specific to the type of data to be entered.[8] For example, for specifying a date, provide a date control instead of a text field, as at *United.com,* the website of United Airlines (Figure 4.4).

> *Provide choice.* The simplest kind of data-type–specific control is a way to choose one from an explicit set of possible values. Menus are one way to present such choices. *RealEstate.com,* unlike the U.S. Postal Service website, provides a menu for choosing a state in which you want to buy a house (Figure 4.5), rather than requir-

Figure 4.3. ***www.USPS.gov*** **(Feb. 2002)—State abbreviation list (displayed by clicking on link in Figure 4.2). Lists state abbreviations, but doesn't allow users to choose one.**

State/Possession	Abbreviation
ALABAMA	AL
ALASKA	AK
AMERICAN SAMOA	AS
ARIZONA	AZ
ARKANSAS	AR
CALIFORNIA	CA
COLORADO	CO
CONNECTICUT	CT
DELAWARE	DE
DISTRICT OF COLUMBIA	DC
FEDERATED STATES OF MICRONESIA	FM
FLORIDA	FL
GEORGIA	GA
GUAM	GU
HAWAII	HI
IDAHO	ID

State abbreviation list is not a menu; it's just a list to look at.

ing typed state abbreviations. If the choices are few and fixed, radiobuttons also work.

> *Augment text fields with data choosers.* If you decide to use a text field, try to provide a way to choose a value for it, such as a calendar for picking dates, as at *NWA.com* (Figure 4.6).

[8]In programmers' terms: Online forms and control panels should be strongly typed, just as many popular programming languages are.

123

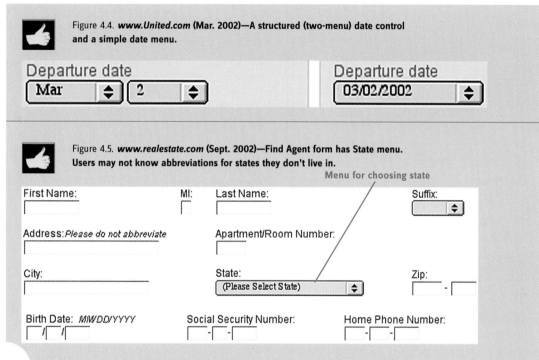

Figure 4.4. **www.United.com (Mar. 2002)—A structured (two-menu) date control and a simple date menu.**

Departure date

| Mar | ▲▼ | | 2 | ▲▼ |

Departure date

| 03/02/2002 | ▲▼ |

Figure 4.5. **www.realestate.com (Sept. 2002)—Find Agent form has State menu. Users may not know abbreviations for states they don't live in.**

Menu for choosing state

First Name: | MI: | Last Name: | Suffix: | ▲▼

Address: *Please do not abbreviate* | Apartment/Room Number:

City: | State: (Please Select State) ▲▼ | Zip: -

Birth Date: *MM/DD/YYYY* | Social Security Number: - - | Home Phone Number: - -

Figure 4.6. **www.NWA.com (Mar. 2002)— A date text field with an optional pop-up date chooser.**

Netscape: NWA Travel Cale...

Mar 2002 | Mar ▲▼ | 2002 ▲▼

S	M	T	W	T	F	S
24	25	26	27	28	1	2
3	4	5	6	7	8	9
10	11	12	13	14	15	16
17	18	19	20	21	22	23
24	25	26	27	28	29	30
31	1	2	3	4	5	6

Enter Departure Date (MM/DD/YY)

03/26/02

When Type-in Is Okay

Requiring data to be typed is often okay or even necessary. It is fine to let users type data if the data is:

> Unstructured, such as new user names, street addresses, descriptions, and comments

> Secure, such as user names and passwords

> Internationally variable, such as telephone numbers or postal codes

> Something users know very well and have typed so often that it is in their finger memory, such as their *own* state or birth date

Blooper 23: Intolerant Data Fields

Sometimes it isn't possible to let people point and click to choose what they want. Sometimes you need to have them type text into a field: search terms, addresses, phone numbers, names, passwords, or comments.

If your website contains text or number type-in fields, your Web software must of course check what people type to make sure it is valid. But to be friendly and helpful, you have to tolerate reasonable variations in what people type. Unfortunately, text fields on many websites are intolerant. Users of such sites often see error messages like the one from *Microsoft.com* (Figure 4.7).

It's Our Way or No Way!

The same client company internal Web application mentioned in the previous blooper provides a good example of a *very* intolerant text field (Figure 4.8).

The Week Ending Date field wants dates in the form DD-MON-YYYY. Notice that the Month part of the pattern is "MON," not "MMM." That, and the character length of the field, suggests that "14-1-2000" would be a valid date.

It isn't. The date *must* be typed with a two-digit day (with a leading zero if the day is nine or less), a hyphen, a three-letter month abbreviation, a hyphen, and a four-digit year. To specify January 4, 2003, you'd have to type "04-jan-2003." Any other form of date provokes a stern error message.

Especially bad is the fact that "valid" dates won't really fit into the date field; they scroll it sideways. This would actually *discourage* people from using the form's only allowed format for dates.

United.com often commits the sin of not accepting data in familiar formats. In Figure 4.9, we see that Frequent Flier numbers are rejected if entered in the format that United itself uses on Frequent Flier cards and printed mileage statements. Another form at this site rejects credit card numbers that include spaces. Those spaces are in those numbers for a *reason*. They make it easier to scan and check the numbers. Let us type them!

Error: AT&T Is an Invalid Company Name

A friend pointed out a frustrating intolerant form at the California state website where citizens apply for unemployment benefits. The application form requires users to name their most recent employers but won't accept characters other than letters and digits. This makes it impossible to specify employer names that include nonalphanumeric characters, such as AT&T and Excite@Home. My friend had to type in her former employers as "ATandT" and "ExciteAtHome," which probably caused other problems in the processing of her application (Figure 4.10).

Amazing Intolerance

An amazing example of form intolerance comes from *Sony.com*. Assume you've bought a Sony product and want to register it. You go to the Product Registration page (Figure 4.11) and type the product number *exactly* as it is

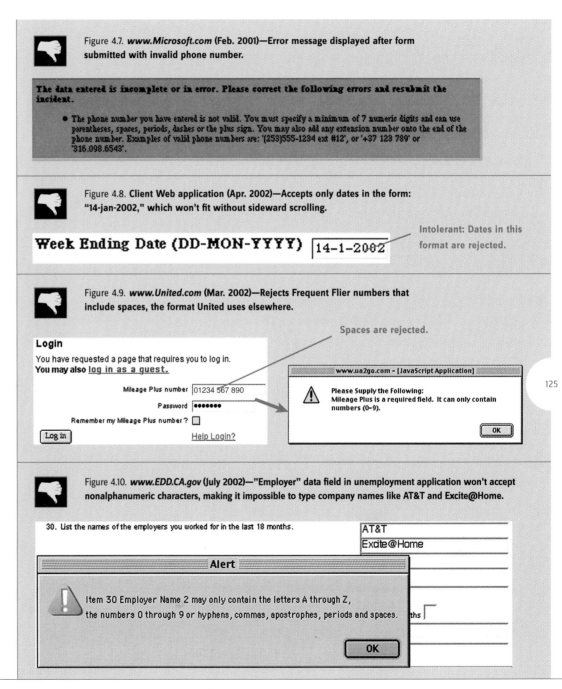

Figure 4.7. ***www.Microsoft.com*** **(Feb. 2001)—Error message displayed after form submitted with invalid phone number.**

The data entered is incomplete or in error. Please correct the following errors and resubmit the incident.

- The phone number you have entered is not valid. You must specify a minimum of 7 numeric digits and can use parentheses, spaces, periods, dashes or the plus sign. You may also add any extension number onto the end of the phone number. Examples of valid phone numbers are: '(253)555-1234 ext #12', or '+37 123 789' or '316.098.6543'.

Figure 4.8. **Client Web application (Apr. 2002)—Accepts only dates in the form: "14-jan-2002," which won't fit without sideward scrolling.**

Week Ending Date (DD-MON-YYYY) `14-1-2002`

Intolerant: Dates in this format are rejected.

Figure 4.9. ***www.United.com*** **(Mar. 2002)—Rejects Frequent Flier numbers that include spaces, the format United uses elsewhere.**

Spaces are rejected.

Login
You have requested a page that requires you to log in.
You may also log in as a guest.

Mileage Plus number `01234 567 890`
Password `••••••`
Remember my Mileage Plus number? ☐
`Log in`   Help Login?

www.ua2go.com - [JavaScript Application]
⚠ Please Supply the Following:
Mileage Plus is a required field. It can only contain numbers (0-9).
`OK`

125

Figure 4.10. ***www.EDD.CA.gov*** **(July 2002)—"Employer" data field in unemployment application won't accept nonalphanumeric characters, making it impossible to type company names like AT&T and Excite@Home.**

30. List the names of the employers you worked for in the last 18 months.
`AT&T`
`Excite@Home`

Alert
⚠ Item 30 Employer Name 2 may only contain the letters A through Z, the numbers 0 through 9 or hyphens, commas, apostrophes, periods and spaces.
`OK`

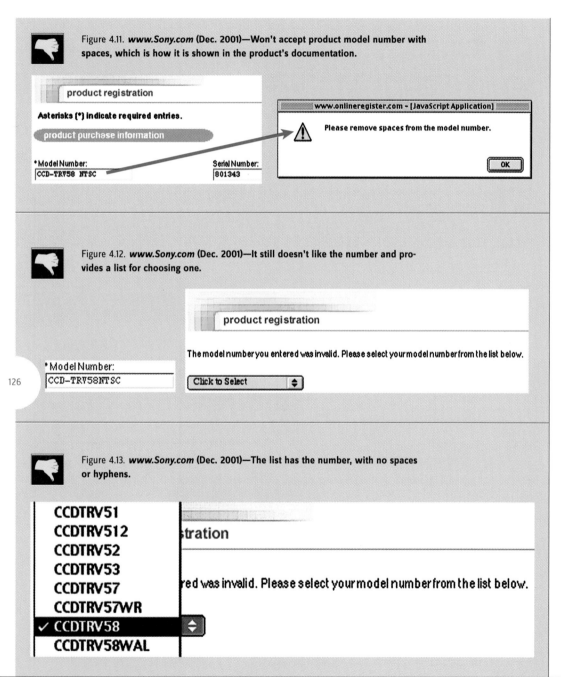

Figure 4.11. *www.Sony.com* (Dec. 2001)—Won't accept product model number with spaces, which is how it is shown in the product's documentation.

Figure 4.12. *www.Sony.com* (Dec. 2001)—It still doesn't like the number and provides a list for choosing one.

Figure 4.13. *www.Sony.com* (Dec. 2001)—The list has the number, with no spaces or hyphens.

shown on the packaging and in the owner's manual: CCD-TRV58 NTSC. You fill out the rest of the form and click Submit. Up pops an error message "Please remove spaces from the model number."

At this point, you might wonder, Why can't they remove the @%&# spaces and go on? But they don't do that, so you remove the space from the model number (Figure 4.12) and click Submit again. Another message appears: "The model number you entered was invalid."[9] The message doesn't explain what is wrong with the model number now, but a menu is provided, allowing you to choose a model number. You might wonder why this menu wasn't provided to start with.

You click open the menu, and there is your model number (Figure 4.13), free not only of spaces, but also of hyphens, which neither error message mentioned. You choose it and sigh with relief as the form is finally accepted. Are experiences like this conducive to customer loyalty?

Form Won't Accept Its Own Example

As comic relief from so many intolerant forms, let's look at one that's so bad it's funny. *Intel.com* is the website of Intel Corporation, maker of computer microchips. The Intel Developer Forum subsite has a Feedback page for sending feedback to the webmaster. The form asks for the URL of the page about which you are providing feedback (Figure 4.14). However, until recently, the URL field wouldn't accept more than 35 characters—which means it wouldn't accept URLs for most of the pages at the site. It wouldn't even fit the *sample* URL at the top of the page!

The irony is, to give them feedback on *this* blooper, you'd have to supply the URL for this feedback page, but you couldn't because the field wouldn't accept it! Fortunately, a recent site update corrected this blooper.

Can't We All Get Along?

Why are all these websites so intolerant and uncooperative? Why are they so picky about what people type? Why can't they even accept data in common formats—even just one—or in formats that the companies themselves use elsewhere?

One common excuse is that it is hard for programmers to write software that can interpret and accept data typed in anything but a single very simple format. Perhaps, but consider how many user hours are wasted for each programmer hour saved. More to the point, consider the traffic and revenue lost because of intolerant, annoying forms. Consider the impression you give your customers when your website rejects model numbers typed *exactly* as they appear in your own packaging and literature. They get the impression that your company is lacking in organization and coordination.

AVOIDING THE BLOOPER

Fortunately, the guidelines for providing user-friendly, tolerant type-in fields are not too complicated.

> *Match field length to data.* The visible length of a field should suggest the length of the data to be typed. It needn't be exact, because that would create ragged looking forms and isn't feasible anyway because of variable-width typefaces. What is important is that fields be (1) long enough to hold their data and (2) not a lot longer than that.

> *Accept common formats.* If the information has a common, accepted format, allow it. If there are several common formats, allow as many as is feasible. For example, a time field could accept times in any of the following formats: 12:30 am, 12:30 AM, 12:30 a, 00:30, 00:30 h.

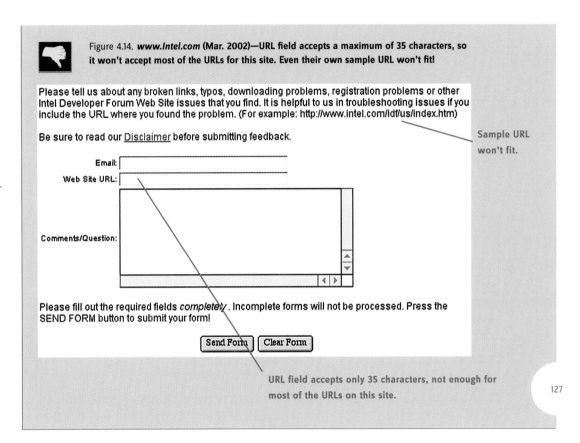

Figure 4.14. *www.Intel.com* (Mar. 2002)—URL field accepts a maximum of 35 characters, so it won't accept most of the URLs for this site. Even their own sample URL won't fit!

Please tell us about any broken links, typos, downloading problems, registration problems or other Intel Developer Forum Web Site issues that you find. It is helpful to us in troubleshooting issues if you include the URL where you found the problem. (For example: http://www.intel.com/idf/us/index.htm)

Be sure to read our <u>Disclaimer</u> before submitting feedback.

Sample URL won't fit.

Email:

Web Site URL:

Comments/Question:

Please fill out the required fields *completely*. Incomplete forms will not be processed. Press the SEND FORM button to submit your form!

Send Form   Clear Form

URL field accepts only 35 characters, not enough for most of the URLs on this site.

127

> *Accept your own formats.* Accept data in the formats you use elsewhere. For example, if your printed product codes look like "ZX-4563.33 QR," your Web forms should accept the codes in that exact same format.

> *Beware of rejecting legitimate data.* Think hard about who might be using your form. Customers from Canada or the United Kingdom, where postal codes include letters, would be greatly annoyed at an order form that required a "zip code" but rejected letters.

[9]This error message appears on the page itself instead of in a pop-up error dialog box. Why are the two error messages displayed differently? And why is the message in the past tense, as if the number entered *was* invalid, but no longer is?

> *Make letter-case irrelevant.* If you expect users to type codes that include letters, and if letter case is not significant for the data, users should be able to type either uppercase or lowercase into the field. Using the previous example, users could type either "zx-45 . . ." or "ZX-45. . . ."

> *Provide a pattern.* Give an example of a valid format, for example, "DD/MM/YYYY," or "Sample Serial #: QP-00275-5559." Put it somewhere right next to the field: above it, below it, or on either side. See Northwest Airlines' website, *NWA.com,* for an example of a data field that provides a pattern (Figure 4.15).

> *Structure text fields.* Unless you must allow different—perhaps international—formats, build the format you want into the form by structuring the text fields. For example, if you are absolutely certain that only U.S. phone numbers will be entered into the form, you can structure it into separate fields for area code and number, as at Bank of America's form (Figure 4.16). If you segment a text field into subfields, you must make it easy for users to move between fields. The Tab key should always move the insertion point from one field to the next. A form can automatically move the insertion point to the next field when the required number of characters has been typed.

Blooper 24: No Defaults

An important design principle for websites, Web applications, and software in general is that the less a user has to specify to get what he or she wants, the better (Johnson 2000). One specific implication of this principle is that choices in forms and control panels should have default values. The default values should be the most likely ones. This frees users from having to set everything explicitly. Instead, they can simply scan the settings, maybe change a few, and proceed.

Unfortunately, this important design principle is not widely known. Millions of websites and Web applications offer choices with no defaults or with defaults that are unlikely to be what users want.

At best, such choices force users to make explicit decisions and choices, consuming valuable time. Often, however, the result of missing defaults is that users overlook the settings, try to proceed, and then either get scolded for omitting required information (Figure 4.17) or end up with results they didn't want.

Figure 4.15. ***www.NWA.com*** **(Mar. 2002)—Date field with a pattern for valid dates.**

Enter Departure Date
(MM/DD/YY)

03/26/02

Figure 4.16. ***www.BankOfAmerica.com*** **(Mar. 2002)—Segments date, social security number, and phone number into subfields.**

Birth Date: *MM/DD/YYYY*

Social Security Number:

Home Phone Number:

Figure 4.17. ***www.Slip.net*** **(July 2001)—Error message displayed when user submits form without changing a menu from its default value.**

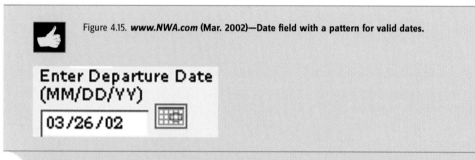

Reasons for Not Providing a Default

On the other hand, some choices offered by websites cannot offer a default value. There are two reasons why this might be so:

> *No useful default value.* For example, a membership application form at an organization's website might have a menu for applicants to indicate their home state. If the organization is nationwide, such as the American Civil Liberties Union (ACLU), there probably is no basis for making any one of the fifty U.S. states the default. However, if the organization is local, such as the San Francisco *chapter* of the ACLU, it would make sense to make California the default state on the membership application.

> *Social, political, or legal requirement.* In some situations, Web designers must try not to offend anyone by being presumptuous. Imagine the trouble a Canadian government website would be in if, in offering visitors a choice of English versus French, it defaulted the choice to English. It would be a *faux pas,* to say the least.

Despite these exceptions, most choice controls on websites should have default values. Let's look at some examples of websites that in one way or another failed to provide defaults for choices.

Radiobuttons with No Default

On the Web, one often sees radiobutton choices that start with none of the buttons selected.

Sometimes, this is simply a bug: the result of the radiobuttons having been defined incorrectly. Often, however, Web designers do this intentionally. They want to do one of the following:

1. Avoid any presumptions about what users will choose, as discussed previously
2. Force users to choose explicitly
3. Allow users *not* to choose (although this reason is much rarer than the first two)

The website of sporting goods retailer L.L. Bean provides examples, from two separate forms, of radiobuttons with no default value (Figure 4.18). In these cases, the lack of defaults makes sense. Defaulting either choice to one of its two values would be at least presumptuous, perhaps even illegal.

Although radiobuttons with no default value may be justifiable in rare cases, they are usually bad design. They violate users' expectations about how radiobuttons work. They violate the logical type of a radiobutton set: a one-from-N choice, not a zero-or-one-from-N choice. They are impossible to set back to their initial unset state. They violate the design guideline that in cases in which no default makes sense, menus are preferable to radiobuttons (see later discussion). Finally, they violate the aforementioned interaction design principle about letting users do as little as possible to get what they want.

129

Figure 4.18. *www.LLBean.com* (Nov. 2000)—Radiobuttons with no valid initial value, from two different forms at the site. In both cases, not having a default is justifiable, perhaps even required.

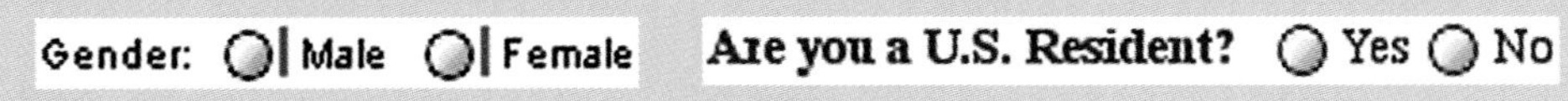

Gender: ◯| Male ◯| Female   **Are you a U.S. Resident?** ◯ Yes ◯ No

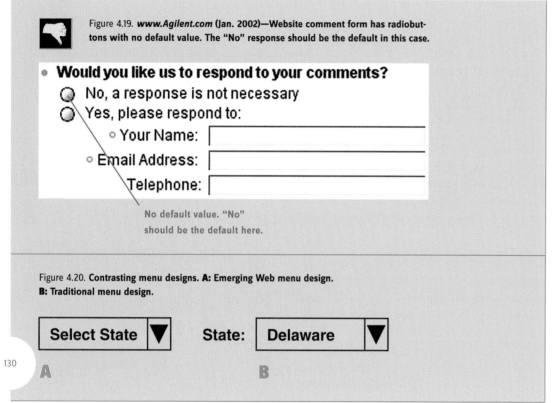

Figure 4.19. *www.Agilent.com* (Jan. 2002)—Website comment form has radiobuttons with no default value. The "No" response should be the default in this case.

● **Would you like us to respond to your comments?**
   ○ **No, a response is not necessary**
   ○ **Yes, please respond to:**
      ○ **Your Name:**
      ○ **Email Address:**
      Telephone:

No default value. "No" should be the default here.

Figure 4.20. **Contrasting menu designs. A: Emerging Web menu design. B: Traditional menu design.**

| Select State ▼ | State: | Delaware ▼ |

A   **B**

Menus with No Default

Drop-down menus with no initial value are even more common on the Web than radiobuttons with no initial value. Generally speaking, this is okay, for two reasons:

1. A menu with no value is not as unnatural as a radiobutton choice with no value. "No value" on radiobuttons means that it is set to *none* of its possible values. In contrast, "No value" on a menu is just one of the values in the menu, albeit a special value.
2. Menus are often used to present more options than radiobuttons can present. Radiobuttons are best for from two to about eight choices.[10] Menus can present dozens of options. The larger number of options—such as in a menu for specifying one's state of residence—makes it less likely that any of them would be a suitable default value.

Bolstering the commonness of menus with no initial value is a newly emerged Web-design idiom in which a menu's initial value is also its label or an instruction to users. For example, a menu to indicate your home state in the United States might be set to a prompt such as "Select State" or "State" (Figure 4.20[A]). This contrasts with the traditional menu design, in which a menu is set to a real value such as "Delaware," with an external label "State" (Figure 4.20[B]).

This new way of designing menus is okay as long as Web designers follow these guidelines:

> It should be used only for menus that have no useful default.

> Menu labels—including the initial value that serves as a prompt—must be carefully worded to make clear what the choice is.

If these two guidelines are *not* followed, the result is menus that needlessly force users to make explicit choices instead

Therefore, designers should have a *very* compelling reason for presenting radiobuttons without a default value. Far too often, no such compelling reason exists.

Look, for example, at *Agilent.com*. The site provides a Feedback page where visitors can comment on the website. In submitting comments, visitors have to specify whether they *do* or *do not* want a response (Figure 4.19). I repeat: "have to specify." There is simply no good reason why this choice could not default to "No, a response is not necessary."

[10]In special cases, carefully designed arrays of radiobuttons can be used to present more choices.

of letting them simply accept defaults, menus that users have to pull open even just to see what the choice is, or both. Sadly, these guidelines are often not followed. Considering the millions of menus on websites worldwide, multiplied by millions of Web users, mind-boggling amounts of Web-user time is being wasted.

A good example of a website that wastes customers' time by failing to provide defaults for menus is the Stanford University Bookstore. The Shopping Cart page has a menu with a long, confusing description and "Please choose" as its initial value (Figure 4.21[A]). The menu's purpose is to allow the store to substitute used books for new books or new books for used books depending on what is in stock. Its values are "yes" or "no." Because of the verbose instruction and the menu's position on the page, it is easy to ignore. However, you can't proceed until you set it (Figure 4.21[B]).

A better design would (1) assign the choice control a default value that allows book substitutions, requiring customers to change the control to *disallow* them, and (2) make the control more prominent. In the following Avoiding the Blooper section, I offer an improved design.

At *LLBean.com,* an online sporting goods and clothing store, I found a more serious example of a menu lacking a valid default for no good reason. I was shopping for a backpacking tent. I found one I liked, looked at its product page (Figure 4.22), then clicked "Add to Shopping Cart." Instead of taking me to my shopping cart, the site displayed an error message: "We're sorry, more information is needed to order this item. Please complete Step 2 then continue your order." I clicked OK and went back to the product page. What had I missed? Step 2 included a Quantity field, which I had left set to the sensible default of 1, but it also included a Color/Style menu, which I had also left as it was.

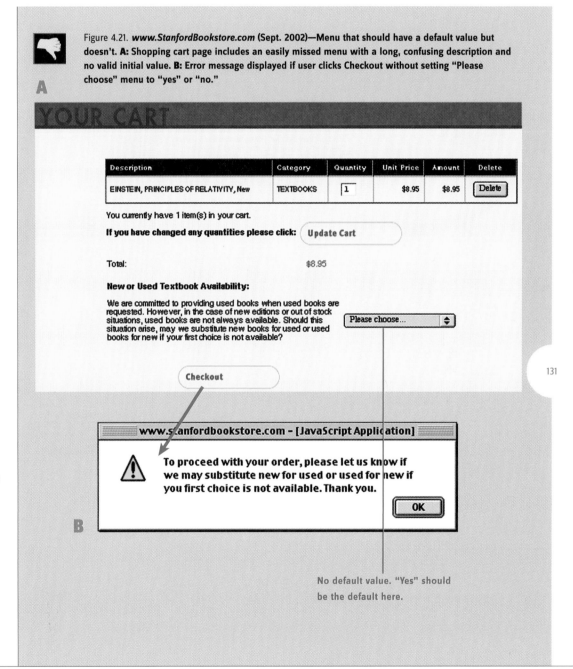

Figure 4.21. *www.StanfordBookstore.com* (Sept. 2002)—Menu that should have a default value but doesn't. A: Shopping cart page includes an easily missed menu with a long, confusing description and no valid initial value. B: Error message displayed if user clicks Checkout without setting "Please choose" menu to "yes" or "no."

131

Figure 4.22. *www.LLBean.com* (Nov. 2000)—Menu with no valid initial value. **A:** The menu in step 2 is initialized to a label "Color/Style," not to a valid value. **B:** This is true even though the product comes in only one color. **C:** If customers try to proceed without setting the Color/Style menu, they get an error message.

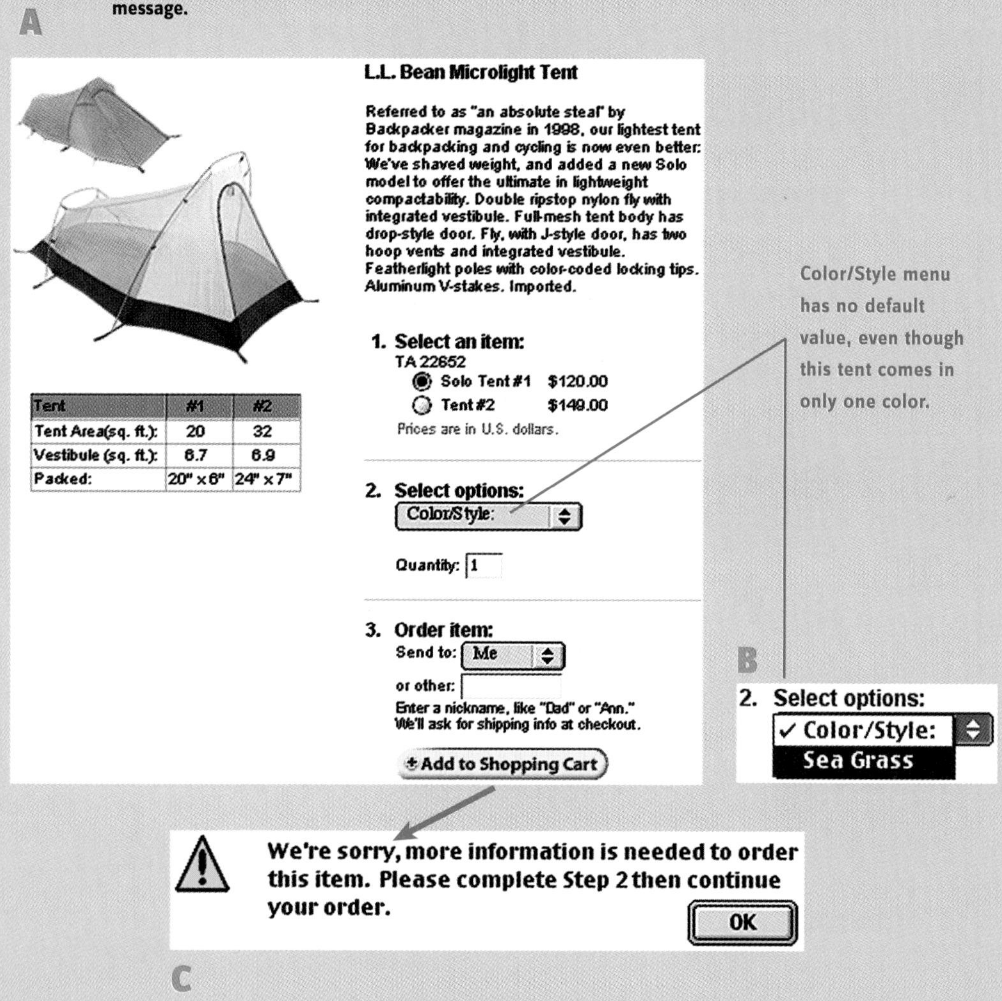

Okay, so I had neglected to choose a color. I opened the menu and saw that the tent comes in only one color: Sea Grass.

Why didn't *LLBean.com* set the menu to "Sea Grass" by default? Because product pages are generated automatically from product databases, so they are designed generically rather than being carefully designed for each product. Different products have different options, so step 2 is generically labeled "Select options" rather than "Select Color." The menu choices are generated dynamically, with an initial value labeling the options for that product. This example shows that automatically generated pages, although they have economic advantages, have strong usability disadvantages, which can translate into economic disadvantages.

L.L. Bean's website also provides another instructive example. Recall the guideline: If menus are designed according to the new Web-design trend of having their initial value be a prompt, the labels—including the prompt value—must be carefully worded to make clear what the choice is. The menus on *LLBean.com*'s credit card application follow the new trend, but the labels are vague: "select" (Figure 4.23). One menu is labeled "Are you:" Users have to open it to see what it sets. It could be about anything: Are you . . . rich? Are you . . . in prison? Are you . . . annoyed by poorly labeled menus?

Similarly, at *Agilent.com*, the lack of initial values in menus, combined with vague labels—"Select"—yields a confusing trio of menus. Do the three menus each represent a product, with product *options* on the menus, or does each menu represent a product *category*, with products on the menu? Customers can't tell. All three menus should have meaningful defaults (Figure 4.24).

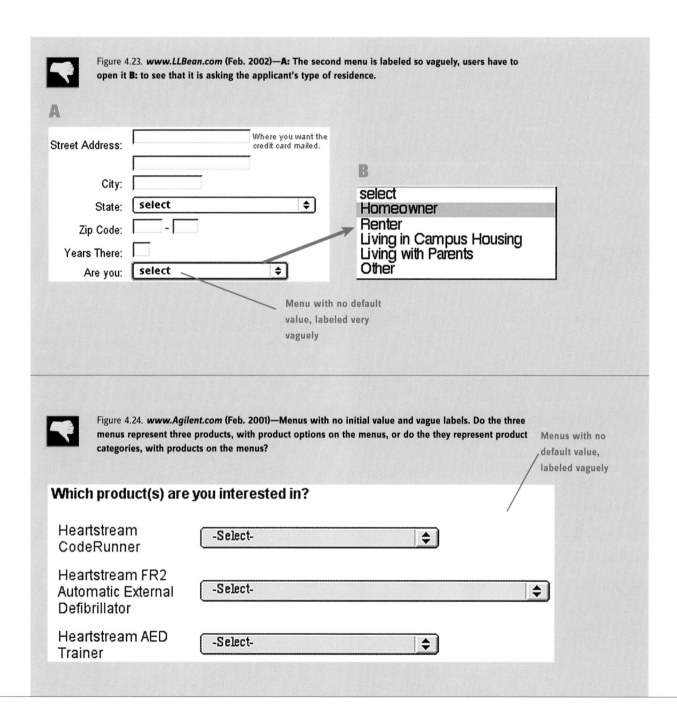

Figure 4.23. *www.LLBean.com* (Feb. 2002)—**A:** The second menu is labeled so vaguely, users have to open it **B:** to see that it is asking the applicant's type of residence.

A

Street Address: [ ] Where you want the credit card mailed.

[ ]

City: [ ]

State: [select ▼]

Zip Code: [ ] - [ ]

Years There: [ ]

Are you: [select ▼]

B

| select |
| Homeowner |
| Renter |
| Living in Campus Housing |
| Living with Parents |
| Other |

Menu with no default value, labeled very vaguely

133

Figure 4.24. *www.Agilent.com* (Feb. 2001)—Menus with no initial value and vague labels. Do the three menus represent three products, with product options on the menus, or do the they represent product categories, with products on the menus?

Menus with no default value, labeled vaguely

Which product(s) are you interested in?

Heartstream CodeRunner   [-Select- ▼]

Heartstream FR2 Automatic External Defibrillator   [-Select- ▼]

Heartstream AED Trainer   [-Select- ▼]

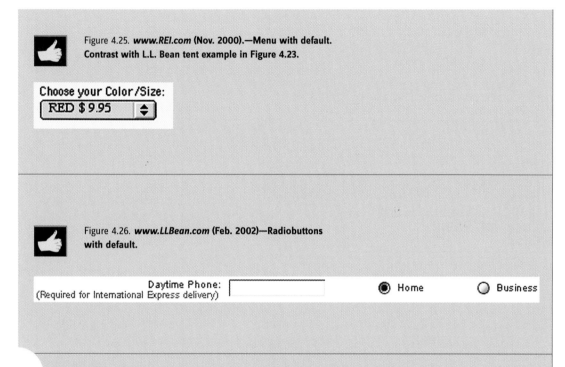

Figure 4.25. *www.REI.com* (Nov. 2000).—Menu with default. Contrast with L.L. Bean tent example in Figure 4.23.

Choose your Color/Size:

RED $ 9.95 ⬍

Figure 4.26. *www.LLBean.com* (Feb. 2002)—Radiobuttons with default.

Daytime Phone: [   ] ● Home   ○ Business
(Required for International Express delivery)

Figure 4.27. *www.UPAssoc.org* (July 2001)—Radiobuttons with default "none" value.

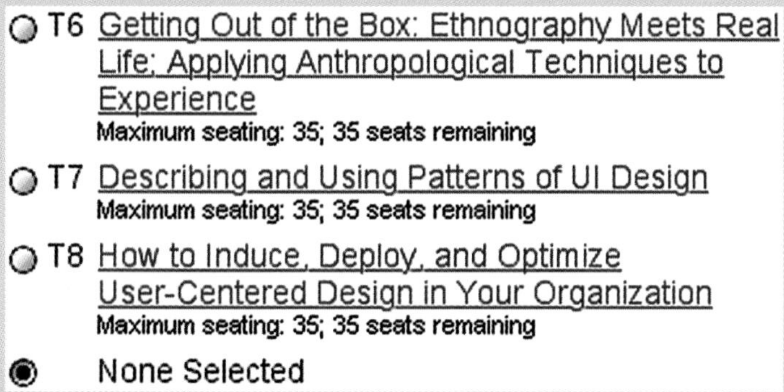

○ T6 Getting Out of the Box: Ethnography Meets Real Life: Applying Anthropological Techniques to Experience
Maximum seating: 35; 35 seats remaining

○ T7 Describing and Using Patterns of UI Design
Maximum seating: 35; 35 seats remaining

○ T8 How to Induce, Deploy, and Optimize User-Centered Design in Your Organization
Maximum seating: 35; 35 seats remaining

● None Selected

AVOIDING THE BLOOPER

In presenting and discussing examples of bloopers concerning defaults, I touched on most of the important design principles for avoiding such bloopers. I now summarize the principles.

Provide a Default Value if Possible

Make it as easy as possible for your site's users to accomplish their goals. One way to do that is to provide default values for as many data fields and choices as possible, so they can focus on just those they need to change.

A good example of providing a default comes from L.L. Bean's competitor, REI. The color choice shown in Figure 4.25 is similar to the previously discussed choice of tent color at *LLBean.com*, where no default is provided (Figure 4.22). Why does REI provide a default color while L.L. Bean does not? The relative popularity of the color options cannot be the reason, as L.L. Bean's tent is available in only one color. Perhaps REI's Web designers were more aware than L.L. Bean's of the value of good defaults.

However, *LLBean.com* does provide defaults for some choices. For example, when asking for a phone number, the site asks whether the number is a home or business phone number, with "Home" as the default (Figure 4.26).

When "None Yet" Is an Important Option, Make It Explicit and Make It the Default

Some choices have to indicate that the user has not yet selected an option. In such cases, it is recommended to make "none" an explicit value and make it the default. A course-registration form on the website of the Usability Professionals Association includes such a choice (Figure 4.27).

When No Default Can Be Assumed, Menus Are Better than Radiobuttons

Sometimes you can't provide a default value for a choice, for pragmatic or political reasons—when asking the user's gender, for example. In such cases, it is better to use a menu than a radiobutton, because, as discussed previously, menus with no value are more natural than radiobuttons with no value. This means that in some cases, you will be using menus even though there are only a few options or even though there would be plenty of space on the page for radiobuttons.

Radiobuttons with no initial value should be avoided. At the very least, using them should require very strong justification.

Use the New Web Menu Style Carefully

The new Web-design trend, in which menus contain their own prompt as a default value, works as long as Web designers follow the two design guidelines stated previously. For convenience, I provide them again here:

1. This type of menu should be used *only* for menus that have no useful default.
2. Menu labels—including the initial value that serves as a prompt—must be carefully worded to make clear what the choice is.

Some Binary Choices Are Better Expressed as Checkboxes

Menus and radiobuttons are not the only way to express choices. When a choice has two clearly opposite values, it can be represented by a checkbox. A checkbox is always either on or off, so it has a default value by definition.

Recall that the Stanford Bookstore's Shopping Cart page had a mandatory "yes/no" choice, presented in a menu initially set to the prompt "Please choose." Let's consider how a checkbox might be used to improve that design.

To improve that page, I would change several things. I would keep only the last sentence of the long instruction paragraph and make it the heading for the control. I would present the new/used substitution question as a checkbox, positioned prominently, with the simple label "Substitutions OK." The checkbox would be checked (on) by default (Figure 4.28).

On the other hand, Web designers should be careful not to misuse checkboxes. Checkboxes should be used *only* for choices for which a particular attribute—such as "italics"—is on or off, true or false, present or absent. They should *not* be used for choices that just happen to have two values, such as alignment (left/right), gender (male/female), or color (black/white). (See Blooper 28: Checkboxes or Radiobuttons, in this chapter.)

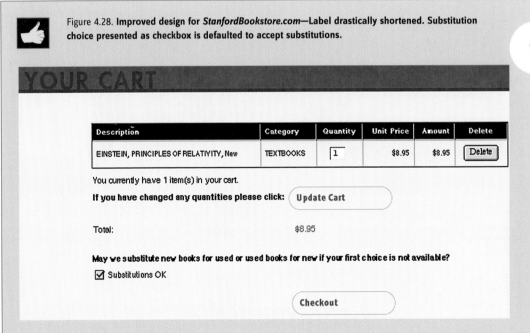

Figure 4.28. **Improved design for *StanfordBookstore.com*—Label drastically shortened. Substitution choice presented as checkbox is defaulted to accept substitutions.**

135

YOUR CART

Description	Category	Quantity	Unit Price	Amount	Delete
EINSTEIN, PRINCIPLES OF RELATIVITY, New	TEXTBOOKS	1	$8.95	$8.95	Delete

You currently have 1 item(s) in your cart.

If you have changed any quantities please click: Update Cart

Total: $8.95

May we substitute new books for used or used books for new if your first choice is not available?

☑ Substitutions OK

Checkout

Figure 4.29. ***www.StanfordBookstore.com*** (Sept. 2002)—State menu defaults to Alabama for a customer of the Stanford University Bookstore, which is in California.

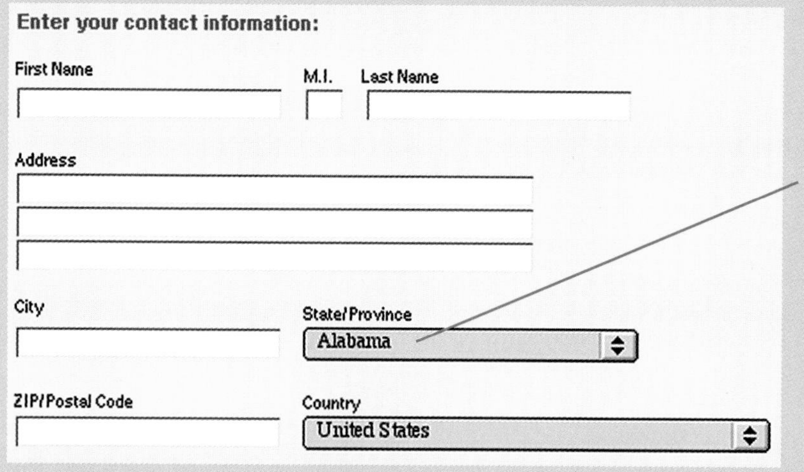

Enter your contact information:

First Name

M.I.   Last Name

Address

City

State/Province

Alabama

ZIP/Postal Code

Country

United States

Default state for book purchase is Alabama, even though Stanford is in California.

136

Figure 4.30. ***www.MKP.com*** (June 2002)—Default search method is "By Author," which is not what most users usually want.

Figure 4.31. ***www.JacksonAndPerkins.com*** (Sept. 2002)—Option to receive email "spam" is checked by default.

Option is at bottom of form, checked by default.

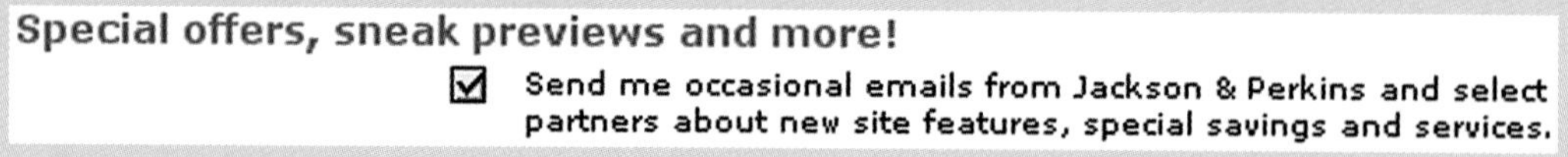

Special offers, sneak previews and more!

☑ Send me occasional emails from Jackson & Perkins and select partners about new site features, special savings and services.

Blooper 25: Faulty Defaults

A default value that is unlikely to be the one users want is potentially more harmful than no default. A user who overlooks a control that has *no* default often gets an error message, but overlooking a *bad* default usually yields an unwanted result.

A common "reason" for a poor default value is that the developers didn't bother to instruct the menu, radiobutton set, or scrolling list to initialize itself to an explicit value, so the control sets its default value to the first value listed.

An example of this comes from the Stanford University Bookstore website. When a user buys a book online, he or she has to supply an address. The State menu defaults to *Alabama* (Figure 4.29)—the first state alphabetically—even though most customers of this site live near Stanford, in *California*. If a customer fails to set the state, the problem might not be caught until the book is returned to the bookstore from an invalid mailing address in Alabama.

While we're on the subject of books, let's examine a poor default on the website of Morgan-Kaufmann Publishers. The home page has a Search function for finding books in its catalog. Under the Search box is a menu for indicating whether you want to search "By Author," "By Title," "By ISBN Number," and so forth. By default, the menu is set to "By Author" (Figure 4.30), probably because it is first in alphabetical order. Unfortunately, that isn't how most visitors to this site will want to search most of the time. "By Title" is much more likely to be what people want. A large number of visitors will either not notice the menu or assume it doesn't matter and make the mistake I've made on this site many times: type a title into the Search box, click Go, and get nothing.

At least *MKP.com's* Search results page tells you *why* it found nothing: "No results found for Author = 'GUI

Design,'" so users don't have to wonder what went wrong. That's better than the feedback provided by many website Search functions: nothing. But users still have to back up, set the menu to "By Subject," and try again.

Evil Defaults

Some defaults in website forms are more than bad, they are downright evil: intentionally set so visitors who fail to notice them will get something they probably don't want.

For example, some sites ask new registrants if their data can be shared with other organizations, with the default set to "yes." Other sites ask whether they can send email announcements, defaulting to "yes." An example of the latter comes from flower vendor *JacksonAndPerkins.com* (Figure 4.31). The option appears at the bottom of its registration form, where people can easily miss it.

Here's one that is even more evil. Let's say a friend of yours uses *Evite.com* to send party invitations. The friend gives *Evite* the email addresses of invitees. *Evite* sends you a message with a link to their site for viewing and responding to the invitation. When you respond, you may or may not notice a checkbox at the bottom of the response form, labeled "Yes, I'd like to receive Evite news and special offers" (Figure 4.32). It is checked unless you uncheck it.

This default amounts to "viral" marketing. People who aren't actual *Evite* customers, but who just received invitations, can be added to *Evite's* marketing list simply by overlooking a checkbox.

Defaults such as those at *JacksonAndPerkins.com* and *Evite* favor a website's *company,* rather than its users.

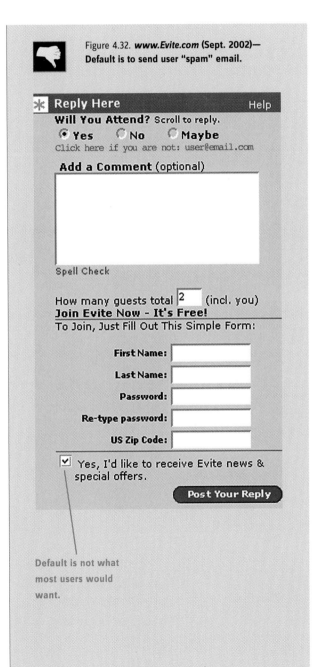

Figure 4.32. *www.Evite.com* (Sept. 2002)— Default is to send user "spam" email.

Default is not what most users would want.

137

Figure 4.33. *www.ThisDayInMusic.com* (Mar. 2001)—Default for the date is "invalid."

Default setting for date is invalid.

Figure 4.34. *www.ACSCSN.org* (Sept. 2002)—Default lets users opt in, not out.

138

If you would like to be contacted by the American Cancer Society regarding programs or information that you may be interested in please check the box below and enter your contact information.

☐ Yes, I would like to be contacted by the American Cancer Society.

[11]Perhaps the user is registered and logged in, so the site "knows" the user's location. Otherwise, the site could guess the location by looking up the IP address in a database that maps addresses to locations.

Rejects Its Own Defaults

The grand prize for the most ridiculous default value goes to—*may I have the envelope, please—ThisDayInMusic.com*, a website in the United Kingdom that, given a date, tells you "What [popular song] was No. 1 in the UK/USA on the day you were born." Leaving it on the default date—1 Jan 1952—I clicked the U.S. flag. Up came an error message "The UK charts began on 14/11/52, the US charts on 1/1/55. Please try again using a valid date." The form scolded me for using its *own* default date (Figure 4.33)!

AVOIDING THE BLOOPER

How do you choose the default value for a choice? Here are several possible ways:

> *Common sense.* Often, simple common sense works. On a form to apply for a San Francisco library card, it's a good bet that applicants live in San Francisco.

> *Experience and site data.* If common sense doesn't suggest a default, perhaps your customer observations or Web logs show that most people pick a certain option. If the site's defaults don't match what people usually choose, change them to save work for users in the future.

> *Based on user's data.* If no single default is suitable for all site users, use different defaults based on whatever you know about a particular user, such as where he or she is located.[11]

> *Arbitrarily.* Finally, if no particular option seems any more likely than any other, there is sometimes no harm in arbitrarily declaring one to be the default.

Don't Be Evil

Set defaults so that they benefit your site's *visitors,* not your organization. Let people opt *in* to having their information shared or receiving email announcements, as the American Cancer Society's website does (Figure 4.34).

Blooper 26: Compulsory Clicking: No Default Text Input Focus

When a form on a Web page requires users to type data, it should automatically place the text input focus in the first text field. This lets Web users start typing immediately.

If a form doesn't set a default input focus, users must move the cursor to a text field and click there before they can start typing. That isn't just an inconvenience; it violates people's expectations: They start typing and . . . nothing. Their keystrokes—and seconds of their valuable time—are wasted. The impact is even worse on blind users and people who don't use a pointing device; they must first *realize* that the insertion point isn't set, then press the Tab key to set it. Unfortunately many designers of forms on the Web are either unaware of the importance of setting the input focus or they regard it as a minor, low-priority detail.

Examples of this blooper can be found all over the Web. The home page of *IEEE.org*, the website of the Institute of Electrical and Electronics Engineers, forces members to move the mouse and click in the User ID field before they can log in (Figure 4.35).

The blooper is especially annoying on Web pages that have only one text field, such as the home pages of *TowerRecords.com*, a record store (Figure 4.36[A]) and *Ford.com* (Figure 4.36[B]), an automobile company. Both of these pages require visitors to click in the one and only text field on the page. Many people don't know this and start typing when the page appears.

A quick check of airline websites—United, Continental, and American (Mar. 2002)—found that none of their home pages set a text input focus. A quick check of three popular Search sites—*Google, Yahoo,* and *AltaVista* (Mar. 2002)—found that *Yahoo* didn't set a text input focus in the Search text field on its main page, whereas *Google* and *AltaVista* did on theirs.

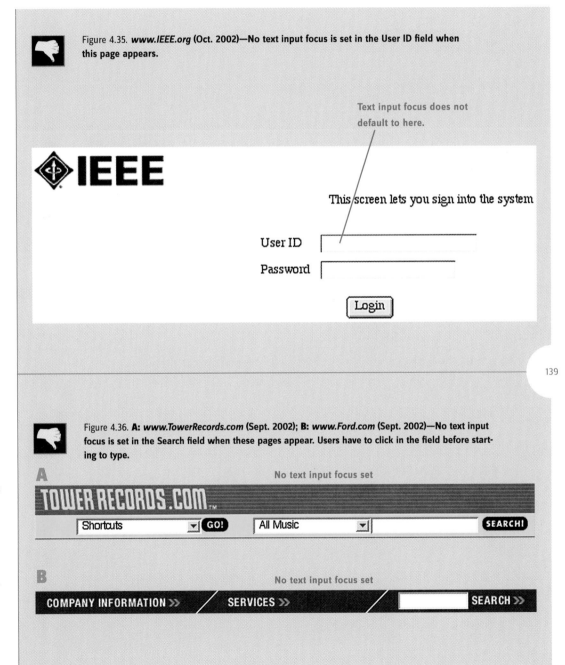

Figure 4.35. *www.IEEE.org* (Oct. 2002)—No text input focus is set in the User ID field when this page appears.

Text input focus does not default to here.

This screen lets you sign into the system

User ID

Password

Login

Figure 4.36. A: *www.TowerRecords.com* (Sept. 2002); B: *www.Ford.com* (Sept. 2002)—No text input focus is set in the Search field when these pages appear. Users have to click in the field before starting to type.

A   No text input focus set

TOWER RECORDS.COM™

Shortcuts ▾ GO!   All Music ▾   SEARCH!

B   No text input focus set

COMPANY INFORMATION ≫   SERVICES ≫   SEARCH ≫

139

AVOIDING THE BLOOPER

The need for online forms to provide a default text input focus is a well-known user-interface design guideline dating back long before the Web—even before the GUI. When a form or a page appears, users should immediately be able to start typing into the first (or only) text field. They should not have to click there first. A site that sets an input focus is *Google.com* (Figure 4.37).

One reason many website forms don't set a default text input focus is that simple HTML forms don't. If you create a form using the standard HTML `<form>` and `<input type = text>` tags, the resulting form will not have a default input focus. Setting an input focus in a text field on a Web page requires using JavaScript or some other scripting language.

The JavaScript required to set a text input focus is not complicated; it's just a tiny amount of code. But many websites don't do it. This may be because the developers don't know how important it is. That's my reason for including this blooper in this book: to explain that it is important. Alternatively, Web developers may not know *how* to set a default input focus. For their benefit, the JavaScript code that does it is provided in the sidebar (Tech Talk: How to Set a Default Input Focus).

Of course, the code works only with Web browsers that handle JavaScript. Some Web developers wish to avoid JavaScript; they want their pages to be based on pure HTML. To them, I'll simply say, Please reconsider this trade-off. The amount of JavaScript required is tiny, but the benefit for users is high.

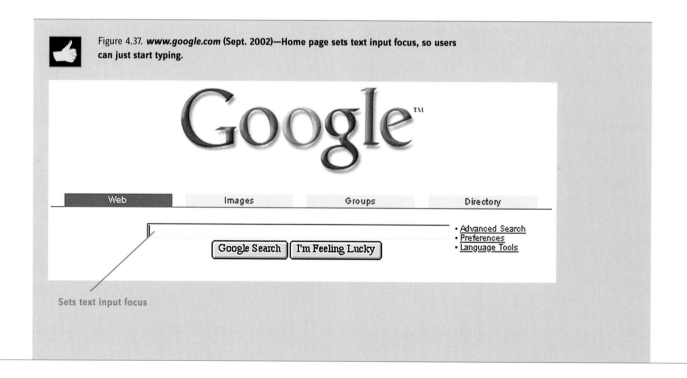

Figure 4.37. *www.google.com* (Sept. 2002)—Home page sets text input focus, so users can just start typing.

Sets text input focus

TECH TALK: HOW TO SET A DEFAULT INPUT FOCUS

Here's how to set an input focus on a Web page using JavaScript.

Suppose a page has a text field named "textField1." Include the following code in the page's `<body>` tag:

```
onLoad="javascript:document.forms[0].
textField1.focus();"
```

This works with version 4.0 or later of either of the two most popular Web browsers: Netscape Navigator and Microsoft Internet Explorer. Here is sample HTML code for a page that sets a default input focus:

```
<html>
  <head>
  <title>Text Input Focus Test</title>
  </head>
  <body bgcolor="white"
    onLoad="javascript:
    document.forms[0].name.focus();">
  <form>
  Name:
  <input type=text name="name"
    size=32 maxlength=35>
  <p>
  Address:
  <input type=text name="addr"
    size=50 maxlength=50>
  </form>
  </body>
</html>
```

In websites that generate pages from templates, the site designer may not know in advance whether a particular page will contain a text field when viewed by a user. In such cases, the code setting an input focus can be placed inside conditional expressions that check whether the page has a form containing a text field by a certain name. Here is an example:

```
{if (document.forms[0] &&
  document.forms[0].search)
  {document.forms[0].search.focus()}}
```

In English, this says, if there is at least one form and that form has a field named "search," then set the input focus there. By embedding this code in the `onLoad` attribute of every page's `<body>` tag, Web developers can ensure that text fields named "search" on any page will have the input focus.

141

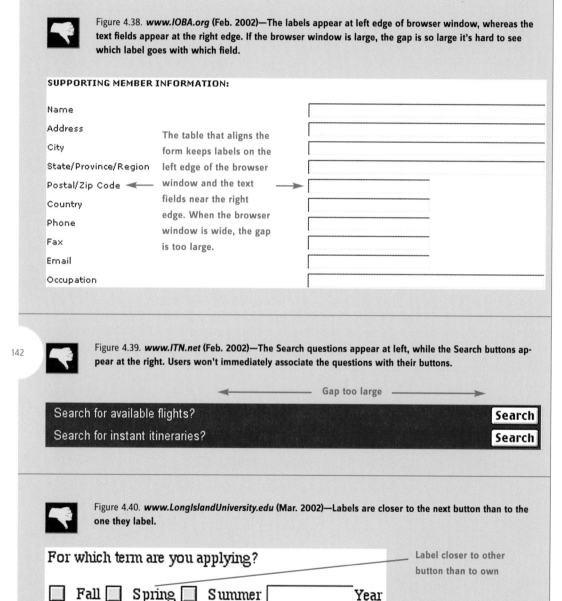

Figure 4.38. *www.IOBA.org* (Feb. 2002)—The labels appear at left edge of browser window, whereas the text fields appear at the right edge. If the browser window is large, the gap is so large it's hard to see which label goes with which field.

SUPPORTING MEMBER INFORMATION:

Name

Address

City
> The table that aligns the form keeps labels on the left edge of the browser window and the text fields near the right edge. When the browser window is wide, the gap is too large.

State/Province/Region

Postal/Zip Code

Country

Phone

Fax

Email

Occupation

Figure 4.39. *www.ITN.net* (Feb. 2002)—The Search questions appear at left, while the Search buttons appear at the right. Users won't immediately associate the questions with their buttons.

← Gap too large →

Search for available flights?   Search

Search for instant itineraries?   Search

Figure 4.40. *www.LongIslandUniversity.edu* (Mar. 2002)—Labels are closer to the next button than to the one they label.

For which term are you applying?

□ Fall □ Spring □ Summer [Year   ]

Label closer to other button than to own

Blooper 27: Lame Label Placement

Forms on the Web often suffer from poor label placement (Johnson, 2000). The result is websites that look sloppy and amateurish and in severe cases may be difficult to use.

Labels Too Far from Field or Control

A severe case can be seen at *IOBA.org,* the website of the Independent Online Booksellers Association (Figure 4.38). The membership form is laid out using an invisible table that keeps the labels at the left edge of the browser window and the type-in fields near the right edge of the browser window. The gap between labels and type-in fields grows as users widen their browser window. If you make your browser full-screen size, it's hard to see which label goes with which field.

A slightly different version of the same problem can be seen at *ITN.net,* a travel-booking website operated by American Express (Figure 4.39). This site's designers obviously expect users to immediately associate the labels with the buttons.

However, that isn't how human vision works. We associate objects based on *proximity* if no other cues are present. Thus, most people initially see this as two questions on the left and two Search buttons—unrelated to the questions—on the right.

Furthermore, we group "nearby" items based on which are *nearest.* A label in a Web-based form might be close to its control but still closer to another control. For example, the labels on checkboxes at Long Island University's website are closer to the *next* checkbox than to their own (Figure 4.40). Some people might think "Fall" goes with the checkbox on its *right,* rather than the one on its left. This would be even more likely if the list of checkboxes were longer.

Inconsistent Horizontal Alignment

A common problem in positioning data labels in forms is inconsistency in whether the labels are left aligned or right aligned. At some sites, labels are aligned differently on different pages of the site, as at Pitsco-LEGOdacta's online store (Figure 4.41).

At other sites, labels are aligned differently in different parts of the same page, as at *TechReview.com* (Figure 4.42).

Whether the inconsistency is within a single page or across different pages, the cause is usually that different developers coded the different forms and didn't coordinate with each other.

Sloppy Vertical Alignment

The most common way for form labels to be misplaced is vertically, relative to their data fields. For example, a credit card application form at *LLBean.com* has labels that are not properly aligned with the data fields (Figure 4.43). This conveys an impression of amateurish design. In extreme cases, it can cause confusion about which label goes with which field.

Labels in Web-based forms often are misaligned because developers don't take the time to align them. They may

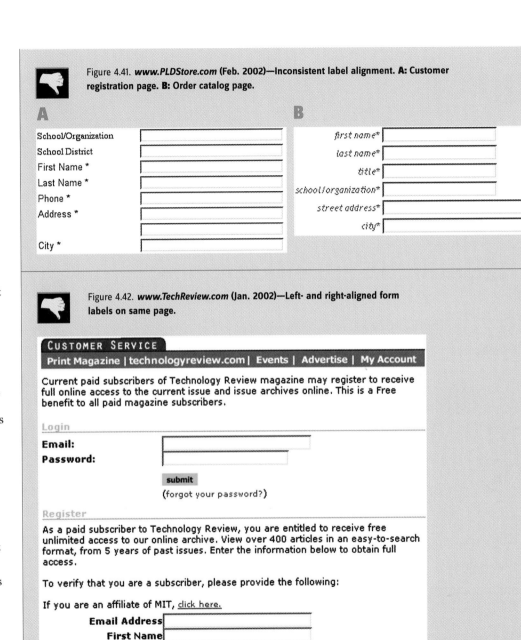

Figure 4.41. *www.PLDStore.com* (Feb. 2002)—Inconsistent label alignment. **A:** Customer registration page. **B:** Order catalog page.

Figure 4.42. *www.TechReview.com* (Jan. 2002)—Left- and right-aligned form labels on same page.

143

Figure 4.43. *www.LLBean.com* (Oct. 2002)—Label baselines are not aligned with baselines of text in the fields.

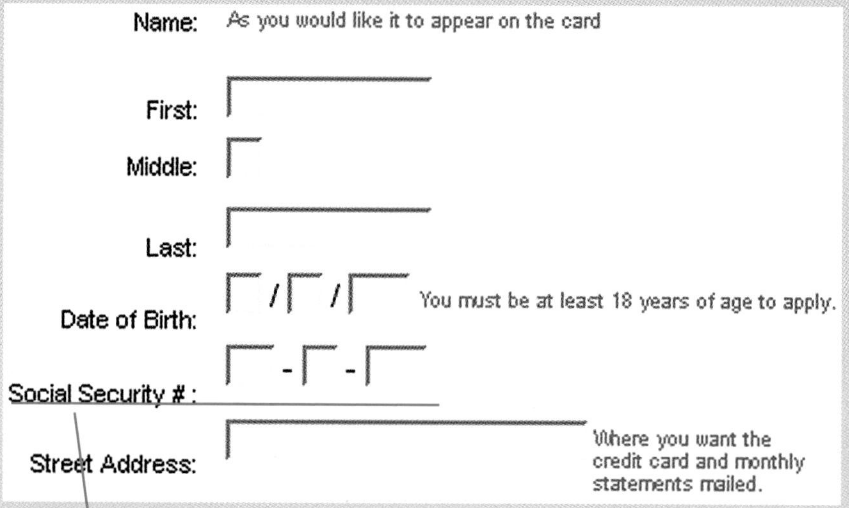

Name: As you would like it to appear on the card

First:

Middle:

Last:

Date of Birth: ⌐ / ⌐ / ⌐   You must be at least 18 years of age to apply.

Social Security # : ⌐ - ⌐ - ⌐

Street Address: ⌐   Where you want the credit card and monthly statements mailed.

Label baseline lower than value baseline

Figure 4.44. *www.Erlbaum.com* (Feb. 2002)—Labels are bottom aligned with data fields and data fields aren't aligned with each other, resulting in an amateurish-looking form.

Sloppy layout yields amateurish-looking form.

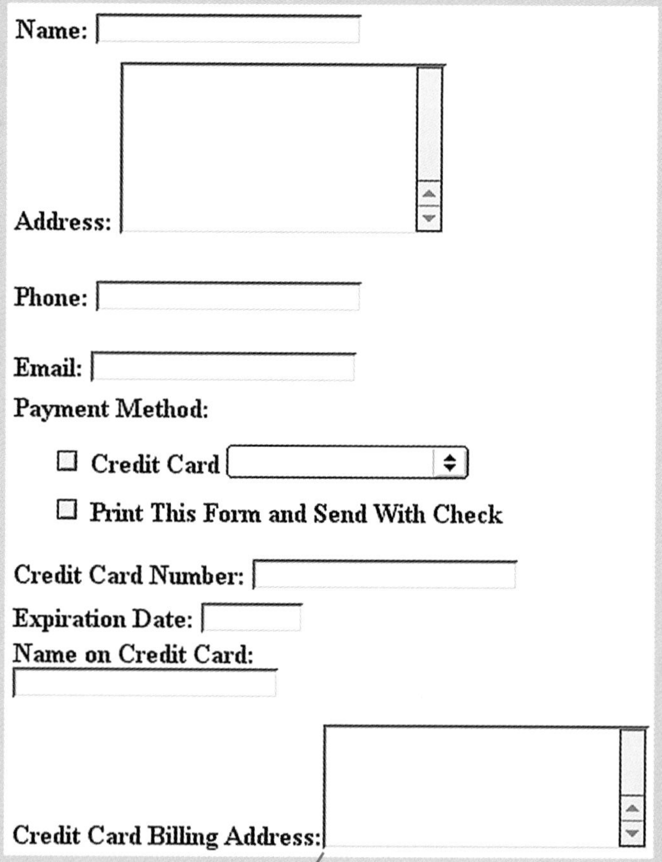

Name:

Address:

Phone:

Email:

Payment Method:

☐ Credit Card ▢ ▲▼

☐ Print This Form and Send With Check

Credit Card Number:

Expiration Date:

Name on Credit Card:

Credit Card Billing Address:

Labels are aligned with *bottoms* of data fields.

intend to improve the alignment when they have more time, but often that is never.

Alternatively, Web developers may *want* to align the components but not know what alignment is best. Until a recent site upgrade, a form at *Erlbaum.com*, a book publisher's website, had the bottoms of labels aligned with the bottoms of the text fields (Figure 4.44). One could also align the vertical middles of the labels with the vertical middles of the text fields or the tops of the labels with the tops of the text fields. However, none of these is the correct alignment.

AVOIDING THE BLOOPER

Here are the guidelines for aligning form labels with their data fields.

Labels Should Be Close to Their Data Fields and Controls

Even though one of our examples of labels being too far from their data fields came from *IOBA.org*, the same site also has an example of doing it right (Figure 4.45). The form for searching for a member bookseller has labels close to their respective data fields. The reason for the difference between the two forms is unclear; probably they were added by two different people.

How could *ITN.net's* designers correct their blooper—labels too far from the Search buttons (see Figure 4.39)? One way is to connect the labels with the buttons visually (Figure 4.46).

Simply adding a visual connection helps, but it still seems odd and unnecessary for the labels to be so far from the buttons. If they were just closer, no visual connector would be needed (Figure 4.47). Therefore, I first moved the labels over to the buttons and eliminated the unnecessary question marks (Figure 4.47[A]). Next, I deleted "Search for" from both labels, since it is redundant with the buttons (Figure 4.47[B]).

Figure 4.45. *www.IOBA.org* (Feb. 2002)—Labels on the member-search form, unlike the new-member registration form, are close to their type-in fields.

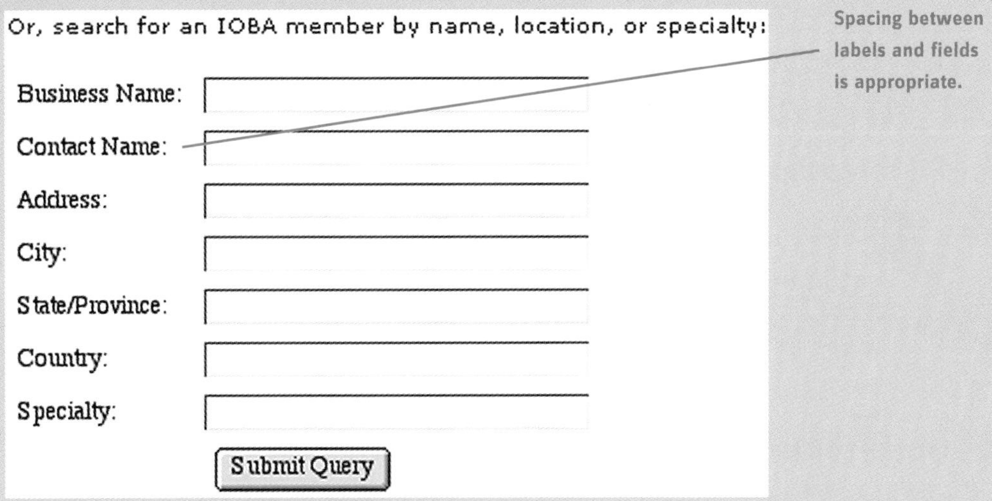

Spacing between labels and fields is appropriate.

145

Figure 4.46. Correction of blooper at *www.ITN.net* (Figure 4.39)—Added visual connection between labels and buttons.

Improved: Visual connection to close gap

Figure 4.47. Correction of blooper at *www.ITN.net* (Figure 4.39)—A: Better: Moved labels next to buttons and deleted question marks. B: Best: Deleted redundant words.

Figure 4.48. **Good label position—A: *www.google.com* (Feb. 2002) Left aligned. B: *www.amazon.com* (Feb. 2002) Right aligned.**

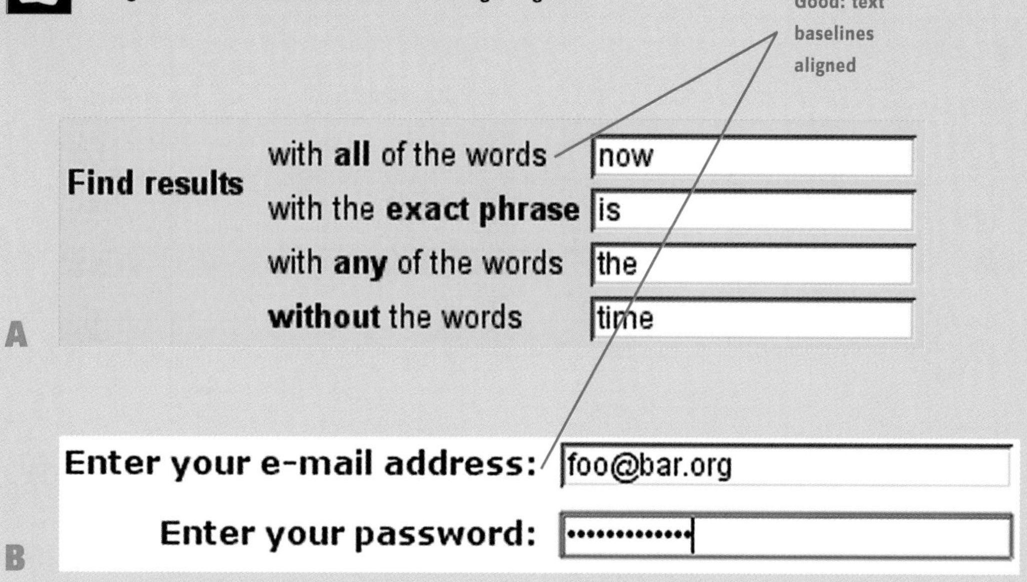

Good: text
baselines
aligned

Find results

with **all** of the words `now`

with the **exact phrase** `is`

with **any** of the words `the`

without the words `time`

A

Enter your e-mail address: `foo@bar.org`

Enter your password: `••••••••••••`

B

146

Figure 4.49. ***www.CharityFocus.org* (Mar. 2001)—One radiobutton used as if it were a checkbox: "I accept the Volunteer Code." Once you turn it on, you can't turn it off.**

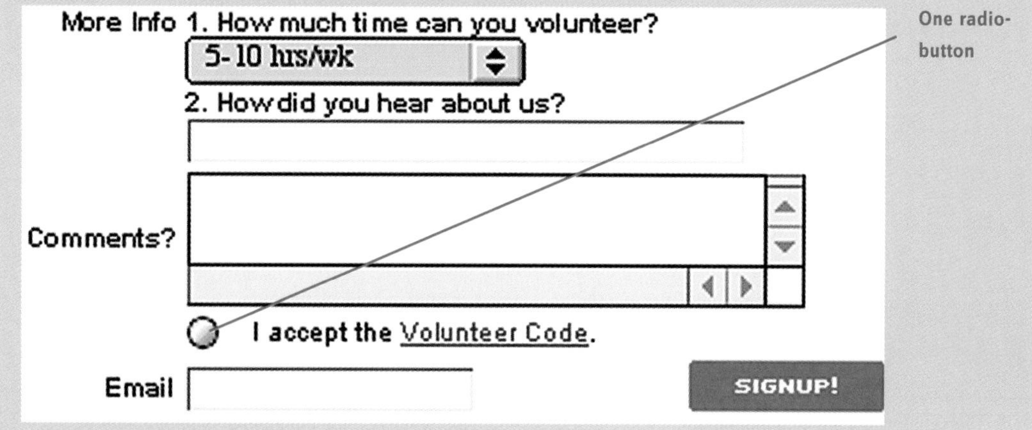

More Info 1. How much time can you volunteer?

`5-10 hrs/wk`

2. How did you hear about us?

One radiobutton

Comments?

I accept the <u>Volunteer Code</u>.

Email

SIGNUP!

Align Labels Consistently, Either Left or Right

Within a website, alignment of form labels should be consistent: either always left aligned or always right aligned. Many designers prefer right alignment because it puts the labels closer to the fields (e.g., Brinck, Gergle, and Wood 2001), but some designers argue that right-aligned labels create a ragged left margin that makes the labels difficult to scan.

Whether you choose left or right alignment isn't actually very important. What is important is that you pick a convention and follow it consistently throughout your site.

Align Baselines of Labels with Baselines of Text in Controls

For correct vertical alignment, all text in a "line" of controls should be positioned so the baselines (bottoms of letters, ignoring descenders as in *p* and *y*) are aligned. This includes the text *inside* the controls (e.g., text fields and menus). Well-positioned *left*-aligned labels can be seen in the Advanced Search page of *Google.com* (Figure 4.48[A]). Well-positioned *right*-aligned labels can be seen in the login page of *Amazon.com* (Figure 4.48[B]).

Blooper 28: Checkboxes or Radiobuttons

Checkboxes and radiobuttons were devised as logically different controls, intended for different situations:

Radiobuttons are for choosing one of several options.

Checkboxes are for on/off choices.

Unfortunately, many GUI and Web development toolkits blur the distinction between them: They treat them as the same component, with an attribute to specify one versus the other. As a result, radiobuttons and checkboxes are sometimes mixed up.

One Radiobutton

The most common result of such confusion is a single radiobutton, all by itself, as if it were a checkbox. An example of this can be seen in a volunteer registration form at the website of *CharityFocus.org* (Figure 4.49). Besides being the wrong control for a yes/no choice, there is no way to turn a single radiobutton *off* once it is *on*.

Aside from developer oversights, a common cause of this blooper is that the website offers a variable number of choices depending on circumstances, but doesn't properly handle the case when only one choice is available.

This is why the online ticket-purchasing service *TicketWeb.com* commits the blooper (Figure 4.50). Normally, they offer ticket buyers a choice of how the tickets should be delivered and present the choices using a set of radiobuttons. However, if you buy tickets too late for anything but Will Call (pick up from box office at event), the site gives you *one* radiobutton. Worse, it's off by default; you have to turn it on before the site will let you proceed (see Blooper 25: Faulty Defaults, in this chapter).

Misusing Checkboxes as if They Were Radiobuttons

The opposite error—using checkboxes where radiobuttons are correct—is almost as common.

One site where it occurs is Long Island University's website, *LIU.edu*. *LIU.edu's* online application form misuses checkboxes for what should be mutually exclusive radiobutton choices. The blooper at this site allows applicants to check both male and female, apply for multiple school terms simultaneously, and answer both yes and no to questions (Figure 4.51).

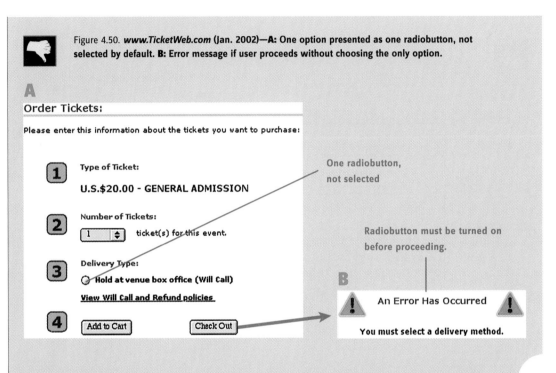

Figure 4.50. *www.TicketWeb.com* (Jan. 2002)—**A:** One option presented as one radiobutton, not selected by default. **B:** Error message if user proceeds without choosing the only option.

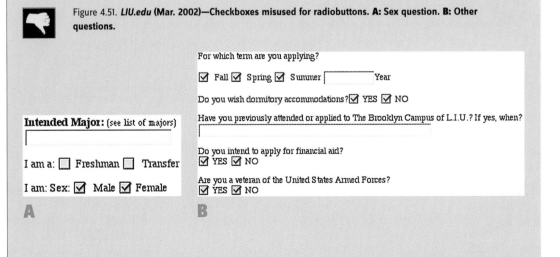

Figure 4.51. *LIU.edu* (Mar. 2002)—Checkboxes misused for radiobuttons. **A:** Sex question. **B:** Other questions.

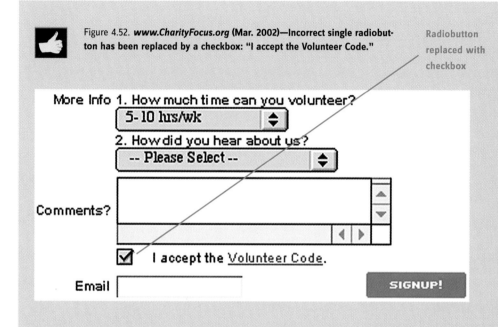

Figure 4.52. **www.CharityFocus.org** (Mar. 2002)—Incorrect single radiobutton has been replaced by a checkbox: "I accept the Volunteer Code."

Radiobutton replaced with checkbox

Figure 4.53. **www.Sibelius.com** (Jan. 2002)—For this software product, only one language option is available: English. Instead of displaying one radiobutton, the language "choice" displays no control and simply indicates which language will be delivered.

Only one option available, so no radiobuttons

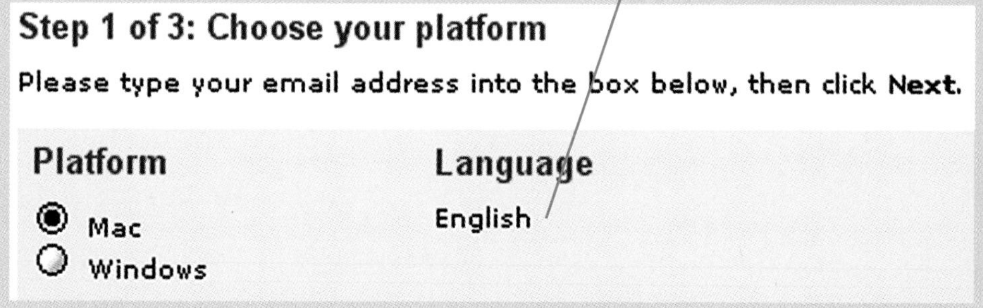

AVOIDING THE BLOOPER

To avoid committing this blooper, developers just need to be aware of the rules for using radiobuttons versus checkboxes. Here they are again:

> *Radiobuttons* are for choosing one of several options.

> *Checkboxes* are for on/off (or yes/no) choices.

If your toolkit of Web controls treats checkboxes and radiobuttons as the same type of component, make sure you set the attribute to get the right type of control. Better toolkits treat the two types of components as distinct, minimizing the chance of confusion.

Checkbox for Yes/No Choice

As an example of correct usage of a checkbox for a single yes/no choice, Figure 4.52 is the corrected form at *CharityFocus.org*. The lone radiobutton has been replaced by a checkbox. The checkbox is on by default. Obviously, they want visitors to accept the Volunteer Code.

When the number of choices is variable, design your form so that it adjusts the presentation from radiobuttons to something else when only one choice is available. What the "something else" should be depends on whether the one choice is optional or mandatory.

One Choice, Optional

When there is only one choice and users can choose it or not, do exactly what you would do if the number of choices were always one: Use a checkbox, not a radiobutton. Whether the checkbox is checked or not by default depends on what you expect the most common response to be.

One Choice, Mandatory

When your website normally offers a one-from-many choice but only one option is currently available and it is mandatory, what do you do? It is tempting to display a checked checkbox and either (1) make it noneditable or (2) have the form flag an error if the user turns the checkbox off and tries to proceed.

However, there is a better solution: Don't present a control at all; just show what will happen. This is how the one-checkbox blooper is avoided at *Sibelius.com,* the website of a music software company (Figure 4.53). On the product download page, it would show a choice of languages if there were a choice, but for this product only an English version is available, so it just says that. Simple and clear.

Radiobuttons for Mutually Exclusive Choices

Long Island University eventually replaced the erroneous checkboxes on its application forms with correct radiobuttons (Figure 4.54).

Blooper 29: Looks Editable but Isn't

A blooper that seems to be growing more common in Web-based forms is standard interactive controls that present data users cannot change. This does not refer to controls that are sometimes active and sometimes inactive (grayed out); it refers to controls that are *never* editable.

At the website of the University of Houston's Clear Lake campus, we see an example of this blooper (Figure 4.55). The scrolling text box looks editable, but it isn't. It displays a brief explanation of the item selected in the "Quick Menu" above it.

More examples of the blooper come from *uBid.com.* The site's "Email Us" form commits the blooper twice (Figure 4.56). First, it uses checkboxes to mark "Required" fields.

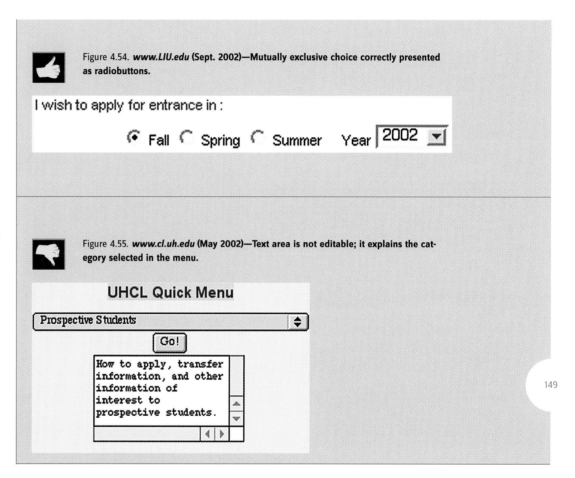

Figure 4.54. *www.LIU.edu* (Sept. 2002)—Mutually exclusive choice correctly presented as radiobuttons.

Figure 4.55. *www.cl.uh.edu* (May 2002)—Text area is not editable; it explains the category selected in the menu.

149

Users might think they can change the checkboxes, but they can't. Further down the form, there is a scrolling text box displaying "Special Instructions." These are instructions for filling out the form and are not editable. The box containing the instructions looks no different from the editable box below it. Highly misleading!

Part of the problem is that some user-interface toolkits allow controls to be set to "noneditable." This encourages Web developers to misuse editable-looking controls to display noneditable data.

Figure 4.56. *www.uBid.com* (Sept. 2002)—Checkboxes misused to indicate required fields. "Special Instructions" text field displays noneditable instructions. Item 3, "Enter Your Message," is editable.

Email Us

Try <u>Tech Help</u> for product support and technical questions.

Emailing uBid is a quick and easy way to receive a prompt response to your inquiry. Simply
and click the "submit" button. You can also search for answers in our comprehensive Help s

1. Select your Subject:

| Bidding/Account |
| Shipping/Order Problems |
| Website Questions |
| General |
| Product Problems |
| Billing Inquires |
| Consumer Exchange |
| Feedback |

Then, select a Request:

| Missing Parts |
| Not as Advertised |
| Defective Merchandise |
| Warranty Information |

2. Please provide your information: Required

First Name: ☑

Last Name: ☑

Email Address: ☑

Email Address (twice for verification): ☑

Login: ☑

Order Number: ☑

Lot Number: ☐

Special Instructions:

Please enter detailed information about how the
product you received was not as advertised on the
site. Please include model number and serial
number.

3. Enter your message in the box below:

Figure 4.57. **Correction of bloopers at *www.cl.uh.edu* and *uBid.com*—
A: Corrected University of Houston form has text in gray box. B: Corrected uBid form has noneditable text checkmarks and text directly on the background.**

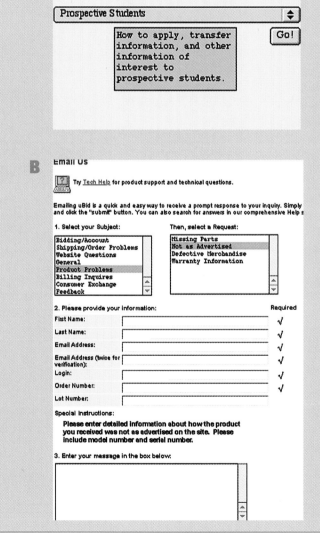

A

UHCL Quick Menu

Prospective Students ⬍

How to apply, transfer
information, and other
information of
interest to
prospective students.

Go!

B

Email Us

Try <u>Tech Help</u> for product support and technical questions.

Emailing uBid is a quick and easy way to receive a prompt response to your inquiry. Simply
and click the "submit" button. You can also search for answers in our comprehensive Help s

1. Select your Subject:

| Bidding/Account |
| Shipping/Order Problems |
| Website Questions |
| General |
| Product Problems |
| Billing Inquires |
| Consumer Exchange |
| Feedback |

Then, select a Request:

| Missing Parts |
| Not as Advertised |
| Defective Merchandise |
| Warranty Information |

2. Please provide your information: Required

First Name: √

Last Name: √

Email Address: √

Email Address (twice for verification): √

Login: √

Order Number: √

Lot Number:

Special Instructions:

Please enter detailed information about how the product
you received was not as advertised on the site. Please
include model number and serial number.

3. Enter your message in the box below:

AVOIDING THE BLOOPER

Noneditable data displayed by a site strictly for users' information should never be displayed in a control that looks operable.

Checkboxes, radiobuttons, menus, sliders, and other controls should never be used for noneditable data. Such controls look operable. Even if they are grayed out (inactive), they look as if they can somehow be made operable.

Noneditable text fields should be avoided, because people don't distinguish them from temporarily inactive text fields: They assume the field can be made editable somehow. When a text data value is display only—never editable by the user—it should be displayed using a text (label) component, not a noneditable text field (Figure 4.57).

Blooper 30: Mysterious Controls

Some forms are just plain mysterious. Three common causes are

> Poor labeling

> Poor layout

> Nonstandard controls

Let's look at some examples of each of these.

Poor Labeling

Internet sites that host email discussion groups (often called "list servers" or "listservs") usually provide a way for list subscribers to change settings affecting their subscriptions. For example,

> Is delivery to you active or temporarily paused, such as for a vacation?

> Are postings sent to you one at a time or in daily digests?

> Should you receive copies of messages you post to the list?

At some listservs, settings such as these are controlled through a website: Subscribers come to the site, log in, and view and change their subscription settings. The user interface that people encounter when they visit their listserv depends on what software the Internet site uses.

One popular listserv software package is *Mailman*. Mailman has a decidedly funky user interface, so any listserv that uses Mailman has a funky user interface. One of Mailman's funkier aspects is the setting for pausing delivery of postings. Put bluntly, it's backward: To *stop* delivery, you turn Disable Delivery *on;* to resume delivery, you turn Disable Delivery *off* (Figure 4.58). The best (and easiest) way to improve this control would *not* be to switch the meanings of *on* and *off,* but to relabel the radiobuttons "Disable" and "Enable," similar to how the third setting (Get MIME) is labeled.

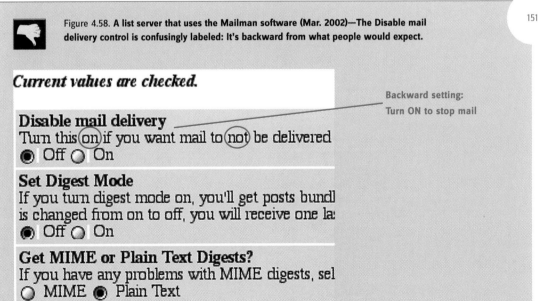

Figure 4.58. **A list server that uses the Mailman software (Mar. 2002)—The Disable mail delivery control is confusingly labeled: It's backward from what people would expect.**

Backward setting:
Turn ON to stop mail

Current values are checked.

Disable mail delivery
Turn this (on) if you want mail to (not) be delivered
◉ Off ○ On

Set Digest Mode
If you turn digest mode on, you'll get posts bundl
is changed from on to off, you will receive one la:
◉ Off ○ On

Get MIME or Plain Text Digests?
If you have any problems with MIME digests, sel
○ MIME ◉ Plain Text

151

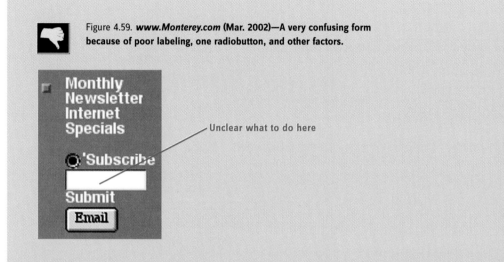

Figure 4.59. *www.Monterey.com* (Mar. 2002)—A very confusing form because of poor labeling, one radiobutton, and other factors.

Unclear what to do here

Figure 4.60. *www.DenPlan.co.uk* (Feb. 2002)—Radiobuttons indicate type of location typed into "Near to" box.

Dentist search

If you want to find a dentist, then Denplan can help you.
Please specify whether you would like to select all Denplan Dentists or Denplan Excel dentists only in the box below. Alternatively, you can telephone us free on **0800 401 402** or use the email feedback facility to request a list, stating which postcode area you want to find a dentist in and Denplan will send a list through the post.

| Mainland UK | | | |

| Please select | All ⇕ | Near to | |
| Among | ○ Places | ○ London Streets | ◉ Postcodes | Search |

Unclear that radiobuttons
are for "Near to" setting

Another poorly labeled form is at *Monterey.com*. Most of the site's pages include a control for subscribing to the organization's newsletter (Figure 4.59). The problem is, the controls are so poorly labeled that most users won't know what to do. The label "Submit" under the text field should be on the button, not under the text field. The "Email" label should be *above* the text field and should be "Email Address" so people know what to type there. There is also a single radiobutton, which cannot be turned off (see Blooper 28: Checkboxes or Radiobuttons, in this chapter). Finally, the nonclickable "bullet" on the "Monthly Newsletter" label is needless clutter.

Poor Layout

On the Dentist Search page of *DenPlan.co.uk,* a website for dental insurance in the United Kingdom, the main problem isn't poor labeling—although there is a bit of that—but poor *layout* of controls. To find a dentist near you, you have to tell it

> Whether you want to see *all* dentists in the area or those for a specific dental plan (menu)

> The location of interest (text field)

> Whether the location you typed is a place, London street, or postcode

As the controls are laid out (Figure 4.60), "Among" looks like an independent control but in fact is closely tied to the "Near to" text field: It controls how it is interpreted. The form could be laid out to show that. Also, the menu ("All" vs. a specific dental plan) is the least important control and as such should not be first.

Poor layout is also the main problem on *Earthlink.net's* page for checking the status of your order for Earthlink's Digital Subscriber Line (DSL) broadband Internet service (Figure 4.61). You're supposed to use one of two sets of controls, but are the two sets left and right or upper and lower? After examining the form for a minute or two, you'll probably figure out that it must be left and right. But why do they have two separate phone number fields? Why not have one phone number field and a choice of whether to identify the order by the credit card or work-order number?

Poor Labeling and Layout

The prize for a challenging combination of poor form labeling *and* layout goes to Hewlett-Packard for the form it provides for changing one's subscription to its newsletter (Figure 4.62).

What is wrong with this form?

> The text "making changes" and "Time to make a change" are meaningless. They just waste space and the reader's time.

> The paragraph of instructions misses its chance to name the newsletter and omits a period after "Thank you."

> It uses different words for the same thing: "the newsletter" and "Incoming." (See Chapter 6, Blooper 45: Variable Vocabulary: Different Words for the Same Thing.)

> The label "E-mail address to unsubscribe" is nowhere near the email address text field. Instead, it's next to the radiobuttons, which are not for specifying an email address.

> The radiobutton labels seem ungrammatical until you figure out that the newsletter must be named "Incoming."

> The purpose of the second radiobutton, "Please continue" (the default), is unclear. Leaving it set here only "continues to send . . . Incoming" if I already subscribe. If I don't currently subscribe, leaving it set here means "continue to not send me Incoming." Why would anyone ever need this middle choice?

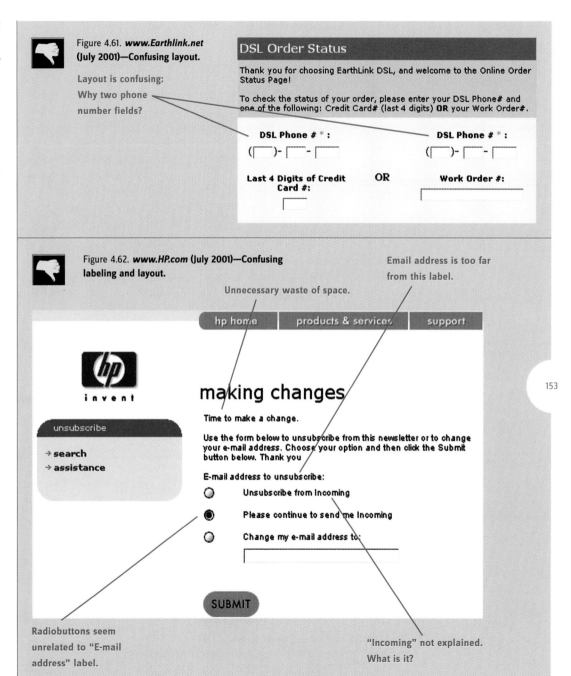

Figure 4.61. *www.Earthlink.net* (July 2001)—Confusing layout.

Layout is confusing: Why two phone number fields?

Figure 4.62. *www.HP.com* (July 2001)—Confusing labeling and layout.

Email address is too far from this label.

Unnecessary waste of space.

Radiobuttons seem unrelated to "E-mail address" label.

"Incoming" not explained. What is it?

153

> There doesn't seem to be a way to subscribe to the newsletter, unless it's typing your email address in the text field and leaving it set to "Please continue to send me *Incoming.*"

Nonstandard Controls

Sometimes websites confuse users by providing unique or unexpected controls in forms and controls panels. *ITN.net* tries to help users choose travel dates by providing a calendar tool (Figure 4.63). However, it's not like the pop-up calendar tools found at many other travel websites. It doesn't pop up; it's right there in the page next to the date control. But there are *two* date controls: Departing or Returning. You have to first indicate which date you want to set by clicking on the arrow next to it. That "connects" the calendar tool to that date. Got that? More importantly, will you remember it while using this form?

Citibank's *CitibusinessOnline.com* website complicates an action that should be simple—identifying yourself to the system (Figure 4.64). Imagine you arrive at this page. You see the menu and are at first not sure what it's for but, by opening it, figure out that it's for indicating what sort of user you are: New User, Guest, Subscriber, and so on. The Enter button is clear: You click it after you've set the menu. But what's that Delete button for? What could there be to delete here, on the login page? The Delete button slows people down *just by being there:* It's a mystery, so they waste time thinking about it and maybe trying it.

AVOIDING THE BLOOPER

How a form is laid out and labeled strongly affects its usability. One cannot place fields and controls on a page, label them haphazardly, and expect good results. Also, websites— especially e-commerce sites—should be wary of altering standard control idioms or introducing new controls unless they have collected extensive test data showing that the new control is usable.

Label Carefully

As an example of how more careful labeling can improve a badly labeled form, Figure 4.65(B) is my improvement of the *Monterey.com* newsletter subscription controls. Contrast it with the original controls (Figure 4.65[A]).

Lay Out Thoughtfully

To show how the clarity of a form can be improved by thoughtful layout, Figure 4.66 shows revisions of *DenPlan's* "Find a Dentist" form (Figure 4.66[A]) and Earthlink's DSL status inquiry form (Figure 4.66[B]). The DenPlan form could be simplified even further by *removing* the radiobuttons and having the site *figure out* what sort of location the user typed, based on syntactic analysis and database comparisons.

Use Common Idioms

ITN.net (see Figure 4.63) is to be commended for providing a way for the site's users to choose dates from a calendar, rather than typing them. However, their design has a severe usability problem: The calendar tool has to be connected to the desired date control before choosing a date. Testing would certainly show that people will have trouble with this.

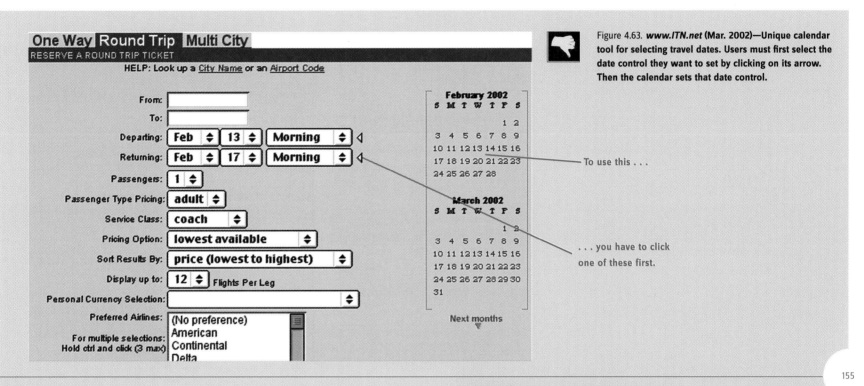

Figure 4.63. *www.ITN.net* (Mar. 2002)—Unique calendar tool for selecting travel dates. Users must first select the date control they want to set by clicking on its arrow. Then the calendar sets that date control.

To use this . . .

. . . you have to click one of these first.

155

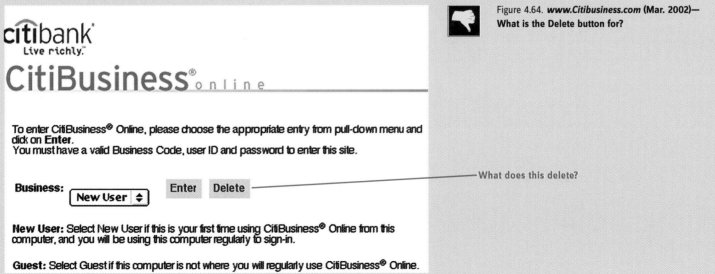

Figure 4.64. *www.Citibusiness.com* (Mar. 2002)— What is the Delete button for?

What does this delete?

Figure 4.65. **Correction of blooper at *www.Monterey.com*— A: Actual newspaper subscription form, with bloopers. B: Improved labeling.**

A

B

Label explains what goes into field.

Figure 4.66. **Correction of bloopers at A: *www.Denplan.co.uk* and B: *www.Earthlink.net*—The new layout for *www.Earthlink.net* makes it clearer that users are supposed to give their DSL phone number and either their credit card number or the work-order number.**

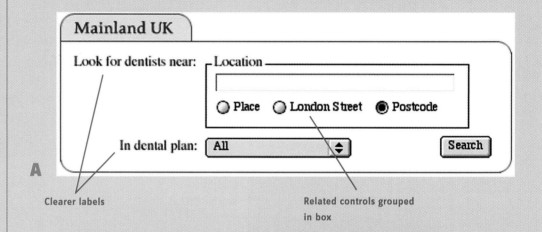

A

Clearer labels

Related controls grouped in box

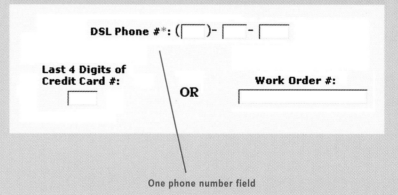

B

One phone number field

There is a more straightforward—and more common—approach to providing a calendar tool for choosing dates. To see an example of it, we need look no further than the Northwest Airlines website we already examined earlier in this chapter (Figure 4.67).

The Web is still evolving. Design idioms and best practices are still emerging. There is certainly room for improvement through creative innovation.

As the Web continues to evolve, less successful design idioms such as ITN's in-panel calendar tool will disappear and more successful ones will proliferate. Successful design idioms for everything from date choosers to shopping carts will be encapsulated in high-level components and made available for easy incorporation into sites. The most successful idioms and components will be adopted into Web browsers, allowing websites to simply state which one they want—supplying details in parameters—and have the browser display it.

However, until successful design idioms are available in component libraries or are incorporated into browsers, Web designers need to be aware of the best ones and use them. Keep in mind that innovation just for the sake of being different is bad on the Web. Finally, before inflicting a new, creative design on the general public, it is wise to test it thoroughly to see whether it really is an improvement.

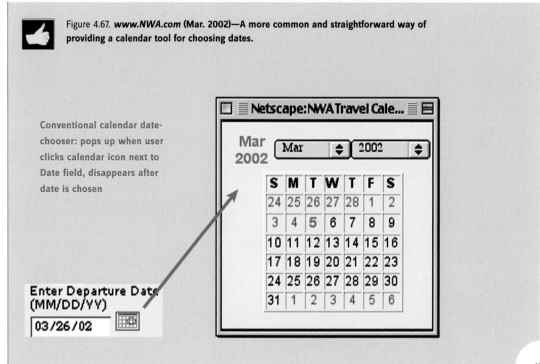

Figure 4.67. *www.NWA.com* (Mar. 2002)—A more common and straightforward way of providing a calendar tool for choosing dates.

Conventional calendar date-chooser: pops up when user clicks calendar icon next to Date field, disappears after date is chosen

157

SEARCH BLOOPERS

In the introduction to this book, I summarized the early days of the Web. Now let's examine the history of Web *search*.

In 1991, before Mosaic sparked the Web's rapid growth, the world's websites could be counted on two hands. There was no need for anything like our present-day search websites and comprehensive Web directories: AltaVista, Excite, Google, Yahoo. The particle physicists who were the primary users of the early Web knew all the sites. To visit a site, they just typed its URL into a browser. However, this only means that there was no need to search for *websites* on the early Web. It doesn't mean that there was no need for search.

The early physics websites had relatively few fixed HTML pages: usually less than a dozen. However, the main purpose of those sites was to provide access to databases—of physicists, physics data, and research paper citations. Those databases were large. Out of necessity, they provided search capabilities. When a user clicked on a Search link (Figure 5.1), a special search window[12] appeared, providing a box into which search terms could be typed. Search results were displayed as a list of links to the actual items,[13] just as they are today. Thus, searching was a part of the Web from the beginning.

As the Web expanded in the late 1990s, it essentially became a gigantic database. One doesn't usually find information in a database by browsing or "surfing." One searches.

[12]A dialog box, not a browser window.

[13]The technique of generating HTML pages to display search results as lists of links was first used at the Stanford Linear Accelerator Center (SLAC).

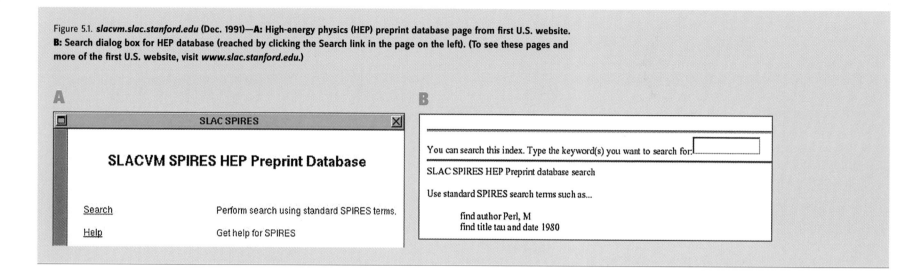

Figure 5.1. *slacvm.slac.stanford.edu* (Dec. 1991)—**A:** High-energy physics (HEP) preprint database page from first U.S. website. **B:** Search dialog box for HEP database (reached by clicking the Search link in the page on the left). (To see these pages and more of the first U.S. website, visit *www.slac.stanford.edu*.)

As more websites came online, the average number of pages per site also increased. Some sites today have more pages than the entire Web had in 1991. Furthermore, many of today's websites provide access to large databases of products, legislation, court decisions, weather, movies, history, sports scores, news, missing persons, and so forth.

Because search capability is so crucial to the Web, searching it has to be easy. People should be able to type words into a text box and, with the click of a button, retrieve links to relevant pages or items. Simple.

Well, it's *supposed* to be simple. Unfortunately, many website search functions don't live up to that ideal (Spool et al., 1999). In this chapter, we'll examine common ways in which search facilities fail to achieve simplicity.

Copyright Mark Parisi.

160

Blooper 31: Baffling Search Controls

Let's imagine you are an evil Web designer, trying to make the search function at your site as difficult as possible to use. How might you do it?

Geeky Search Options

One way would be to label the search controls in your site using technical concepts and jargon from the information-retrieval and database subfields of computer science. For example, you could ask site users to choose between "key-word" search and "text search," as the websites of the Association of Computing Machinery (*ACM.org*) and the Institute for Global Communications (*IGC.org*) used to do (Figure 5.2). Faced with such a choice, many people will either waste time staring at the controls trying to decide which setting is right for their query or just leave it as it was set, whether or not that is correct for their search.

ACM might be excused for making this distinction: Its website is targeted at computer professionals. However, IGC has no such excuse: Its website is aimed at a much broader demographic. Fortunately, IGC eventually realized that this was poor design and simplified its search controls considerably. Even ACM eventually eliminated the need for users to specify keyword versus text search (although, as discussed later, it introduced other complexities).

SBC, the parent company of several regional phone companies in the United States, has a website that used to make a similar but more blatant mistake: forcing people to specify whether the search terms they typed were "literal text" or "boolean" expressions (Figure 5.3). Few visitors to *SBC.com* would know what "boolean" means. Like IGC, SBC eventually corrected this blooper.

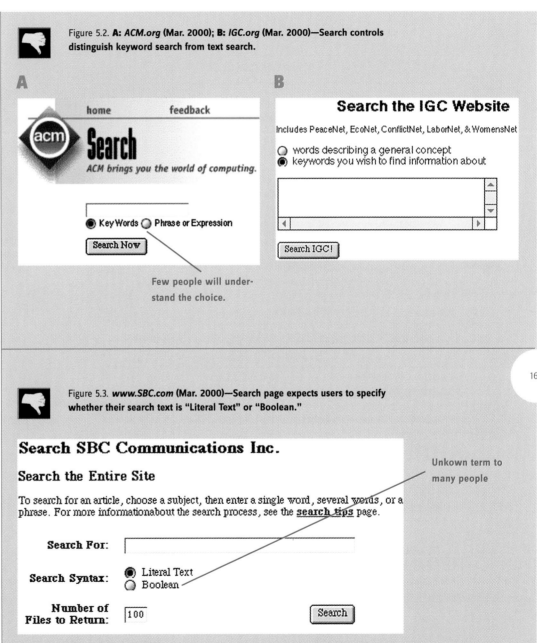

Figure 5.2. **A:** *ACM.org* **(Mar. 2000); B:** *IGC.org* **(Mar. 2000)—Search controls distinguish keyword search from text search.**

A

B

Few people will understand the choice.

Figure 5.3. *www.SBC.com* **(Mar. 2000)—Search page expects users to specify whether their search text is "Literal Text" or "Boolean."**

Unkown term to many people

By now you may be hypothesizing that using geeky termi-nology in website search controls is an affliction of organi-zations with three-letter names. Before you run off to check the FBI, CIA, and KGB websites, let me counter that hy-pothesis with an example from a company with a four-letter name: Dice. *Dice.com's* job-search function provides a choice between searching for "all of the . . . keywords," "any of the keywords," and "boolean expression" (Figure 5.4).

On the other hand, *Dice.com's* blooper isn't as serious as those in the aforementioned sites: Its "boolean" option is hidden in a menu, so people who don't bother to open the menu never see it.

Insider Terminology

Continuing to imagine ourselves as evil Web designers, let's consider another way to thwart people who hope to find something using our site's search facility. Even without re-sorting to geeky terminology, we can stymie users by label-ing the search options using *insider* terminology—words users wouldn't know unless they are as familiar with the site as the designers are.

For example, consider the website of the state of California's Department of Motor Vehicles. It's a subsite of *CA.gov*, the California state government site. The search function offers a choice between searching "this site" and "My CA," with "My CA" as the default (Figure 5.5). My CA is your own personalized "California home page" containing links to the parts of *CA.gov* you use often.

Whoever designed these search controls *must* know that many visitors to the DMV's website won't have seen the main State of California home page, where the opportunity to create a My CA page is offered. For example, I got to *DMV.ca.gov* by searching Google for "CA DMV." Even visi-tors who *have* been to the main California home page may not have a My CA page because they didn't create one. Therefore, for many visitors to the DMV pages, the "My CA" choice will be either meaningless or not applicable.

Worse, "My CA" is the *default*. Many visitors will type text into the *DMV.ca.gov's* Search box, hit the button, and be pre-sented with a list of hits that aren't from the DMV subsite, but are from other parts of *CA.gov*. For example, searching for "drivers' license" returns a list of press releases from the governor's office that mention licenses rather than links to

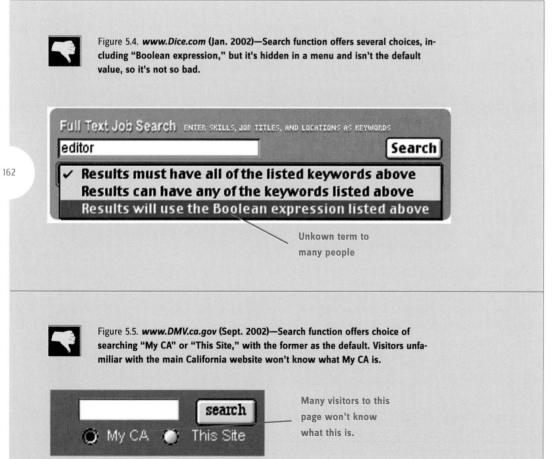

Figure 5.4. *www.Dice.com* (Jan. 2002)—Search function offers several choices, in-cluding "Boolean expression," but it's hidden in a menu and isn't the default value, so it's not so bad.

Unkown term to many people

Figure 5.5. *www.DMV.ca.gov* (Sept. 2002)—Search function offers choice of searching "My CA" or "This Site," with the former as the default. Visitors unfa-miliar with the main California website won't know what My CA is.

Many visitors to this page won't know what this is.

the DMV's pages about drivers' licenses. That isn't how website search functions usually work. Usually, a site's search function searches *that* site, at least by default (see also Chapter 4, Blooper 25: Faulty Defaults).

"Unique" Search Controls

A third method the evil Web designer has for thwarting users who try to use a site's search facility is to devise such original, unfamiliar controls that no one will have seen anything similar before and so won't know how they work. Take for example the "Restrict by Area Code" search option provided at *Dice.com* (Figure 5.6). Presumably, this control restricts the search to a particular area code or codes, but I'll bet few users figure out how to set it.[14]

I mentioned earlier that the *ACM.com* Search page was revised to eliminate the need for site users to choose between keyword and text ("phrase") search. Unfortunately, they added two very unusual search fields: "Specify a Domain Name" and "Specify a Base URL" (Figure 5.7). I'm a computer professional, and I can't tell what these fields are for, even though examples are provided.

Why should I give a domain name, when I'm *at* the domain I want to search: *ACM.org*? And what does "Base URL" mean? The example given isn't a URL, it's just a *piece* of one. Finally, the extra fields are marked "optional," but it's unclear whether they can be used alone or only in concert with the "Keywords and Phrases" field. In short, it was an improvement to combine keywords and phrases into one field, but the highly unusual new fields cancel out any improvement in usability.

[14]Answer: You can restrict the search to between one and five area codes by typing one area code into each box.

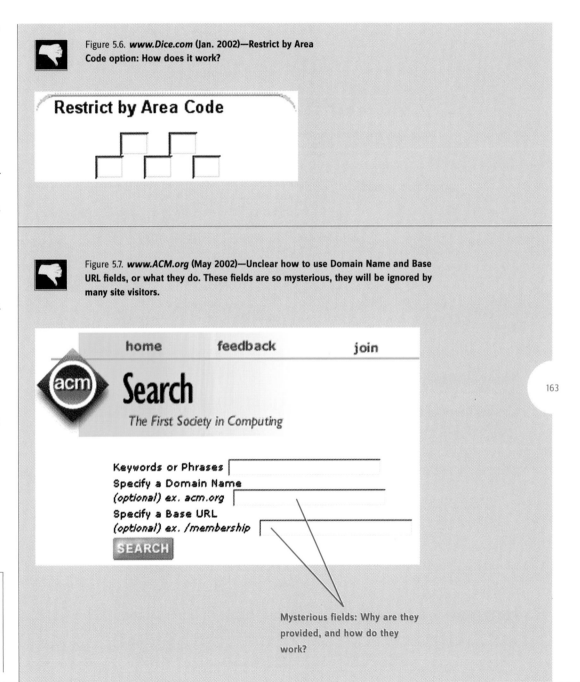

Figure 5.6. *www.Dice.com* (Jan. 2002)—Restrict by Area Code option: How does it work?

Figure 5.7. *www.ACM.org* (May 2002)—Unclear how to use Domain Name and Base URL fields, or what they do. These fields are so mysterious, they will be ignored by many site visitors.

Mysterious fields: Why are they provided, and how do they work?

163

The prize for unusual search controls goes to *NPR.org*, the website of National Public Radio in the United States (Figure 5.8). Its Search page formerly presented a bewildering array of options and made command buttons look like radiobuttons. No one to whom I showed this page understood what the choices were, much less how to operate them.

Web developers might assume that users will "figure out" the unusual search controls eventually, but that's a naive view of how people use the Web. First, people probably wouldn't use *NPR*'s search function often enough to "figure it out." It's only one of dozens—maybe hundreds—of websites they use, after all. Second, as Krug (2000) points out in the book *Don't Make Me Think*, people don't figure out software and websites they don't understand; they just muddle through. On this page, they would simply type something into the text box and hit Enter (or maybe the Search button), ignoring everything else.

AVOIDING THE BLOOPER

The guidelines for designing search controls that won't confuse users are straightforward: keep it simple, use nontechnical language, and optionally, focus the search controls on specific site content.

Keep It Simple

The easiest way to keep search controls simple is to provide just one Search box and no options. *Sears.com* provides an example (Figure 5.9[A]). So does *Amazoon.com* (Figure 5.9[B]). Search controls can't get much simpler than this.

For searching the entire Web, Google has without question the simplest controls (Figure 5.10). There are options (presented as tabs and links), but the most commonly used option, search the Web, is the default.

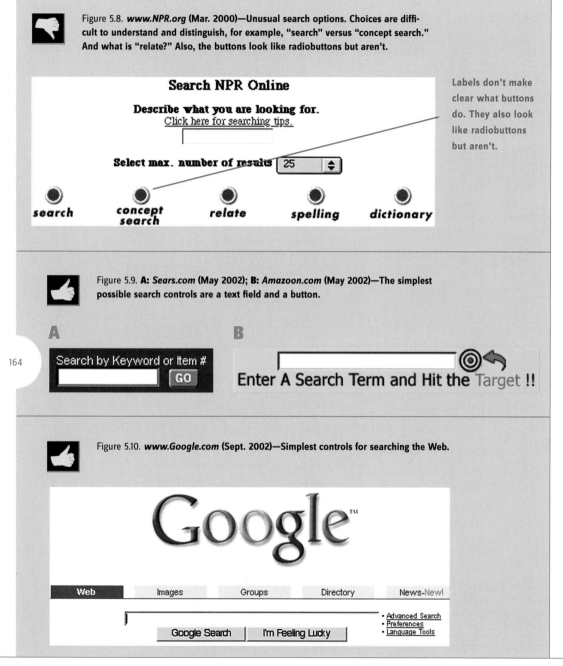

Figure 5.8. **www.NPR.org (Mar. 2000)—Unusual search options. Choices are difficult to understand and distinguish, for example, "search" versus "concept search." And what is "relate?" Also, the buttons look like radiobuttons but aren't.**

Labels don't make clear what buttons do. They also look like radiobuttons but aren't.

Figure 5.9. **A:** *Sears.com* **(May 2002); B:** *Amazoon.com* **(May 2002)—The simplest possible search controls are a text field and a button.**

Figure 5.10. **www.Google.com (Sept. 2002)—Simplest controls for searching the Web.**

Use Nontechnical Language

If the search function must include more options—and they often must—Web designers can keep the controls simple by avoiding technical jargon. Use language meaningful to the people who visit the site. The advanced search options at the state of California's main website, in contrast to those on the California DMV's home page, are clear and sensible (Figure 5.11).

Similarly, SBC's new site clearly does a better job than its old one of sticking to familiar terminology. The "boolean" option is gone (Figure 5.12).

Focus on Specific Site Content

A third way to make a search function easy to use is to consider what people will usually be looking for at the site and focus the search function on helping them find that. For example, an e-commerce site's search facility could focus on product search. This of course ignores the possibility that some people might want to find the organization's privacy policy or postal mailing address, but that may be fine, assuming those things can be easily found without searching.

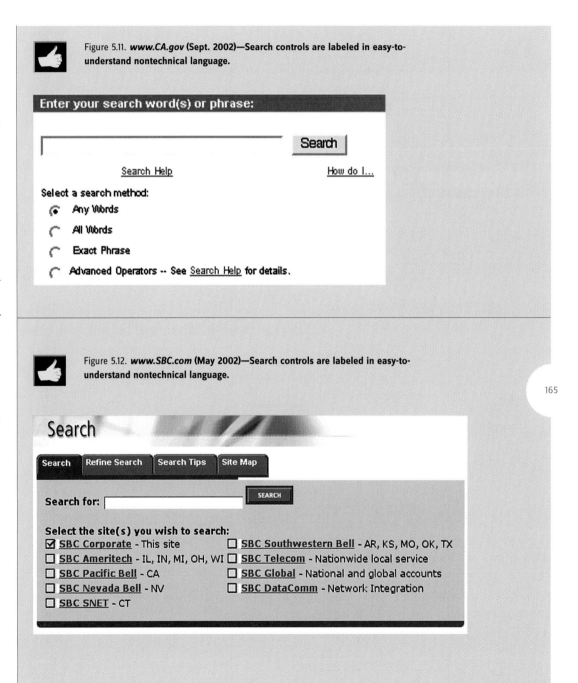

Figure 5.11. **www.CA.gov** (Sept. 2002)—Search controls are labeled in easy-to-understand nontechnical language.

Figure 5.12. **www.SBC.com** (May 2002)—Search controls are labeled in easy-to-understand nontechnical language.

165

Figure 5.13. **www.SharperImage.com** (Nov. 2000)—Task-focused search function finds products only.

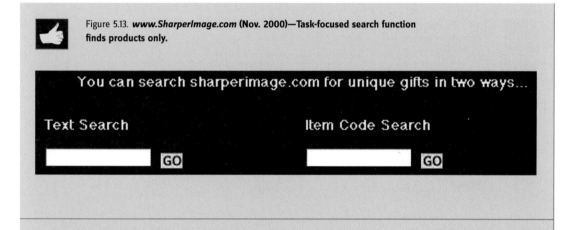

This approach can be seen at *SharperImage.com*. The search function is explicitly for finding products (Figure 5.13). It won't find links pertaining to jobs at Sharper Image, corporate news, or other non–product topics. The site covers such topics, but they must be found by following links from the home page. That is okay: The main thing visitors come to the site looking for is products.

The label "Text Search" is a bit geeky; I would label it "Product" instead. But otherwise, this is a good design. If you know the name of the product, you use one field; if you have a catalog and know the item code, you use the other field. Nice.

NPR, which used to have a horribly confusing search function (see Figure 5.8), redesigned it to focus on what most visitors look for: stories they heard on the radio. The new task-focused controls are a clear improvement in usability over the old ones, even though they won't find everything at the site (Figure 5.14). NPR's *old* search controls might in principle have provided access to more of the site's content, but in practice they provided access to *less,* because people couldn't figure out how to use them.

Figure 5.14. **www.NPR.org (May 2002)**—Task-focused search function finds radio stories only.

Other examples of search functions tailored to a site's content are as follows:

> Many news, historical, and scientific archives provide ways to search for items by dates or date ranges.

> Some poetry sites provide ways to search for words rhyming with specified words or for rhyming words that occur in the same poem.

166

Blooper 32: Dueling Search Controls

Even when the controls for a website's search function are simple, site visitors often encounter another problem: more than one set of search controls from which to choose. "Which ones should I use?" "Are these different or the same?" "Do they search through the same data?" These are questions that arise in the minds of site visitors when they are faced with competing search controls. As explained in *Don't Make Me Think* (Krug 2000), competing search controls cause users to stop thinking about their work and start thinking about how to operate the website.

Gotcha: Wrong One!

CNN.com, the website of the well-known television news company, provides a good example of competing search controls and how they can confuse people (Figure 5.15). Visitors to this site could easily mistake the Search button at the top of the page—the one labeled with a magnifying glass—for the site's search function. In fact, that Search button brings up a search engine for searching the entire Web.[15] CNN's Search box is somewhat "buried" just under the big red *CNN.com* logo. It is further "disguised" by the word "SEARCH" in it, making it look like a button rather than a text field. When I've shown people this site and asked them to find a news story using the search function, they almost always try the top Search button first.

So Many Search Boxes, So Little Time

Another news organization, the *Los Angeles Times* newspaper, has two competing Search boxes on its home page, *LATimes.com* (Figure 5.16[A]). Here, however, the problem is that it is unclear how they differ. The one at the upper left of the page is labeled "Search," and the one at the lower left is labeled "Archives," "Enter Keyword," and "Detailed Search." But the upper Search box can find articles in the site's news archives, which are presumably the same

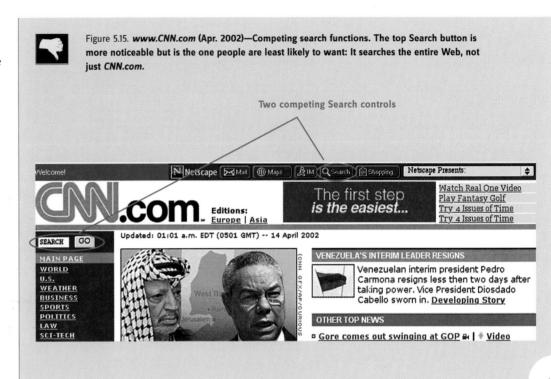

Figure 5.15. *www.CNN.com* (Apr. 2002)—Competing search functions. The top Search button is more noticeable but is the one people are least likely to want: It searches the entire Web, not just *CNN.com*.

Two competing Search controls

167

"archives" to which the lower Search box refers. What then is the point of the lower Search box?

To compound the duplication, when the site displays search results, it includes a Search box to make it easy to search again (Figure 5.16[B]). Thus, after a search, the fixed portions of the page—with their two competing Search boxes—now compete with a *third* Search box. It seems likely that the search results portion of the page was designed without the knowledge that it would appear embedded in a page that already has a Search box.

[15]The entire top row of buttons on *CNN*'s home page is supplied by Netscape, a CNN sponsor.

Figure 5.16. **www.LATimes.com**
(Feb. 2002)—Competing search
functions. **A:** Two Search boxes
are on home page. **B:** Three
Search boxes are on the Search
results page.

Competing
search controls

Competing search controls

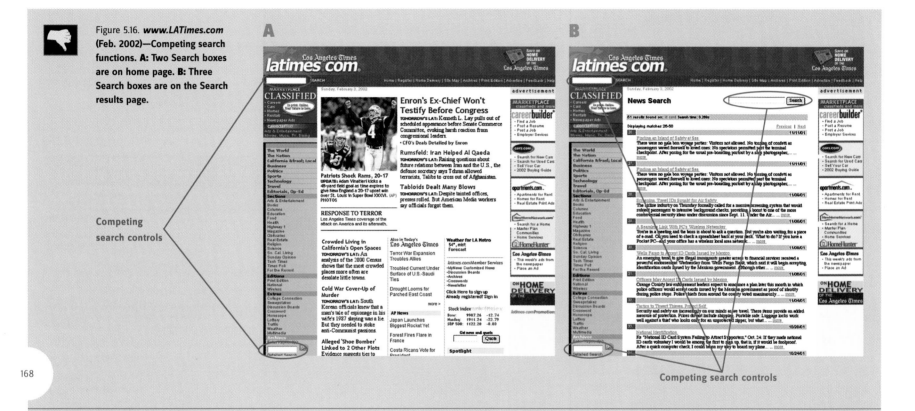

Figure 5.17. **www.CPSR.org**
(Jan. 2002)—Competing search
functions, "Quick Site Search"
versus "Complete Search,"
force users to make a choice
despite not knowing the
trade-offs, if any.

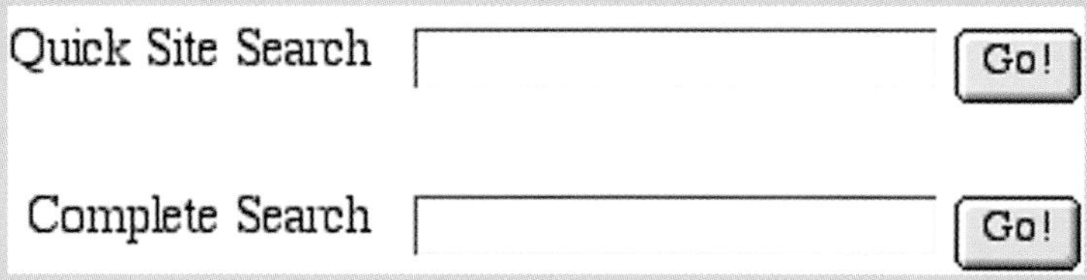

Hmm . . . Which One's Best?

The website of Computer Professionals for Social Responsibility, *CPSR.org,* exhibits an interesting variation of the "Dueling Search Controls" blooper. The home page has two Search boxes, one labeled "Quick Site Search," the other labeled "Complete Search" (Figure 5.17). The two search functions use different search engines and are labeled differently, but the differences between them aren't clear enough to allow site visitors to decide rationally which one to use. For example, is the Quick Search *in*complete? Is the Complete Search significantly *slower?*

To answer these questions, I tested both Quick Search and Complete Search to compare their response time and completeness. It turns out that the Quick Search is not much faster than the Complete Search and sometimes is *more* complete, returning more hits for the same search terms.

The site's designers may have provided two search functions because they understand the implementation differences and considered the speed-versus-completeness trade-off to be significant. Or maybe they just couldn't decide which one was better and so included both. The bottom line is that the differences between *CPSR.org's* two search functions do not seem important enough, or even reliable enough, to warrant burdening users with deciding which one to use.

AVOIDING THE BLOOPER

Web designers may have reasons for providing multiple competing search functions on a single Web page. However, providing multiple search functions has *costs* that must be weighed against the benefits. The costs boil down to this: The search functions compete for attention.

If the competing search functions are *different,* as on the *CNN* and *CPSR* home pages, one cost is that people might use the wrong one. They might notice the wrong one first and use it, overlooking the correct one. Even if they see both, they might not know how they differ—or even that they differ—and choose the wrong one for their intended search.

If the search functions are the *same,* as on *LATimes.com,* users must *decide* which one to use. Decisions cost time and distract people from their own tasks (Raskin 2000).

Less Is More

For search functions, as for user interfaces in general, less is more. In fact, for Search boxes on a page, the best number is one. More than one causes confusion, delay, and error.

If you are considering putting two or three copies of the same Search box on a page because you aren't sure where visitors will look, don't. Really. Place just one Search box prominently, in one of the standard places: top left under the logo, top right, or lower left under the navigation column. And make sure users recognize it as a Search box.

If you plan to include a function for searching the entire Web (as at *CNN.com*), heed this advice from Nielsen and Tahir (2001):

> *Don't offer a feature to "Search the Web". . . . Users will use their favorite search engine to do that, and this option makes search more complex and error-prone.*

If you want to provide different search functions for searching different data sources, such as general site content *versus* news articles *versus* stock prices, design them to look *completely* different. First, consider making everything

169

other than the general site Search box a link to a separate page. Second, if that isn't acceptable, design each Search box to look as specific to its own search domain as possible. None of the special-purpose Search boxes should look like a general site–Search box (Figure 5.18[A]). For example, a function for looking up stock quotes could be sized to fit only company stock symbols, and its button could be labeled "Get Quote" instead of "Search" (Figure 5.18[B]).

Finally, if you are providing two search functions to give users a choice between search implementations having different characteristics, first question whether that is the real reason. If the real reason is that the developers can't decide which implementation *they* prefer, choose one arbitrarily and consider the other one "exploratory development." If the intent to offer users a choice is sincere, ask whether users really care. Even if they do, don't offer the choice on your home page. The home page should have one general Search box, period. Options should be confined to the Advanced Search page. Even there, the choice should be presented as an option affecting a single Search box, rather than as multiple competing Search boxes.

Blooper 33: Hits Look Alike

Imagine that you've just used a website's search function to find something. You typed search terms into a text box and are now looking at a list of matching items, often referred to as "hits." Think about how you evaluate the list of hits. Do you carefully read each item, scrutinizing every detail? Do you click on each item one by one? Of course not! You quickly scan the list, looking for "hits" that look promising.

Now imagine once again that you are an evil Web designer. You want to make it as difficult as possible for people to scan search results looking for promising items. How could you do that? Behold two important techniques of the evil designer!

1. *Bury differences in a sea of similarity.* Make all the hits look similar, so people have to carefully examine each one to see what it's about and how it differs from other items. For example, you could load each listed item with marketing hype or database output that is the same for every item. That'll slow them down!

2. *Force them to click on items.* The absolute best way to prevent people from scanning search results is to make the found items look *exactly* alike. Then the only way to check an item's relevance is to actually follow the link to wherever it goes, consuming the user's valuable time while the browser fetches the page.

Many Web search functions use these "techniques" so well, they seem to have been designed by evil designers *trying* to make life difficult for visitors.

For example, in 1999, the search site *Lycos.com* returned a list of items that looked so similar that it was difficult to distinguish them or find the important information in each (Figure 5.19[A]). Since then, the problem of item similarity has been reduced (Figure 5.19[B]).

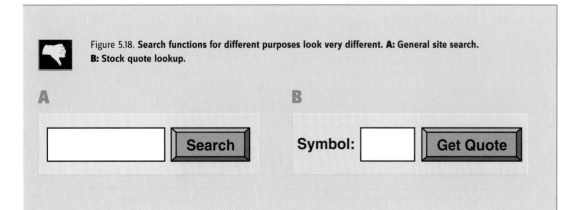

Figure 5.18. **Search functions for different purposes look very different. A: General site search. B: Stock quote lookup.**

A

B

170

Turning to searching *within* websites, let's first examine results from a search at *DigiGuide.com,* an online television guide (Figure 5.20). It uses the first of the evil designer's techniques: burying differences in similarity. *DigiGuide's* search results increase the similarity of found items by starting every item with "DigiGuide: The Best TV Guide." Not only is marketing hype inappropriate here—we're already at the site—but repeating it for every item is beyond useless and beyond annoying; it reduces usability by increasing the similarity of items. In addition, the detailed text underneath each item starts with the item's position in the site's information hierarchy, which for search results is almost guaranteed to make items more similar.

What about the second evil technique: making found items look so alike that the only way to check their relevance is to click on them? In late 2001, *SiliconValley.com* provided an example of that. Figure 5.21 shows the results of searching for articles about "usability."

Given results such as these, a person could easily assume that a faulty search engine had returned several links to the same item (see also Blooper 34: Duplicate Hits, in this chapter, and Chapter 3, Blooper 17: Deceptive Duplicate Links). In fact, there is a difference between the returned items: their file size. However, that difference is hard to spot and not very useful for deciding which articles are relevant.

SiliconValley.com must have realized that this search facility was hurting its bottom line. In early 2002, the company replaced it with one that displays more reasonable results.

Figure 5.19. *www.Lycos.com*—Results of a search for "acoustic guitar." **A:** (early 1999) Hits look very similar, so it's hard to tell which ones are good. **B:** (Mar. 2002) Hits look more different, so it's easier to scan the list.

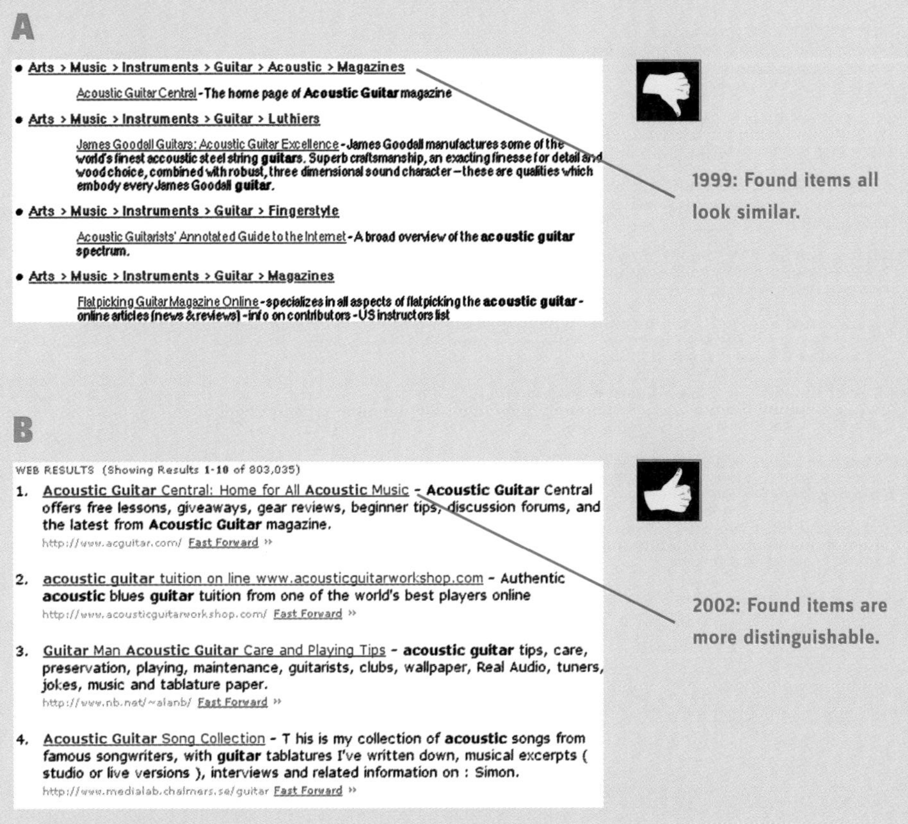

A

1999: Found items all look similar.

B

2002: Found items are more distinguishable.

Figure 5.20. *www.DigiGuide.com* (Feb. 2002)—Results of a search for "software" begin each item with marketing text, making differences hard to see.

Results of your search for the words: 'software'

⊳ DigiGuide: The Best TV Guide - Tutorial - Auto-Update
Home » Tutorial Index » Auto-Update Auto-Update DigiGuide version 5.0 provides a much-improved listings and software update...

▷ DigiGuide: The Best TV Guide - Tutorial - How to use Auto-Update
Home » Tutorial Index » How to use Auto-Update How To Use Auto-Update Enabling Auto-Update Enable Auto-Update does just t...

▷ DigiGuide: The Best TV Guide - Tutorial - Printing - New Stuff for DigiGuide 5.0
Home » Tutorial Index » Printing » New Stuff for DigiGuide 5.0 New Stuff For DigiGuide 5.0 Printing Printing within ...

▷ DigiGuide: The Best TV Guide - Tutorial - Reminder Options
Home » Tutorial Index » Reminder Options Reminder Options There are a fair number of options for reminders and thankfully y...

▷ DigiGuide: The Best TV Guide - Tutorial - What happens when a reminder happens
Home » Tutorial Index » What happens when a reminder happens What Happens When a Reminder Happens When a reminder event occ...

▷ DigiGuide: The Best TV Guide - Customer Comments
Home » Customer Comments Customer Comments "When I downloaded Digiguide for the first time, I thought, this is brilliant, it ...

▷ DigiGuide: The Best TV Guide - What is DigiGuide?
Home » What is DigiGuide? What is DigiGuide? DigiGuide is a TV guide for your PC, an electronic Interactive Programme Guide s...

▷ DigiGuide: The Best TV Guide - Knowledgebase: Get new listings
Home » DigiGuide Knowledgebase How Can I Get New Programme Listings For DigiGuide? DigiGuide 4.0 sports a new method for gett...

▷ DigiGuide: The Best TV Guide - Knowledgebase: Video Plus issues

Repeated marketing hype makes all results harder to distinguish.

Figure 5.21. *www.SiliconValley.com* (Oct. 2001)—All "hits" look the same. Are they the same, or do they just look alike? Can't tell without clicking on them.

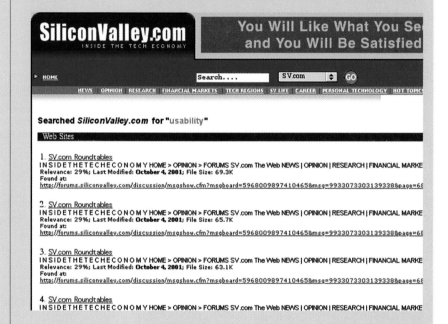

AVOIDING THE BLOOPER

How do we avoid letting the evil designer within us compromise our otherwise good intentions? Easy: just invert the evil designer's rules.

1. *Show and stress important data.* Minimize repetition between listed items. Most of each item should be information that lets people *distinguish* items from one another. The distinguishing data for each item should be emphasized. Additional information, if it must be shown, should be deemphasized. In information-theoretical terms, cut the visual *noise* and focus users' attention on the *information* in each item.

2. *Minimize the need to click.* Ideally, people should have to follow links for found items *only* to actually get the item (purchase, read). They should not have to follow links just to decide which item(s) they want.

Amazon.com provides an example of useful search results (Figure 5.22). The information shown for items allows quick discrimination between them. There is neither too much information nor too little.

AltaVista shows good results for a full Web search (Figure 5.23). Excerpts from the content containing the search terms are shown, with the search terms highlighted. This helps users quickly judge and compare the items' relevance. Additional hits from the same site are indented to help users see what comes from where. Repeated text—for example, the "Translate" link—is present but deemphasized.

 Figure 5.22. *www.Amazon.com* (Sept. 2002)—Search "hits" show and stress discriminating information. Users needn't try links to find relevant ones.

Most popular results for **brinck** :

1. **The Aleutian Kayak: Origins, Construction, and Use of the Traditional Seagoing Baidarka** -- by Wolfgang Brinck; Paperback **Our Price: $13.97** -- Or <u>buy used</u> from $10.18

2. **Usability for the Web: Designing Web Sites that Work** -- by Tom Brinck, et al; Paperback **Our Price: $34.97** -- Or <u>buy used</u> from $32.50

3. **The Boy Next Door** -- by Gretchen Brinck; Mass Market Paperback **Our Price: $6.50** -- Or <u>buy used</u> from $2.99

 Figure 5.23. *www.AltaVista.com* (Oct. 2002)—Search "hits" highlight the search term in context and indent hits from the same site.

AltaVista found 978 results <u>About</u>
<u>**Joe Pass**: Solo **Jazz Guitar** - MIDI Classics</u>
Joe Pass: Solo **Jazz Guitar**. by - **Joe Pass** Media: VIDEO. "Solo **Jazz Guitar**" features: chromatic chords, voice movements, common tones, adding color...
www.midi-classics.com/v/v2209.htm • <u>Translate</u>
<u>More pages from www.midi-classics.com</u>

    <u>**Jazz Guitar** Sampler - MIDI Classics</u>
    Jazz Guitar Sampler. by - Django Reinhardt , Mike Stern , **Joe Pass** Jazz is one of which is still developing and growing to this day. This sampler of some of the...
    www.midi-classics.com/b/b9062.htm • <u>Translate</u>

<u>**Jazz Guitar** Central/Fingerstyle</u>
A step by step method for learning **Jazz Guitar** -beginning to advanced players. Fingerst Walk. Did you ever wonder how **Joe Pass**, Tuck Address, and Charlie...
carbon.cudenver.edu/~pmusso/html/walkin.html • <u>Translate</u>

<u>Brent Stuntzner: Carpentry contractor, evolving luthier, and musician</u>
Offering free jazz transcriptions and information concerning my efforts and goals as a ...
www.stuntzner.brent.org/ • <u>Related pages</u> • <u>Translate</u>
<u>More pages from www.stuntzner.brent.org</u>

Figure 5.24. **www.LATimes.com** (Feb. 2002)—**A:** Two items look alike, but the first link works and the second link is "broken." **B:** Two true duplicates.

A

| 12. | 01/20/02 |

Mexican ID Card Gains Status, and Long Lines of Applicants
The matricula consular , an identification card the Mexican government has given expatriates for more than a century, has recently become highly sought after, with lines of applicants wrapping around city blocks each workday at Mexican consulates in... ... more

| 13. | 01/20/02 |

Mexican ID Card Gains Status, and Long Lines of Applicants
The matricula consular, an identification card the Mexican government has given expatriates for more than a century, has recently become highly sought after, with lines of applicants wrapping around city blocks each workday at Mexican consulates in Santa... ... more

B

| 44. | 09/05/01 |

Napa's Big Squeeze
Msgr. John Brenkle opened the door at the rectory here one recent morning to pick up the newspaper and almost tripped over a man sleeping on the doorstep with the welcome mat pulled over his shoulders for warmth. Brenkle suggested that the Mexican... ... more

| 46. | 09/05/01 |

Napa's Big Squeeze
Msgr. John Brenkle opened the door at the rectory here one recent morning to pick up the newspaper and almost tripped over a man sleeping on the doorstep with the welcome mat pulled over his shoulders for warmth. Brenkle suggested that the Mexican... ... more

Figure 5.25. **www.VitaminShoppe.com** (Feb. 2002)—Search for "wild yam" yielded duplications in the Product Categories section of the results.

>Home >Advanced Search >Search Results

Search Results for: "wild yam"

Wild yam plants are found across the midwestern and eastern United Mexico), and Asia. Several different species exist, all possessing sin

Read more

Product Categories | Brands | Products | Health Guide

Duplicate hits

Product Categories

‣ Wild Yam
‣ Wild Cherry

‣ Wild Yam
‣ Wild Cherry

Brands

‣ **Weleda**
   All Products

Blooper 34: Duplicate Hits

If it's bad for a search facility to return several items that look alike, it must be worse for a search facility to return multiple listings for the same item, right? Yes and no.

Recall our discussion of *true* versus *false* versus *stealth* duplicates (see Chapter 3, Blooper 17: Deceptive Duplicate Links). The basic principle is not to mislead. If two links look the same, they should go to the same place. If they look different, they should go to different places. If they look the same but go to different places (false duplicates), or if they look different but go to the same place (stealth duplicates), they are misleading.

In one sense, a search facility that returns several copies of the same item isn't as bad as one that returns deceptively similar-looking items. It at least doesn't mislead people: Items that look the same *are* the same.

However, in another sense, returning multiple copies of the same item is a worse blooper. Spool et al. (1999) tested several website search functions on Web users and found that "users didn't like it when the search engine returned multiple instances of the same link." The presence of duplicates in the results greatly lowers people's confidence in a search function. They consider it to be buggy, which in a way it is. If people have low confidence in a search function, they won't use it.

Both false and true duplicate hits can be seen at *LATimes.com* (Figure 5.24). A search for "ID cards" yielded a long list of articles. Items 12 and 13 look almost exactly alike but aren't: Item 12 links to an article, and item 13 is an invalid link. Since the headline and lead sentence are the same for the two items, one wonders what item 13 used to point to, if not the same article as item 12. Items 44 and 45 point to the same article and so are true duplicates. Though not as confusing as false duplicates, their presence in the results doesn't inspire confidence in the site's search facility.

LATimes.com, including the search facility, was recently updated, but unfortunately the problem of duplicate hits in search results persists.

At *VitaminShoppe.com,* one can see a different type of duplicate search hit. This site's search facility returns the usual list of products, below categories in the company's product hierarchy that match the user's search terms. However, something inside the search facility seems buggy: Under Product Categories, we have "Wild Yam" and "Wild Cherry" each listed twice (Figure 5.25).

AVOIDING THE BLOOPER

The usual cause of Duplicate Hits is quite different from that of Blooper 33 (Hits Look Alike). Results lists of hard-to-distinguish items are the fault of poor user-interface design. In contrast, duplicate hits are the fault of poor *back-end* design:

> Databases that are so poorly organized, they contain duplicates

> Middleware that doesn't detect duplicates found via different routes

> Server-side applications that don't attempt to organize what the database and middleware return before presenting it to users

This blooper thus provides a clear example of back-end flaws causing a usability problem. Therefore, the main design guideline for avoiding duplicate search hits is as follows:

Ensure that either the database doesn't contain duplicates or the search facility can filter them out before presenting results to users.

Web-development managers, take note: This means that website usability is the responsibility of *back-end* developers *and* Web designers.

Blooper 35: Search Myopia: Missing Relevant Items

When you use a website's search facility, you expect it to show you everything related to the search terms and settings you give it. You expect it not to miss anything relevant.[16] In the data-retrieval field, a search facility's ability to fetch *all* relevant items is known as its *recall.*

Search facilities that miss relevant items are bad for two reasons. First, they mislead people into believing that everything of interest has been found, when it hasn't. Second, they risk losing users' confidence. If Web users see evidence that a website's search facility misses relevant items, they lose confidence in it—and perhaps in the site or company as a whole—and therefore use it less.

Missing relevant items is such a serious blooper for a search facility that one might expect to find it only in websites thrown together on shoestring budgets by kids, impoverished nonprofit organizations, or family businesses. Not so! This blooper is found even in websites of well-known companies.

The blooper can be found at *iFilm.com.* I used the Search box on the site's home page to look for films by Joe Bini, an independent filmmaker. It found several films about guys named Joe, but no Joe Bini (Figure 5.26[A]). A friend had already told me that Joe Bini *is* listed at *iFilm,* so I doubted the search results. Besides, Bini's an award-winning filmmaker; he *must* be in there. I tried again with quotes around the name. Not surprisingly, I got *nothing*—not even films about guys named Joe (Figure 5.26[B]). It gave the message "Your search for 'Joe Bini' found no results. *What's next?*"

[16]You also want the search facility *not* to show you items of little or no relevance to your search specification, but that's a separate issue, discussed in Blooper 36: Needle in a Haystack: Piles of Irrelevant Hits, in this chapter.

A

Joe Bini not found

B

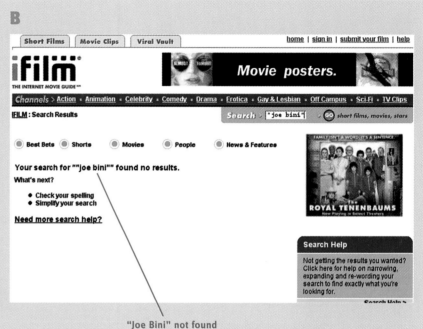

"Joe Bini" not found

But he's in there.

C

Figure 5.26. *www.iFilm.com* (Jan. 2002)—**A:** Search for Joe Bini doesn't find his listing at the site. **B:** Adding quotes finds even less. **C:** Listing for Joe Bini is found by browsing.

CRAN AND LERMA — by nik scott

Panel 1: YOU'RE SAYING I CAN FIND MY MR RIGHT ON THE NET? / NOTHING EASIER

Panel 2: I'LL DO A SEARCH / SEARCHING FOR MR RIGHT

Panel 3:
- MR RIGHT BRAIN
- MR SELF RIGHTEOUS
- MR GOD GIVEN RIGHT
- MR FRIGHT
- MR RIGHT WING MILITIA
- MR DOWNRIGHT NASTY

Copyright © 2000 Nik Scott.

I thought, *What's next is that I'm giving up on this useless search and will browse the site.* I saw the box on the lower right asking, "Not getting the results you wanted?" and offering to help me refine my search, but I didn't think it would help. After all, how much more specific could one be than the guy's *name?*

Eventually, by browsing the site's categories, I found *iFilm's* listing for Joe Bini (Figure 5.26[C]). Even though the item is filed under "People: Joe Bini," it apparently is not indexed by that name for search purposes.

InfoWorld.com, an online technology news service, has a search facility that fails to find articles when given search terms that should match. In this case, I had come back to the site to find an article I found there previously. I knew the article was titled "White House Nixes Controversial National ID Notion." I searched for it using "white house nix"—quoted and unquoted—without success (Figure 5.27[A and B]). (We will ignore the strange "estimated total number of results . . . ") Unwilling to believe that the article had been removed, I tried "white house nixes." Oddly, that worked (Figure 5.27[C]). Normally in search functions, "nix" matches "nixes"—and "nixed," "nixing," and "Nixon"— but *InfoWorld.com's* search function apparently doesn't work that way.

Figure 5.27. ***www.InfoWorld.com*** **(Feb. 2002)—A** and **B:** Fruitless searches for a known article using the first few words of its title. **C:** Spelling "nixes" in full found the article.

A

The estimated total number of results for the search of "white house nix" is 2

Technology issues get campaign attention
... no Internet tax" position -- has promised to **nix** new Internet taxes at least through ... new
online taxes, but touts **White House** efforts to put the current ... March 03, 2000

Presidential candidates weigh in on technology for Super ...
... to be a Net tax foe, promising to **nix** new Net taxes at least until 2004 ... no new online taxes but points to **White House** efforts to put legislation in place ... Feburary 28, 2000

B

InfoWorld.com found no results for ""white house nix""

C

The estimated total number of results for the search of "white house nixes" is 1

White House nixes controversial national ID notion
... **White House nixes** controversial national ID notion By Jennifer Jones September 27, 2001 11:45 am PT, ... September 27, 2001

177

AVOIDING THE BLOOPER

Like the solution to Blooper 34 (Duplicate Hits), the solution to this one focuses on the *back end*—the servers that store and retrieve data for a website—rather than on the front end—the design and organization of the site's pages.

Search facilities that fail to find data in the database can result from software bugs. However, that is not the usual cause of the problem. As the examples suggest, overlooked data more often results from the following:

> *Poorly indexed data,* such as inadequate or inaccurate keywords on items

> *Weak search methods,* such as relying completely on keywords or accepting only whole-word matches

One obvious solution to such problems is to index the content more carefully, thoroughly, and consistently. With multiple people adding content, the chances of them doing it inconsistently or insufficiently are higher, leading to diminished search accuracy. Indexing content carefully, thoroughly, and consistently means adding content—along with the data required to index it[17]—to the back-end system in a controlled way.

For example, when adding content items to the database, designers or content editors should try to anticipate and include, as keywords attached to the items, all the terms people might use to search for them. A site keyword lexicon listing allowable keywords and their meanings—and indicating which ones are synonyms—can help content editors choose consistent, predictable keywords for new content (Rosenfeld and Morville 2002).

During site design and development, conduct tests to see how typical visitors to the site will look for items. Such testing need not be expensive, as early testing can be done very cheaply, without a computer, using questions on paper,

such as the following: Suppose you wanted to find an article about XYZ; what search terms would you use to find it?

After a site is in use, it is of course not feasible to pretest keywords whenever new content is added. However, it *is* feasible and advisable to evaluate how easily site users find what they are looking for and what sorts of search terms they use. This can be done either by conducting periodic user tests or by having the site monitor usage of its search function.

Another solution is to use stronger search methods. Some methods rely completely on keywords. If keyword-only searches miss too much of your site's data, don't rely solely on this type of search. Search the actual text of the content or at least the title and abstract or lead paragraph. And if a user types partial words for search terms, find everything that matches them (within reason, of course). The goal is to maximize the search function's ability to find relevant items without significantly increasing its tendency to return irrelevant ones (discussed in the following blooper).

Blooper 36: Needle in a Haystack: Piles of Irrelevant Hits

Just as you don't want a search facility to miss relevant items, you don't want it to return a lot of stuff that isn't really relevant to your search terms. Search facilities are measured not only by their *recall*—ability to find all relevant items—but also by their *precision,* or ability to exclude irrelevant items. On the Web, search facilities are also measured by their ability to sort results by relevance, so the most relevant items are listed first.

Unfortunately, search facilities that bury relevant items in irrelevant and barely relevant ones are even more common than search facilities that overlook relevant items. Irrelevant items are an annoying distraction even when rel-

---

[17]Referred to as *metadata.*

atively few in number, especially if presented as if they were relevant. Conversely, a large number of low-relevance items isn't too harmful if all the relevant items are listed before them. What's worst is when a search facility returns a large number of items *and* fails to order them by actual relevance to the user's search terms.

Spurious Matches as Distractions

United Airlines' website provides a good example of how spurious search results can distract and delay users (Figure 5.28). If you search for a flight to Minneapolis, instead of a list of flights, you first get a page that reads:

> Uncertain City/Airport Name: More than one city were found matching with your destination entry of 'minneapolis" in our databases. Please select an airport in or nearby the city of your choice from the following list. Otherwise go back and specify a different entry.

For now we'll ignore the poor English (" . . . one city were found . . . ") and focus on the fact that only one of the airports listed has anything to do with "Minneapolis: St. Paul International." Multiple choices might make sense if Minneapolis had more than one airport, but it doesn't. The other six airports listed are not only not in Minneapolis; they are in states nowhere *near* Minnesota! Furthermore, their names aren't even similar to "Minneapolis." Why these match the given destination is unclear. But they do, so anyone who uses *United.com* to book a flight to "Minneapolis" is forced to make this entirely unnecessary choice.

Figure 5.28. **www.United.com (Feb. 2002)—A:** A search for a flight to Minneapolis turns up **B:** seven matches: One is Minneapolis, but the other six are irrelevant.

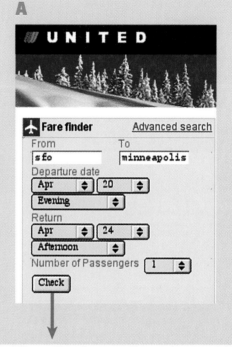

Uncertain City/Airport Name: More than one city were found matching with your destination entry of **"minneapolis"** in our database. Please select an airport in or nearby the city of your choice from the following list. Otherwise go back and specify a different entry.
City: Minneapolis

Select	State/Country	Airport	Distance (miles)	No. of airlines
Select	Minnesota, USA	St Paul International (Minneapolis, MN)	...	18
Select	Kansas, USA	Salina (Salina, KS)	17	1
Select		Mid-Continent (Wichita, KS)	78	9
Select		Eppley Airfield (Omaha, NE)	147	13
Select	North Carolina, USA	Tri-Cities Regional (Bristol/Johnson City/Kingsport, TN)	29	3
Select		Hickory (Hickory, NC)	36	1
Select		Municipal (Asheville/Hendersonville, NC)	44	4

A Book Search Results

We found 21 titles with the keywords **ellen isaacs**.

▶ More titles from our network of out of print book dealers with the keywords **ellen isaacs**.

Below are 1 - 21 of the 21 titles sorted in **bestselling order**.

Re-sort this list in [A-Z by Title] or [Publication Date] order.

1. **Canadian Writers and Their Works**: Fiction
In Stock: Ships within 24 hours
Robert Lecker (Editor), Jack David (Editor), Ellen Quigley (Editor), Isaac Bickerstaff (Illustrator) / Hardcover / General Distribution Services, Inc. / January 1990
Our Price: $45.00 — [Add to Cart]

2. **Canadian Writers and Their Works**: Fiction
In Stock: Ships within 24 hours
Robert Lecker (Editor), Jack David (Editor), Ellen Quigley (Editor), Isaac Bickerstaff (Illustrator) / Hardcover / General Distribution Services, Inc. / January 1989
Our Price: $45.00 — [Add to Cart]

3. **Canadian Writers and Their Works**: Fiction
In Stock: Ships within 24 hours
Robert Lecker (Editor), Jack David (Editor), Ellen Quigley (Editor), Isaac Bickerstaff (Illustrator) / Hardcover / General Distribution Services, Inc. / January 1991
Our Price: $45.00 — [Add to Cart]

4. **Canadian Writers and Their Works**: Fiction
Robert Lecker (Editor), Jack David (Editor), Ellen Quigley (Editor), Isaac Bickerstaff (Illustrator) / Hardcover / General Distribution Services, Inc. / January 1988
This title is not prese... this title may be availa... dealers.

B 18. **Canadian Writers and Their Works**. Poetry Series, Vol. 4
In Stock: Ships within 24 hours .
Robert Lecker (Editor), Jack David (Editor), Ellen Quigley (Editor), Isaac Bickerstaff (Illustrator) / Hardcover / General Distribution Services, Inc. / January 1990
Our Price: $45.00 — [Add to Cart]

19. **Canadian Writers and Their Works** : Poetry Series, Vol. 8
In Stock: Ships within 24 hours .
Robert Lecker (Editor), Jack David (Editor), Ellen Quigley (Editor), Isaac Bickerstaff (Illustrator) / Hardcover / General Distribution Services, Inc. / August 1992
Our Price: $45.00 — [Add to Cart]

20. **Designing from Both Sides of the Screen**: How Designers and Engineers Can Collaborate to Build Cooperative Technology
In Stock: Ships within 24 hours .
Ellen Isaacs, Alan Walendow, Alan Walendowski / Paperback / New Riders / December 2001
Our Price: $35.99, You Save 20% — [Add to Cart]

21. **Isaac Asimov**: Scientist and Storyteller
Ellen Erlanger / Library Binding / Lerner Publishing Group, The / April 1988
This title is not prese... this title may be availa... dealers.

180

Figure 5.29.
www.BarnesAndNoble.com
(Jan. 2002)—**A:** A look at the top of the search results shows results sorted in "bestselling order," not by relevance. **B:** At the bottom of the results, the best matching book is listed as item 20 of 21 items.

Results not in order of relevance; best-matching hit is 20th in list

Poor Results Order

A good example of search results being poorly ordered comes from online bookstore *BarnesAndNoble.com*. I searched for book author "Ellen Isaacs." The search facility found 21 books (Figure 5.29). As the results page indicates, the books are sorted not by relevance to the given search terms, but by "bestselling order." In this order, books by Ellen Quigley (editor) and Isaac Bickerstaff (illustrator) are at the top of the list, and Ellen Isaacs' book doesn't appear until item 20. In other words, the book that best matches the search terms is 20th in a list of 21. Doesn't that seem odd?

The results page provides buttons that resort the list alphabetically by title or by publication date, but not by relevance to the search terms. Imagine if the search facility had found 50 books, or 100, sorted by best-selling order.

VitaminShoppe.com provides a similar example in a different product domain. The user searched for "glucoseamine sulfate" (Figure 5.30). Everything it found matched at least one of those words, which is good. What isn't good is that products matching *both* words did not appear in the results list until item *eight*. Quoting the search terms didn't help. Clearly, relevance to a user's search terms is not the default order of *VitaminShoppe.com's* search results.

Searching for a Job at *Dice.com*

The search facility at *Dice.com* returns many irrelevant job descriptions *and* orders them poorly. Someone I know searched for "editor." It found 133 job listings supposedly matching that word. The first thirty were as follows:

1. Strong Project Editor

2. Freelance Video Editor

3. Resource Kit Technical Editor

4. Medical Managing Editor

5. Web Copy Editor

6. Freelance Editing/Final Cut Pro/Avid/Photoshop

7. Technical Documentation Editor/analyst

8. Senior Circuit Design Engineer

9. Technical Writer

10. Senior Circuit Design Engineer

11. Clarify Technical Lead/Senior Programmer

12. Photo Editor

13. IC Mask Layout Designer

14. Medical Writer/Editor

15. Filmbox Editor

16. IC Layout Mask Design Contractor

17. Senior Circuit Design Engineer SRAM, PLL, I/O

18. Backend Design Engineer

19. Clarify Tech Lead

20. Senior Technical Writer-HTML Editor

21. Oracle Application Serv Admin

22. Jr. UNIX Database Administrator-Shell Scripting, SQL, Unix Ad

23. Sr. Analog and RFIC Layout Designer

24. Product Developer

25. Unix Operator Consultant

26. Senior Analog Layout Designer

27. Senior SQL Server DBA/Biztalk

28. Sr. Mask Layout Engineer

29. Senior IC Mask Designer-Microprocessor products

30. Web Developer w/BizTalk and .Net

The first seven job titles actually contain the word "editor," which is good, but after that, the results go downhill fast.

The titles of jobs 12, 14, 15, and 20 contain the word "editor," but for some reason they weren't placed before many items that don't contain "editor" and seem irrelevant. Finally, none of the jobs in items 21 through 133 seem even remotely relevant to the term "editor."

Figure 5.30. *www.VitaminShoppe.com* (Jan. 2002)—A search for "glucoseamine sulfate" gave the first seven items matching only "sulfate," and the actual hits start at item 8.

Search Results for: "glucoseamine sulfate"

Product Categories

- Vanadyl Sulfate
- Glucosamine Single
- Glucosamine Combinations
- N-acetyl Glucosamine
- Chondroitin Sulfate
- Glucosamine/Chondroitin
- Glucosamine & Chondroitin
- Glucosamine

Products

Displaying products 1-10 of 150
The products listed below are exact matches for your search as well as the names of products that sound similar. To resort, click on any column header.

*SO - Special Orders are not regularly stocked items and will be shipped within 10-14 days at no additional charge.

Brand & Name	Strength	Size	Retail	Our Price	Save	Qty	
Source Naturals, Inc. Chondroitin Sulfate* (SO)*	0 0 MG	30 Each (Tablet)	$11.98	$8.98	25%	1	Add to Cart
Ultimate Nutrition Vanadyl Sulfate	10 mg	150 Each (Tablets)	$15.95	$11.16	30%	1	Add to Cart
Douglas Lab/Amni Vanadyl Sulfate	8 Mg	90 Each (Tablets)	$15.00	$12.00	20%	1	Add to Cart
Country Life Vanadyl Sulfate	5000 Mcg	180 Each (Capsule)	$16.50	$13.20	20%	1	Add to Cart
Country Life Vanadyl Sulfate	5000 Mcg	90 Each (Capsule)	$9.60	$7.68	20%	1	Add to Cart
Vitamin Shoppe Vanadyl Sulfate	2 Mg	300 Each (Tablets)	$23.95	$14.37	40%	1	Add to Cart
Vitamin Shoppe Vanadyl Sulfate	2 Mg	100 Each (Tablets)	$8.95	$5.37	40%	1	Add to Cart
Carlson Laboratories Glucosamine Sulfate	0 0 MG	180 EA (CH/T)	$49.90	$39.92	20%	1	Add to Cart
Carlson Laboratories Glucosamine Sulfate	0 0 MG	60 EA (CH/T)	$18.80	$15.04	20%	1	Add to Cart
Vitamin Shoppe	0	60 Each	$18.95	$11.37	40%	1	Add

True hits don't start until item 8.

181

AVOIDING THE BLOOPER

Extraneous irrelevant hits usually occur for the same reasons as missed items: poor indexing and weak search methods. Poor ordering of results is usually due to faulty metrics for rating the relevance of items.

Again, this is a *back-end* implementation problem that strongly affects the usability of a website. Therefore, the best remedy is a back-end design process that is just as focused on users and their tasks as the front-end design process is. Back-end developers may squirm at this, but it is crucial: You cannot slap a user-friendly front end on a back end that was designed with no thought to usability and usefulness for actual user tasks.

Incorrect keywords on data items can totally destroy the accuracy of an otherwise good search engine. Erroneous keywords sometimes get attached to data items when new items are copied from old ones haphazardly. Sometimes it happens because the people hired to add content to the site don't really understand the site's central topic.

As with Blooper 35 (Search Myopia: Missing Relevant Items), the obvious remedy to this blooper is better procedures and oversight for adding indexing and maintaining content. Further, a lexicon of allowed keywords can help reduce randomness in assigning keywords to content items (Rosenfeld and Morville 2002). The goal is to ensure that keywords on items are accurate and useful.

Blooper 37: Hits Sorted Uselessly

In some website search functions, items either match the criteria or they don't; matching is not a matter of degree. For example, a real-estate website might offer a way to search for available homes by postal code. All homes for sale in the postal code area *match* the search criterion and so are included in the results, and all are equally relevant. Homes outside the indicated postal code area are *not* relevant and so aren't in the results.

For that type of search function, found items should be ordered in a way that is useful to site users. Let's look at examples of website search results in which items are ordered in not-so-useful ways.

HauteAtHome.com, an online vendor of gourmet meals, provides a clear example of the blooper. When you click on

Figure 5.31. www.*HauteAtHome.com* (Jan. 2002)—Fine Entree's results page lists items alphabetically, but by their decorous names. Lamb Crown Roast isn't under *L*, it's under *C* for "chili-infused."

Fine Entrées

Page 1 of 2 --<u>1</u> <u>2</u>

SKU	Name	List Price
41600279	CHILI-INFUSED, HONEY-CRUSTED LAMB CROWN ROAST	$130.00
41600305	CLASSIC BEEF WELLINGTON	$65.00
41600298	CORNBREAD STUFFED PORK CHOPS	$62.00
41600175	FOIE GRAS & TRUFFLE-STUFFED QUAIL	$78.00
41600280	FRENCH DEBONED STUFFED TURKEY	$135.00
41600320	ITALIAN ROASTED LEG OF LAMB - BACK ORDERED 01/14/02	$62.00
41600100	JULIENNE VEGETABLE-STUFFED TENDERLOIN	$83.00
41600330	LAMB PINWHEELS WITH SPRING VEGETABLES	$39.00
41600260	POUSSIN PATé EN CROÛTE	$48.00
41600290	RABBIT TART PROVÉNCAL	$41.00

Results ordered uselessly

a food category on this website, you effectively search its database of available dishes, with the category as the search criterion. The result is a table listing all the dishes in that category (Figure 5.31).

How is the table ordered? Alphabetically, of course! That seems reasonable, except that the alphabetization is based on the full, ingredient-laden, haute-cuisine name of the dish instead of the main ingredient. Thus, Lamb Crown Roast is alphabetized under *C,* rather than *L,* because its full name is "Chili-Infused Honey-Crusted Lamb Crown Roast." Likewise, Stuffed Turkey is alphabetized under *F,* for "French Deboned Stuffed Turkey."

This makes dishes hard to find in the list if you have a specific main ingredient in mind, such as lamb. It also means dishes with the same main ingredient aren't listed together; they are scattered willy-nilly throughout the list.

For a more complex example of this blooper, let's look at the website of the Feldenkrais Guild. It has a "Find a Feldenkrais Practitioner" page, with a typical search form: data fields, a menu for choosing how the results will be sorted, and a button to start the search (Figure 5.32). The sorting options are as follows: by name, city, and zip code. So far, this is all good.

The page also has links for quickly listing all practitioners in a specific state. For example, clicking the California link is the same as typing "CA" into the form's City field and clicking Find. Except for one difference: The state links have no "Sort by" option. The results are always sorted by city. This is closer to the problem but isn't quite it.

The problem is that once the search results are listed, you can't change the order. There is no sort-order menu on the results page (Figure 5.33). You can go back to the Find page and specify a different order using the form, but if you use the state links again, the results order is always the same: by city.

Figure 5.32. *www.Feldenkrais.com* (Oct. 2002)—Page for finding a Feldenkrais practitioner includes two ways to search: using the form at the upper right or clicking on a state at the bottom.

Find a FELDENKRAIS® Practitioner

SEARCH

BROWSE

United States
Canada
International

About the Practitioners:

All practitioners have completed a Professional *Feldenkrais* Training Program and have been initially certified by their trainers, and continue to develop their skills through further study and training in order to meet yearly certification requirements.

Beside each practitioner's name is the year of graduation (or "SA" – "Student Associate" having completed two years, and are authorized to teach *Awareness Through Movement®* lessons).

Zip/Postal Code [　　　]
City [CA]
State [　　　]

First Name [　　　]
Last Name [　　　]

Country [United States ▼]
Sort By [Name ▼]

[Clear] [Find]

United States

Alabama	Idaho	Nebraska	Tennessee
Alaska	Illinois	Nevada	Texas
Arizona	Indiana	New Hampshire	Utah
Arkansas	Iowa	New Jersey	Vermont
California	Kansas	New Mexico	Virginia
Colorado	Kentucky	New York	Washington
	Louisiana	North Carolina	West Virginia
	Maine	North Dakota	Wisconsin

Searching by link always sorts results by city.

Searching by form offers choice of sort order.

183

Figure 5.33. **www.Feldenkrais.com** (Oct. 2002)—Results of a search for practitioners in California **A:** by using a search form, by practitioner name and **B:** by clicking on the California link, by city name.

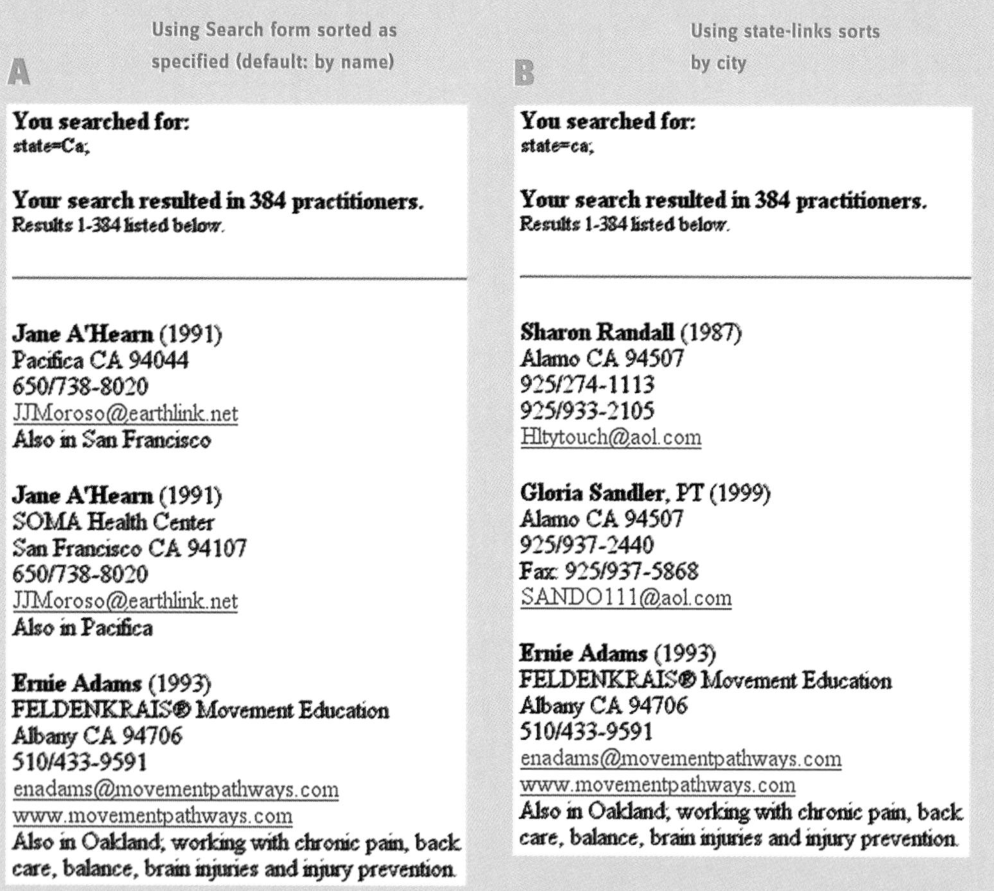

A Using Search form sorted as specified (default: by name)

B Using state-links sorts by city

A

You searched for:
state=Ca;

Your search resulted in 384 practitioners.
Results 1-384 listed below.

Jane A'Hearn (1991)
Pacifica CA 94044
650/738-8020
JJMoroso@earthlink.net
Also in San Francisco

Jane A'Hearn (1991)
SOMA Health Center
San Francisco CA 94107
650/738-8020
JJMoroso@earthlink.net
Also in Pacifica

Ernie Adams (1993)
FELDENKRAIS® Movement Education
Albany CA 94706
510/433-9591
enadams@movementpathways.com
www.movementpathways.com
Also in Oakland; working with chronic pain, back care, balance, brain injuries and injury prevention.

B

You searched for:
state=ca;

Your search resulted in 384 practitioners.
Results 1-384 listed below.

Sharon Randall (1987)
Alamo CA 94507
925/274-1113
925/933-2105
Hltytouch@aol.com

Gloria Sandler, PT (1999)
Alamo CA 94507
925/937-2440
Fax: 925/937-5868
SANDO111@aol.com

Ernie Adams (1993)
FELDENKRAIS® Movement Education
Albany CA 94706
510/433-9591
enadams@movementpathways.com
www.movementpathways.com
Also in Oakland; working with chronic pain, back care, balance, brain injuries and injury prevention.

184

This means that the state links are useful or not depending on *why* you are searching. If you are trying to find a practitioner *near* you, the links are useful because sorting by city is useful. On the other hand, if you have been referred to a specific practitioner in California and want to find how to contact him or her, a list of hundreds of practitioners sorted by city is nearly useless.

This design forces site users to plan ahead: to choose whether to use the form or the links depending on their purpose in searching. Requiring users to plan ahead is a very bad idea in websites or user interfaces in general. Users simply won't do it—remember Steve Krug's main design guideline: "Don't make me think!" (Krug 2000). In the case of the Feldenkrais website, that means people can easily end up with search results in the wrong order for their purpose.

AVOIDING THE BLOOPER

The issue is how to order found items that are equal in relevance to the search criteria. It is a blooper to order them in an arbitrary way that doesn't support users' goals.

One way to avoid the blooper is to determine—by interviewing people typical of the site's intended users or by employing simple common sense—what the most helpful order is and use that order. For example, it seems obvious that ordering dinner entrees by their full haute-cuisine names is not helpful, but ordering them by the name of their primary ingredient—beef, chicken, lamb, pork, and so on—would be. To show this, I reordered the *HauteAtHome* results table (Figure 5.34). In addition to reordering the entrees, I added a "Meat" column to the table to make the ordering criterion clearer.

This static solution works if one results order will satisfy everyone all the time. That may be true for websites like *HauteAtHome.com,* where there is really only one plausible use of the search results. It would not work, however, for websites like *Feldenkrais.com,* where there are multiple possible uses of the search results. For such websites, the solution is to let users specify the sort order, either before the search, after it, or both.

When search results are listed in tables, the best way to let users reorder the list is to make the column headers be links, which, when clicked, reorder the table according to that column (Figure 5.35).

In most websites, search results are not listed in tables, but in lists. The Feldenkrais website is an example. In such a case, separate ordering controls—buttons, links, menus—can be added above the results list, as in my redesign of the Feldenkrais Search results page (Figure 5.36).

Blooper 38: Crazy Search Behavior

Some website search facilities exhibit seemingly nonsensical, "crazy" relationships between the search criteria you give them and the results they return. For example, suppose you searched at an online pet store for "siamese cats" and got 42 hits, then searched for "cats" and got *no* hits. You'd probably say "Huh?," not believe the results of the second search, and try it again. Unfortunately, this sort of "crazy" behavior is common enough that I consider it a blooper.

Use More Stringent Criteria, Find More

"Crazy" search behavior was found at *Erlbaum.com,* the website of Lawrence Erlbaum Associates (Figure 5.37). Its Search page provides text fields for Title, Author, and ISBN, and menus for Subject. Suppose you want to check whether developmental psychologist Dan Osherson has published any books with Erlbaum. If you search for Author = "osherson," you get nothing. If you try again, adding a

Figure 5.34. **Improvement of *HauteAtHome.com.*—Items are ordered more sensibly.**

SKU	Meat	Name	List Price
41600305	BEEF	CLASSIC BEEF WELLINGTON	$65.00
41600100	BEEF	JULIENNE VEGETABLE-STUFFED TENDERLOIN	$83.00
41600260	CHICKEN	POUSSIN PATE EN CROUTE	$48.00
41600279	LAMB	CHILI-INFUSED, HONEY-CRUSTED LAMB CROWN ROAST	$130.00
41600330	LAMB	ITALIAN ROASTED LEG OF LAMB-- BACK ORDERED 01/14/02	$62.00
41600330	LAMB	LAMB PINWHEELS WITH SPRING VEGETABLES	$39.00
41600298	PORK	CORNBREAD STUFFED PORK CHOPS	$62.00
41600290	RABBIT	RABBIT TART PROVENCAL	$41.00
41600280	TURKEY	FRENCH DEBONED STUFFED TURKEY	$135.00
41600175	QUAIL	FOIE GRAS & TRUFFLE-STUFFED QUAIL	$78.00

185

Figure 5.35. **Improvement of *HauteAtHome.com.* Column headers are links that reorder the table by that column.**

SKU	Meat	Name	List Price
41600305	BEEF	CLASSIC BEEF WELLINGTON	$65.00
41600100	BEEF	JULIENNE VEGETABLE-STUFFED TENDERLOIN	$83.00

Lets users reorder results

Figure 5.36. **Improvement of *Feldenkrais.com*—Menu is added to allow users to reorder the results.**

Figure 5.37. ***www.Erlbaum.com* (Feb. 2002)—In searching for "osherson" A: specifying only the author yields no hits. B: Specifying the author and other criteria yields many hits, though none by Osherson.**

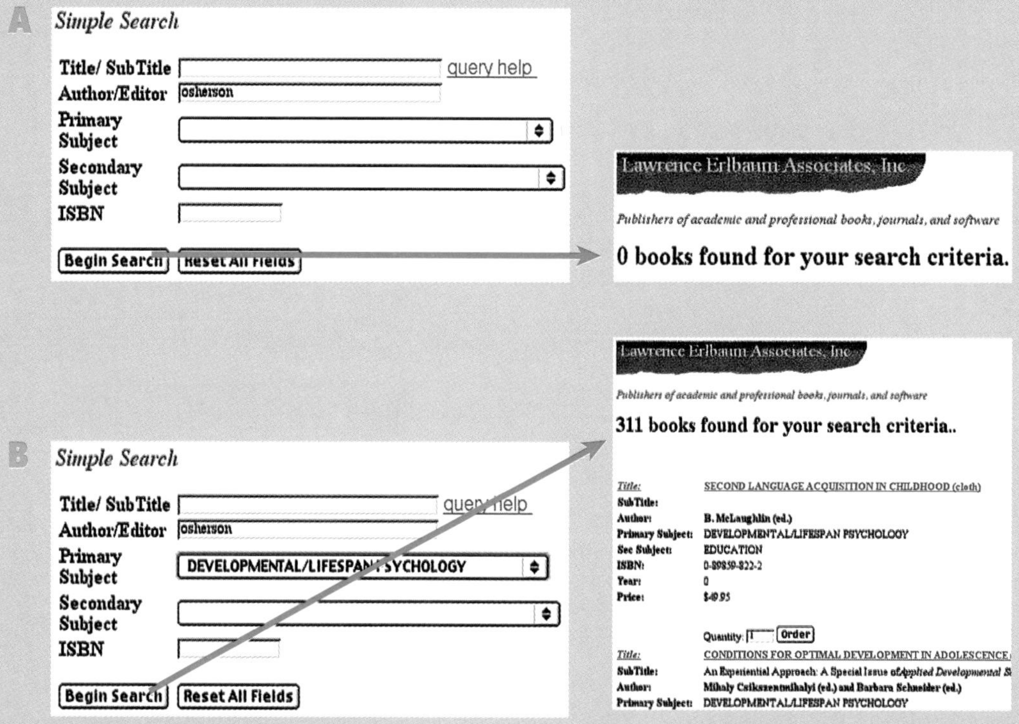

You searched for:
state=ca;

Your search resulted in 384 practitioners.
Results 1-384 listed below.

Order by: [City ◆]

Lets users reorder results

Sharon Randall (1987)
Alamo CA 94507
925/274-1113
925/933-2105
Hltytouch@aol.com

Gloria Sandler, PT (1999)
Alamo CA 94507
925/937-2440
Fax: 925/937-5868
SANDO111@aol.com

Ernie Adams (1993)
FELDENKRAIS® Movement Education
Albany CA 94706
510/433-9591
enadams@movementpathways.com
www.movementpathways.com
Also in Oakland; working with chronic pain, back care, balance, brain injuries and injury prevention.

A

Simple Search

Title/ SubTitle [   ]   query help
Author/Editor [osherson]
Primary Subject [◆]
Secondary Subject [◆]
ISBN [   ]

[Begin Search] [Reset All Fields]

Lawrence Erlbaum Associates, Inc

Publishers of academic and professional books, journals, and software

0 books found for your search criteria.

B

Simple Search

Title/ SubTitle [   ]   query help
Author/Editor [osherson]
Primary Subject [DEVELOPMENTAL/LIFESPAN PSYCHOLOGY ◆]
Secondary Subject [◆]
ISBN [   ]

[Begin Search] [Reset All Fields]

Lawrence Erlbaum Associates, Inc

Publishers of academic and professional books, journals, and software

311 books found for your search criteria..

Title: SECOND LANGUAGE ACQUISITION IN CHILDHOOD (cloth)
SubTitle:
Author: B. McLaughlin (ed.)
Primary Subject: DEVELOPMENTAL/LIFESPAN PSYCHOLOGY
Sec Subject: EDUCATION
ISBN: 0-89859-822-2
Year: 0
Price: $49.95

Quantity: [1] [Order]

Title: CONDITIONS FOR OPTIMAL DEVELOPMENT IN ADOLESCENCE:
SubTitle: An Experiential Approach: A Special Issue of Applied Developmental S
Author: Mihaly Csikszentmihalyi (ed.) and Barbara Schneider (ed.)
Primary Subject: DEVELOPMENTAL/LIFESPAN PSYCHOLOGY

criterion, such as Primary Subject = Developmental/ Lifespan Psychology, you get a long list of books, but none by Osherson. With *more* criteria, you get *more* hits, which are not books by the specified author. Huh?

A possible reason for *Erlbaum.com's* odd behavior is discussed under "Avoiding the Blooper." Whatever the cause, the behavior of this search facility does not match what most people would expect.

Legitimate Spelling Finds Nothing

At *RadioShack.com,* when you search for "videotape," you find no videotape, just three products that are related, more or less, to videotape (Figure 5.38[A]). But if you search for "video tape" (two words), you find several categories of products, including videotape. Huh? "Videotape"

is at least as common a spelling as "video tape," if not more so. (See also Blooper 35: Search Myopia: Missing Relevant Items, in this chapter.)

AVOIDING THE BLOOPER

As the two examples of this blooper suggest, "crazy" search behavior has diverse causes, and therefore diverse solutions.

Erlbaum.com's odd behavior is probably caused by combining search criteria nonintuitively: returning items matching *any* of the criteria, even if they match only the optional criteria and not the "main" one. When people add optional criteria to a search specification, it is more reasonable to assume that they want to find items matching *all* of the criteria. The sidebar (Tech Talk: Combining Search Criteria) discusses this in more technical terms.

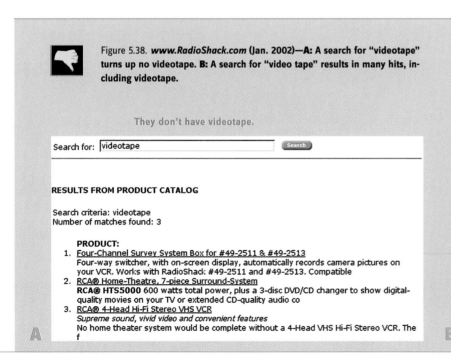

Figure 5.38. *www.RadioShack.com* (Jan. 2002)—**A:** A search for "videotape" turns up no videotape. **B:** A search for "video tape" results in many hits, including videotape.

They do have video tape.

187

They don't have videotape.

Search for: videotape   [Search]

RESULTS FROM PRODUCT CATALOG

Search criteria: videotape
Number of matches found: 3

PRODUCT:
1. Four-Channel Survey System Box for #49-2511 & #49-2513
   Four-way switcher, with on-screen display, automatically records camera pictures on your VCR. Works with RadioShack #49-2511 and #49-2513. Compatible
2. RCA® Home-Theatre, 7-piece Surround-System
   RCA® HTS5000 600 watts total power, plus a 3-disc DVD/CD changer to show digital-quality movies on your TV or extended CD-quality audio co
3. RCA® 4-Head Hi-Fi Stereo VHS VCR
   Supreme sound, vivid video and convenient features
   No home theater system would be complete without a 4-Head VHS Hi-Fi Stereo VCR. The f

A

RESULTS FROM PRODUCT CATALOG

Search criteria: video tape
Number of matches found: 696   [◄ Previous Page]   [Next Page ►]

CATEGORY:
11. Security Books & Videos
12. Tapes
13. TV/Audio/Video
14. Video
15. Video Cards
16. Video Converters
17. Video Distribution Systems
18. Videos
19. Videos/Educational

PRODUCT:
20. :CRQ 3-Channel Wireless Audio Link
    Take advantage of Digital:Convergence audio cues!

    Just like the familiar cues you see in printed media (like the RadioShack Internet-Ready

21. 1.25V/1000mAh 'AA' Hi-Capacity™ Ni-Cd Batteries Pk/2
    1.25V/1000mAh 'AA' Hi-Capacity™ Ni-Cd Batteries Pk/2 are the ideal choice for high-current equipment such as RC cars, cordless tools, portab
22. 1.3-Megapixel Digital Camera

B

TECH TALK

TECH TALK: COMBINING SEARCH CRITERIA

When specifying criteria for a computer search, people often specify more than one criterion. Sometimes they want the search to find items matching *any* of the criteria, and sometimes they want it to find only items that match *all* of the criteria.

Computer scientists have technical terms for these two ways of combining search criteria: *OR* and *AND*.

> OR: Find items that match any of the criteria. For example, search for books authored by Osherson OR books about developmental psychology.

> AND: Find items that match *all* of the criteria. For example, search for books that are authored by Osherson AND are about developmental psychology.

Using this terminology, we can say that when people give multiple search criteria, they normally expect them to be ANDed unless they say otherwise. Any search function that ORs multiple search criteria without providing a strong indicator that it is doing so will seem odd to users.

The implication for design: Search functions should AND criteria together, at least by default and perhaps with no option to do otherwise. If it is necessary to let users specify ORed searches, provide it as an option.

At *RadioShack.com,* a difference in results between searching for "videotape" versus "video tape" is most likely due to inadequate indexing of the data. The solution: adding all plausible spellings as keywords.

The unifying principle for avoiding "crazy" search behavior is to design search facilities to behave according to user expectations. That means finding out what users expect or at least *testing* the facility to see if it often makes users say "Huh?"

Blooper 39: Search Terms Not Shown

When examining the results of a Web search, people need to know what they searched for so they can make sense of the results. But of course they *know* what they searched for because they specified the search criteria only moments ago, before they hit the Search button. Yeah, sure!

Unfortunately, people aren't perfect:

> When they have a lot on their minds—as they often do when surfing the Web—they can forget what they just asked for.

> If they plan to search for something five different ways, they can lose track of which one they just did.

> They can mistype a search term without realizing it.

Web designers know this because they *are* people: They suffer from the same lapses as anyone else. But if they know this about people, why do so many websites display search results without showing the criteria that produced them?

For example, the job-hunting service *Dice.com* indicates only how many jobs it found matching "your query," without reminding you what the query was (Figure 5.39). Dice's search function tends to return a wide variety of job types,

so users may want to double-check the search criteria they gave it. At the very least, they will often want to refine the search to cut out unrelated jobs. Unfortunately, neither of these is easy to do because the search criteria aren't shown.

Erlbaum.com commits the same blooper on its Search results page (Figure 5.40). It says, "1 books found for your search criteria . . . , " but it doesn't show what the search criteria were.

Figure 5.39. *www.Dice.com* (Jan. 2002)—Search terms are not shown with results. In this case, the term was "editor."

Doesn't remind users what the query was

189

Figure 5.40. **www.Erlbaum.com** (Feb. 2002)—Search terms are not shown with the results.

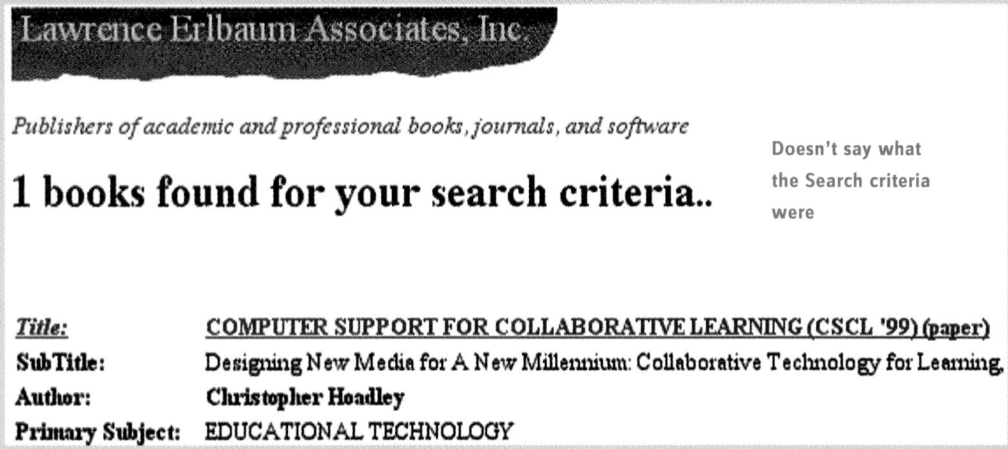

Lawrence Erlbaum Associates, Inc.

Publishers of academic and professional books, journals, and software

Doesn't say what
the Search criteria
were

1 books found for your search criteria..

Title: COMPUTER SUPPORT FOR COLLABORATIVE LEARNING (CSCL '99) (paper)
SubTitle: Designing New Media for A New Millennium: Collaborative Technology for Learning
Author: Christopher Hoadley
Primary Subject: EDUCATIONAL TECHNOLOGY

Figure 5.41. **A:** *Feldenkrais.com* (Jan. 2002); **B:** *VitaminShoppe.com* (Jan. 2002)—Search terms are shown with the results.

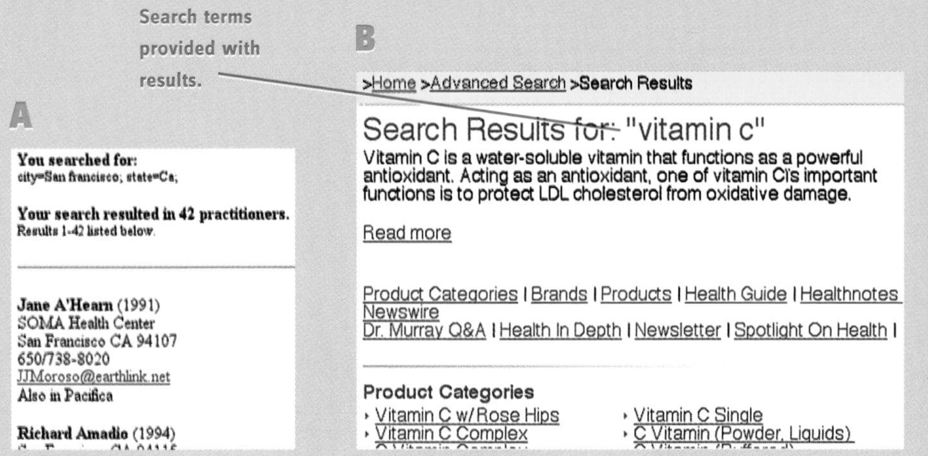

Search terms
provided with
results.

A

B

>Home >Advanced Search >Search Results

Search Results for: "vitamin c"

Vitamin C is a water-soluble vitamin that functions as a powerful antioxidant. Acting as an antioxidant, one of vitamin C's important functions is to protect LDL cholesterol from oxidative damage.

Read more

Product Categories I Brands I Products I Health Guide I Healthnotes Newswire
Dr. Murray Q&A I Health In Depth I Newsletter I Spotlight On Health I

Product Categories
▸ Vitamin C w/Rose Hips   ▸ Vitamin C Single
▸ Vitamin C Complex   ▸ C Vitamin (Powder, Liquids)

You searched for:
city=San francisco; state=Ca;

Your search resulted in 42 practitioners.
Results 1-42 listed below.

Jane A'Hearn (1991)
SOMA Health Center
San Francisco CA 94107
650/738-8020
JJMoroso@earthlink.net
Also in Pacifica

Richard Amadio (1994)

AVOIDING THE BLOOPER

People are not computers. They often won't remember what they asked for and they mistype things. Website search functions therefore need to show them what search criterion they gave to get the results they are looking at (Brinck, Gergle, and Wood 2001). *Feldenkrais.com* and *VitaminShoppe.com* show that it can be done (Figure 5.41).

Even better is to display the search terms in editable form so users can modify them on the results page to refine their search or try a different one. The search facility on Stanford University's website does this (Figure 5.42), although it may be hard to see at first glance because the results page is somewhat cluttered.

Blooper 40: Number of Hits Not Revealed

Another important piece of information often missing from Web search results is the number of found items, referred to in the industry as "hits."

Earlier, I showed that the search facility of *DigiGuide.com* (see Figure 5.20) includes a lot of duplicated information in its results (Blooper 33: Hits Look Alike). *DigiGuide's* search results has another problem: It doesn't say how many items were found (Figure 5.43). There isn't even an indication of how many *pages* of results were found—just an uninformative "next" button. Users have to scroll and page through the results to see whether their search found a few, a few dozen, or a few hundred items. Not very customer friendly.

Figure 5.42. **www.Stanford.edu** (Jan. 2002)—Search terms, which are editable, are shown with the results.

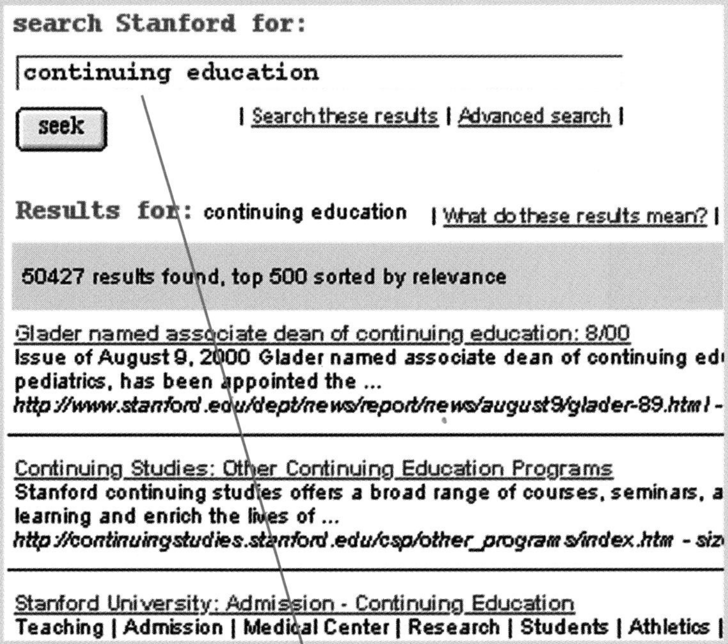

search Stanford for:

| continuing education |

[seek] | Search these results | Advanced search |

Results for: continuing education | What do these results mean? |

50427 results found, top 500 sorted by relevance

Glader named associate dean of continuing education: 8/00
Issue of August 9, 2000 Glader named associate dean of continuing ed
pediatrics, has been appointed the ...
http://www.stanford.edu/dept/news/report/news/august9/glader-89.html -

Continuing Studies: Other Continuing Education Programs
Stanford continuing studies offers a broad range of courses, seminars, a
learning and enrich the lives of ...
http://continuingstudies.stanford.edu/csp/other_programs/index.htm - siz

Stanford University: Admission - Continuing Education
Teaching | Admission | Medical Center | Research | Students | Athletics |

Editable search terms provided with
results, so user can revise Search

Figure 5.43. **www.DigiGuide.com** (May 2002)—The number of hits is not shown with results.

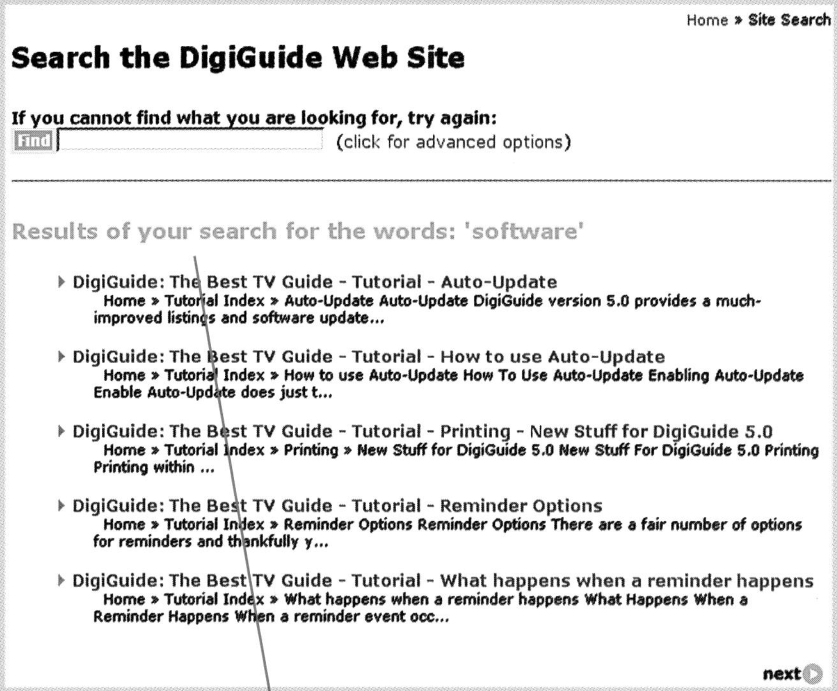

Home » **Site Search**

Search the DigiGuide Web Site

If you cannot find what you are looking for, try again:
[Find] [   ] (click for advanced options)

Results of your search for the words: 'software'

▸ **DigiGuide: The Best TV Guide - Tutorial - Auto-Update**
   Home » Tutorial Index » Auto-Update Auto-Update DigiGuide version 5.0 provides a much-improved listings and software update...

▸ **DigiGuide: The Best TV Guide - Tutorial - How to use Auto-Update**
   Home » Tutorial Index » How to use Auto-Update How To Use Auto-Update Enabling Auto-Update Enable Auto-Update does just t...

▸ **DigiGuide: The Best TV Guide - Tutorial - Printing - New Stuff for DigiGuide 5.0**
   Home » Tutorial Index » Printing » New Stuff for DigiGuide 5.0 New Stuff For DigiGuide 5.0 Printing Printing within ...

▸ **DigiGuide: The Best TV Guide - Tutorial - Reminder Options**
   Home » Tutorial Index » Reminder Options Reminder Options There are a fair number of options for reminders and thankfully y...

▸ **DigiGuide: The Best TV Guide - Tutorial - What happens when a reminder happens**
   Home » Tutorial Index » What happens when a reminder happens What Happens When a Reminder Happens When a reminder event occ...

next ▶

Number of hits not given

191

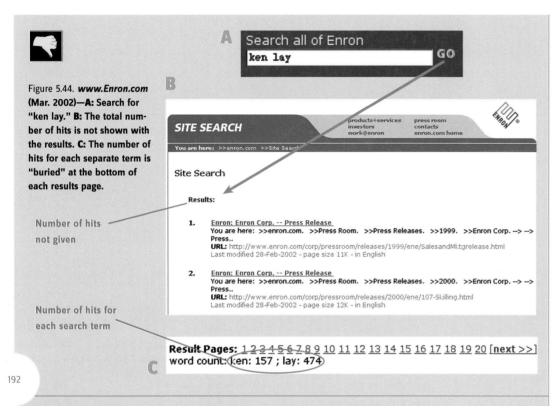

Figure 5.44. **www.Enron.com**
(Mar. 2002)—A: Search for
"ken lay." B: The total num-
ber of hits is not shown with
the results. C: The number of
hits for each separate term is
"buried" at the bottom of
each results page.

Number of hits
not given

Number of hits for
each search term

192

Figure 5.45.
www.Amazon.com (Sept.
2002)—Both the search
terms and the number of
hits are shown with the
results.

Search terms
and number
of hits shown

Close, but No Cigar

Some websites don't show the total number of hits with search results but do provide some information that lets users judge the quantity of results. Sorry, that's not good enough: It requires too much mental effort. Web designers should avoid making users think about anything but their own goals.

For example, Enron's website comes tantalizingly close to showing a total hit count but doesn't quite do it. In addition to a list of results pages, it shows how many items matched *each* of the given search terms (Figure 5.44). So close, but yet, so far!

AVOIDING THE BLOOPER

How hard can it be to show the number of hits? Lots of sites do it, such as *Amazon.com* (Figure 5.45).

Brinck, Gergle, and Wood (2001) list pieces of information search results must include in order to be usable. The number of hits is one of them. Search results should therefore follow Amazon's example and show the exact number of hits—as well as the search terms—above the list of results.

PART III BLOOPERS IN THE PRESENTATION OF THE WEBSITE

TEXT AND WRITING BLOOPERS CHAPTER 6

The Web began as a way for researchers—mainly physicists—to share data, analyses, and conclusions with each other. The primary form of information on the early Web was text. In fact, the first Web browser could not display graphics—only text.

Despite the emergence of browsers and browser plug-ins that display images and structured graphics and play audio and video recordings, the dominant form of information on the Web is still text. Text makes up not only the bulk of website *content,* but also the bulk of the *user interface* for accessing the Web: navigation links, button labels, error messages, help information, setting labels, setting values, and search terms.

The dominance of text on the Web makes it important to get the text in your website right. If the text in your website is wordy, hard to understand, inconsistent, or error ridden, chances are your site will be perceived by visitors as being of low quality.

Unfortunately, a lot of bad text can be found on the Web. Let's look at some of the most common textual bloopers and how to avoid them.

Blooper 41: Too Much Text

By far the most common mistake to make with text on the Web is to have too much of it. "Blocks of Text" is one of Nielsen's top ten Web-design mistakes for 2002 (see *UseIt.com*).

Needless text is bad anytime (Strunk and White 1979) but is especially bad on the Web. People don't read websites, they scan them. They scan for words and pictures that match their goals (Krug 2000). Verbose link labels, instructions, and messages just slow people down and "bury" important information.

In Chapter 4, I showed a Checkout page at *StanfordBookstore.com* that asks a question and provides a poorly defaulted menu to answer it (see Chapter 4, Blooper 24: No Defaults). The question itself (Figure 6.1) is an example of too much text.

At the Association of Computing Machinery's website, members are asked to log in. An invalid log in results in a long and confusing error message (Figure 6.2). The last bullet point contains a *triple* negative!

Figure 6.1. **www.StanfordBookstore.com** (Sept. 2002)—Question is too wordy.

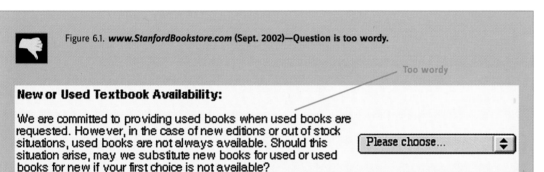

New or Used Textbook Availability:

We are committed to providing used books when used books are requested. However, in the case of new editions or out of stock situations, used books are not always available. Should this situation arise, may we substitute new books for used or used books for new if your first choice is not available?

Too wordy

Please choose...

Figure 6.2. **www.ACM.org** (Sept. 2002)—Login error message is too long.

Too long

Warning: The email address/client number you have provided is not found within our system. Please do the following:

- If you are presently a non-member subscriber, please check the email address and click *Try Again* .
- If you have your non-member client number available please use it and click *Try Again* .
- To locate your non-member subscriber client number, contact the Member Services Department at 1-800-342-6626(US/Canada), 212-626-0500(Global); or email acmhelp@acm.org
- If you are not a non-member subscriber please click *Non-Member Account*.

Triple negative

Lengthy Links

Textual links, when too long and especially when in lists of links, can be difficult for users to scan. If text is repeated in adjacent links, "scannability" and legibility suffer even more. A long list of links from the California Department of Motor Vehicles' (DMV) website shows this (Figure 6.3). Some of the headings on the page are also unnecessarily wordy. The first heading, for example, needlessly duplicates the phrase "Driver License Information" from the page title just above it.

AVOIDING THE BLOOPER

Text should be reduced to the bare essentials: no more than is necessary to convey the intended meaning. Good text on the Web is similar to good text in presentation slides. Thus Web designers should do the following:

> Keep link labels short: ideally 1 to 3 words.

> Avoid long passages of prose.

> Use headings, short phrases, and bullet points.

Figure 6.3. **www.DMV.ca.gov (Jan. 2002)—Long textual links are hard to scan, especially in lists and with text repeated in adjacent links.**

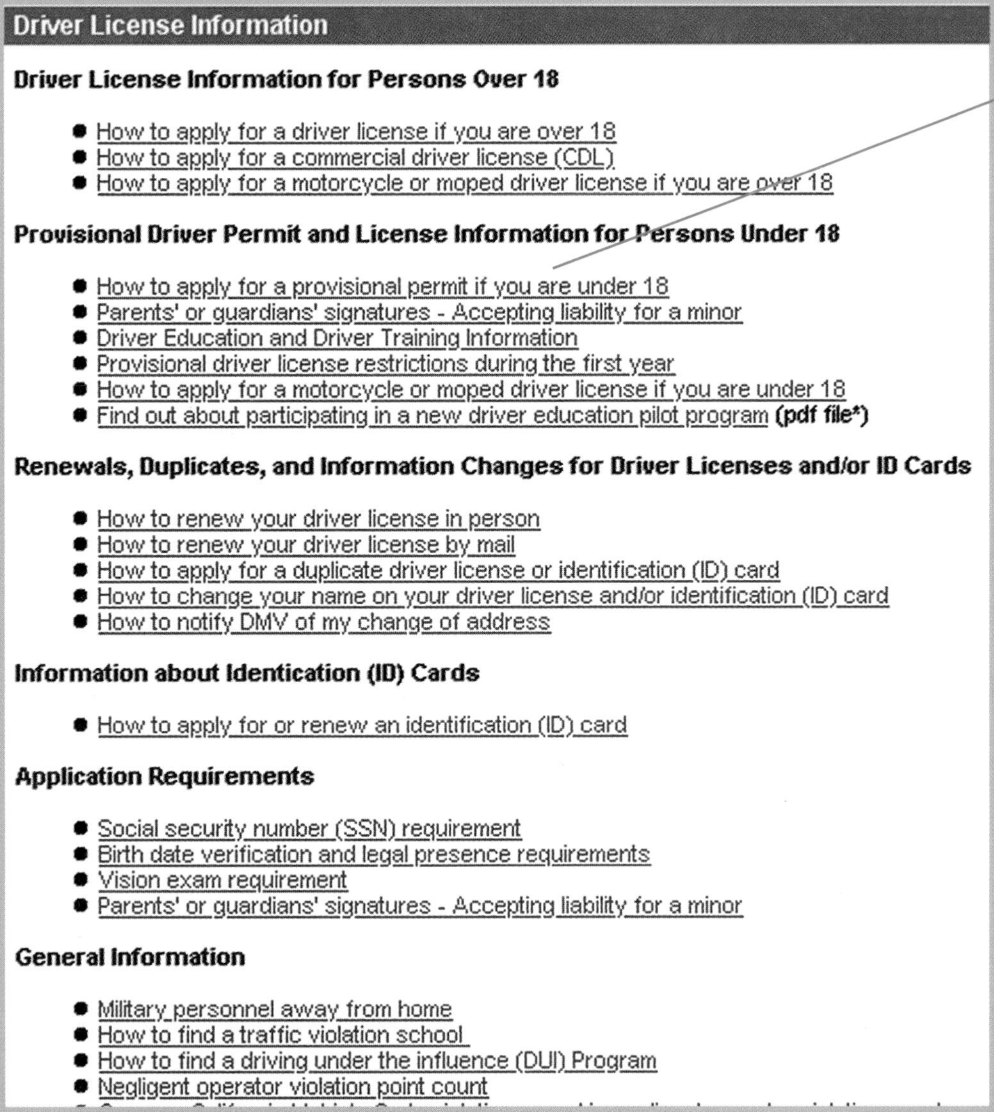

Driver License Information

Driver License Information for Persons Over 18

- How to apply for a driver license if you are over 18
- How to apply for a commercial driver license (CDL)
- How to apply for a motorcycle or moped driver license if you are over 18

Long textual links are hard to scan.

Provisional Driver Permit and License Information for Persons Under 18

- How to apply for a provisional permit if you are under 18
- Parents' or guardians' signatures - Accepting liability for a minor
- Driver Education and Driver Training Information
- Provisional driver license restrictions during the first year
- How to apply for a motorcycle or moped driver license if you are under 18
- Find out about participating in a new driver education pilot program **(pdf file*)**

Renewals, Duplicates, and Information Changes for Driver Licenses and/or ID Cards

- How to renew your driver license in person
- How to renew your driver license by mail
- How to apply for a duplicate driver license or identification (ID) card
- How to change your name on your driver license and/or identification (ID) card
- How to notify DMV of my change of address

Information about Identication (ID) Cards

- How to apply for or renew an identification (ID) card

Application Requirements

- Social security number (SSN) requirement
- Birth date verification and legal presence requirements
- Vision exam requirement
- Parents' or guardians' signatures - Accepting liability for a minor

General Information

- Military personnel away from home
- How to find a traffic violation school
- How to find a driving under the influence (DUI) Program
- Negligent operator violation point count

197

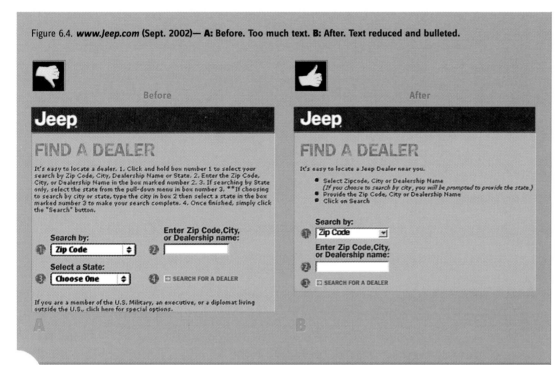

Figure 6.4. *www.Jeep.com* (Sept. 2002)— **A: Before. Too much text. B: After. Text reduced and bulleted.**

Figure 6.5. **Improved design for *StanfordBookstore.com*—Label drastically shortened.**

> May we substitute new books for used or used books for new if your first choice is not available?
> ☑ Substitutions OK

Web-design authors Jakob Nielsen and Steve Krug both recommend brevity. Nielsen (1999) provides guidelines similar to those listed previously. Krug (2000) warns that long passages of prose won't be read and suggests that web designers "get rid of half of the words on each page, then get rid of half of what's left."

Examples of Cutting Needless Text

An excellent illustration of how wordy text can be cut comes from automaker *Jeep.com*. In September 2002, it revised the "Find A Dealer" page to simplify it and reduce its verbosity (Figure 6.4). A lengthy paragraph was reduced to one sentence and three bulleted steps. Jeep also eliminated another blooper: It didn't need both zip code *and* state (see Chapter 2, Blooper 9: Requiring Unneeded Data).

The lengthy question on *StanfordBookstore.com's* Checkout page could be reduced to one sentence, with a checkbox for responding (Figure 6.5).

Even the shortened question is too long, because it covers both *new* and *used* book orders. It is asked at checkout and so could be simplified if made to depend on what the customer ordered. For example,

May we substitute used books if no new books are available?

If the customer ordered both new and used books, the site could ask two separate questions.

Avoiding Long Lists of Links

Lengthy links can be avoided by doing the following:

> Confining the link to the most important phrase of a sentence

> Removing repeated text from the links, putting it into a subheading

Lists of links can also be made easier to scan by spacing items more. If these design rules were applied to the California DMV's page, a more easily scanned list of links would result (Figure 6.6).

The Real Goals: Scannability and Clarity

It is important to realize that brevity is not itself a goal. Brevity is only a means to designers' true goals: ease of comprehension and navigation, scannability, and clarity. Brevity on the Web is advisable because of empirical observations that Web users do not read Web pages; they scan them. The point of brevity is to facilitate users' ability to comprehend and navigate by scanning.

If a designer forgets this and strives for brevity for its own sake, usability can suffer (Raskin 2000). Needlessly limiting button or link labels to one word, for example, can appear to users as cryptic arbitrary codes that they have to learn in order to use a website. To paraphrase Albert Einstein, text on the Web should be as brief as possible, but no briefer.

Blooper 42: Speaking Geek

Text in websites and Web applications, as in desktop software, is often written in programmers' technical jargon, making it incomprehensible to the software's intended users. This is known as "speaking Geek" (Johnson 2000).

Although Web developers come from a wide variety of backgrounds, many have programming backgrounds. When writing text for websites, they often use programmers' jargon. Why? There are several reasons:

> They don't realize it's jargon.

> They can't express themselves in nontechnical terms.

> They expect computer users to learn the jargon.

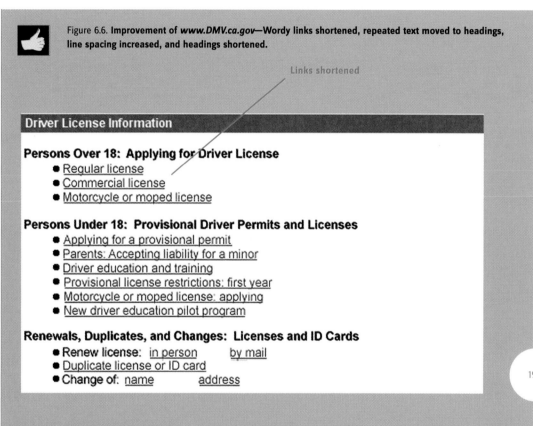

Figure 6.6. **Improvement of** *www.DMV.ca.gov*—**Wordy links shortened, repeated text moved to headings, line spacing increased, and headings shortened.**

Links shortened

Driver License Information

Persons Over 18: Applying for Driver License
- Regular license
- Commercial license
- Motorcycle or moped license

Persons Under 18: Provisional Driver Permits and Licenses
- Applying for a provisional permit
- Parents: Accepting liability for a minor
- Driver education and training
- Provisional license restrictions: first year
- Motorcycle or moped license: applying
- New driver education pilot program

Renewals, Duplicates, and Changes: Licenses and ID Cards
- Renew license: in person   by mail
- Duplicate license or ID card
- Change of: name   address

199

> They directly expose low-level software-to-software communication—for example, java exceptions—instead of translating it into terms related to what the user is doing.

> They don't have time: "Someone will fix this before we go live!"

> The site is poorly designed: It exposes implementation concepts that aren't easily "painted over."

© Bill Griffith. Reprint with special permission of King Features Syndicate.

Figure 6.7. **www.Earthlink.net** (Sept. 2001)—Asks user to enter three pieces of information into only two fields. Most users won't know what the domain is or that it is part of the email address.

Please enter your email address, domain, and password:

Email address: [   ]

Password: [   ]

[Submit]

Geek speak

Geek speak can appear anywhere there is text in a website. Sometimes it's in instructions the site provides. Sometimes it's in error messages. Sometimes it's in the names of commands site users have to invoke to accomplish anything. Let's look at examples of each.

Geeky Instructions

Earthlink.net gives subscribers a way to create a "vacation" message that will automatically be sent in reply to incoming email, as well as a way to turn vacation auto-reply on and off. If you are a subscriber, you access your vacation settings by going to *Earthlink.net* and typing your email address and password (Figure 6.7). The instructions say to "enter your email address, domain, and password"—three pieces of information—but the form provides only *two* text boxes. Software developers know that the domain is *part* of the email address, but I doubt that my aunt Geraldine and others like her know that, or even what "domain" means in this context.

In this case, the Geek speak is entirely superfluous: The word "domain" could be dropped from the instruction with no loss. In fact, the entire instruction could be dropped with no loss, because the field labels are enough.

Website instructions sometimes also speak Geek by using graphical user interface (GUI) toolkit terms for parts of the user interface. Programmers often forget that words like "field," "icon," "drop down," and "dialog" either are unknown or mean something else to most English speakers. The terms "drop down" and "dialog" are actually *double* jargon: They are abbreviations for longer jargon terms: "drop-down menu" and "dialog box," respectively. Perhaps programmers assume that learning GUI component names is a necessary part of learning how to use a computer. If so, they are wrong. Figure 6.8 shows excerpts from three websites that use the GUI toolkit jargon terms "field," "icon," and "dialog": *FinancialEngines.com, OfficeMax.com,* and *Galor.com* (Figure 6.8).

Even worse than using GUI toolkit jargon is using it *incorrectly.* The San Mateo County (California) Department of Transportation's *TransitInfo* search page instructs users to "type a query in the Search dialog" (Figure 6.9). The problem is, there is no dialog box—only a text field on a regular Web page. A dialog box is a little window that pops up to collect data from the user or display a message. If you're going to use implementation toolkit jargon, at least get the component names right!

Geeky Error Messages

Another obvious place for Geek speak to show up is in error messages. A classic example of a geeky error message is from the website of an organization that should know better. The Association of Computing Machinery's Special Interest Group on Computer-Human Interaction (ACM SIGCHI) is all about making computers easier to use. Every year, SIGCHI holds a conference. The CHI conference pages at ACM's website allow people to register online until about 2 weeks before the conference. After that, online registration is closed; additional attendees must register at the conference. In 2002, if someone tried to register online for CHI 2002 after online registration had closed, the site displayed the helpful message: "RegMaster Error 105: Cannot open CHI02closed.txt" (Figure 6.10). Clearly, some internal Web-server message is being displayed by the site.

Even if SIGCHI fixed the message to say something sensible like "Sorry: Online registration for CHI 2002 closed on April 8. Please register at the conference," they would still be

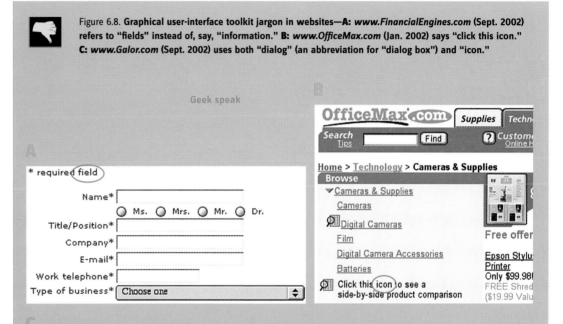

Figure 6.8. **Graphical user-interface toolkit jargon in websites—A:** *www.FinancialEngines.com* **(Sept. 2002) refers to "fields" instead of, say, "information." B:** *www.OfficeMax.com* **(Jan. 2002) says "click this icon." C:** *www.Galor.com* **(Sept. 2002) uses both "dialog" (an abbreviation for "dialog box") and "icon."**

201

Figure 6.9. **www.TransitInfo.org (Dec. 2001)—Geek speak that isn't even correct: Calls a text field a "dialog."**

Geek speak that isn't even correct.

Search for Bay Area Transit Information

Main Menu : **Search**

This is an index of the information on this server. Please type a query in the search dialog. You may use compound searches, such as: **fare**

	Search

Figure 6.10. **www.ACM.org/chi2002 (Apr. 2002)—Message informing user that the deadline for online registration for the ACM CHI2002 conference has passed.**

RegMaster Error 105: Cannot open CHI02closed.txt.

Figure 6.11. **www.Audi.com (Feb. 2002)—A: Global Home page, with Continent and Country menus. B: Error message resulting from clicking arrow button without having chosen continent and country.**

A

Welcome to the Audi World Site

Method Not Allowed

An error has occurred.

B

Audi worldwide	Language	Audi News
Please select	▶ Deutsch	▶ Audi Glossary
		New on our Site
		▶ Growth defies trend
Continent ▾		Market share increased
Country ▾		▶ Read more news
▶		

committing a blooper (see Chapter 2, Blooper 13: Dead-end Paths: *Now* you tell me!). The site should say up front that online registration is closed, and no longer provide links for that, instead of letting people follow links to online registration and then telling them registration is closed.

On the home page of *Audi.com,* menus are provided to let users go to sections of the site designed for specific countries. Select a continent and a country, then click the arrow button to go there. What if someone clicks the arrow without first choosing a continent and a country? The fancy pages with car pictures are replaced by a stark gray geekism: "Method Not Allowed," no doubt referring to a Java programming language method (Figure 6.11). Perhaps realizing that this message might not help visitors understand what they did wrong, *Audi.com* adds the helpful comment: "An error has occurred." Danke sehr!

A special case of a geeky error message comes from *Feldenkrais.com.* If a visitor uses the site's search function, but the search function finds nothing matching the user's search terms, it displays an error message and a very geeky one at that (Figure 6.12). Of course, the main problem is not the geekyness of the message, but that not finding anything is treated as an error.

Geeky Commands

A good example of speaking Geek in commands comes from a client company's internal Web application for logging hours worked on a project. When a user first signs in, the site lists recently submitted hours and expenses and provides commands for viewing more of the history. The command for logging new hours is called "Create a new record" (Figure 6.13).

Why is the command called "Create a new record" instead of something more task-related such as "Log hours"? Because in order to log new hours, the back end has to

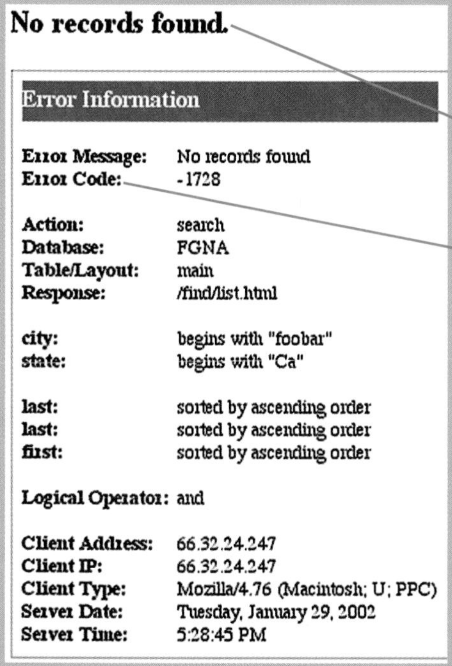

No records found.

Error Information

Error Message:	No records found
Error Code:	-1728
Action:	search
Database:	FGNA
Table/Layout:	main
Response:	/find/list.html
city:	begins with "foobar"
state:	begins with "Ca"
last:	sorted by ascending order
last:	sorted by ascending order
first:	sorted by ascending order
Logical Operator:	and
Client Address:	66.32.24.247
Client IP:	66.32.24.247
Client Type:	Mozilla/4.76 (Macintosh; U; PPC)
Server Date:	Tuesday, January 29, 2002
Server Time:	5:28:45 PM

Figure 6.12. *www.Feldenkrais.com* (Oct. 2002)—Error message exposes internal software communication.

Null results shouldn't be an error.

Geek speak

203

Figure 6.13. **Client Web application (Apr. 2002)—Command "Create a new record" is implementation focused, not task focused.**

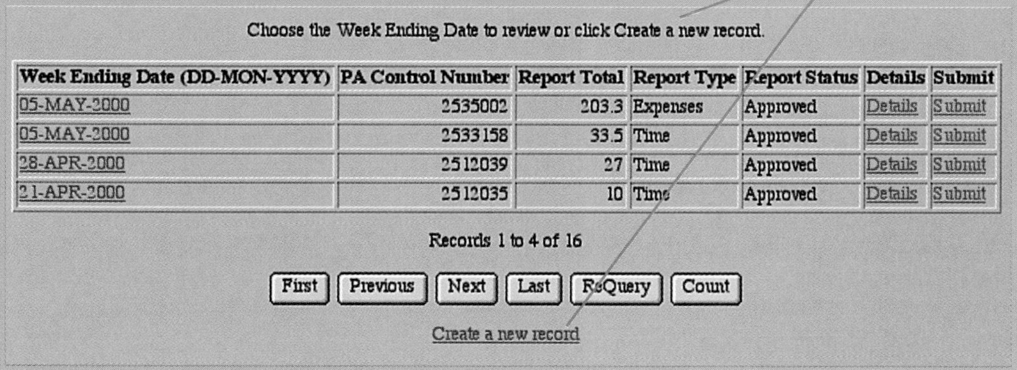

Geek speak

Choose the Week Ending Date to review or click Create a new record.

Week Ending Date (DD-MON-YYYY)	PA Control Number	Report Total	Report Type	Report Status	Details	Submit
05-MAY-2000	2535002	203.3	Expenses	Approved	Details	Submit
05-MAY-2000	2533158	33.5	Time	Approved	Details	Submit
28-APR-2000	2512039	27	Time	Approved	Details	Submit
21-APR-2000	2512035	10	Time	Approved	Details	Submit

Records 1 to 4 of 16

[First] [Previous] [Next] [Last] [ReQuery] [Count]

Create a new record

create a new data record. The implementation has crept into the user interface. However, users don't want to "create a new record." They want to log work hours. Therefore it might take them a while to figure out how to log their hours.

Nice Try, But No Cigar

Many websites—especially e-commerce sites—are front ends for large, complex transaction-processing systems. In such sites, it is nearly impossible to predict all the ways a user can arrive at a given page, especially since Web users often navigate using their Back and Forward buttons. The site can also experience internal failures, both minor and major. It is therefore difficult to ensure that all instructions and error messages are task focused and helpful.

As examples, let's examine two different error conditions that can occur at *United.com.* In one situation, a user logged in, accessed his frequent-flyer account, backed out without doing anything, visited other websites, and then returned to United's home page and logged in again (Figure 6.14). From the site's point of view, the user is still logged in from before but is trying to log in again.[18] The message tries to explain in plain language what the user should do: log out. Nonetheless, my mother-in-law probably wouldn't understand this. For one thing, she probably wouldn't know what an "active session" is. It is also unclear what it means to "register an existing . . . account." Most people's reaction to a confusing message would be to hit the Back button. In this case, that happens to be what United wants them to do anyway, so this message might be okay. On the other hand, it also asks users to log out. People rarely explicitly log out of websites. Instead, they just back out or send their browser to another site. If this situation arises frequently, United should reexamine it and try to devise a better solution.

In the second situation, the user specified his flight details, then selected one of the resulting itineraries to get a price. According to the error message, something in the back-end system prevented it from pricing the itinerary (Figure 6.15). "Reservation system internal error" is a bit too geeky to meet the "retail product quality" standard. Consumers would never buy a car or TV that displayed "internal system error" messages. Still, it isn't a horrible message, and the rest of the message suggests in plain language what the user should do: Try a different flight. However, that "try a different flight" suggestion is also troubling because it is so likely to be wrong. For example, this customer tried several flights and got the same message for all of them. He had no way to tell whether the problem was a transient glitch or a restriction on what itineraries can be priced.

---

[18]The site detects that the user returned by checking for a "cookie" that it gave the user's browser during the first visit.

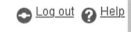

Figure 6.14. *www.United.com* (Apr. 2002)—User logged into site twice. Problem description is a bit geeky, but instructions at least make a good attempt to be helpful.

Register at
united.com

Log out   Help

You currently have an active united.com session. Please log out prior to attempting to register an existing Mileage Plus account.

Please press the **"Back"** button in your browser to return to the previous screen. Or, you may continue to navigate through the site using the left-side navigation links.

AVOIDING THE BLOOPER

Geek speak must go! Web users aren't captive, so they are even more sensitive to geekisms than users of desktop software. If anything confuses or annoys them, they can leave at any time.

How to avoid speaking Geek can be summarized as follows[19]:

> *Know your users.* Interview representatives of your target user population to learn their vocabulary for the tasks your site covers. Don't expect people to learn a new vocabulary—even just a few new terms—to use your site. They won't, and you'll be the loser.

> *Develop a site lexicon.* Create a list of all the terms and their corresponding meanings that will appear in the site. Base the list on the users' tasks and vocabulary. Follow it religiously and keep it current as the site changes. Assign a team member—preferably a technical writer—to be the keeper and enforcer of the lexicon.

> *Keep implementation terms out.* This includes GUI component names like *dialog, icon, field,* and *drop down.* It includes technical terms like *proxy server, SSL encryption,* and *authenticate.* It includes internal exception symbols and program code like *array_index_out_of_range, javascript error: file.open() failed,* and *illegal method.*

> *Provide solutions for errors.* Engineers like to describe the problem. Users want to know the solution. Of course describe the problem—in terms related to what the user was doing—but also suggest a course of action, as is shown in an excellent error message from Southwest Airlines' website (Figure 6.16).

[19]See Johnson (2000).

Figure 6.15. *www.United.com* (Apr. 2002)—Internal glitch caused task failure. Problem description is a bit geeky, but instructions at least make a good attempt to be helpful.

✈ **Flights** Modify Flight		E-Fares ╷ Award travel

We Can't Price/Book This Itinerary

We had trouble pricing or completing your reservation for the following reason:

Reservation system internal error - cannot price this itinerary, please try a different flight.

Please try double checking all your information, and/or rebuilding your itinerary. If you continue to have problems, please let us know.

Thanks!

Back

205

Figure 6.16. *www.Southwest.com* (Sept. 2002)—Great error message. Describes the problem in users' vocabulary and suggests what to do.

www.southwest.com

WHAT HAPPENED?

You did not fill in all the required information:
*You did not select a departure date for a return flight

WHAT YOU NEED TO DO:

Go back to the previous page and complete your selection.

> *Put the right people on the job.* The root cause of Geek speak in software and websites is a management blooper: assigning the job of writing command names, instructions, and messages to programmers. Programmers are skilled in writing software code, not text. The writing of software text should be assigned to people who have the right training and skills: user-interface designers or technical writers, preferably the latter.

> *Test the text on users.* The text in a website should be tried on representative users before the site is put on the Web. One nice thing about text is that it can be tested using paper-and-pencil tests or not-yet-connected static pages; you don't have to wait for the site to be finished. Another nice thing about text is that even if problems are discovered close to the release date, they are usually easy to fix.

Situations such as the two that occurred at *United.com* are admittedly difficult. In both cases, *United.com* made a reasonable attempt to avoid speaking Geek to its customers. However, that still wasn't good enough for a mass consumer market. Here are some thoughts on how *United.com* might have better handled these situations.

In the first case, someone who still had an active session from a previous login tried to log back into the site. I see two possible solutions:

> If you view the situation from the user's point of view rather than the website's, it shouldn't be considered a problem. From the user' viewpoint, he left *United.com* and then returned. He didn't know he was still logged in. The site should either just forget about the previous session and let the guy log in again or treat his new login as "unnecessary" and take him back to where he was before. Either way, a geeky error message is avoided because there is no error.

> If it is necessary to consider this an error condition, rewrite the message in less technical language. For example,

You are already logged in from a previous visit. You can either resume your last visit to *United.com* or you can start again. <u>Resume</u> <u>Start Again</u>

Note the use of the less-technical word "visit" instead of the geeky term "session."

In the second case, the site encountered an "internal error." Without knowing what the actual problem was, it is hard to know what the message should say. Whatever the problem, the message should be clearer about whether it is temporary or not. In other words, if the customer tries again later, will the site be able to price the itinerary or is there something about the itinerary that prevents it from being priced, ever?

"You can access me by saying simply 'Agnes.' It is not necessary to add 'dot com.'"

Blooper 43: Calling Site Visitors "User"

One form of speaking Geek is so common that I consider it a blooper of its own: websites that refer to site visitors as "users."

"Users" is what we—software and Web *developers*—call people who use our systems. It's a fine term to use when we are talking with other developers. It's part of our professional jargon—our way of communicating succinctly with peers. But "users" is *not* how people refer to themselves. Well, maybe *heroin* and *cocaine* users refer to themselves as "users," but nobody else calls themselves that.

Websites should be designed from the point of view of the people who will *use* the website, not that of the site's designers or developers. Therefore, websites that call users "user" to their face are committing a blooper.

Consider *BarnesAndNoble.com* and *BookPool.com*. Both use the word "user" to refer to the people who visit their sites (Figure 6.17). Barnes&Noble's Computer Books page uses the ambiguous phrase "Home Users"—does this mean people who use homes, people who use computers at home, or people who use *BarnesAndNoble.com* at home? Almost as bad, *BookPool.com* calls its visitors "Past Users" or "New Users" depending on whether they've registered.

A more blatant form of the blooper is exhibited by *FinancialEngines.com:* It doesn't just call site visitors "user," it makes them refer to *themselves* as "user." The home page commits the normal form of the blooper by asking "First time users" to "start here" (Figure 6.18[A]). The Advice page asks visitors to classify themselves to help guide the site's investment advice, with "An individual user" as one of the available options (Figure 6.18[B]).

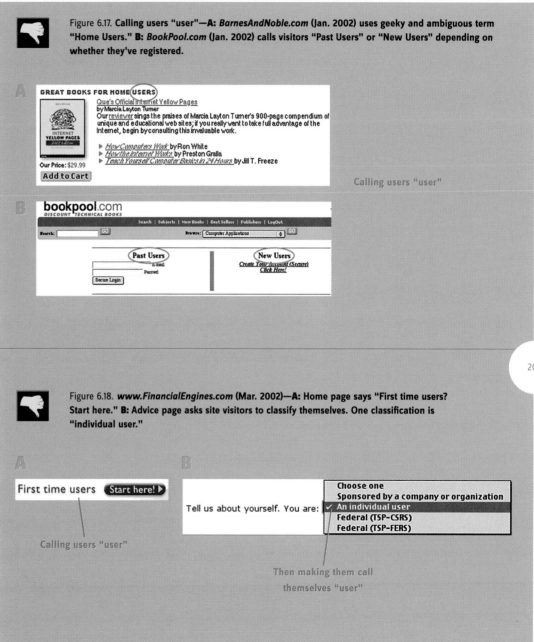

Figure 6.17. **Calling users "user"—A:** *BarnesAndNoble.com* **(Jan. 2002) uses geeky and ambiguous term "Home Users." B:** *BookPool.com* **(Jan. 2002) calls visitors "Past Users" or "New Users" depending on whether they've registered.**

Calling users "user"

Figure 6.18. *www.FinancialEngines.com* **(Mar. 2002)—A: Home page says "First time users? Start here." B: Advice page asks site visitors to classify themselves. One classification is "individual user."**

Calling users "user"

Then making them call themselves "user"

207

Figure 6.19. **www.Amazon.com** (Jan. 2002)—**A:** Home page says "New Customer? Start here." **B:** Login page uses the term "customer."

A

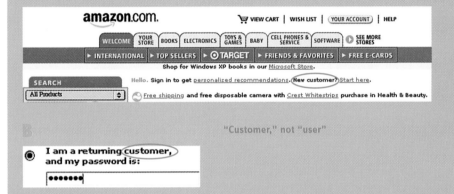

"Customer," not "user"

B

Calling users "user" to their face is an easy mistake to make: "User" is developers' jargon for people who use the website. If a development team doesn't explicitly *think* about this and choose a more appropriate word, "users" is the word that will be used. That's why this blooper is so common. Other websites that (as of February 2002) call their users "user" include *Continental.com, eBay, ITN.net, Learn2.com,* and *VitaminShoppe.com.*

AVOIDING THE BLOOPER

As easy as it is to make this blooper, it's just as easy to avoid or correct it. It just takes awareness and a few moments of thought.

In contrast to *BarnesAndNoble.com* and *BookPool.com,* their competitor *Amazon.com* uses the more appropriate and less geeky term "customer" (Figure 6.19).

It is instructive to look at two contrasting subsites of *Yahoo.com:* One commits the blooper; the other avoids it. *Yahoo Maps* greets unregistered visitors with "Welcome, Guest User" (Figure 6.20[A]). *Yahoo Weather* greets them with "Hello, Guest" (Figure 6.20[B]). *Yahoo Weather's* greeting is shorter and less geeky. Yahoo—and other companies—should consider corporate standards for addressing site visitors.

Using sensible words like "customer" and "member" instead of "user" costs next to nothing. Any company or organization could do it. Three more websites that avoid the blooper are *AmericanAirlines.com* (Figure 6.21[A]), *HauteAtHome.com* (Figure 6.21[B]), and *WalMart.com* (Figure 6.21[C]).

Because this blooper is so easily avoided and corrected, there is *no valid excuse* for calling users "user" in a website.

208

Figure 6.20. **www.Yahoo.com** (Apr. 2002)—**A:** *maps.Yahoo.com:* "Welcome, Guest User." **B:** *weather.Yahoo.com:* "Hello, Guest."

A **B**

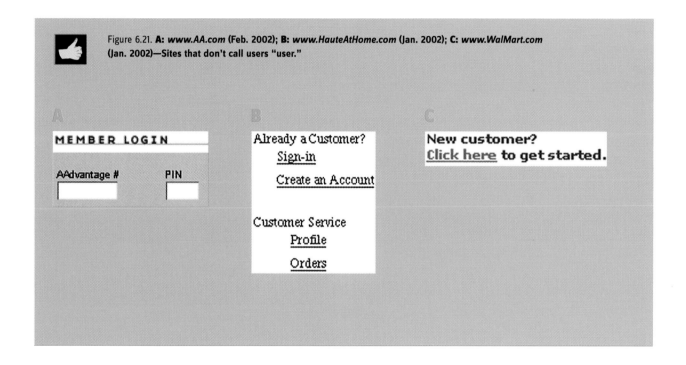

Figure 6.21. **A: *www.AA.com*** (Feb. 2002); **B: *www.HauteAtHome.com*** (Jan. 2002); **C: *www.WalMart.com***
(Jan. 2002)—Sites that don't call users "user."

Blooper 44: Insider Jargon

Speaking Geek is using *computer* jargon inappropriately. Computer jargon isn't the only kind of jargon. Every business—plumbers, real-estate agents, florists, grocers, airlines, taxicabs, doctors, caterers, you name it—has its own specialized jargon for communication between people in the profession.

Many sites on the Web confuse visitors by using the jargon of industry "insiders," even though the site's intended users aren't industry insiders and don't know the jargon. For example, a San Francisco real-estate website might describe an apartment as a "5R boxcar w/ illegal inlaw down,"[20] which wouldn't mean much to most apartment seekers.

Both speaking Geek and insider jargon are the result of website text being written by the wrong people. They differ in who those wrong people are. For speaking Geek, the culprits are the site's *engineers.* For insider jargon, the culprits are the *business* experts—marketing, sales, purchasing—who know the site's business inside and out. If they fill the site with their industry's insider jargon, most customers won't understand it.

HauteAtHome has a website that lists its offered dishes and lets customers place orders (Figure 6.22). The website lists the available dishes in tables, and for each dish has an SKU number. Did you know that "SKU" is a retail-industry term for "stock keeping unit?" Probably not. Most catalogs would

[20]It means the apartment has five rooms arranged along a long central hallway, and a separate studio apartment in the basement for which no building permit was obtained.

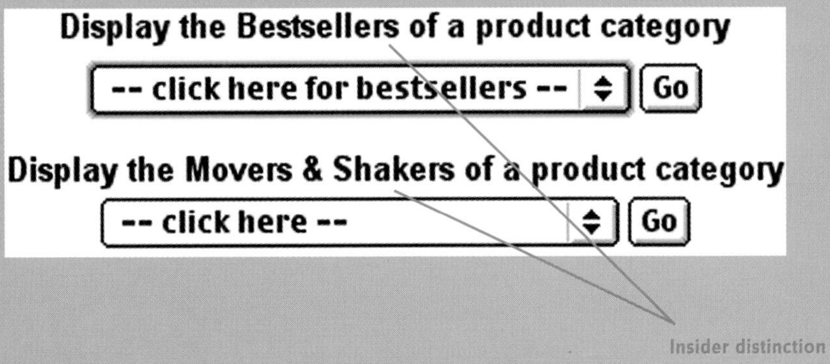

label this "item number" or "item code." This might seem minor, but envision yourself on the phone with a customer-service agent asking you for the "SKU" of the product you ordered but didn't receive.

Another e-commerce site, *ZBuyer.com*, provides a menu of all its product categories and a button for displaying the "Bestsellers" in the chosen category (Figure 6.23). That seems useful. However, ZBuyer confuses the issue by also providing another menu, right under the first, for displaying the "Movers & Shakers" in a specified category. You might wonder what the difference is between a "Bestseller" and a "Mover & Shaker." If you were a ZBuyer insider, you'd know that "Bestsellers" are the most popular products, while "Movers and Shakers" are products whose popularity is rapidly *changing* (presumably rising).

The best example of insider jargon is from *Connectix.com* (Figure 6.24). To submit a question to the customer-service department, Connectix customers must "create a new incident." "Incident" is an industry term for a customer problem report requiring a response.[21] Maybe Connectix customers will understand that and maybe they won't, but there is worse jargon here. To create an incident, customers have to indicate which product their incident is about. Connectix products are listed in two separate menus, labeled "Fee products" and "Free products." Customers probably assume this refers to whether they paid for the product or downloaded it for free, but they quickly find that the products in the two menus don't match that assumption. In fact, "fee" versus "free" is Connectix customer-support

Figure 6.22. **www.HauteAtHome.com** (Jan. 2002)—Lists of foods available for ordering include a number labeled "SKU," an insider term. Most customers don't know or care what it means.

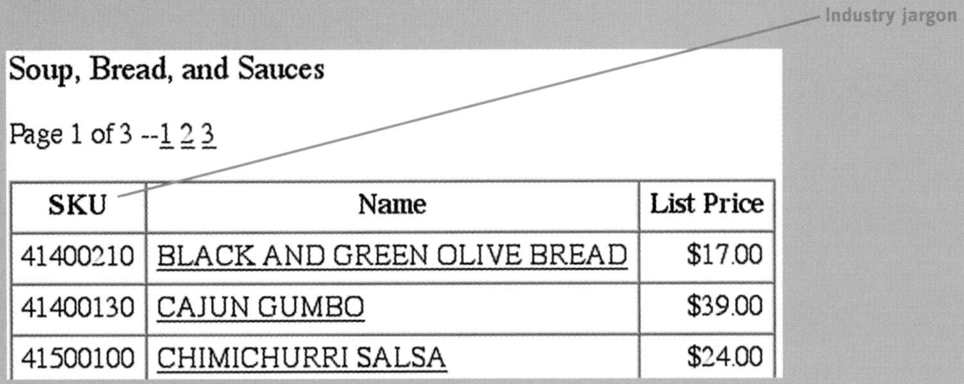

Industry jargon

Soup, Bread, and Sauces

Page 1 of 3 --<u>1</u> <u>2</u> <u>3</u>

SKU	Name	List Price
41400210	BLACK AND GREEN OLIVE BREAD	$17.00
41400130	CAJUN GUMBO	$39.00
41500100	CHIMICHURRI SALSA	$24.00

Figure 6.23. **www.ZBuyer.com** (Feb. 2002)—Makes a distinction between the "Bestsellers" and the "Movers & Shakers" in a product category. Unless you work at ZBuyer, you probably don't know the difference.

Display the Bestsellers of a product category

── click here for bestsellers ── ◆ Go

Display the Movers & Shakers of a product category

── click here ── ◆ Go

Insider distinction

[21]Another common software-industry term for this is "action requests" (ARs).

jargon for whether a fee is charged for *service* for that product or not. Obviously, these terms are based on Connectix's point of view, not their customers'.

AVOIDING THE BLOOPER

The methods for keeping your site free of insider jargon are similar to those for keeping it free of Geek speak.

First, the site's vocabulary should be based on that of its intended users, not the vocabulary of experts in your site's business. This means you have to study representatives of your hoped-for users and learn their vocabulary. That vocabulary should be used to construct a site lexicon, which in turn should be used to govern the terminology that appears in the website.

Second, experienced technical writers—not experts in your site's business—should write, test, and maintain all text on the site that isn't contributed by users. That includes instructions, messages, link labels, field labels, command names, mouse-over pop-ups, and any other text that appears on the site.

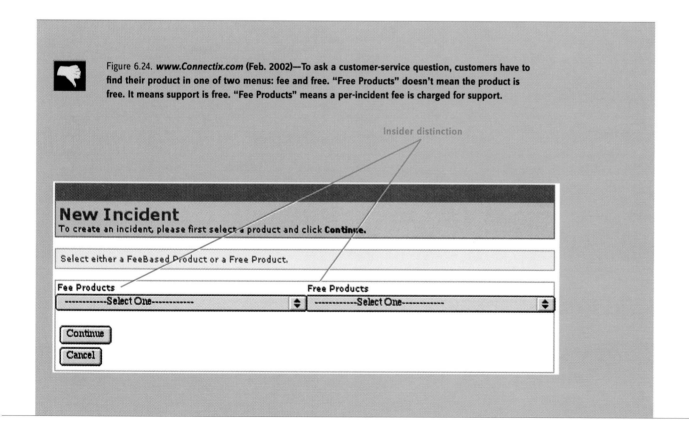

Figure 6.24. *www.Connectix.com* (Feb. 2002)—To ask a customer-service question, customers have to find their product in one of two menus: fee and free. "Free Products" doesn't mean the product is free. It means support is free. "Fee Products" means a per-incident fee is charged for support.

Figure 6.25. *www.DigiGuide.com* (Apr. 2002)—**A: Customer-support home page describes FAQ pages. B: The FAQ page is labeled "Knowledgebase" and "Common Questions."**

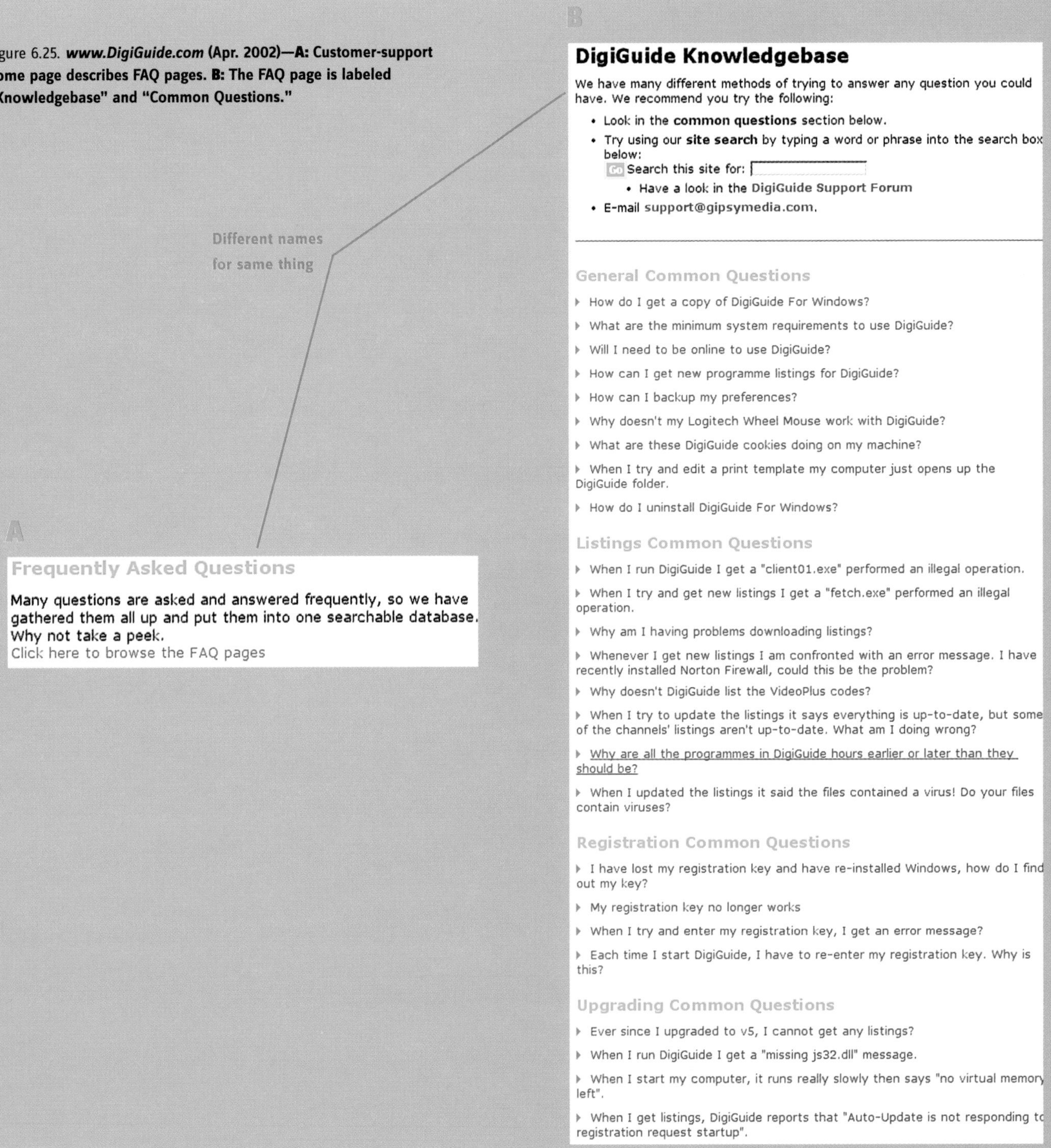

Different names
for same thing

A

Frequently Asked Questions

Many questions are asked and answered frequently, so we have gathered them all up and put them into one searchable database. Why not take a peek.
Click here to browse the FAQ pages

B

DigiGuide Knowledgebase

We have many different methods of trying to answer any question you could have. We recommend you try the following:

- Look in the **common questions** section below.
- Try using our **site search** by typing a word or phrase into the search box below:
  Go Search this site for: [_____]
    - Have a look in the **DigiGuide Support Forum**
- E-mail support@gipsymedia.com.

General Common Questions

▸ How do I get a copy of DigiGuide For Windows?

▸ What are the minimum system requirements to use DigiGuide?

▸ Will I need to be online to use DigiGuide?

▸ How can I get new programme listings for DigiGuide?

▸ How can I backup my preferences?

▸ Why doesn't my Logitech Wheel Mouse work with DigiGuide?

▸ What are these DigiGuide cookies doing on my machine?

▸ When I try and edit a print template my computer just opens up the DigiGuide folder.

▸ How do I uninstall DigiGuide For Windows?

Listings Common Questions

▸ When I run DigiGuide I get a "client01.exe" performed an illegal operation.

▸ When I try and get new listings I get a "fetch.exe" performed an illegal operation.

▸ Why am I having problems downloading listings?

▸ Whenever I get new listings I am confronted with an error message. I have recently installed Norton Firewall, could this be the problem?

▸ Why doesn't DigiGuide list the VideoPlus codes?

▸ When I try to update the listings it says everything is up-to-date, but some of the channels' listings aren't up-to-date. What am I doing wrong?

▸ Why are all the programmes in DigiGuide hours earlier or later than they should be?

▸ When I updated the listings it said the files contained a virus! Do your files contain viruses?

Registration Common Questions

▸ I have lost my registration key and have re-installed Windows, how do I find out my key?

▸ My registration key no longer works

▸ When I try and enter my registration key, I get an error message?

▸ Each time I start DigiGuide, I have to re-enter my registration key. Why is this?

Upgrading Common Questions

▸ Ever since I upgraded to v5, I cannot get any listings?

▸ When I run DigiGuide I get a "missing js32.dll" message.

▸ When I start my computer, it runs really slowly then says "no virtual memory left".

▸ When I get listings, DigiGuide reports that "Auto-Update is not responding to registration request startup".

Blooper 45: Variable Vocabulary: Different Words for the Same Thing

A very common blooper that greatly degrades people's ability to learn and use websites and Web-based applications is using different terms for the same concept in different places. It is about the best way possible to confuse people with text.

DigiGuide.com includes a page that answers frequently asked questions. The common name for such a page is "FAQ." On the Customer Support home page, that's what they call it (Figure 6.25[A]). But on the FAQ page itself, it's called a "Knowledgebase" containing "Common Questions" in various categories (Figure 6.25[B]). Visitors to this site can't be sure whether these terms refer to the same thing or not.

Some websites even use different terms for a single concept on the *same page. Erlbaum.com* lets customers find and order books. On the Book Search page, the function was until recently labeled both "search" and "query" (Figure 6.26).

ZBuyer.com provides two adjacent sets of search controls, each with its own button to start the search (Figure 6.27). One of the start buttons is labeled "Search," but the other is labeled "Go." There is no apparent reason for this difference, other than perhaps that the two sets of controls were added by different programmers.

AVOIDING THE BLOOPER

Caroline Jarrett, an authority on user interface and forms design, suggests this design rule for terminology in software and websites:

Same name, same thing; different name, different thing.

This means that terms in websites (and desktop software) should map one-to-one onto concepts. Strictly. Never use

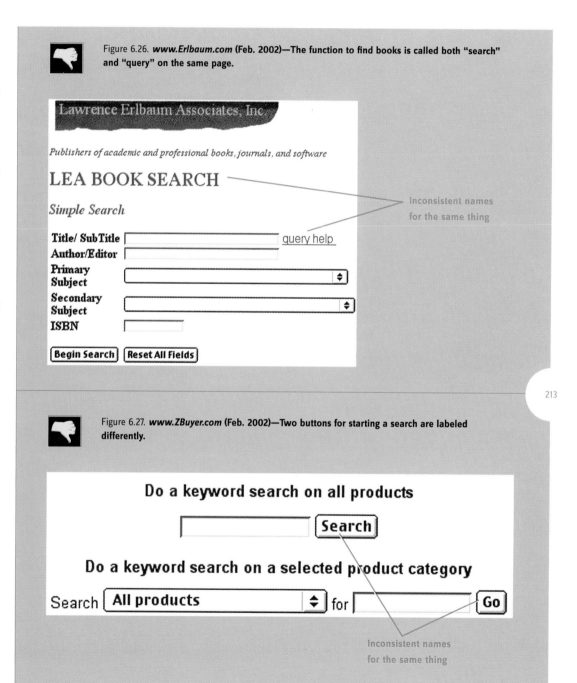

Figure 6.26. *www.Erlbaum.com* (Feb. 2002)—The function to find books is called both "search" and "query" on the same page.

Lawrence Erlbaum Associates, Inc.

Publishers of academic and professional books, journals, and software

LEA BOOK SEARCH

Simple Search

Title/ SubTitle _____ query help
Author/Editor _____
Primary Subject _____
Secondary Subject _____
ISBN _____

Begin Search   Reset All Fields

Inconsistent names for the same thing

Figure 6.27. *www.ZBuyer.com* (Feb. 2002)—Two buttons for starting a search are labeled differently.

Do a keyword search on all products

[   ] Search

Do a keyword search on a selected product category

Search [All products] for [   ] Go

Inconsistent names for the same thing

213

the same term for different concepts, and never use different terms for the same concept.

I'm beginning to repeat myself, but the best way to avoid using inconsistent terms for concepts is to create a site lexicon and enforce it. Enforcing it means assigning someone the job of enforcer. Although that word conjures up images of burly men carrying violin cases, it's better if the enforcer is friendly and well liked. Here's one side of a phone conversation between the designated lexicon enforcer and a programmer:

Hey, Sally, it's Phil. Got a minute? On your pages in our customer-service website, you use the term "bug report" for when customers submit a problem. But our agreed-upon term for that is "action request," remember? That's what we call them everywhere else in the site. It's also what's in the site lexicon. Where's the lexicon? At the project's intranet website. So can you please change "bug report" to "action request" on all your pages? We're running some usability tests on Thursday, so I'm hoping you can make these changes by Wednesday. You will? Great, thank you!

Had DigiGuide's development team created and used a website lexicon, it might have been more evident that the FAQ page should be titled "Frequently Asked Questions." The repeated term "Common Questions" on topic subheadings, instead of being changed to "Frequently Asked Questions," could simply be dropped.

Similarly, use of a site lexicon could fix the *Erlbaum.com* search page (see Figure 6.26) by changing the "query help" link to "Search help" or just plain "Help."

Reconciling the *ZBuyer.com* search controls (see Figure 6.27) is a bit more complicated. A site lexicon would help ensure that both buttons had the same label, but in this case I would suggest simply removing the upper Search box and button. The default value of the lower control's category menu makes it equivalent to the upper control, so two sets of controls aren't needed.

Blooper 46: Inconsistent Style

Related to inconsistent terminology, we have the blooper of inconsistent writing *style*. Many websites and Web applications exhibit stylistic inconsistencies in the text of instructions, link text, product descriptions, buttons labels, page titles, and so on. Common inconsistencies include the following:

> Labeling some links or buttons as actions (verbs or verb phrases) but others as objects (nouns or noun phrases), for example, "Show History" versus "Details"

> Using terse, "telegraphic" language for some form-field labels, for example, "Desired delivery date," but wordy language for others, for example, "Please specify the address to which the flowers are to be delivered"

> Using title case (e.g., "Privacy Policy") for some links, sentence case (e.g., "Investor info") for others, and lower case (e.g., "contact us") for still others

> Ending some but not all sentences (e.g., in instructions or error messages) with periods

While inconsistent writing style may not diminish the usability of a website as much as inconsistent terminology does, it certainly diminishes the impression site visitors get of the company or organization that owns the website.

Some Examples

Figure 6.28 is an excerpt from a form on *FinancialEngines.com*. Are fields in this form labeled with (a) questions, (b) commands, (c) simple nouns, or (d) all of the above? If you answered "d, all of the above," you're right! Why isn't the third field labeled "What is your zip code?" Why isn't the fourth one labeled "What is your e-mail address?"

Alternatively, why aren't the first two and the last one just nouns: "First name," "Last name," "E-mail address"?

Form fields should be labeled as briefly and simply as possible. In this example, all should be labeled as simple nouns, as "Zip code" is.

The Association for Computing Machinery's website, *ACM.org,* is fairly consistent in its writing style, but in a few places there are glaring inconsistencies. One such place is on the site's Search page. In addition to the usual search controls, the site offers several specialized searches, which search specific information sources or archives (Figure 6.29). The problem is that the wording of the links to these different searches is inconsistent.

Three of the links identify their information resource as belonging to ACM, for example, "Search the ACM Portal Now"; two don't, for example, "Search the Online Guide Now." Presumably, these are all ACM information resources, so it isn't really necessary to include "ACM" in the links. However, if they really wanted to mention ACM, they should have included it in *all* of these links. Furthermore, the first three links end with the word "Now," such as "Search the ACM Digital Library Now." The last two links don't say "Now"; does that mean that they don't search when you click on them, but sometime *later?* There is no apparent reason for these inconsistencies in writing; they were probably just added at different times by different people, with no oversight to maintain consistent writing style.

Many websites list product or topic categories. Often, category names are links to the indicated page or section. Such labels should be written in a consistent style but often are not. *ZBuyer.com* provides an example of inconsistent

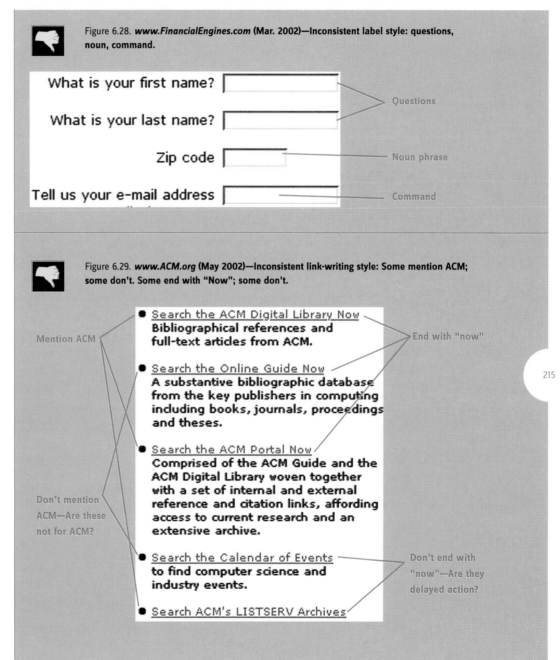

Figure 6.28. *www.FinancialEngines.com* (Mar. 2002)—Inconsistent label style: questions, noun, command.

Figure 6.29. *www.ACM.org* (May 2002)—Inconsistent link-writing style: Some mention ACM; some don't. Some end with "Now"; some don't.

215

Figure 6.30. **www.ZBuyer.com (Mar. 2002)—Inconsistent label style: simple nouns, noun phrases, proper names, sentences.**

- Camera & Photo
- Products
- See all our Canon binoculars
- See all Night Owl gear

- astronomy and birding titles
- See more Education & How-To software
- Really Cool Stuff
- Michael Lewis

- Binocular glossary
- Telescope glossary
- Binocular buying guide
- Telescope buying guide

Figure 6.31. **www.AmericanExpress.com (Jan. 2002)—Inconsistent capitalization used in A: labels on trip preference controls and B: link text.**

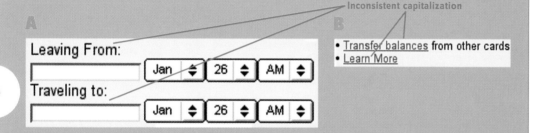

Inconsistent capitalization

A

B

Leaving From:

| Jan ▲▼ | 26 ▲▼ | AM ▲▼ |

Traveling to:

| Jan ▲▼ | 26 ▲▼ | AM ▲▼ |

- Transfer balances from other cards
- Learn More

Figure 6.32. **www.ZBuyer.com (Feb. 2002)—Inconsistent capitalization of link labels.**

- Camera & Photo
- Products
- See all digital camera bundles
- See all Olympus cameras
- See all Kodak digital cameras

- Camera & Photo Travel store
- Editor's Recommendations
- An Introduction to Digital Photography
- Digital Camera Buying Guide

- Ask the Editor: How Many Pixels Do I Need?
- Digital Camera Definitions
- Recommended Digital Camera Accessories
- graphics software

product category names (Figure 6.30). Chapter 1 discusses the oddness of some of the categories in this list. In this chapter, the focus is on writing style.

Some categories are simple nouns such as "Camera & Photo" and "Products." Others are sentences such as "See all our Night Owl gear." Another includes the word "titles." These links appear to have been written by different people, with no guidelines for how category links should be written, no management oversight over the result, and no recognition of the unprofessional impression such a hodge-podge of writing styles conveys to customers.

Inconsistent Capitalization

One aspect of writing style is how text is capitalized. A surprisingly large number of websites seem to pay no attention to capitalization. New text is often added without regard for what is already in the site.

Consider two examples from *AmericanExpress.com*. In one example, one of two similar labels uses title case, and the other uses sentence case (Figure 6.31[A]). In the other example, two similar links are capitalized differently (Figure 6.31[B]).

Similar inconsistency in capitalization style can be seen at ZBuyer (Figure 6.32). These links were probably added at different times by different people, with no site stylebook for guidance, no management oversight, and no effort to check how already present links were capitalized. ZBuyer's parent company, *Amazon.com,* whose site does follow strict capitalization rules, should consider making those rules company-wide.

AVOIDING THE BLOOPER

The rules for achieving stylistic consistency in a website's text are as follows:

> *Develop or adopt a style guide.* The *Chicago Manual of Style* (Grossman 1993) is a classic style reference for print publishers. Although it lacks guidelines for many aspects of designing websites, its guidelines for text are just as applicable to the Web as to print media. A style guide designed specifically for the Web is the *Yale Web Style Guide* (Lynch and Horton 2002), which is a good one to use if your organization has none of its own. It is available both as a printed book and on the Web at *info.med.yale.edu/caim/manual/index.html*. Brinck, Gergle, and Wood (2001), in their chapter on writing for the Web, provide a brief example of a style guide.

> *Put a writer in charge of reviewing all text on the site.* One person should oversee all the non–user-contributed text on the site, and that person should be a writer or editor. In addition to that person, a development manager should be responsible for general site quality and usability.

> *Look at what's already there when adding new text.* Don't add new links, messages, commands, or instructions without paying attention to how similar ones already on the site are written.

Capitalization

Achieving consistency in the text on a website may seem like a trivial concern. However, it isn't. Committing this blooper—or the next one, Blooper 47: Typos and Grammos: Sloppy Writing—conveys to users of your site that your organization is careless, inattentive to detail, and semiliterate. That's a bad impression to give if you want the visitor to become a customer, member, or repeated user.

The four styles of capitalizing text are as follows:

> *Sentence case:* The initial word is capitalized, with everything else in lower case except proper names and acronyms.

> *Title Case:* All words start with capital letters except articles (e.g., "a," "an," "the"), conjunctions (e.g., "or," "and"), and prepositions (e.g., "in," "after," "below").

> *lower case:* All letters are in lower case.

> *UPPER CASE:* All letters are in upper case.

Capitalization styles should be used consistently within a website. This doesn't mean all text should use the same capitalization style. Text serves many different roles: site title, page title, category heading, instruction, product description, textual content, link label, button label, error message, mouse-over tool-tip, and more. How text should be capitalized depends on the role it serves. Titles should of course be in title case. Prose text should be in sentence case.

However, many of the other roles for text have no predetermined capitalization style. For example, for navigation links and button labels, Web designers are free to define capitalization style rules however they like. The bottom line is that text that serves a particular role should be capitalized consistently.

Blooper 47: Typos and Grammos: Sloppy Writing

Even if the writing at a website isn't geeky and inconsistent, it may still be careless and awkward—in a word, sloppy. When use of the Internet and Web began to explode in the mid-1990s, some pundits predicted a renaissance of writing skills, as more and more people began writing emails, participating in chat rooms, creating Web pages, and so on. Instead, we seem to be seeing how many

217

Figure 6.33. *www.ValcoElectronics.com* (Jan. 2002)—**A:** FAQ page: Questions 4 through 6 are ungrammatical, and answer 5 has a typo. **B:** The Product page has a spelling error.

A   Sloppy writing

VALCO ELECTRONICS.COM 1-800-673-2244
ONLINE STORE   1-337-546-0090

HOME | CATALOG | WHATS NEW | F.A.Q. | TRACK A PACKAGE

Established in 1973

Have a look at our **Specials!** Please read our **Shipping Policy**.
Chat Live with our Sales Representatives via Yahoo Instant Messenger Service
Add valcoweb and valcotronics to your friends list.

Listed below are frequently asked questions.

✦ *How much freight will be added to my order ?*

We only charge what UPS or the USPO will charge to process your order. When your package is ready to ship it is placed on a UPS scale the freight charge is automatically included into your bill. We can give you an accurate estimate if you provide us with your zip code.

✦ *Do you mail out catalogs?*

In order to continue to bring you the best possible prices we only issue catalogs to our dealers. We carry many accessories which are currently not on our WebPages, just give us a call and we will be happy to help answer any questions you may have. 1-800-673-2244

✦ *What payment methods do you accept ?*

We accept all Major credit cards and money orders.

✦ *I live in another country can you ship to me, do I have to pay import taxes and how long will it take to get my order ?*

Yes we can ship out of the US. Import Taxes are different for each country, check with your local government on import taxes, you are responsible for any extra taxes or fees added to your order by your government. To ship out of country can take anywhere from 2 to 4 weeks to receive your order. View our international information page, click here.

✦ *I live in the US do I have to pay sales tax on my order ?*

Only persons living in Louisiana or subject to sales tax.

✦ *I am nervous about ordering from the internet what assurance can you give me.*

We have been in business since 1973 . We ship packages all over the world to customers like yourself. We can provide you with your package tracking number, so you can track your package from the time it leaves our warehouse till the time it reaches your door. We can understand why people and companies are willing to show the entire world how quasi-literate and careless they are.

One example comes from *ValcoElectronics.com*'s FAQ page (Figure 6.33[A]). For the moment, ignore the page's odd, hard-to-scan formatting. Notice instead the ungrammatical run-on sentences in the fourth, fifth, and sixth questions, such as, "I live in the US do I have to pay sales tax on my order?" Notice the misspelling in the answer to question five: "Only persons living in Louisiana or [sic] subject to sales tax." A product page at the same site contains a blatant spelling error (Figure 6.33[B]).

Whatever language or languages a website targets, the text in it should be written—or at least edited—by skilled writers of that language. Since Valco is clearly targeting English-speaking customers, text in its site should have been written or checked by people trained to write well in English.

Poor writing can also be seen at *Connectix.com*. The site's instructions for upgrading Connectix's product Virtual PC from Windows 95 to Windows 98 contain several grammatical and typographical errors (Figure 6.34), such as "more then suggested." Connectix may use technical writers and copy editors to write software manuals, but it apparently does not use them to write website text.

It would not be surprising to find sloppy writing on someone's personal website of baby pictures or vacation stories. What is surprising is poorly proofread, poorly written text on websites of well-known companies, organizations, and institutions. Even the prestigious U.S. National Academies, which includes the U.S. National Academy of Sciences and National Research Council, is not immune (Figure 6.35).

Figure 6.34. *www.Connectix.com* (Feb. 2002)—Poor writing and capitalization: "reason why," "more then suggested," product name "windows" not capitalized.

Sloppy writing

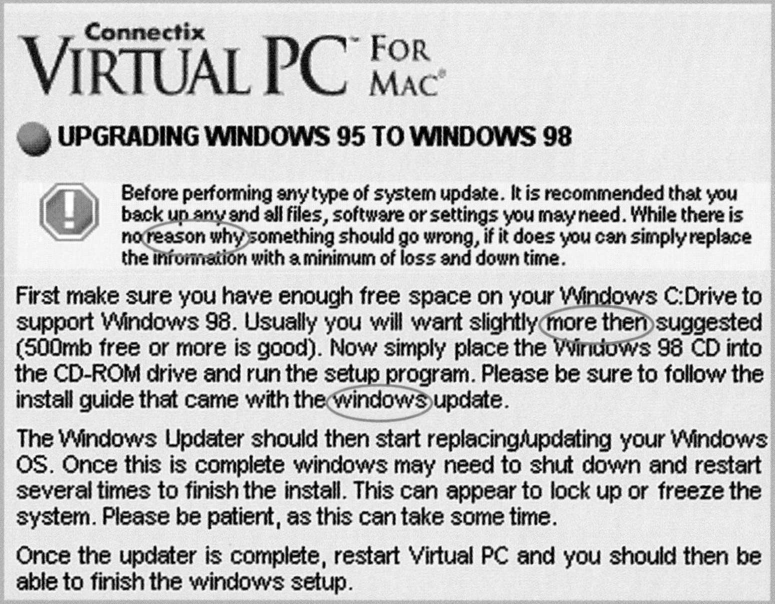

Figure 6.35. *www.NationalAcademies.org* (Apr. 2002)—Typo: "The web site that you have requested does not exit."

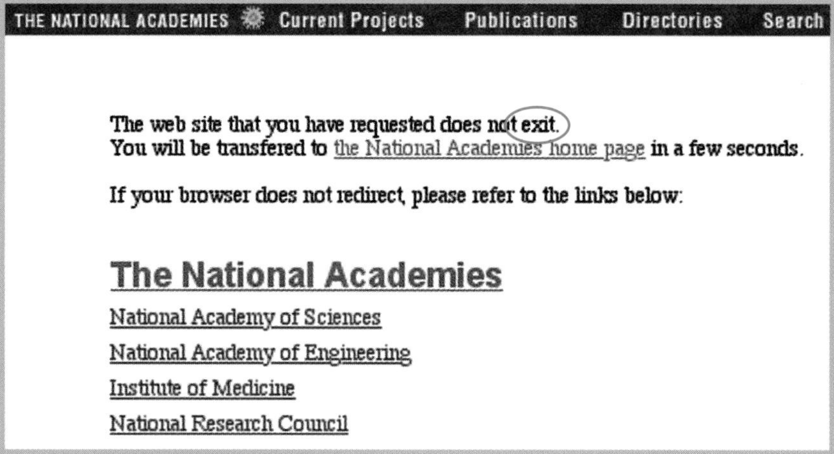

219

AVOIDING THE BLOOPER

Sloppy writing at a website is a surface-level blooper that is usually caused by two deeper bloopers:

> *Management blooper:* assigning the job of writing website text to people unskilled at writing in the target language

> *Process blooper:* failing to proofread and edit all text in the site: content, button labels, links, tool-tips, menu items, error messages—all text

To avoid committing the "sloppy writing" blooper, make sure your organization doesn't commit the underlying management and process bloopers. Assign the job of writing website text to people who are trained to write well: technical writers and editors. Then leave time to review and improve the text before putting the site up on the Web.

If the writing on your website is sloppy, people will notice it, and the impression they will have of your company or organization won't be good. That's why you want to pay attention to this. If the writing on the site is good, your reward will be that people won't notice it.

CHAPTER 7

LINK APPEARANCE BLOOPERS

The next chapter discusses bloopers in the graphic design and layout of websites—how they are presented. Before we get to those, let's examine a specific type of graphic design bloopers: those concerning how *links* are presented. Links may be the most important aspect of the Web: They are the primary form of navigation. They are what makes it a web.

If links are the primary form of navigation on the Web, shouldn't link-presentation bloopers be considered a special type of *navigation* blooper? Yes. But didn't we just say link-presentation bloopers are a type of *graphic design* blooper? Yes, we did. There is no contradiction. Link-presentation bloopers are simultaneously graphic design bloopers and navigation bloopers. That is why link-presentation bloopers warrant their own chapter.

Blooper 48: Links Don't Look Like Links

Because links are the primary means of navigating on the Web, Web users should be able to tell what is a link and what is not. This is based on a more general design principle: Users of interactive systems should be able to tell at a glance what can be manipulated and what cannot.

Here, I discuss links that because of poor presentation mislead people into believing they are *not* links. The next blooper covers *non*-links that because of poor presentation mislead people into believing they *are* links.

Textual Links

All Web users and designers know the convention for displaying textual links: underlined, preferably in blue or a similar color. However, some websites ignore this convention. Let's look at some examples.

At *Stanford.edu*, textual links are not underlined. Instead, they are displayed in a bold, red font (Figure 7.1[A]). This is already a problem, because most Web users won't immediately recognize the red text as links. However, it gets worse: Non-link text is emphasized by making it—you guessed it—bold and red (Figure 7.1[B]). Users of *Stanford.edu* won't be able to tell links from emphasized non-links.

Poorly marked links can also be seen at *Monterey.com* and *WisconSUN.org*. At *Monterey.com*, the link "Site Guide" appears in a unique font (Figure 7.2[A]). It looks neither like other links nor like a heading. At *WisconSUN.org*, the links appear in blue but are not underlined (Figure 7.2[B]). They stand out less than the yellow headings above them, which aren't links.

A slightly different form of the blooper can be seen at the website of Wiesner Brothers (Figure 7.3). In the line of contact information at the bottom of the site's home page,

Figure 7.1. **www.*Stanford.edu* (Jan. 2002)—A:** Textual links not underlined; marked in bold, red font. **B:** Non-link text emphasized in bold, red font.

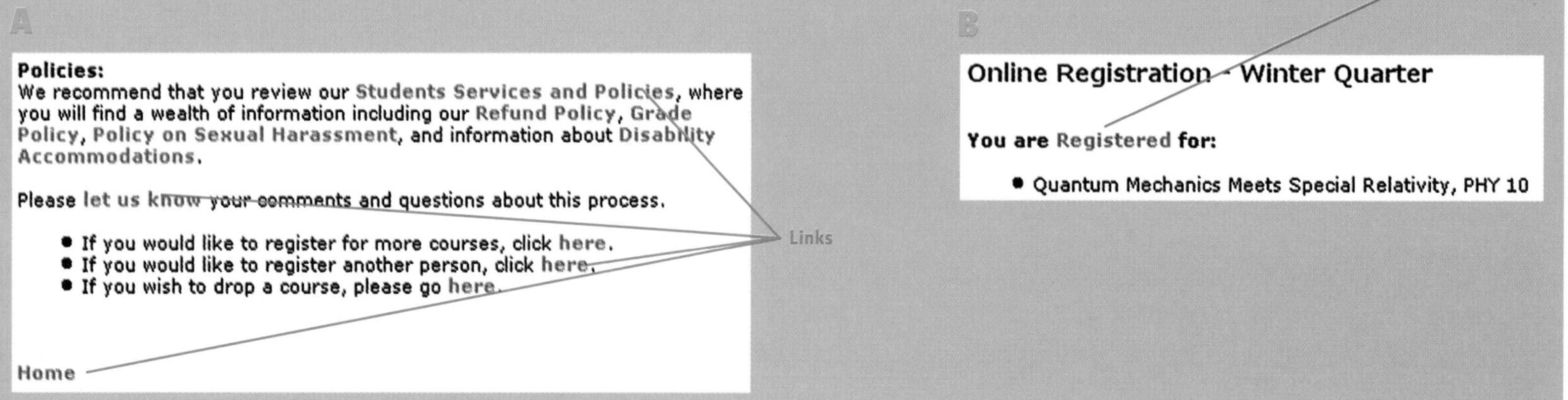

A

Policies:
We recommend that you review our Students Services and Policies, where you will find a wealth of information including our Refund Policy, Grade Policy, Policy on Sexual Harassment, and information about Disability Accommodations.

Please let us know your comments and questions about this process.

- If you would like to register for more courses, click here.
- If you would like to register another person, click here.
- If you wish to drop a course, please go here.

Home

Links

B

Not a link

Online Registration – Winter Quarter

You are Registered **for:**

- Quantum Mechanics Meets Special Relativity, PHY 10

Figure 7.2. **Unclear links—A: *www.Monterey.com* (Jan. 2002) "Site Guide" link is in a unique font, unlike other links. B: *www.WisconSUN.org* (Jan. 2002) Links are blue but not underlined. They are easy to miss.**

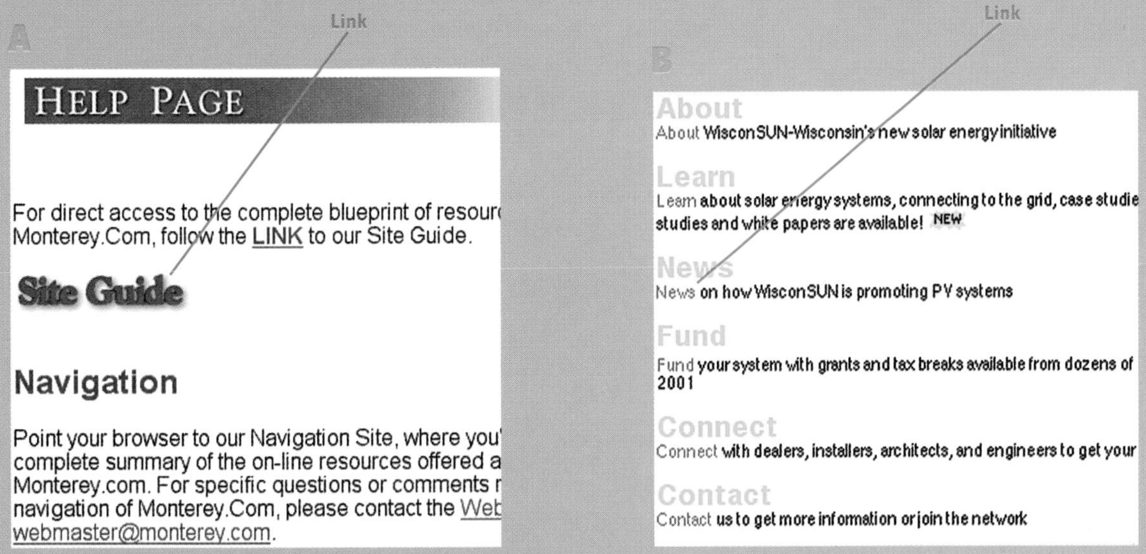

A

Link

HELP PAGE

For direct access to the complete blueprint of resourc[e]
Monterey.Com, follow the LINK to our Site Guide.

Site Guide

Navigation

Point your browser to our Navigation Site, where you'
complete summary of the on-line resources offered a
Monterey.com. For specific questions or comments r
navigation of Monterey.Com, please contact the Web
webmaster@monterey.com.

B

Link

About
About WisconSUN-Wisconsin's new solar energy initiative

Learn
Learn about solar energy systems, connecting to the grid, case studie
studies and white papers are available! NEW

News
News on how WisconSUN is promoting PV systems

Fund
Fund your system with grants and tax breaks available from dozens of
2001

Connect
Connect with dealers, installers, architects, and engineers to get your

Contact
Contact us to get more information or join the network

Figure 7.3. ***www.WiesnerBros.com* (Feb. 2002)—Address and email address are links but are poorly marked.**

Link

2402 Victory Blvd. Staten Island, NY 10314 [click here for driving directions]   (718) 761.5141 fax (718) 698.6294   info@wiesnerbros.com

nothing is underlined to mark it as a link. The street address (and the "click here" text following it) and the email address are links, but it takes peering closely at the small line of text to determine that (see Blooper 52: "Click <u>Here</u>": Burying Links in Text, in this chapter).

At *Stanford.edu, WisconSUN.org,* and *WiesnerBros.com,* the links are encoded as ordinary link tags, but with attributes set to inhibit the default underlining and color. At *Monterey.com,* an image of text was used in place of a textual link. Why? A common excuse is that the default appearance of textual links clashes with the page's graphic design and color scheme. In other words, usability is often sacrificed for the sake of better graphic appearance. In my opinion, usability is more important than graphic appearance. However, even if we concede that graphic design considerations sometimes trump usability, one would have to make the case that the graphic appearance actually benefited from the trade-off. Except for the WiesnerBros site, I don't think it did. Thus, for at least three of these examples, usability was sacrificed for nothing.

Graphical Links

Graphical links can be "disguised" as non-links just as textual links can. By default, image links are surrounded by a blue border. In many websites, the blue border is turned off. Again, the usual excuse is that the blue border messes up the visual design. Never mind that turning the border off leaves users with few hints that the image is a link.[22]

As an example, look at these product offerings at *Amazon.com* (Figure 7.4). The pictures are links, but that isn't apparent from how they appear. In this case, the image links go to the same page as the nearby underlined textual link, so the consequences of this blooper aren't terrible. If, however, the images were the *only* links to their respective pages, the consequences of the blooper would be more serious, because some users would never find the pages to which the images link.

Buttons

Most "buttons" displayed on the Web are actually just image links or image maps divided into link areas. Only a small proportion of buttons on the Web are actual button controls, such as the standard browser form-submit buttons. Thus, Web buttons can easily be designed poorly, so they don't look like buttons.

As an example, consider *HotelDiscount.com.* Customers specify when they need a hotel room and what sort of room they want, and then send the site off to search for suitable

224

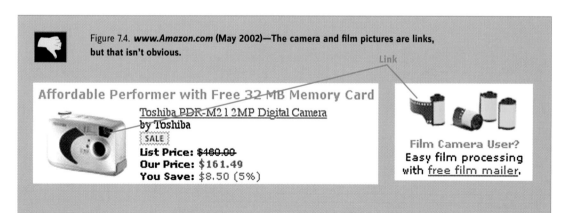

Figure 7.4. *www.Amazon.com* (May 2002)—The camera and film pictures are links, but that isn't obvious.

[22]The only hint is the cursor's changing shape, which most Web users don't notice.

rooms (Figure 7.5). I wonder how many visitors to this site set the search controls and then waste several seconds trying to find a "Go" or "Search" button. By a process of elimination, users might figure out that the blue area labeled "Display ONLY Available Hotels" must be the Search button. The odd label doesn't help: There is no option to display *un*available hotels, even if that somehow made sense.

AVOIDING THE BLOOPER

One could argue that Web users can distinguish links from non-links by watching the shape of the cursor as they move it around the screen. But that ignores the fact that most Web users, especially nontechnically trained ones, don't watch the cursor or notice changes in its shape. Furthermore, it is bad user-interface design to require users to move the pointer over components to check whether they are clickable. User interfaces, including websites and Web applications, should make the clickability of screen components obvious at first glance.

The easiest—and usually best—way to ensure that links look like links is to follow the conventions.

Underline Textual Links, Preferably in Blue

Amazon.com's home page shows how it should be done (Figure 7.6). There is no mistaking any of the textual links on this page. Even though *Amazon* uses other color schemes on other pages, the link colors remain the same: blue for not-yet-followed ones, magenta for already-followed ones. Usability is more important here than preserving a color scheme.

Graphical Buttons Should Look Like Buttons

Buttons constructed from images should look clearly like buttons. *Monterey.com* may not display textual links clearly (see Figure 7.2[A]), but buttons on its home page do look like buttons (Figure 7.7).

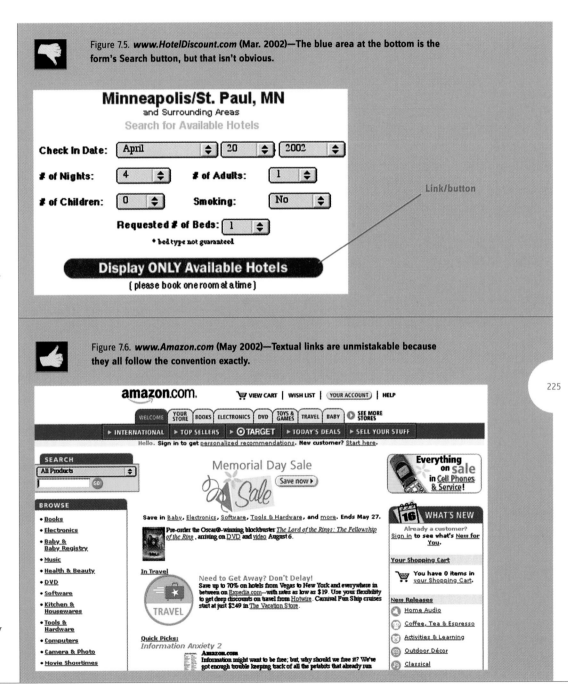

Figure 7.5. ***www.HotelDiscount.com*** (Mar. 2002)—The blue area at the bottom is the form's Search button, but that isn't obvious.

Link/button

Figure 7.6. ***www.Amazon.com*** (May 2002)—Textual links are unmistakable because they all follow the convention exactly.

225

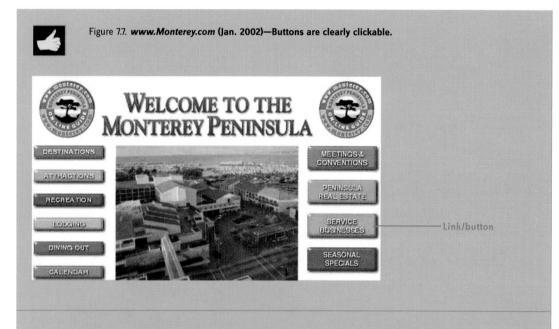

Figure 7.7. **www.Monterey.com (Jan. 2002)—Buttons are clearly clickable.**

Link/button

Figure 7.8. **Image links marked as links. A: www.ACM.org/sigchi (Nov. 2000)—Image with border is a link; other images aren't links. B: www.Sears.com (Nov. 2000)—Instructions above the array of images indicate that the images are links.**

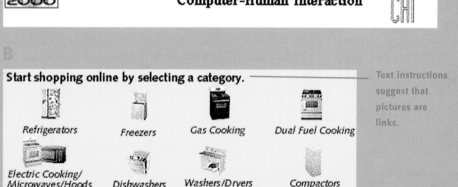

A

Link

Not a link

B

Text instructions suggest that pictures are links.

Other Image Links Should Be Marked as Links

Image links that aren't buttons, such as photographs, should be marked as links. One way is to *display* them with the default blue border, as *ACM.org* does (Figure 7.8[A]). Another way is to *label* them as links, as *Sears.com* used to (Figure 7.8[B]), but unfortunately no longer does.

Blooper 49: Non-Links Look Like Links

Having discussed the blooper of links not looking like links, we now turn to the opposite blooper: non-links looking like links. It's not clear which one is worse. Not letting people know where to click makes them miss things they might have found useful. Fooling them into clicking on things that aren't clickable wastes people's time and annoys them.

Underlined Non-Link Text

Because textual links on the Web are usually marked by underlining the link text, the most obvious way to trick Web users into clicking on text that isn't a link is to <u>underline it</u>. The text needn't even be blue to attract clicks: Even though blue is the usual color for links, textual links on the Web vary enough in color that experienced Web users tend to assume that *anything* underlined is a link.

At *Dice.com*, a job-hunting website, text headings are underlined. If the heading is a link, the underlining is red; otherwise, it is black (Figure 7.9). This may seem reasonable, but since 10% of men have some sort of color blindness, it is unwise to use simple color differences to mark important distinctions (see Chapter 8, Blooper 58: Shades of Beige: Color Differences Too Subtle).

Figure 7.9. **www.Dice.com** (Jan. 2002)—**A:** Headings that are links are red and underlined. **B:** Headings that are not links are black and underlined, creating potential for users to mistake them for links.

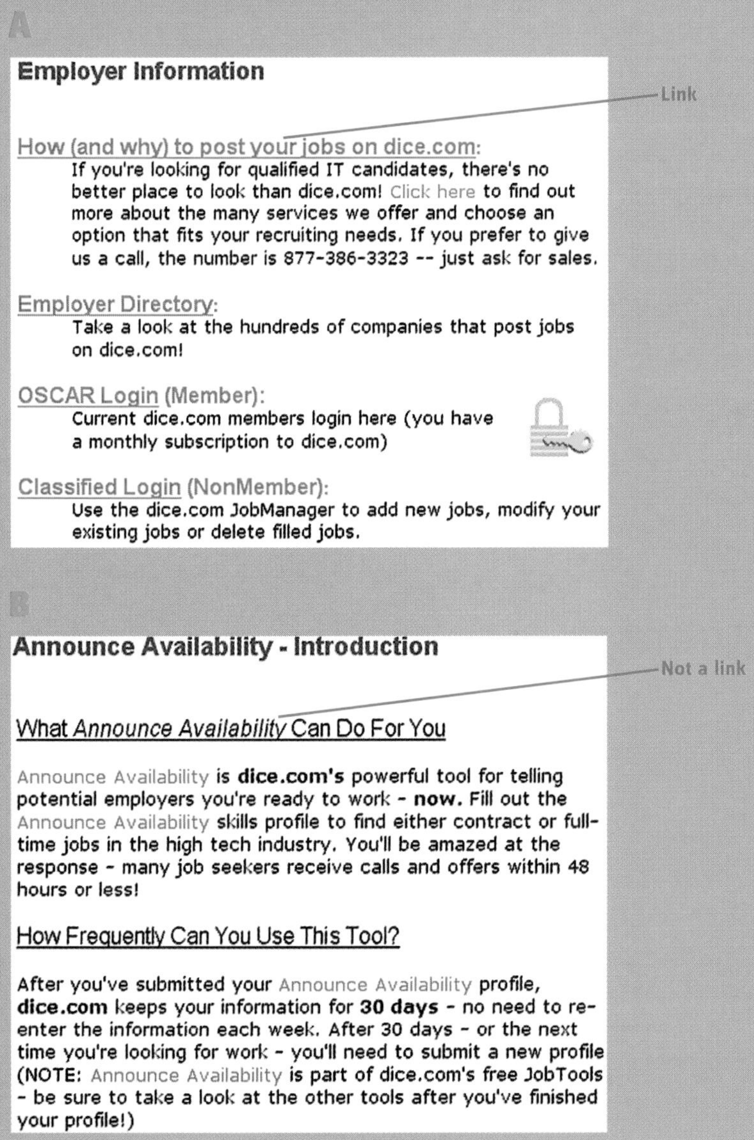

A

Employer Information

Link

How (and why) to post your jobs on dice.com:
If you're looking for qualified IT candidates, there's no better place to look than dice.com! Click here to find out more about the many services we offer and choose an option that fits your recruiting needs. If you prefer to give us a call, the number is 877-386-3323 -- just ask for sales.

Employer Directory:
Take a look at the hundreds of companies that post jobs on dice.com!

OSCAR Login (Member):
Current dice.com members login here (you have a monthly subscription to dice.com)

Classified Login (NonMember):
Use the dice.com JobManager to add new jobs, modify your existing jobs or delete filled jobs.

B

Announce Availability - Introduction

Not a link

What *Announce Availability* Can Do For You

Announce Availability is **dice.com's** powerful tool for telling potential employers you're ready to work - **now.** Fill out the Announce Availability skills profile to find either contract or full-time jobs in the high tech industry. You'll be amazed at the response - many job seekers receive calls and offers within 48 hours or less!

How Frequently Can You Use This Tool?

After you've submitted your Announce Availability **profile, dice.com** keeps your information for **30 days** - no need to re-enter the information each week. After 30 days - or the next time you're looking for work - you'll need to submit a new profile (**NOTE:** Announce Availability is part of dice.com's free JobTools - be sure to take a look at the other tools after you've finished your profile!)

Misleading underlined non-link text is sometimes found in documents that were repurposed from print media to Web pages without adjustments for the Web medium. An example is a book review from *Dr. Dobb's Journal* that was put on its website (Figure 7.10). The irony is that underlining book titles is a leftover from typewriters, which were incapable of italics. It is no longer necessary, even in print media.

Underlined non-links are also seen in text written specifically for the Web. *Enron.com* and *UPAssoc.org* both underline some of the headings at their websites in *blue,* much like links are marked (Figure 7.11). Some visitors to these sites will mistake the headings for links.

Graphics Look Clickable, but Aren't

If graphic images attract users' clicks but aren't really clickable, we have another form of the "Non-Links Look Like Links" blooper. Like underlined text, graphical elements having a button-like shape and/or a 3D appearance will appear to most Web users to be clickable "buttons."

Examples of misleading 3D graphics can be seen at the websites of the Comdex computer conference and Galor, a software company. On *Comdex.com's* home page (Figure 7.12[A]), the topic headings on the left side (e.g., "Upcoming Events") look like clickable buttons but are not. They are just display graphics intended to make the head-

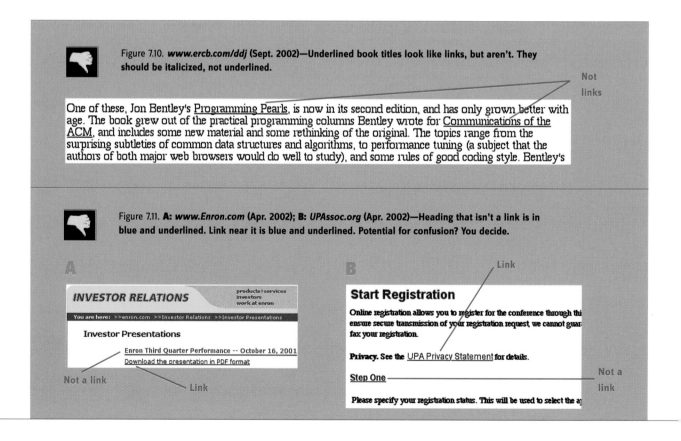

Figure 7.10. ***www.ercb.com/ddj*** (Sept. 2002)—Underlined book titles look like links, but aren't. They should be italicized, not underlined.

Not links

One of these, Jon Bentley's Programming Pearls, is now in its second edition, and has only grown better with age. The book grew out of the practical programming columns Bentley wrote for Communications of the ACM, and includes some new material and some rethinking of the original. The topics range from the surprising subtleties of common data structures and algorithms, to performance tuning (a subject that the authors of both major web browsers would do well to study), and some rules of good coding style. Bentley's

Figure 7.11. **A: *www.Enron.com* (Apr. 2002); B: *UPAssoc.org* (Apr. 2002)—Heading that isn't a link is in blue and underlined. Link near it is blue and underlined. Potential for confusion? You decide.**

A

INVESTOR RELATIONS products+services investors work at enron

You are here: >>enron.com >>Investor Relations >>Investor Presentations

Investor Presentations

Enron Third Quarter Performance -- October 16, 2001
Download the presentation in PDF format

Not a link
Link

B

Link

Start Registration

Online registration allows you to register for the conference through thi ensure secure transmission of your registration request, we cannot guar: fax your registration.

Privacy. See the UPA Privacy Statement for details.

Step One

Not a link

Please specify your registration status. This will be used to select the a

ings stand out. Similarly, the "Comdex Fall Countdown" heading is not a button. Home and Register *are* buttons. *Galor.com's* splash page (Figure 7.12[B]) has four "icons" that look like separate buttons but aren't. Together, they simply make up the company logo.

Similarly, *Dice.com* has an area on the left (headed in yellow) that looks like a secondary navigation bar subordinate to the top row of tabs (Figure 7.13). However, it isn't a secondary navigation bar; it's just a table of contents for the article on the right. Nothing on it is a link.

Graphic images that aren't links can attract clicks even without looking button-like or 3D. An example is *OfficeMax.com*. The "Browse" navigation bar on the left of product-category pages uses a magnifying glass icon to indicate that side-by-side product comparisons are available for certain product categories (Figure 7.14). However, at the bottom of the list is the same icon, with the same size and color saturation and the label "Click this icon to see a side-by-side comparison." Visitors to this site might take this instruction literally, clicking the inactive legend rather than the real icon.

AVOIDING THE BLOOPER

Web designers can avoid non-links that look like links by following two simple rules:

> Don't underline non-links.

> Deemphasize nonclickable graphics.

Don't Underline Non-Links

On the Web, only links should be underlined. Don't underline textual headings. Don't use underlining for ordinary emphasis. Don't assume that color alone is enough to distinguish link underlining from "ordinary" underlining.

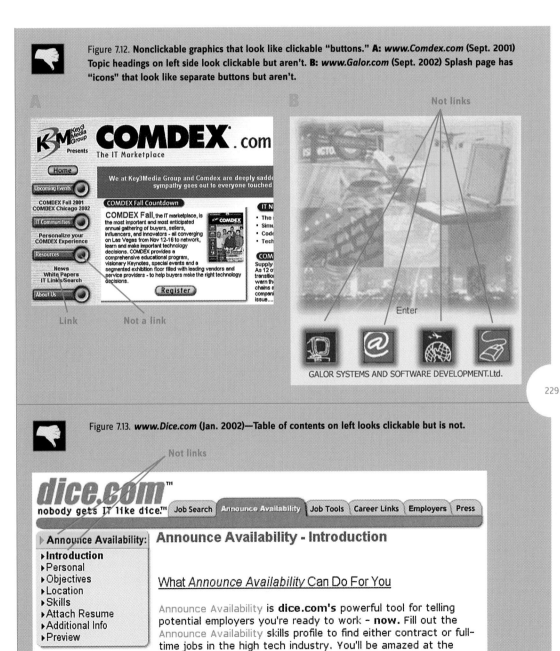

Figure 7.12. **Nonclickable graphics that look like clickable "buttons." A:** *www.Comdex.com* **(Sept. 2001) Topic headings on left side look clickable but aren't. B:** *www.Galor.com* **(Sept. 2002) Splash page has "icons" that look like separate buttons but aren't.**

Figure 7.13. *www.Dice.com* **(Jan. 2002)—Table of contents on left looks clickable but is not.**

229

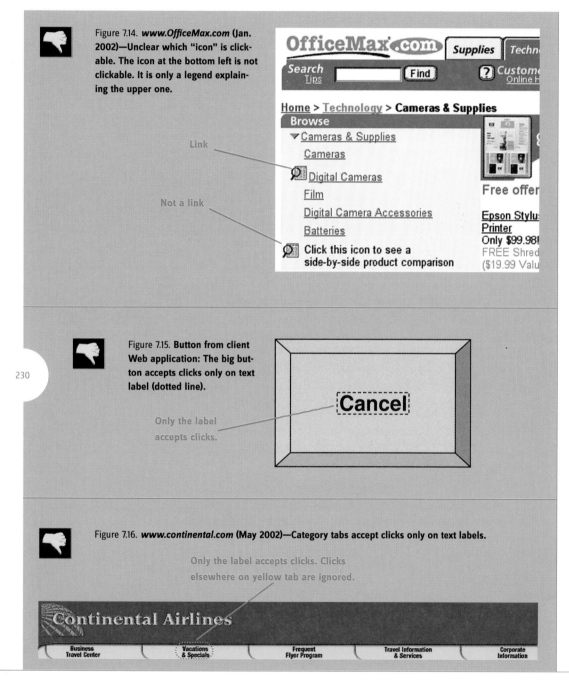

Figure 7.14. ***www.OfficeMax.com*** **(Jan. 2002)—Unclear which "icon" is clickable. The icon at the bottom left is not clickable. It is only a legend explaining the upper one.**

Link

Not a link

Figure 7.15. **Button from client Web application: The big button accepts clicks only on text label (dotted line).**

Only the label accepts clicks.

Figure 7.16. ***www.continental.com*** **(May 2002)—Category tabs accept clicks only on text labels.**

Only the label accepts clicks. Clicks elsewhere on yellow tab are ignored.

When text written for other media—print, electronic documents—is "repurposed" for the Web, the conversion process should include changing underlined text to use other means of emphasizing text, such as HTML's `<EM>` or `<STRONG>` tags or emphasis styles. In printed text, titles of publications such as books and periodicals are often underlined, but only when italics is unavailable. Because italics is available on the Web, publication titles should be underlined only if they are links.

Don't Make Non-Links 3D

Graphic elements that are not clickable should not appear three dimensional (3D). On-screen items that are 3D attract clicks very strongly.

Blooper 50: Bizarre Buttons: Click Target Smaller than It Seems

A few years ago, a company asked me to review the user interface of an intranet Web application it had developed. I did and found an interesting problem: The application had large buttons all over its pages, but those buttons accepted clicks only directly on the (small) text labels in the middle of the buttons (Figure 7.15). Clicks anywhere else on the buttons were ignored.

I explained that users would *hate* these buttons, and some would have trouble hitting the label. I advised the company to change the buttons to accept clicks over their entire area. The developers resisted, claiming that the toolkit they were using wouldn't let them fix the problem, and that users would "get used to it."

I doubted users would get used to it, because most other on-screen buttons they encounter—on the Web and elsewhere—allow clicking anywhere on the button. Not to mention that the small labels were much harder to hit than the buttons. I appealed to management, and eventually the bizarre buttons were fixed.

Since then, this blooper has grown increasingly common on the Web and in intranet Web applications.

For example, Continental Airlines' website has tabs at the top of its home page for navigating to the site's functional areas (Figure 7.16). As in many websites, the tab width adjusts according to the width of the visitor's browser window. However, only the text labels of the tabs respond to mouse-over and mouse-clicks.

RealEstate.com exhibits an even more misleading form of the blooper. In the Quick Find navigation bar on the left of the home page (Figure 7.17), the "buttons" change color when the cursor is over any part of them, strongly suggesting that the entire button is clickable. However, only the text labels on the buttons accept clicks.

Adding to the confusion, the links in the home page's *top* navigation bar *don't* have the blooper: They respond to clicks anywhere inside their black box. So users can click anywhere on the buttons in the top navigation bar but have to hit the text labels in the Quick Find bar. Got that? There's more: On *other* pages in the site, the top navigation bar *does* commit the blooper, by accepting clicks only exactly on the button labels (Figure 7.18). This sort of inconsistency can easily occur if each navigation bar is implemented by a different programmer, with no coordination between them.

Until *RealEstate.com* is purged of this blooper or at least is made consistent regarding where users can click, its visitors will have trouble remembering which navigation bar works which way.

This blooper can be seen at *many* other websites: *Acer.com, SDExpo.com, CRLA.net, CSMonitor.com, RitzCameras.com,*

Figure 7.17. *www.RealEstate.com* (Sept. 2002)—**A:** Quick Find "buttons" accept clicks only on text labels; those in top navigation bar accept clicks anywhere in box. **B:** Quick Find "buttons" change color when pointer enters any part of the "button."

Accepts clicks anywhere in box

Changes color when pointer is over any part of "button"

Accepts clicks only directly on label

Figure 7.18. *www.RealEstate.com* (Sept. 2002)—Navigation "buttons" across top accept clicks only on the text labels.

Accepts clicks only directly on label

231

Figure 7.19. **This navigation bar follows the blooper recipe.**

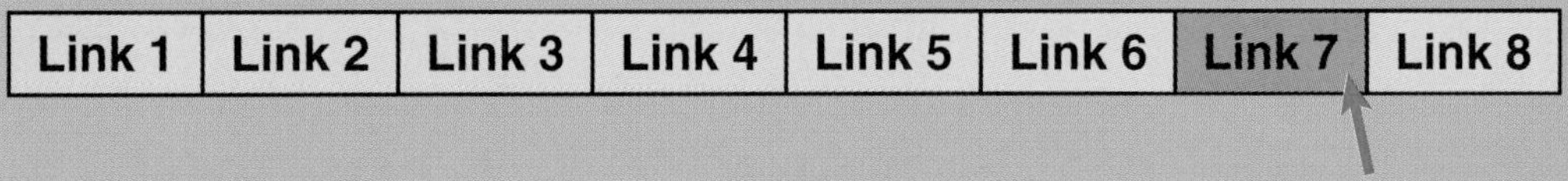

| Link 1 | Link 2 | Link 3 | Link 4 | Link 5 | Link 6 | Link 7 | Link 8 |

Figure 7.20. **These navigation bars don't follow the blooper recipe. A: Links not enclosed in visible table cells. B: Links not completely enclosed. C: Links enclosed but underlined as links.**

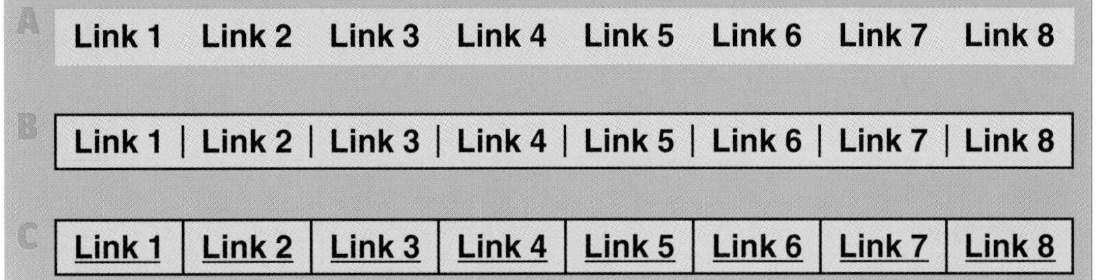

A Link 1   Link 2   Link 3   Link 4   Link 5   Link 6   Link 7   Link 8

B | Link 1 | Link 2 | Link 3 | Link 4 | Link 5 | Link 6 | Link 7 | Link 8 |

C | Link 1 | Link 2 | Link 3 | Link 4 | Link 5 | Link 6 | Link 7 | Link 8 |

Figure 7.21. **www.IRS.gov (Sept. 2002)—Top navigation bar links are underlined and not individually boxed.**

Internal Revenue Service The Digital Daily

DEPARTMENT OF THE TREASURY

Tax Stats | About IRS | Careers | FOIA | The Newsroom | Accessibility | Site Map | Español | Help

to name only a few. In some cases, the misleading user-interface component is simulated buttons; in others, it's simulated tabs.

Recipe for the Blooper

This blooper usually occurs in navigation bars constructed from HTML tables containing text links. This is a simple and therefore common way to construct a navigation bar. Each text link is in its own cell of the table (Figure 7.19). In navigation bars constructed this way, only the text labels are clickable.

In such a case, to have the blooper, simply do the following:

> Make the internal table borders visible so each link is completely enclosed in a box.

> Turn underlining off for the link labels so they won't look like regular links.

> Optionally, make the boxes change color when the cursor moves anywhere into them.

Just follow this simple recipe, and you too will have the blooper: boxes that look like buttons but don't act like buttons.

AVOIDING THE BLOOPER

If you construct a navigation bar using an HTML table, the obvious way to avoid presenting misleading link targets is to *not* follow the recipe. By subverting either or both of the first two parts of the recipe, you make it clear that only the text labels are clickable. Therefore,

> Keep the table borders invisible, or at least don't completely separate the links (Figure 7.20[A, B]).

> Leave underlining of the link labels turned on (Figure 7.20[C]). Better, leave them the standard blue link color.

The U.S. Internal Revenue Service website, *IRS.gov,* avoids the blooper by underlining the text labels and not putting each navigation-bar item in a separate boxed area (Figure 7.21). This makes clear that only the underlined textual links are clickable.

For Image Links

The aforementioned recipe is not the only way to commit this blooper. Not all navigation bars are constructed from text in tables. When Web designers want a navigation bar to look like an array of buttons, they often build it using either a table of images or an image map. In such cases, designers should follow these guidelines to ensure that the "navigation-bar buttons" behave like buttons:

The preferred way to build a button array is to arrange individual button images using stylesheets or tables. Make each button image a whole-image link by enclosing the IMG tag in a link <A> tag.

If you use an image map to present an array of buttons,[23] make the extent of each button clear and design the map so that entire buttons are mapped as links. If the buttons widen when the site visitor widens the browser window, the width of the mapped link must be a run-time calculation.

Many websites achieve buttons that are clickable anywhere by using one of these solutions. For example, the home page of *IEEE.org,* the website of the Institute of Electrical and Electronic Engineers, shows both vertical and horizontal navigation bars in which the entire area of every button is clickable (Figure 7.22).

The blooper is also avoidable in navigation bars that simulate tabs rather than buttons. An example is *OfficeMax.com* (Figure 7.23). Tabs on this navigation bar accept clicks anywhere in their outlined area.

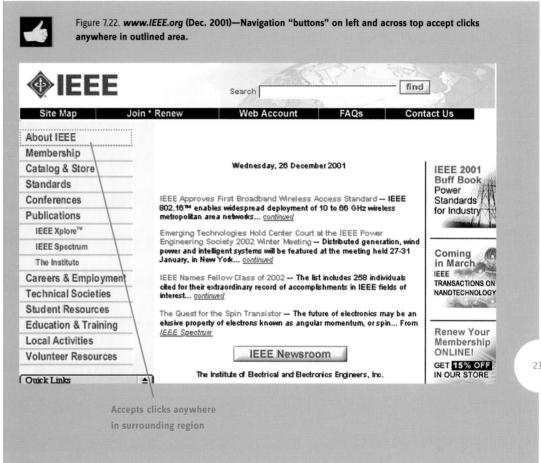

Figure 7.22. *www.IEEE.org* **(Dec. 2001)—Navigation "buttons" on left and across top accept clicks anywhere in outlined area.**

Accepts clicks anywhere in surrounding region

233

[23]Image maps are not well regarded by usability experts, because they increase page-download times and hinder accessibility to blind and motor-impaired people. Nonetheless, some designers use them.

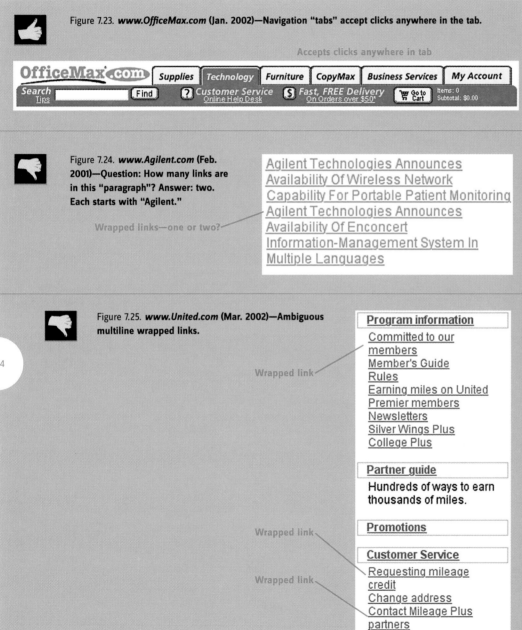

Figure 7.23. ***www.OfficeMax.com*** **(Jan. 2002)—Navigation "tabs" accept clicks anywhere in the tab.**

Accepts clicks anywhere in tab
OfficeMax.com
Supplies
Technology
Furniture
CopyMax
Business Services
My Account
Search
Tips
Find
Customer Service
Online Help Desk
Fast, FREE Delivery
On Orders over $50*
Go to Cart
Items: 0
Subtotal: $0.00

Figure 7.24. ***www.Agilent.com*** **(Feb. 2001)—Question: How many links are in this "paragraph"? Answer: two. Each starts with "Agilent."**

Wrapped links—one or two?
Agilent Technologies Announces
Availability Of Wireless Network
Capability For Portable Patient Monitoring
Agilent Technologies Announces
Availability Of Enconcert
Information-Management System In
Multiple Languages

Figure 7.25. ***www.United.com*** **(Mar. 2002)—Ambiguous multiline wrapped links.**

Program information
Committed to our
members
Member's Guide
Rules
Earning miles on United
Premier members
Newsletters
Silver Wings Plus
College Plus
Partner guide
Hundreds of ways to earn
thousands of miles.
Promotions
Customer Service
Requesting mileage
credit
Change address
Contact Mileage Plus
partners
Contact United
Wrapped link
Wrapped link
Wrapped link

Blooper 51: Wrapped Links: How Many?

When a textual link on the Web consists of more than one word, it may be wrapped to two or more lines. Whether it is wrapped depends on the width of the browser window, the width of the link's containing area of the page, the text font size, and other factors.

Wrapped links create ambiguity and confusion—how many separate links *are* there?—and are difficult to scan quickly. In general, they should be avoided but can work if the ambiguity is minimized by proper graphic design.

Unfortunately, many Web designers don't realize how much wrapped links harm the usability of a website and so make no effort to avoid them or minimize their impact.

A good illustration of the ambiguity of multiline links is provided by *Agilent.com* (Figure 7.24). By scrutinizing this "clump" of text carefully, site visitors might be able to figure out that it contains two links, each beginning with the company name: "Agilent." However, that puts far too much of a burden on site users. It should be designed so it is clear at a glance where links begin and end.

A somewhat different example of confusing multiline links comes from the website of United Airlines. On the frequent-flier customer page is a list of links, some of which are wrapped (Figure 7.25). Because the line spacing is the same between items and within them, customers might not be sure how many links there are unless they notice the capitalization.

When links are in horizontal rows rather than vertical lists, links at the ends of lines may wrap to the next line, causing a slightly different sort of ambiguity. *RadioShack.com* provides an example (Figure 7.26): Five of the links in this list of product categories are split across lines. Careful visual analysis is required here to determine what the links are.

AVOIDING THE BLOOPER

The most straightforward way to avoid the blooper is to simply not let links wrap. Vertical lists of links can be placed in containing areas that are wide enough that no link wraps.

Of course, a design rule that textual links should not wrap conflicts with another important Web design rule: that text should be as fluid as possible to accommodate different-sized browser windows and different font choices by users. Fixing a page's layout so firmly that no multiword links ever wrap would result in inflexible layout and font size, which are themselves bloopers (see Chapter 8, Blooper 54: Tiny Text). There is no general solution to this conflict. Designers must simply attempt to minimize the incidence of all the conflicting bloopers through sensible page layout and reasonable default font sizes.

In specific cases, solutions are available. For example, the wrapping of links at *RadioShack.com* (see Figure 7.26) could be avoided through the use of *nonbreaking spaces* between words in multiword links. However, nonbreaking spaces don't help when there is only one link per line, as in the *Agilent* example.

When multiline links are unavoidable, the ambiguity they cause can be reduced or even eliminated through spacing and bulleting. Screen excerpts from *Albany.co.uk* and *IBM.com* show that if line spacing *between* links is greater than that *within* links, ambiguity about the number of links can be eliminated (Figure 7.27). The *IBM* example shows that the spacing between links need not be much greater than that within links to result in a noticeable improvement.[24]

[24]However, the IBM example is not good in all respects: White text on a light-blue background is very hard to read.

Figure 7.26 ***www.RadioShack.com*** (Feb. 2002)—Some multiword links are wrapped at ends of lines, causing ambiguity about the number of links.

Adapters | Automotive Electronics | Cassette Decks | Cassette Recorders, Handheld | CD Changers | CD Players, Portable | CD Writers | Clock Radios | Cords & Cables | Digital Recorders | Headphones & Essentials | Headset Radios | Home Speakers | Home-Theater Systems | Home-Theater/ Stereo Receiver | Jacks, Plates, Posts, Switches | Miscellaneous | MP3 Players & Accessories | Plugs & Couplers | Portables & Boom Boxes | Radios | Recording Tape & CDs | Replacement Speakers | Shelf Systems | Speaker Essentials | Turntables

Wrapped links

Figure 7.27. **A:** ***www.Albany.co.uk*** (Feb. 2002); **B:** ***www.IBM.com*** (Jan. 2002)—Multiline wrapped links with reduced ambiguity due to greater inter-item spacing.

Latest Updates

Albany Software Offers Cycle Touring Club a Safe Route

Thomas Telford connects with Albany

Animal charity PDSA chooses ALBACS for TV campaign

→ Select a country

→ Home / home office
→ Small business
→ Government
→ Education
→ Industries

· Developers
· IBM Business Partners
· Jobs at IBM
· Investors
· Journalists

235

Figure 7.28. ***www.BarnesAndNoble.com*** (Jan. 2002)—Bulleted links can reduce ambiguity when some links wrap onto multiple lines.

Gift Certificates

FEATURED SUBJECTS
- Art, Architecture & Photography
- Audiobooks
- Computers
- Cooking
- History
- Kids
- Mystery
- Nonfiction
- Romance
- Science Fiction
▶ Browse All Subjects

Figure 7.29. ***www.CRLA.net*** (Feb. 2002)—Link embedded in text instead of just having the label "Bylaws Change" be the link.

Bylaws change

To view the bylaws change, please click on this link.

Unnecessary

Bulleting links is even better than spacing for reducing ambiguity, as is shown by an excerpt from bookseller *BarnesAndNoble.com* (Figure 7.28). However, bulleted items may not fit the graphic style of a particular website.

Blooper 52: "Click <u>Here</u>": Burying Links in Text

Many professionally developed websites look as if they were developed by amateurs. One thing that really conveys that impression is links embedded in prose text. The oft-seen "click <u>here</u>" is the most familiar example, but there are others.

Amateurish

It is common to see such links in personal and family websites. For example,

> Our family trip this year was to Yosemite National Park in California. For photos, click <u>here</u>. For photos of our previous vacations, click <u>here</u>.

When I see "click here" links in a professionally designed website, I consider it a blooper. In my opinion, such links are too informal and amateurish for a professionally developed website.

For example, the College Reading & Learning Association has on its home page a link labeled "<u>please click on this link</u>" (Figure 7.29). Link labels don't have to *say* they are links, and they needn't say "click me." When links look like links, Web users know what to do.

Buried

Not only do such links give site visitors an impression of an amateurish design, they can be hard to spot. Earlier in this chapter, we saw a nonunderlined "click here" link at *WiesnerBros.com* that was very well hidden (see Figure 7.3).

Pitsco-legodacta.com also has a hidden "click here" link. The site begins with a splash page (Figure 7.30). The link from there to the home page is easily missed. It would make much more sense to make the entire logo—maybe even the entire page—a link to the home page.

Even when links are underlined or colored differently from the surrounding text, they can be hard to spot. Try to find the link to buy a bus ticket at *Greyhound.com* (Figure 7.31[A]) or the link to a list of speakers at *SDExpo.com* (Figure 7.31[B]).

Figure 7.30. ***www.Pitsco-legodacta.com*** **(Feb. 2002)—Link from Splash page to home page is hard to spot.**

Link to Home

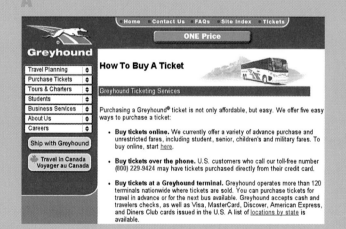

Figure 7.31. **"Click here" links. A: *www.Greyhound.com* (Jan. 2002)— The link to buy tickets is hard to find. B: *www.SDExpo.com* (Feb. 2002)—The link to the faculty list is buried.**

A

B

237

Uninformative

Most importantly for usability, even when embedded "click here" links can be spotted in the surrounding text, they are uninformative. People usually scan a Web page for information or links matching their goals. If they spot a "click here" link, all they see is that they are supposed to click there. The link label doesn't say what the link does. Users must read the surrounding text to determine that.

Look at an example from Yale University's alumni subsite. In a small font are some very wordy instructions with a "click here" link (Figure 7.32; see also Chapter 6, Blooper 41: Too Much Text). Try to figure out quickly where the link goes. This blooper occurs despite Yale's excellent Web style guide (Lynch and Horton 2002), which says that the link should be on the *heading*.

Figure 7.32. **www.aya.Yale.edu (June 2002)—Long instructions with "click here" link.**

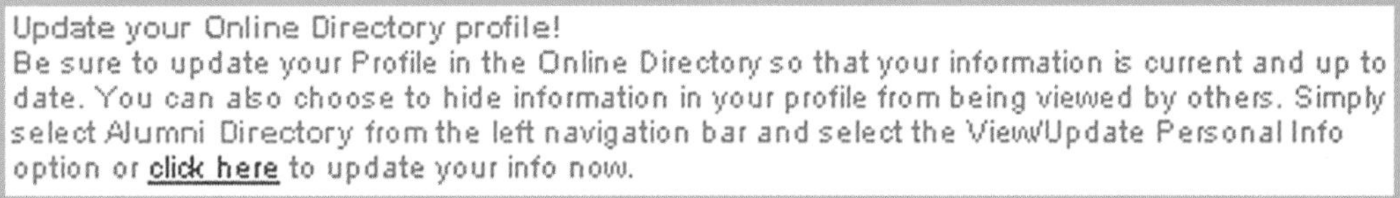

Update your Online Directory profile!
Be sure to update your Profile in the Online Directory so that your information is current and up to date. You can also choose to hide information in your profile from being viewed by others. Simply select Alumni Directory from the left navigation bar and select the View/Update Personal Info option or <u>click here</u> to update your info now.

Figure 7.33. **www.Standord.edu (Jan. 2002)—"Click here" links in bulleted items.**

Please **let us know** your comments and questions about this process.

- If you would like to register for more courses, click **here**.
- If you would like to register another person, click **here**.
- If you wish to drop a course, please go **here**.

Also forcing users to read around the links, Stanford University's website uses verbose bulleted items with "click <u>here</u>" links (Figure 7.33). It would be *much* more effective to list—and link—only crucial phrases: "Register for <u>more courses</u>," "Register <u>another person</u>," "<u>Drop</u> a course."

AVOIDING THE BLOOPER

Websites of companies, nonprofit organizations, and government agencies should be less chatty and verbose than personal and family websites. With the exception of articles that compose a site's primary content, such as news articles or member postings, prose text should be minimized so people can scan pages easily (Krug 2000; see also Chapter 6, Blooper 41: Too Much Text). Sites should be designed for maximum clarity and usability.

"Click <u>here</u> for details" is poor Web design. Instead, the link should consist of just the most important word or phrase, for example, "<u>Details.</u>" More generally, links should not be buried in prose paragraphs. There is one exception, discussed later, after some examples of avoiding the blooper.

Northwest Airlines' website provides a nice before/after contrast. In February 2002, *NWA.com's* Map Center page included both a "click <u>here</u>" link and several heading-style links: "Seat Maps," "Maps and Directions," and so on (Figure 7.34[A]). The "click <u>here</u>" link was in fact a "stealth duplicate" of the "Maps and Directions" link; that is, it went to the same place. Later that year, *NWA.com* eliminated the "click <u>here</u>" link (Figure 7.34[B]; see also Chapter 3, Blooper 17: Deceptive Duplicate Links).

The Macromedia website's Contact Macromedia page shows how links should be done (Figure 7.35). The page *could* have stated "For directions to Macromedia Headquarters, click <u>here</u>." For the different categories of contact information, they *could* have put the link on some words in the brief description. Wisely, they didn't. The

Figure 7.34. **Eliminating a blooper at *www.NWA.com*. A:** Feb. 2002: "Click here" link at lower left goes to the same place as "Maps and Directions" link in middle of page. **B:** May 2002: "Click here" link is gone.

A

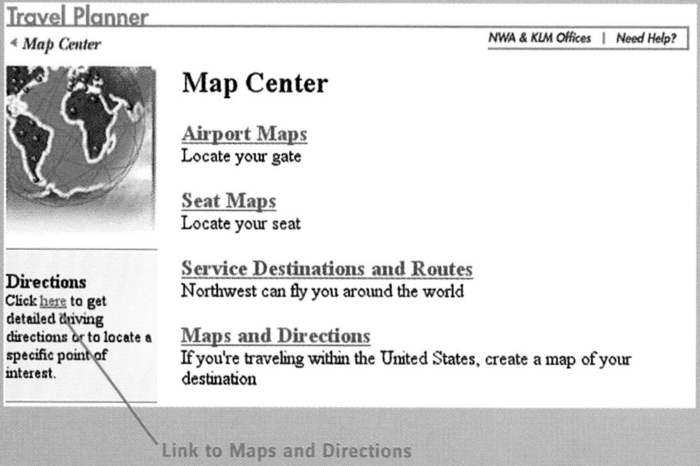

Travel Planner
◀ *Map Center*   NWA & KLM Offices | Need Help?

Map Center

Airport Maps
Locate your gate

Seat Maps
Locate your seat

Service Destinations and Routes
Northwest can fly you around the world

Maps and Directions
If you're traveling within the United States, create a map of your destination

Directions
Click here to get detailed driving directions or to locate a specific point of interest.

Link to Maps and Directions

B

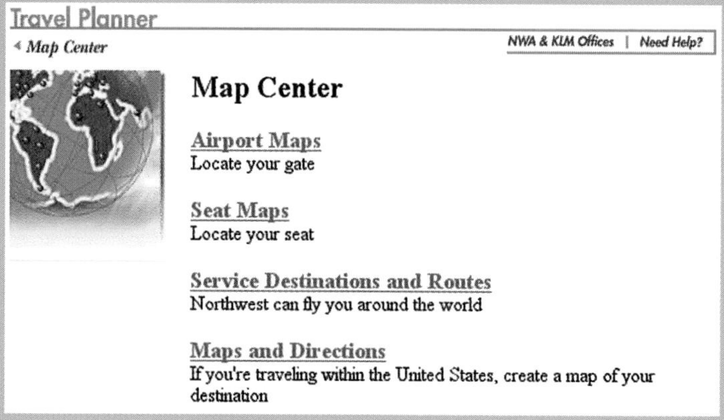

Travel Planner
◀ *Map Center*   NWA & KLM Offices | Need Help?

Map Center

Airport Maps
Locate your gate

Seat Maps
Locate your seat

Service Destinations and Routes
Northwest can fly you around the world

Maps and Directions
If you're traveling within the United States, create a map of your destination

239

Figure 7.35. *www.Macromedia.com* (June 2002)—Links to directions and to the various categories of information are presented as headers, not as "click here" links.

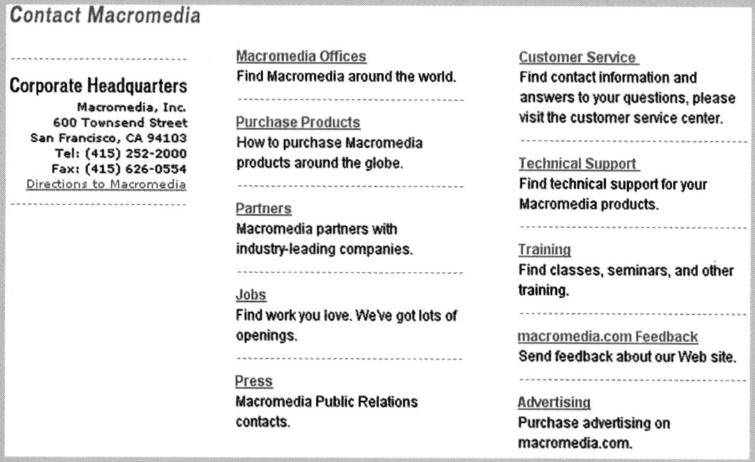

Contact Macromedia

Corporate Headquarters
Macromedia, Inc.
600 Townsend Street
San Francisco, CA 94103
Tel: (415) 252-2000
Fax: (415) 626-0554
Directions to Macromedia

Macromedia Offices
Find Macromedia around the world.

Purchase Products
How to purchase Macromedia products around the globe.

Partners
Macromedia partners with industry-leading companies.

Jobs
Find work you love. We've got lots of openings.

Press
Macromedia Public Relations contacts.

Customer Service
Find contact information and answers to your questions, please visit the customer service center.

Technical Support
Find technical support for your Macromedia products.

Training
Find classes, seminars, and other training.

macromedia.com Feedback
Send feedback about our Web site.

Advertising
Purchase advertising on macromedia.com.

Instead of	Make Links Stand Out	
Click here for a description of this collection.	Employee Skills Collection	Description
If the item you want is not listed above, check the next 10 or the previous 10 items.	Previous 10 items	Next 10 items
House: 3 BR, 2 BA, near public transit. Asking $123,000. Click here for details.	House: 3 BR, 2 BA, near public transit. Asking $123,000.	Details
Your shopping cart currently contains 3 items, with a total cost of $76.45.	Shopping cart: 3 items Total cost: $76.45	View Cart Contents
Click here for information on priority settings and response time.	Priority settings and response time	

Table 7.1   **Examples of Embedded Textual Links, and How to Avoid Them**

headers are the links. The links stand out, so the page is easy to scan.

Table 7.1 provides additional examples of this blooper, along with alternative designs that avoid it.

Exception: Links between Documents

The only links that don't cause usability problems when embedded in text are cross-links between documents.

[25]Sometimes called "hypertext links," but that term is potentially confusing, because it sometimes refers to *all* links on Web pages.

These are links between elements of the information *content* of sites, rather than links for navigating the site.[25] The following are some examples:

> Terms to their definitions

> Names to corresponding illustrations

> Text to comments on that text

> Cross-references between online manuals or help files

Blooper 53: Been There, Done That? Can't Tell

Web browsers keep track of pages they have visited and normally display followed links in a different color from unfollowed ones. This lets users see whether a link goes somewhere they've already been.

When links *don't* show whether a user has already visited the page they point to, the navigability of the site suffers and users unintentionally revisit pages they've already seen. This problem is worse when links to the same page are labeled differently (see Chapter 3, Blooper 17: Deceptive Duplicate Links). Because downloading Web pages takes time, unintended second visits to the same page waste time.

As important as links are for navigating the Web, it is amazing that so many websites and Web-based applications don't mark already-followed links. They don't allow site visitors to see whether they've "been there, done that." Normally, this happens for one of three reasons: The designer prevents link-color change, the designer uses nonstandard link colors, or the designer disables marking of image links.

Designer Prevents Link-Color Change

A common excuse for not allowing link colors to change when visited is that it would ruin the site's color scheme. A site designed with this mind-set specifies the link color—rather than letting it be set by visitors' browsers—and does not specify a different "followed-link" color. The result: To preserve a color scheme, the Web designer has made it impossible for users to see where they've been. In my opinion such priorities are wrong.

An example of unchanging link colors comes from the website of the California Department of Motor Vehicles (Figure 7.36). None of the links at this site change color after having been followed.

A similar, though less cluttered, fixation on preserving colors can be seen at *Andersen.com*. In addition to being barely recognizable as links, the orange links on Andersen's home page never change color (Figure 7.37).

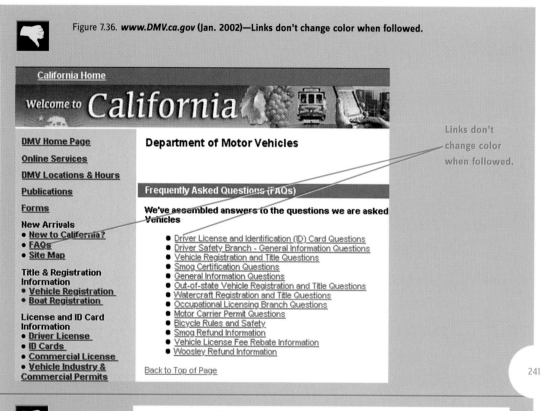

Figure 7.36. *www.DMV.ca.gov* (Jan. 2002)—Links don't change color when followed.

Links don't change color when followed.

Figure 7.37.
www.Andersen.com
(Mar. 2002)—Links
always remain orange.

Links don't change color when followed.

Figure 7.38. **www.OfficeMax.com** (Feb. 2002)—"Bread-crumb" links change color when followed, but the links in the category list below don't.

Home > Furniture > **Filing Cabinets & Safes**

Browse

▼Filing Cabinets & Safes — Change color

　HON Filing Cabinets

　Home/Executive File Cabinets

　Vertical File Cabinets　　　Exec

　Lateral File Cabinets　　　Fabric

　Mobile Files　　　　　　　Only $ — Don't change color

　File Cabinet Accessories　Save

　Safes

Figure 7.39. **www.Yosemite.org** (Dec. 2000)— Which links here have been followed, and which have not?

242

VIRTUAL YOSEMITE

Check out the new, secure Yosemite Store

Live Webcam ——— Nonstandard colors, so can't tell which have been followed

Tuolumne in Winter

Scenic Views

360-Degree Panoramas

Yosemite Music

Jobs at the Yosemite Assocation

An odd example of the blooper can be found at *OfficeMax.com:* Some links change color after being followed, and others don't (Figure 7.38). In particular, the links in the navigation "bread-crumb" path at the top of each page change color, but the links in the list of subcategories do not.

Designer Uses Nonstandard Link Colors

At some websites, links do change color after being followed, but the link-marking colors are so unconventional that users can't tell which color indicates "not followed" and which indicates "followed."

Yosemite.org used to display unfollowed links in dark brown and followed links in light brown (Figure 7.39). Unless site visitors remembered what colors the links were originally, they couldn't tell which links they had visited. Some visitors might even assume that the brighter links—the light brown ones—are the *un*followed ones and the darker ones are the followed. *Yosemite.org's* approach to eliminating the blooper is evaluated in the following Avoiding the Blooper section.

Sometimes a site's color scheme is preserved by using very similar colors for unfollowed and followed links. Often, this means the colors will be difficult to distinguish, especially for Web users who are color blind (see Chapter 8, Blooper 58: Shades of Beige: Color Differences Too Subtle). Try to tell which links at *Enron.com* (Figure 7.40) have been followed. Regardless of your perceptual abilities, you'll have difficulty.

Image Links Not Marked

Image links are of course not underlined. Simple individual image links can have a border around them, which defaults to blue in most browsers. Usually, however, they have no border. The reason: Web designers tend not to like borders around their site's images, so they disable them for all image links. This of course means users cannot see which image links they've followed. HTML also does not provide a way to mark links that are part of an image map.

AVOIDING THE BLOOPER

Web users should be able to tell whether they have previously visited the destination of a link. Website designers should try very hard to ensure that links convey that information. Setting link colors makes it likely that users' ability to distinguish visited links from unvisited links will be disabled.

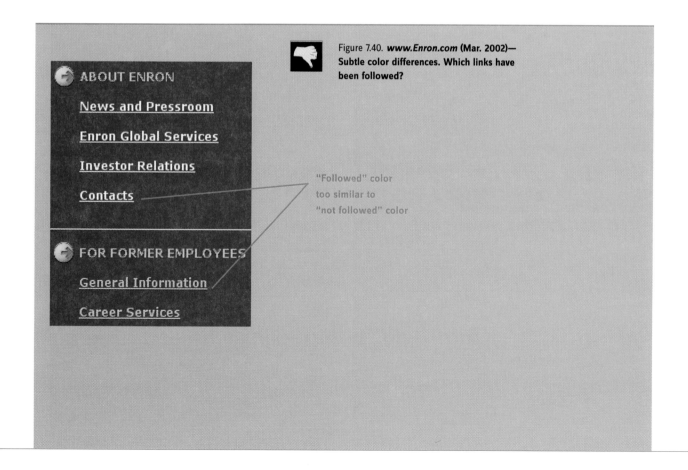

Figure 7.40. *www.Enron.com* (Mar. 2002)— Subtle color differences. Which links have been followed?

"Followed" color too similar to "not followed" color

243

Figure 7.41. **A:** *Amazon.com* (May 2002); **B:** *CPSR.org* (May 2002)—Standard link colors are used so followed links are easily distinguished from unfollowed ones.

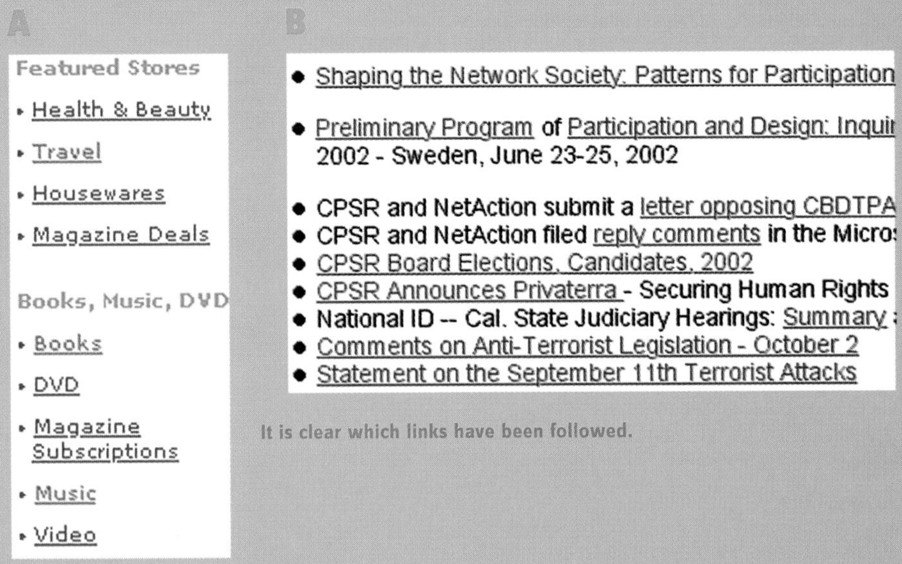

A

Featured Stores

▸ Health & Beauty

▸ Travel

▸ Housewares

▸ Magazine Deals

Books, Music, DVD

▸ Books

▸ DVD

▸ Magazine
 Subscriptions

▸ Music

▸ Video

B

● Shaping the Network Society: Patterns for Participation

● Preliminary Program of Participation and Design: Inquir
 2002 - Sweden, June 23-25, 2002

● CPSR and NetAction submit a letter opposing CBDTPA
● CPSR and NetAction filed reply comments in the Micro:
● CPSR Board Elections, Candidates, 2002
● CPSR Announces Privaterra - Securing Human Rights
● National ID -- Cal. State Judiciary Hearings: Summary :
● Comments on Anti-Terrorist Legislation - October 2
● Statement on the September 11th Terrorist Attacks

It is clear which links have been followed.

Use Standard "Unfollowed" and "Followed" Colors

At *Amazon.com* and *CPSR.org*, site visitors can easily see which links have been followed and which have not, because unfollowed links appear in the default blue (Figure 7.41).

At Least Make Clear Which Links Have Been Followed

As described, *Yosemite.org* formerly used confusing colors for "followed" versus "unfollowed" links, and as a result, users couldn't tell which color meant which. The recently improved site still uses nonstandard link colors but makes clearer through careful color design which color means "unfollowed" and which means "followed." Links that have been followed are dimmed (grayed; Figure 7.42).

Finally, designers should avoid choosing a color for "followed" links that is too similar to the color used for "unfollowed" links. Your users will thank you—not just the color blind ones.

Figure 7.42. ***www.Yosemite.org*** **(Dec. 2000)—Which links here have been followed, and which have not?**

Camping Information

Camping Reservations

Yosemite Valley Campgrounds

Group Campgrounds

Campgrounds Outside Yosemite Valley

Camping Rules and Regulations

Camping Services

YosemiteSites.com

Better link colors:
gray is clearly
visited.

CHAPTER 8

GRAPHIC AND LAYOUT BLOOPERS

Our final category of Web bloopers includes graphic design and layout bloopers. These are mistakes in how Web-page components appear and where they are placed. They are about presentation rather than functionality.

Graphic design and layout bloopers—and how to avoid them—could fill a book all by themselves. There seems to be an infinite number of ways to mess up the presentation of Web content and controls, and Web designers have stumbled across many of them.

However, graphic design and layout issues are already well covered in other Web-design books. Many focus *exclusively* on that, as if there were nothing else to Web design. In *this* book, graphic design and layout is only one aspect of Web design. I left it for last for two reasons:

1. *Usability focus.* This book focuses on usability. Graphic design and layout can affect a site's usability but more often affect users in other ways, such as brand-recognition, organizational image, aesthetics, and trust. Regarding such issues I am no expert and defer to people who are (Flanders and Willis 1997; Flanders 2001; Mullet and Sano 1995).

© Bill Griffith. Reprint with special permission of King Features Syndicate.

2. *Easy to fix.* Graphic design and layout bloopers are right out on the surface. Once recognized, they are typically easy to fix compared with other types of bloopers. This makes them somewhat less important than bloopers whose roots extend into the site architecture and back-end servers.

Even with a focus on graphic design and layout bloopers that affect usability, there were far too many candidate bloopers to include them all. Those that made it into the book are the ones that (1) affect users the most and (2) for which good examples had been found.

Blooper 54: Tiny Text

Of all the bloopers described in this book, tiny text is the number one most common. Most websites exhibit this blooper somewhere in their pages. More people send me complaints about this blooper than any other.

What's wrong with tiny text? People who have impaired vision can't read it. That is a significant portion of the population. As people age, the minimum font size they can read increases. Most people older than 45 years can be considered "visually impaired" for reading small-print text.

[26] The browsers used to collect the examples in this section were Netscape Navigator 4.76, Netscape Navigator 6.2, and Internet Explorer 5.0, all for the Macintosh. Browser and operating system differences are discussed later in this section.

Users Are Older than the Developers

Think of startup companies full of 20-something skateboarders hacking out investment websites that will be used mainly by people who are approaching retirement, and you'll begin to understand the problem.

A good example comes from *FinancialEngines.com,* an investment planning service. The image (Figure 8.1)—like all those for this blooper—is shown full size. It has not been reduced at all from what was displayed in the browser, in this case Netscape Navigator 4.76.[26] The heading on

FinancialEngine's Demo page invites visitors to "Take a closer look." Even with a closer look, I doubt many potential customers can read this. We can only wonder why the text on this page is so small. It certainly isn't for lack of space.

Text that can't be read might as well not be there. It is safe to say that much of the text in many websites is functionally "not there" for a large proportion of the population.

A lack of space also cannot be the reason for tiny fonts in flight schedules at *FrontierAirlines.com* (Figure 8.2). Some people will see this table as a lot of empty space punctuated by small bits of indecipherable black and blue marks.

Tiny Fonts in Forms

Tiny fonts can also be seen—or for many users, not seen—on the Web in the field labels of data-entry forms. Returning to *FinancialEngines.com,* the explanations of

Figure 8.1. ***www.FinancialEngines.com*** **(Sept. 2002)—Most of the text is too small to read.**

items in the financial forecast application form are so small, they won't be helpful to many would-be customers (Figure 8.3).

Tiny Fonts in Links

Tiny text fonts are bad enough in Web content, but they are worse when the tiny text appears in links that people are supposed to use to navigate the website. People must be able not only to read links but also to click on them. Some visitors to the Consumer Information page of the Federal Reserve Bank of Chicago website will have difficulty doing either (Figure 8.4).

Okay, bankers like fine print, but check out the Contact links at *Comdex.com,* the website of a computer confer-

248

Figure 8.2. *www.FrontierAirlines.com* (Sept. 2002)—Tiny, nonadjustable fonts in flight schedule. Many users will have trouble reading this.

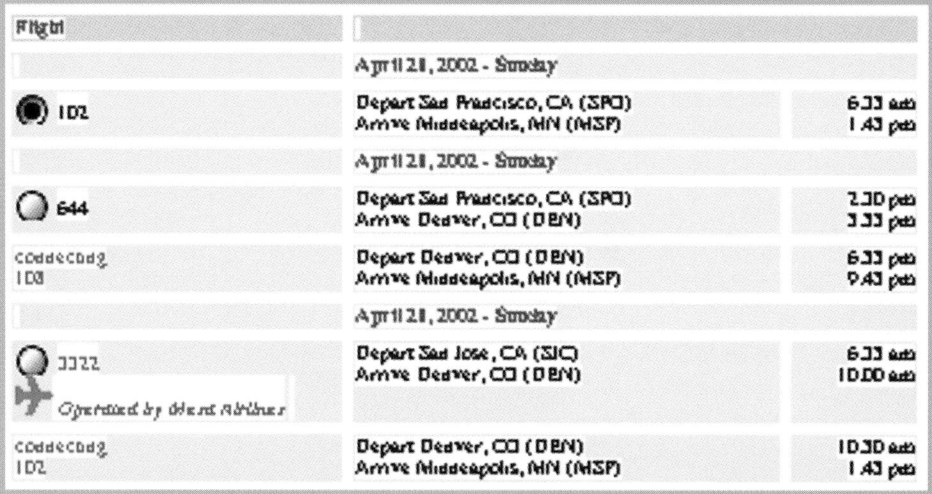

Figure 8.3. *www.FinancialEngines.com* (Sept. 2002)—Tiny fonts in an online application form.

ence (Figure 8.5). How are people supposed to read and hit these?

Web Users Seldom Resize Fonts

Most Web browsers have controls for changing the size of text. However, they work only at sites that don't set explicit font sizes. Some browsers let you override explicit website font settings, displaying your preferred fonts and sizes instead. In theory, both kinds of browser font controls let you choose larger sizes if you can't read text in the size specified by a site's designer.

In practice, most Web users never adjust or override fonts in their browser. Most have *no idea* how to do it. Even knowing how to adjust the browser's font settings may not help, because many websites render browser controls impotent by embedding text in images. Instead of adjusting fonts, most people simply avoid websites they can't read.

Text Size Depends on Operating System and Browser

Ensuring the legibility of text on a website is complicated by the fact that text in a given font size can appear in different screen sizes for people who use different operating systems and Web browsers.

One difference is between Windows PCs and Macintoshes. Put briefly, Windows PCs normally display text 33% larger than Macintoshes do. Therefore, text on a website that is small but legible when viewed from a Windows PC may be illegibly small when viewed from a Mac. More recent Web browsers for the Mac, such as Internet Explorer (IE) 5 and Netscape Navigator 6, correct for this difference, but older Mac browsers, such as IE 4 and Navigator 4, do not. The difference can be seen in excerpts from *Intel.com* and *Microsoft.com* (Table 8.1). More detail on this is in the sidebar, Tech Talk: Ensuring Text Is Legible on All Computers and Browsers.

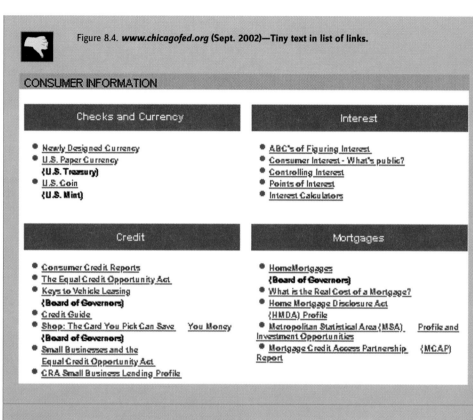

Figure 8.4. *www.chicagofed.org* (Sept. 2002)—Tiny text in list of links.

Figure 8.5. *www.Comdex.com* (Sept. 2001)—List of links displayed in tiny typeface. The links also aren't underlined.

249

Website	Navigator 4.76	IE 5.0
Intel Corporation; *www.Intel.com* (Mar. 2002)	New! Intel® Integrated Performance Primitives 2.0 The Intel Software Products Group is excited to release the Intel® Integrated Performance Primitives 2.0 for Windows* and Linux* and to announce the new Intel service and support program for Intel® IPP.	**New! Intel® Integrated Performance Primitives 2.0** The Intel Software Products Group is excited to release the Intel® Integrated Performance Primitives 2.0 for Windows* and Linux* and to announce the new Intel service and support program for Intel® IPP.
Microsoft Corporation; *www.Microsoft.com* (Jan. 2002)	Product Families Windows Office Servers Developer Tools	**Product Families** Windows Office Servers Developer Tools

Table 8.1 **Comparing Displayed Text Size: Navigator 4.76 vs. Internet Explorer 5.0 (Mac)**

DILBERT reprinted by permission of United Feature Syndicate, Inc.

Many websites are designed and tested using Windows only. The market dominance of Windows PCs ensures that most of the feedback developers receive will be from Windows users. Developers may not realize that the fonts on their site aren't legible to Mac users.

Text Size Depends on Screen Resolution

Even if everyone had the same computer and browser, differences in people's monitor size and chosen screen resolution—640 × 480, 800 × 600, 1024 × 768, and so on—would cause differences in the screen size of a particular website's text. On a 9-inch monitor, 12-point text looks smaller than it does on a 19-inch monitor. Similarly, at high screen resolution (1024 × 768), 12-point text looks smaller than it does at low resolution (640 × 480).

The bottom line: Many factors affect the absolute size of text displayed in a Web browser. Designers do not have total control over it. The challenge is to make sure everyone you want to read the text can.

Excuses for Displaying Tiny Fonts

When told that the fonts on their website might be too small, Web developers often offer excuses. Here are the most common excuses, with my usual response:

> *I can read it. What's the problem?*—The problem is that your intended customers are mostly Baby Boomers approaching retirement, but everyone at your company comes to work on a scooter. Whether developers can read the text is irrelevant. The question is, can the intended users read it?

> *It looks fine in Windows*—How many Macintosh users visit your site? Do you know? Do you care whether they can read the site?

> *We need all this information on here.*—Well, if your users can't read the information, it isn't there, is it?

> *It's not my fault; the text is in an image.*—Send the image back to whoever made it and tell them you need the text in the image to be larger. Better yet, don't embed the text in an image; use actual HTML text (styled as required).

> *It's big enough in low resolution.*—Have you determined how many of your intended customers use high-res versus low-res monitors? If not, you should. Otherwise you have no basis for your choice of font size.

AVOIDING THE BLOOPER

One might ask how websites intended for seniors handle fonts. The website of the American Association of Retired People uses a straightforward approach: Most of its text can be resized by the user's browser. But since most Web users don't know how to adjust text size, that approach may not be good enough.

A better approach can be seen at *SeniorNet.org* (Figure 8.6[A]), a website that promotes use of the Internet by seniors. Even though the default fonts used on its website are a reasonable size, the site's designers realized that some seniors still might not be able to read the text. They also realized that many Web users—regardless of age—never adjust or override the font size in their browser. To increase the number of seniors who will be able to read the text at the site, *SeniorNet's* home page includes a button labeled "Enlarge Text Size," which does exactly that (Figure 8.6[B]).

251

Figure 8.6.
www.SeniorNet.org (Sept. 2002)—**A:** Default font size, with "Enlarge Text" link (top). **B:** Font size increases after clicking "Enlarge Text." Clicking "Shrink Text" restores "normal" text size.

A

Text-Only | Enlarge Text | Email Page | Print Page | Help

SeniorNet. *Bringing Wisdom to the Information Age*

Home | Discussions & Chat | Enrichment Centers | Courses | Galleries | Learning Centers | Research | Sponsors & Specials | About Us

You are here: Home

The nonprofit SeniorNet provides adults 50+ access to and education about computer technology and the Internet to enhance their lives and enable them to share their knowledge and wisdom.

Search SeniorNet

Search!

Current Features

The Skoll Community Fund has awarded SeniorNet $250,000 to support a year-long public outreach campaign promoting the benefits of computers and the Internet. The campaign will direct adults 50+ to SeniorNet Learning Centers where they can take classes and to our web site where they can join our vibrant community.

SENIORNET IS MADE POSSIBLE BY:

YOU

CLICK TO JOIN TODAY!

SeniorNet Polls

Do you communicate with friends and family most by:
○ Email

B

Text-Only | Shrink Text | Email Page | Print Page | Help

SeniorNet. *Bringing Wisdom to the Information Age*

Home | Discussions & Chat | Enrichment Centers | Courses | Galleries | Learning Centers | Research | Sponsors & Specials | About Us

You are here: Home

The nonprofit SeniorNet provides adults 50+ access to and education about computer technology and the Internet to enhance their lives and enable them to share their knowledge and wisdom.

Search SeniorNet

Search!

Current Features

The Skoll Community Fund has awarded SeniorNet $250,000 to support a year-long public outreach campaign promoting the benefits of computers and the Internet. The campaign will direct adults 50+ to SeniorNet Learning Centers where they can take classes and to our web site where they can join our vibrant

join today!

click here to join!

SeniorNet Polls

Do you communicate with friends and family most by:
○ Email

Although SeniorNet's approach makes good sense in its case, it is probably overkill for websites designed for more general audiences. For such sites, I recommend the following rules for displaying text:

> *Let users adjust the font size.* Avoid setting absolute font sizes. To vary font sizes in your site, use semantic tags (such as (H)>) and relative font sizes (such as SIZE = 3 or SIZE = medium). Avoid embedding text in images unless you know it's big enough for everyone in your intended audience to read.

> *Ten-point minimum.* If you must set font sizes, never ever use fonts smaller than 10 point. Repeat: never. Twelve point is even safer.

> *Design for high-resolution displays.* If your site's fonts are large enough to be easily read on high-resolution displays, they'll be even larger and more visible for people who have low-resolution displays.

> *Test it!* The only way to know whether the text is large enough is to test it on the sort of people you want to use your website. If your intended users have trouble reading the text, it's too small. You should also test the site on as many computer platforms, with as many of the popular browsers as you can.

253

TECH TALK

TECH TALK: ENSURING TEXT IS LEGIBLE ON ALL COMPUTERS AND BROWSERS

Content in a Web page may appear larger or smaller on a computer screen than it will appear when printed. The screen size of content depends on many factors, including monitor size and screen resolution. For example, a line that prints as 1-inch long would appear longer than 1 inch on a very large screen (e.g., 25-inch) or on a low-resolution display (e.g., 640 × 480). The same 1-inch line would appear shorter than 1 inch on a very small screen (8 inch) or a high-resolution display (1024 × 768). This can be seen by holding a ruler up to the computer screen and comparing it with a ruler displayed on the screen by software: The rulers usually won't match.

Another factor that affects content size—though only text—is "text resolution."[27] Windows uses a different text resolution than MacOS. This difference can cause text on a website to look smaller when viewed on a Mac than when viewed on a Windows PC.

Text resolution is the number of screen pixels used to show one printed inch of text on the screen. MacOS uses 72 screen pixels for one printed inch of text. Windows uses 96.

Typographers measure typeface size in "points." Seventy-two points make one inch. A 72-point typeface would print as 1 inch high; a 36-point one would print as $1/2$ inch high.

The Mac's scheme equates screen pixels with typographer "point" sizes: 1 point = 1 pixel. In Windows, 1 point = 1.333 pixels. A 72-point letter, which would print as 1 inch tall, would be 72 pixels tall on a Mac screen, but 96 pixels tall on a Windows PC. The number of inches on the actual screen spanned by these pixels of course depends on the monitor size and screen resolution, but, if all of that is equal, a given font size will appear 33% larger on a Windows PC than on a Mac.

Table 8.2 shows, for font sizes set for a Windows PC, the approximate effective font size when the same text is displayed on a Mac that is using MacOS's default text resolution.

Recent Web browsers for the Mac, such as IE 5 and Netscape Navigator 6, automatically correct for this difference by using a default text resolution of 96 pixels per printed inch. In such browsers, text looks the same size on a Mac as on a Windows PC. Older Mac browsers, such as IE 4 and Navigator 4, are stuck with the Mac's native text resolution: 72 pixels per printed inch, with no way to change it. Therefore, Mac users with old browsers will see smaller text on websites than their friends who have Windows or more recent browsers.

There are several methods to ensure that a site's text is displayed at a reasonable size for all visitors:

1. Avoid font sizes less than 14 point. This is the simplest approach, but the most limiting.

2. Use a script to check which browser users have, and apply a different style sheet—specifying larger fonts—for older browsers than for newer ones.

3. When defining font sizes in style sheets, use the predefined logical font-size keywords—medium, large, x-large, xx-large—instead of absolute point sizes. Avoid the smaller logical sizes—small, x-small, xx-small—because they appear too small on some computers.

4. When defining font sizes in style sheets, use pixels (px) as the unit rather than points. Sizes specified in pixels bypass text-resolution scaling and so appear the same on Macs as on Windows PCs. The disadvantage of this approach is that fonts set in pixels cannot be resized by users. That is a significant disadvantage.

Each approach has advantages and disadvantages. I recommend the first method.

Windows PC	Macintosh
8 pt (illegible)	6 pt (illegible)
9 pt (illegible)	7 pt (illegible)
10 pt	8 pt (illegible)
12 pt	9 pt (illegible)
14 pt	11 pt
16 pt	12 pt
18 pt	14 pt
24 pt	18 pt

Table 8.2 **Effective Font Sizes on a Mac Corresponding to Font Sizes Designed for Windows**

[27] That is my name for it: Netscape Navigator calls it "display resolution" and Microsoft Internet Explorer calls it "resolution," both of which can easily be confused with screen resolution, something else entirely.

Blooper 55: Camouflaged Text

Text of any font size can be made difficult to read by placing it over a background that is heavily patterned or that contrasts poorly with the text color.

Text on Patterned Background

To see how a patterned page background can make text difficult to read, examine the mortgage calculator from the website of the Federal Reserve Bank of Chicago (Figure 8.7). The field labels in the calculator would be quite legible over a plain white background (see Avoiding the Blooper), but their legibility is greatly reduced by a patterned background, even a relatively faint one. In their zeal to give the calculator a background appropriate for home mortgages, the site's designers allowed graphic design considerations to supersede usability.

Poor Contrast between Text and Background

Even if the background of a Web page consists of a single solid color, the legibility of text displayed over it can be harmed by insufficient contrast between the text color and the background color. No one would expect users to be able to read text the same color as the background,[28] but some Web designers seem to expect users to read text that isn't very different from the background color.

Take *Microsoft.com,* for example, which often displays error messages in black text on a saturated red background (Figure 8.8). The red is of course to signal an error. Unfortunately, black text on a red background is devilishly difficult to read. The small (10-point) text font doesn't help.

Figure 8.7. *www.ChicagoFed.org* **(Feb. 2002)—Background of mortgage calculator makes it difficult to read the control labels.**

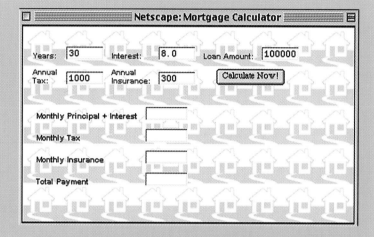

Figure 8.8. *www.Microsoft.com* **(Feb. 2001)—Poor contrast between text and background makes the text difficult to read.**

The data entered is incomplete or in error. Please correct the following errors and resubmit the incident.

- The phone number you have entered is not valid. You must specify a minimum of 7 numeric digits and can use parentheses, spaces, periods, dashes or the plus sign. You may also add any extension number onto the end of the phone number. Examples of valid phone numbers are: '(253)555-1234 ext #12', or '+37 123 789' or '316.098.6543'.

255

[28]In fact, Web designers sometimes use text that is the same color as the background, so search engines will find it (and use it to index the site) but human visitors will not.

A less-legible error message was displayed by the original website of candy vendor Russell Stover (Figure 8.9). Before the site was updated, its registration form displayed error messages in red on a dark blue-green background, making the message very hard to read.

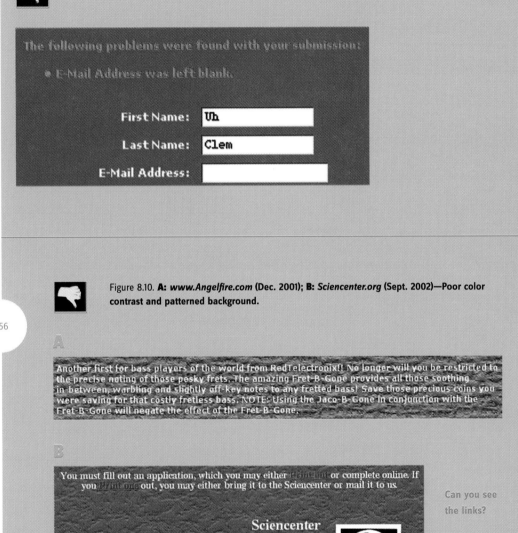

Figure 8.9. **www.RussellStover.com (Feb. 2001)—Red text on dark blue background.**

Figure 8.10. **A: www.Angelfire.com (Dec. 2001); B: Sciencecenter.org (Sept. 2002)—Poor color contrast and patterned background.**

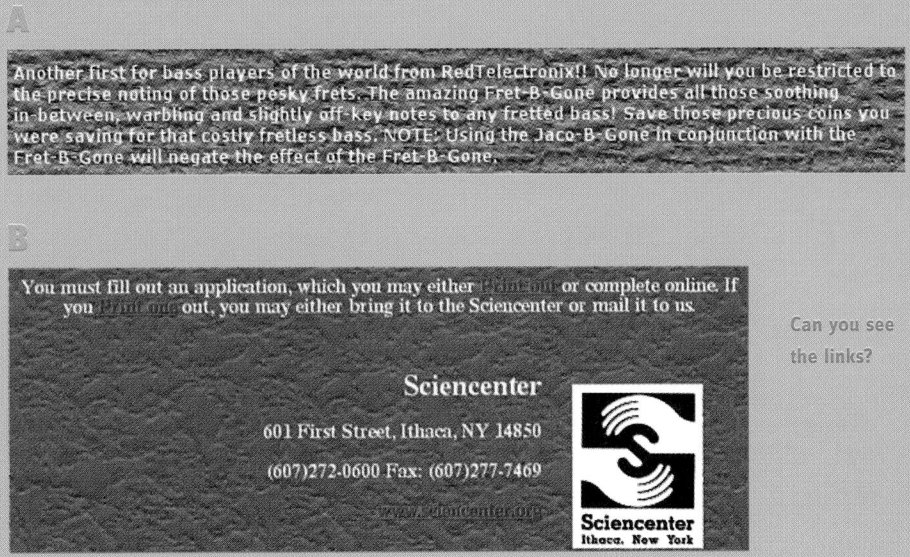

Can you see the links?

Patterned Background *and* Poor Contrast

Because patterned backgrounds and poor color contrast are each common variations of this blooper, it is not surprising that some sites commit *both* variations. Two examples come from *Angelfire.com,* a portal and Web-hosting service, and *Sciencenter.org,* a science learning center in New York. Angelfire, in a subsite, puts white text over a rough brown background (Figure 8.10[A]). Sciencenter has a patterned blue background on all its pages, which not only degrades the legibility of the white text but also makes the blue link labels almost impossible to see (Figure 8.10[B]).

AVOIDING THE BLOOPER

Assuming that a website's primary purpose is to convey information or to let users manipulate data, text on the site should be highly legible. To ensure that text is legible against its background, designers need only follow these guidelines:

> *Use solid backgrounds.* Avoid using patterned backgrounds under text. If you feel your site or certain pages of it absolutely must have patterned backgrounds, make them extremely faint, like watermarks, and design them to have large unpatterned areas over which you can place text.

> *Dark on light beats light on dark.* All other things being equal, dark text on a very light background is more legible than light text on a dark background due to perceptual "bleeding" from the background into the text. However, light text on a dark background can work if the

contrast is great enough and the text is bold enough to withstand the "bleeding."

> *Black on white is ideal.* If legibility were the only concern, the best combination is black text on a white background. Of course, legibility is not the only concern: The Web would be far too bland if all text were black on white. It is, however, good to keep the ideal in mind when choosing text and background colors. Thus, for text, *darker* is better, and for backgrounds, *lighter* is better.

For example, the legibility of the text in the Federal Reserve Bank of Chicago's mortgage calculator can be improved by simply "bleaching" the background to white (Figure 8.11[B]). Compare that with the actual calculator (Figure 8.11[A]).

Similarly, I can improve the legibility of Microsoft's error message while retaining the use of red to signal an error. I used red text on a white background instead of black text on a red background, and while I was at it, I increased the font size from 10 to 12 points (Figure 8.12). Compare the result to the actual *Microsoft.com* message (see Figure 8.8).

Exception: Artistic Sites

Not all websites are primarily for conveying information or manipulating data. Some aim mainly to engage or entertain. According to graphic design expert Kevin Mullet, "Such sites leave a lot more latitude for the designer, since contrast levels may come into play as an aesthetic element, exploiting figure-ground ambiguity for artistic effect."

This of course refers to sites that *are* art or entertainment, rather than sites that *present* art or entertaining content. The latter are not an exception to the normal rules about text versus background, because people must be able to use the site efficiently.

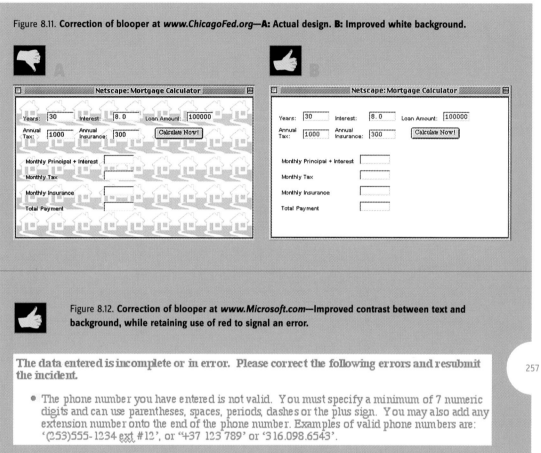

Figure 8.11. **Correction of blooper at *www.ChicagoFed.org*—A: Actual design. B: Improved white background.**

Figure 8.12. **Correction of blooper at *www.Microsoft.com*—Improved contrast between text and background, while retaining use of red to signal an error.**

The data entered is incomplete or in error. Please correct the following errors and resubmit the incident.

• The phone number you have entered is not valid. You must specify a minimum of 7 numeric digits and can use parentheses, spaces, periods, dashes or the plus sign. You may also add any extension number onto the end of the phone number. Examples of valid phone numbers are: '(253)555-1234 ext #12', or '+37 123 789' or '316.098.6543'.

257

Blooper 56: Centering Everything

One sign of a neophyte Web designer or developer is a tendency to center text, controls, and other elements on the page. It may be because HTML and website layout tools make centering easy, and some Web designers haven't yet learned that centering is usually a bad idea.

Figure 8.13. ***www.VitaminShoppe.com*** **(Jan. 2002)—Centered legal disclaimer is harder to read than it would be if it were left aligned.**

© 2002 The Vitamin Shoppe

The products and the claims made about specific products on or through this site have not been evaluated by The Vitamin Shoppe or the United States Food and Drug Administration and are not approved to diagnose, treat, cure or prevent disease. The information provided on this site is for informational purposes only and is not intended as a substitute for advice from your physician or other health care professional or any information contained on or in any product label or packaging. You should not use the information on this site for diagnosis or treatment of any health problem or for prescription of any medication or other treatment. You should consult with a healthcare professional before starting any diet, exercise or supplementation program, before taking any medication, or if you have or suspect you might have a health problem. Please view our full Terms of Use Agreement for more information and the terms and conditions governing your use of this site.

Figure 8.14. ***www.NHASP.org*** **(Jan. 2002)—Everything is centered, making it hard to scan. Centering bulleted lists makes the bullets useless.**

258

Mission Statement
The mission of NHASP as the professional association of school leaders is to provide services to its members by supporting their professional development and leadership for the purpose of continually improving the quality of education for all learners in New Hampshire.

NHASP LINKS:

- NHASP Principal of the Year 2002 - Nominations Closed
  - 2002 Principal of the Year Nomination Schedule
  - Leadership of Association
  - President's Report
  - Message from the Executive Director of NHASP
  - Executive Board Members
  - Task Forces, listed and defined
  - Conference & Other Important Dates
  - Education Directory
  - NHASP Services and Information
  - Past Presidents List
  - Profile of 2001 Principals of the Year
  - NHASP Constitution
  - Annual Conference - June 26-28, 2002, Eagle Mt. House, Jackson, NH
- Teacher Job Fair - Bow High School - May 4, 2002! ($5.00 Processing Fee for All Participants)
  - Administrative Job Vacancies (openings listed as of 1/17/2002)

Links to Helpful Information:

- National Organizations
- New Hampshire Organizations
- Useful Links of All Kinds
- Education Tools
- New Hampshire Minimum Standards for Schools
- Block Scheduling Information
- E-Rate Information

Listserv Info

That explanation is supported by a similar phenomenon of the mid-1980s, when word-processing software became widely available: For a few years, most party invitations, brochures, wedding announcements, and garage-sale fliers had all their text centered. Why? Because it was suddenly possible. Eventually however, computer users learned that centering should be used sparingly. The phenomenon subsided.

Another explanation is that invisible HTML tables are often used as vehicles for laying out Web pages. The HTML standard is for the content of table cells to be *left* aligned by default, but some Web development tools automatically set the alignment to *centered* by default. With such tools, if the developer doesn't specify otherwise, text or other cell content will be centered.

Centering Text

Prose text written in a left-to-right
language such as English
is harder to read when centered than
when left aligned.[29] The reason has to do
with the way our eyes are trained to scan back
and forth over lines of text.
When lines don't start in the same horizontal position,
reading is disrupted. See what I mean?

Despite the difficulty of reading centered text, many websites display large blocks of centered prose. Witness, for example, a legal disclaimer at *VitaminShoppe.com* (Figure 8.13).

[29]For right-to-left languages, *right*-aligned text is preferred over centered.

Centering Bullets

Bulleted text suffers from centering more than prose text does. Bullets are supposed to mark list items. Centering bulleted items "buries" the bullets, effectively neutralizing them. It requires slow, laborious zigzag eye movements.

Nonetheless, it is easy to find centered bullets on the Web. The New Hampshire Association of School Principals website has an example. Not only is its mission statement centered, but the bulleted list of links is too (Figure 8.14).

Centering Controls

If it can be placed on a Web page, it can be centered. This holds for controls and for text and other Web "content." Many Web designers do, either because they think centered controls are good or because center alignment is the default setting for their Web development tool.

For example, check out the search controls at *ZBuyer.com* (Figure 8.15). The labels of the controls and the controls themselves are laid out in a column, centered. Besides being ugly, this layout makes the "Go" and "Search" buttons harder to see than they would be if they were all aligned with each other.

Centering Everything

Our grande finale example of centering comes from the package-tracking page of *ValcoElectronics.com* (Figure 8.16). This page centers *everything*: prose text, controls, and links.

AVOIDING THE BLOOPER

If new Web designers and developers are the primary perpetrators of excessive centering, it might be tempting to just wait until everyone has enough experience to understand that centering should almost never be used. Of course, that

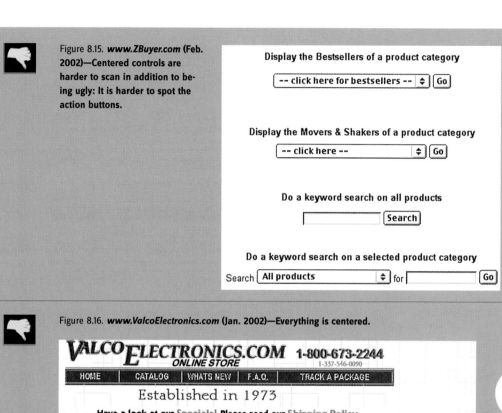

Figure 8.15. *www.ZBuyer.com* (Feb. 2002)—Centered controls are harder to scan in addition to being ugly: It is harder to spot the action buttons.

Figure 8.16. *www.ValcoElectronics.com* (Jan. 2002)—Everything is centered.

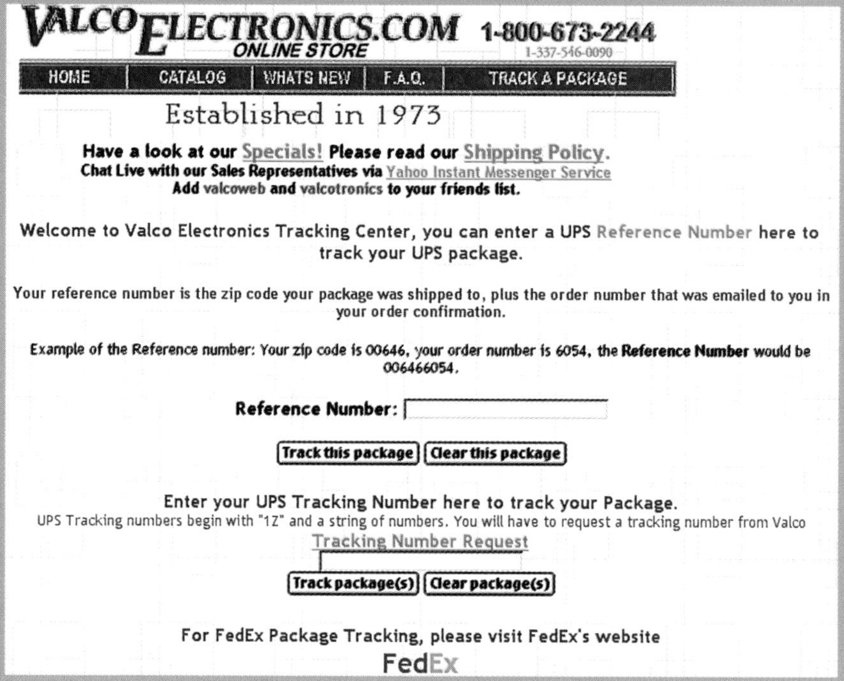

259

may be a long wait. The Web will always have newcomers. We may be doomed to an eternity of centered Web content. Maybe instead, the World Wide Web Consortium should remove center alignment from HTML and its successors.

Assuming a perpetual supply of new Web designers and that HTML will continue to offer center alignment, the next best option is education, on a massive scale. I will do my part by providing rules about centering. The basic rule is, *don't*.

In case you need more detail, here are additional rules:

> *Don't center prose.* Prose text should never be center aligned. It should be left aligned[30] or justified. Single-line headings and poetry are the only text that should be centered, and even those should be done only sparingly: Many headings are left aligned, and poetry is often not centered.

> *Left-align bullets.* Bulleted lists should be aligned so the bullets are aligned; otherwise, the effectiveness of using bullets is greatly reduced. Itemized lists in general should not be centered.

> *Don't accept bad defaults.* Don't center content just because it is the default in your Web development tools. The World Wide Web Consortium, which defines HTML, had good reasons for making left alignment the official default for content in table cells. If your Web development tool has center alignment as its default, it is wrong; you should change the default or use a different tool.

Blooper 57: Unobtrusive Error Messages

The previous bloopers in this chapter are ways in which websites and Web-based applications make text—including error messages—difficult to read. At some websites, the legibility of error messages is overshadowed by a more serious

problem: Users don't even notice messages. The most common reason for this is some combination of the following:

> *Badly placed:* off in a corner where people are not looking

> *No error symbol:* just text, no stop sign, large exclamation point, red X, or something of this sort

> *Font too small and/or plain:* message text that looks just like most other text on the page

> *No blinking or movement:* text that just appears, doing nothing extraordinary to get users' attention

Take, for example, the login page of a client's internal Web application. If the login information is invalid, the Login page reappears, displaying an error message (Figure 8.17). Can you spot the message? It's in the upper left corner of the page. The placement, size, and color of the message make it easy to miss. Users who mistype their PIN probably waste several seconds—or more—wondering why they are still at the login screen.

Citibank's online banking service displays error messages that are even easier to miss. For example, if a customer enters invalid data into their online bill-payment form, an error message is displayed (Figure 8.18). Can you find it? Hint: It isn't even on the Web page. It's in the browser's status bar, on the left, in a small, plain font. The message is not very helpful: "Error on page."

A few bloopers back, I showed an example from Russell Stover's old website of poor color contrast between text and background. I didn't say where that hard-to-read registration-error message appeared. It appeared at the top of the form, at the left edge of the page. Figure 8.19 shows the registration form with and without the error message. It might seem reasonable to display error messages in that position,

260

[30]If the text is in a language that is written from right to left, it should be right aligned.

Figure 8.17. **Client Web application (July 2002)—Error message is easy to miss. Can you spot it?**

Invalid Pin No. Please try again.

Login

For best results, Netscape Navigator 3.x or higher is recommended.

ID [   ]

Pin No [   ]

Change your PIN

[Login] [Cancel]

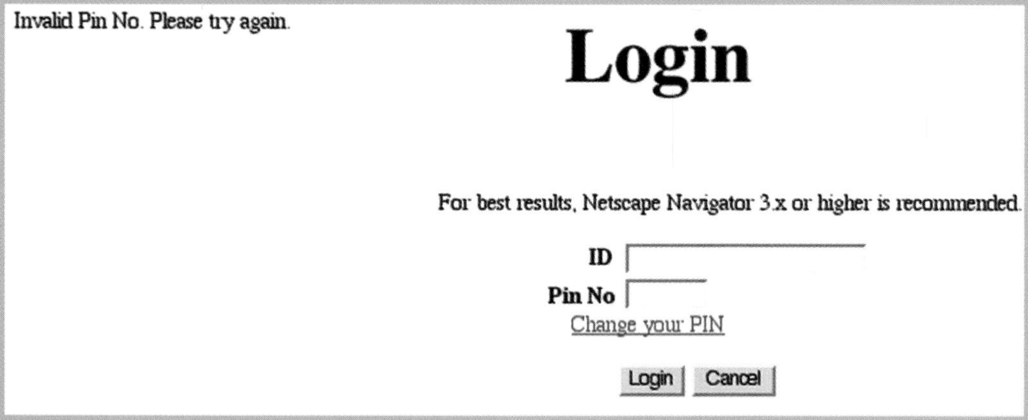

Figure 8.18. ***www.Citibank.com* (Jan. 2002)—Error message is very easy to miss. Can you spot it? It's also not very informative.**

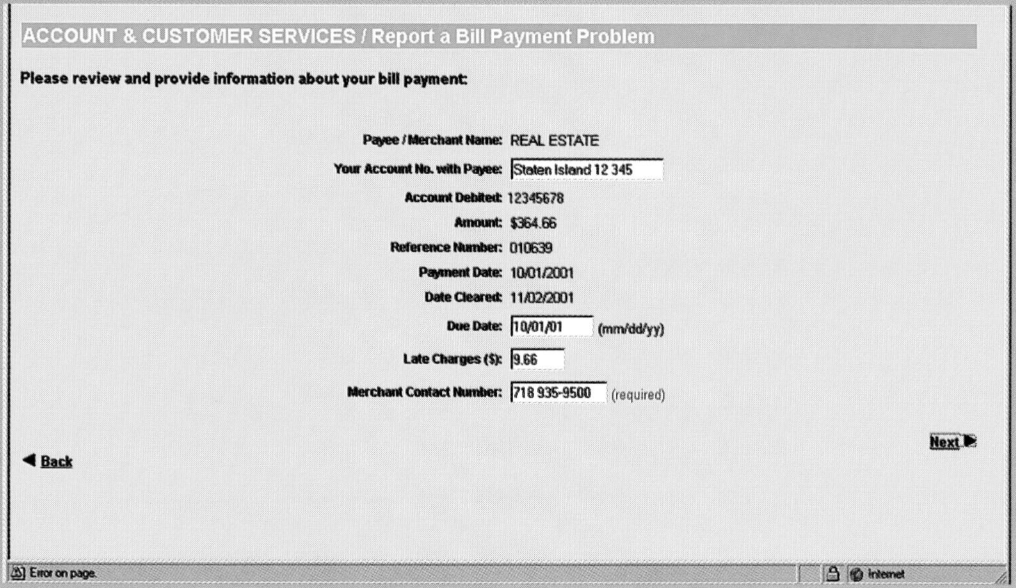

ACCOUNT & CUSTOMER SERVICES / Report a Bill Payment Problem

Please review and provide information about your bill payment:

Payee / Merchant Name:	REAL ESTATE
Your Account No. with Payee:	Staten Island 12 345
Account Debited:	12345678
Amount:	$364.66
Reference Number:	010639
Payment Date:	10/01/2001
Date Cleared:	11/02/2001
Due Date:	10/01/01 (mm/dd/yy)
Late Charges ($):	9.66
Merchant Contact Number:	718 935-9500 (required)

◀ **Back**

Next ▶

Error on page.   Internet

Figure 8.19. **www.RussellStover.com (Feb. 2001)—A: Registration form. B: Form with error message.**

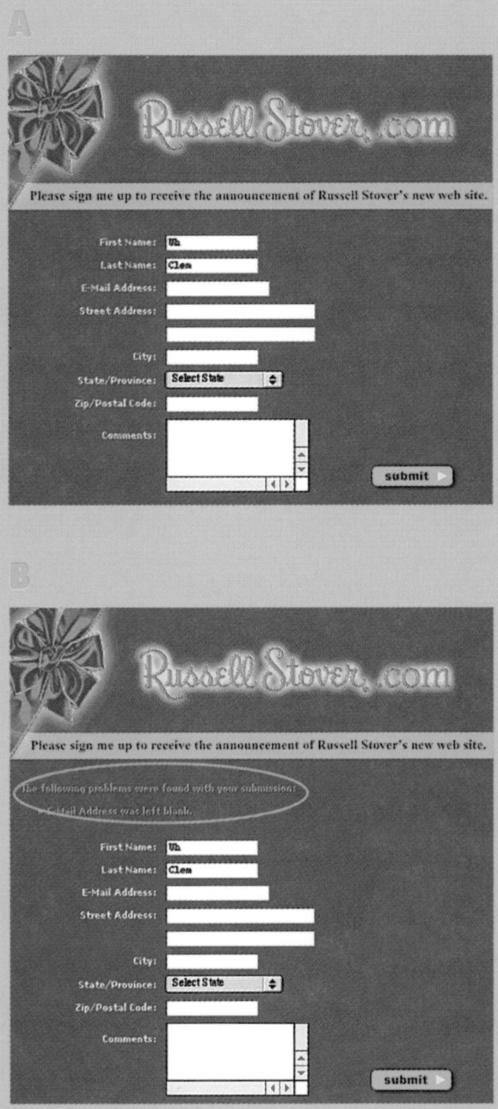

but a user looking at the Submit button or the form fields might miss the poorly contrasting message text.

If the message appeared in this position in a larger font, a color that contrasted better with the background, or inside a box with a different background color and an error symbol, it probably would be sufficiently noticeable. However, in this position, with such poor contrast, I'm sure many visitors to this site initially overlooked the message and wondered why the Submit button just redisplayed the form.

AVOIDING THE BLOOPER

Before I explain how to present error messages that users will notice easily, let's look at a site that does it well. The website of Recreational Equipment has a multipart form for ordering merchandise (Figure 8.20[A]). When customers try to submit the form with invalid data, it is redisplayed with error messages (Figure 8.20[B]), as in the preceding examples. However, the error messages are displayed in red in a separate section that is hard to overlook. Furthermore, the erroneous data fields are highlighted in red and marked with asterisks. No one could miss this.

Let's consider what is wrong with the error messages displayed by Russell Stover (see Figure 8.19[B]) and the internal web application (see Figure 8.17). Both put the message at the upper left of the Web page. That might seem a good place for error messages. There is a fairly well-known design rule for graphical user interfaces (GUIs) that important data and settings should be placed at the upper left of a window (Johnson 2000).

However, that rule doesn't apply to error messages on Web pages, for the following reasons:

> When a Web browser displays a page, the page content is not the top of the window. It is below the browser controls. Items at the extreme top left of a Web page can be

Figure 8.20. *www.REI.com* (Nov. 2000)—**A:** Billing Address specification form. **B:** Same form with error messages listed and highlighted.

Errors are listed in red in separate section and also are highlighted and marked in form.

A

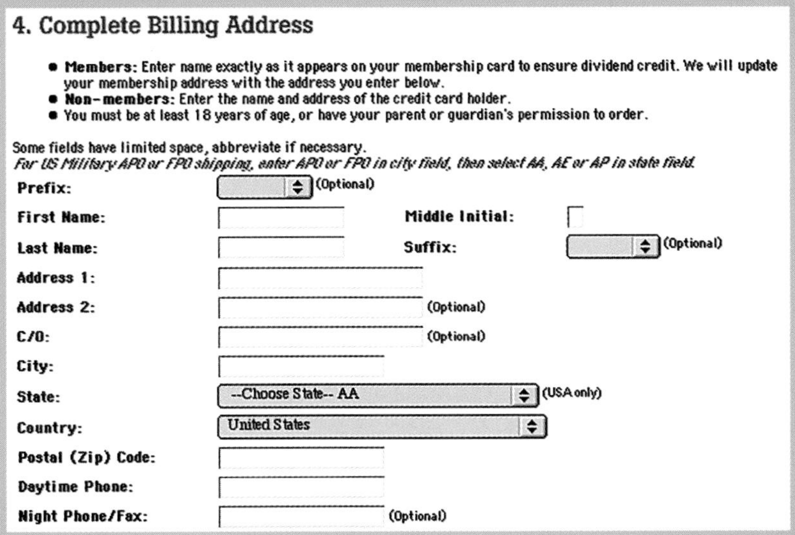

4. Complete Billing Address

- **Members:** Enter name exactly as it appears on your membership card to ensure dividend credit. We will update your membership address with the address you enter below.
- **Non-members:** Enter the name and address of the credit card holder.
- You must be at least 18 years of age, or have your parent or guardian's permission to order.

Some fields have limited space, abbreviate if necessary.
For US Military APO or FPO shipping, enter APO or FPO in city field, then select AA, AE or AP in state field.

Prefix:	[▼] (Optional)
First Name:	[ ] Middle Initial: [ ]
Last Name:	[ ] Suffix: [▼] (Optional)
Address 1:	[ ]
Address 2:	[ ] (Optional)
C/O:	[ ] (Optional)
City:	[ ]
State:	[--Choose State-- AA ▼] (USA only)
Country:	[United States ▼]
Postal (Zip) Code:	[ ]
Daytime Phone:	[ ]
Night Phone/Fax:	[ ] (Optional)

B

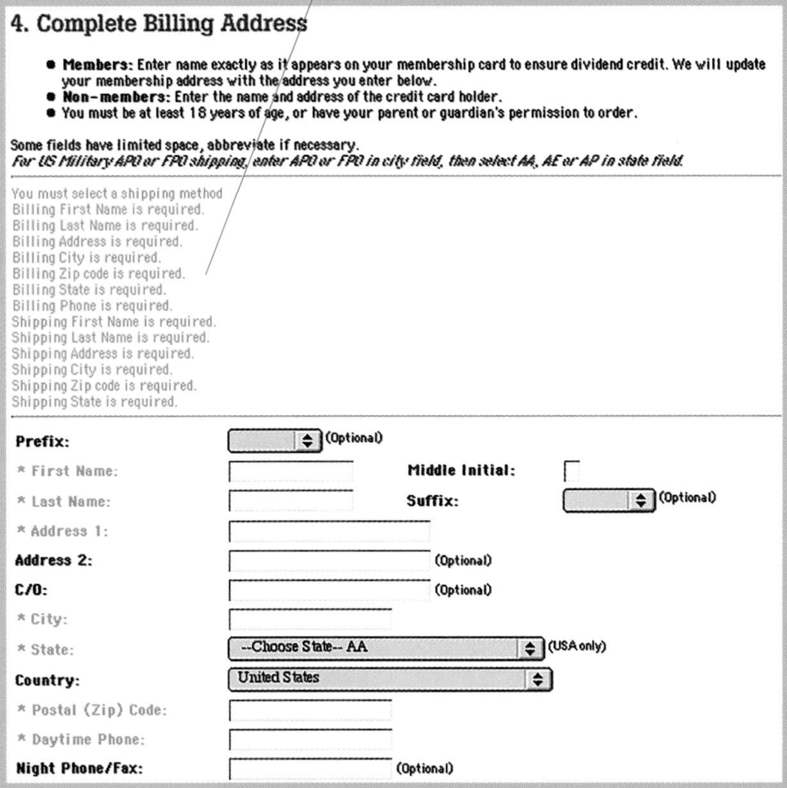

4. Complete Billing Address

- **Members:** Enter name exactly as it appears on your membership card to ensure dividend credit. We will update your membership address with the address you enter below.
- **Non-members:** Enter the name and address of the credit card holder.
- You must be at least 18 years of age, or have your parent or guardian's permission to order.

Some fields have limited space, abbreviate if necessary.
For US Military APO or FPO shipping, enter APO or FPO in city field, then select AA, AE or AP in state field.

You must select a shipping method
Billing First Name is required.
Billing Last Name is required.
Billing Address is required.
Billing City is required.
Billing Zip code is required.
Billing State is required.
Billing Phone is required.
Shipping First Name is required.
Shipping Last Name is required.
Shipping Address is required.
Shipping City is required.
Shipping Zip code is required.
Shipping State is required.

Prefix:	[▼] (Optional)
* First Name:	[ ] Middle Initial: [ ]
* Last Name:	[ ] Suffix: [▼] (Optional)
* Address 1:	[ ]
Address 2:	[ ] (Optional)
C/O:	[ ] (Optional)
* City:	[ ]
* State:	[--Choose State-- AA ▼] (USA only)
Country:	[United States ▼]
* Postal (Zip) Code:	[ ]
* Daytime Phone:	[ ]
Night Phone/Fax:	[ ] (Optional)

263

Figure 8.21. **Correction of blooper in client Web application—Message appears near fields that must be retyped, in large red font, and the fields are highlighted.**

Login

For best results, Netscape Navigator 3.x or higher is recommended.

! Invalid PIN Number. Please login again.

ID [   ]
Pin No [   ]
Change your PIN

Login Cancel

Figure 8.22. **Correction of blooper at www.RussellStover.com—Message is next to relevant data field and data field is highlighted. Message is also less verbose and has better color contrast.**

"buried" by the clutter of the browser controls and by elements on the Web page.

> The GUI rule concerns where users usually look first when a window appears. But the error messages we are discussing are displayed on the *same page* the user has just finished filling out and submitting. By the time users submit the form, they are not looking at the top left; they're looking at the Submit button or the form itself.

When the page redisplays showing the form again, users might not see an error message in the upper left. Instead, they wonder why they didn't move on to the next step.

The aforementioned internal Web application's Login page could be improved by moving the error message closer to where users would be looking and marking the fields that need to be reentered. Even though only the PIN was invalid, the system requires users to reenter both items for security reasons. I therefore put the error message next to the ID field and highlighted both data fields (Figure 8.21).

To correct the blooper at *RussellStover.com*, I shortened the error message and put it next to the offending data field (Figure 8.22). I also highlighted the field to be reentered.

Guidelines for Attracting Attention to Error Messages

Having seen examples of avoiding and correcting the blooper, we can now consider guidelines for ensuring that users notice error messages on Web pages:

> *Put where users are looking.* Human peripheral vision is poor and gets poorer with age. Try to put the error message near where users were probably looking when the error was detected.

> *Put near the error.* If the error is in a specific field or control on the page, place the message near there.

> *Use red.* Red traditionally indicates something is wrong and so is a good color in which to say, "Error!"

> *Use error symbol.* If possible, start every error message with a symbol that signifies an error. Common error symbols are a big red X, a stop sign, or a large exclamation point.

Those are the normal techniques for making error messages noticeable. Sometimes however you need the "heavy artillery": techniques borrowed from desktop software (Johnson 2000) that can make error messages nearly impossible to ignore:

> *Beep.* Emit a brief sound to let users know something is amiss. It's obviously best to use the standard "error" sound for the users' platform.

> *Flash or wiggle briefly.* Human peripheral vision for stationery objects is very poor. However, because humankind evolved in an environment in which we had to avoid predators, peripheral vision is very good at noticing anything that changes or moves. Automatically and quickly, we look directly at whatever drew our attention. Thus, flashing and animation can be used to draw attention to error messages. However, both flashing and animation are distracting and annoying if continuous and so should *always* be stopped after a half a second or so. If you can't stop them, don't use them.

> *Use dialog box.* Error messages can be displayed in dialog boxes, which are small windows that pop out of the browser and get "in the users' face." These can be either true dialog boxes or they can be small browser windows displayed without browser controls.

These desktop software techniques are effective but are rarely feasible in websites. They are more common in Web applications, which in many ways resemble desktop applications.

Blooper 58: Shades of Beige: Color Differences Too Subtle

Few people who design or develop websites have training in human factors, ergonomics, human–computer interaction, or human perception. As a result, the Web is full of sites that rely on subtle color differences to convey important information. Such sites cause problems for a large number of users, for several reasons:

> *Color blindness.* A significant proportion of the general population has some sort of color blindness. Approximately 10% of men do, and although the percentage is much lower for women, it is not zero. Color blindness is an inability to distinguish certain colors. The most common form of color blindness is red-green, with blue-yellow a distant second.

> *Poor ability to distinguish pale colors.* For all people, the paler (less saturated) two colors are, the harder it is to tell them apart.

> *Variation between color displays.* Computer monitors vary in how they display colors. Something that looks yellow on one display may look beige on another. Colors that are clearly different on one monitor may look almost the same on another.

> *Gray-scale displays.* As more personal digital assistants (PDAs), mobile phones, and other appliances are used to access the Web, the number of gray-scale displays displaying websites will increase.

> *Display angle.* Some computer monitors, particularly liquid crystal displays (LCDs), work much better when viewed straight on than when viewed from an angle. When LCD monitors are viewed at an angle, colors—and color differences—often are altered.

265

Figure 8.23. **www.ITN.net** (Jan. 2002)—Current step in airline reservation process is marked using a subtle color. A: Step 1. B: Step 2.

A

B

Figure 8.24. **www.Connectix.com** (Jan. 2002)—The difference in color between followed and unfollowed links is too small.

Home | Knowledge Database | *Answer Path* Online Help Guide | Forums | Product Support Downloads | Support Options | Register - New User | Login

Color as a Navigation Aid

A good example of relying on subtle color differences comes from *ITN.net,* an online travel subsidiary of American Express. The site allows customers to make airline reservations. Making an airline reservation takes several steps. While a reservation is being made, the site shows all the steps across the top of the page and marks the current step in a different color (Figure 8.23). The problem is that the color that marks the current step is so subtle that many people, either because of their vision or because of their computer display, won't be able to see it. Can you?

Perhaps the most common use of color on the Web is to distinguish unfollowed links from already-followed ones. As discussed in the previous chapter, sites in which links *don't* change color when followed are committing a blooper (see Chapter 7, Blooper 53: Been There, Done That? Can't Tell). If a site sets different colors for unfollowed and followed links, it technically avoids *that* blooper. However, if the two colors are so similar that users can't tell them apart, the site is committing the blooper of relying on color differences that are too subtle.

For example, consider a navigation bar at *Connectix.com* (Figure 8.24). Can you tell which two links have been traversed?[31] Not only are the two colors too similar, but the only thing colored is the text characters, which are very thin and so don't provide much area for showing the color. Color patches are harder to distinguish the smaller they are, but this is not widely known among Web designers and developers. The result is websites with colored lines 1-pixel thick and colored text in small nonbold fonts, making colors virtually indistinguishable.

[31]Forums and Product Support Downloads.

Color in Web Content

The preceding examples of relying on subtle color differences were concerned with navigation in websites. Color is also often used—and abused—to convey information in Web *content*.

The Federal Reserve Bank of Chicago provides a graph showing how short-term interest rates have fluctuated in recent years. It actually graphs three rates: Federal Funds rate, Discount rate, and 3-month T-bill rate (Figure 8.25). Each quantity is plotted in its own color. The problem is that some visitors to the site will have trouble distinguishing the colors, especially the red versus the blue. Compounding the problem is that the color patches shown in the color legend are so small that they won't help many people.

AVOIDING THE BLOOPER

The blooper—"relying on subtle color differences"—can be avoided in two ways, each focusing on a different key term in the blooper:

1. *Don't rely* solely *on color.* Use color redundantly with other cues. If you use color to mark something, mark it in another way as well.

2. *Avoid* subtle *color differences.* Make the color differences gross enough that they are unmistakably different. Colors should differ in *saturation* and *brightness* as well as in *hue.* One way to test whether colors are different enough is to print them on a gray-scale printer. If you can't tell the colors apart when printed in grays, they aren't different enough (Brinck, Gergle, and Wood 2001).

Following these guidelines, I strengthened the marking of the current step at *ITN.net* (Figure 8.26). Instead of relying solely on color, I used both color and a bold outline around the step's number and name, so even a color blind person could see what step he or she was on. I also used a very

Figure 8.25. ***www.ChicagoFed.org*** **(Nov. 2000)—Graph uses different colors for different plots on same axes. Some users may not be able to distinguish them.**

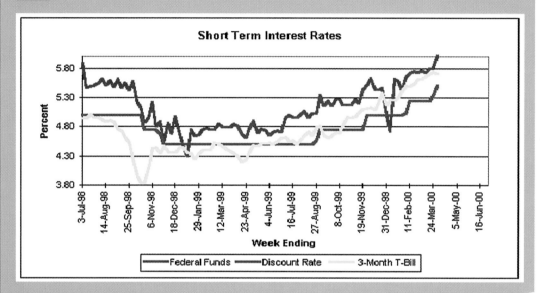

267

Figure 8.26. **Correction of blooper at *www.ITN.net*—Current step is highlighted in two ways: color and bold border. Color used to mark current step is not subtle.**

unsubtle yellow instead of beige as the marking color, to draw users' attention.

Another graph at the Federal Reserve Bank of Chicago uses gray-scale "colors" to show how the average annual income varies across the United States (Figure 8.27). This is a well-designed graph. Any sighted person could read it, even people with colorblindness, a gray-scale display, or a faulty color monitor.

Blooper 59: Dead or Alive: Active Buttons Look Inactive

There is one specific use of color differences that most Web users, because they also use desktop software, are accustomed to: inactive controls that appear "grayed out." Graying controls to indicate that they are inactive is a long-standing convention in desktop software. Websites and Web applications can exploit this convention, and users' familiarity with it, to their advantage. The flip side is that websites and Web-based applications that violate this convention risk confusing and confounding their users.

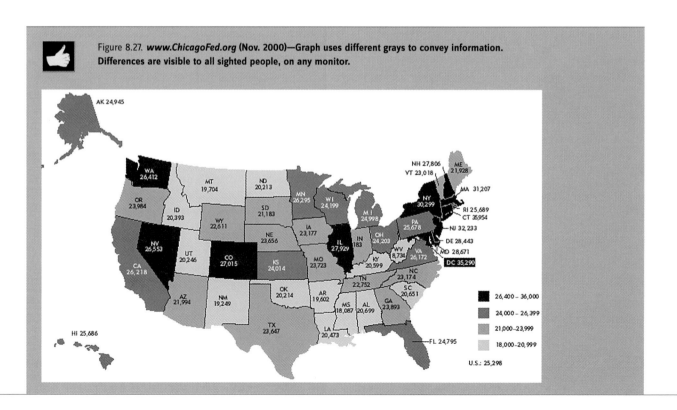

Figure 8.27. *www.ChicagoFed.org* (Nov. 2000)—Graph uses different grays to convey information. Differences are visible to all sighted people, on any monitor.

There are two ways to violate the convention:

> Active controls and links that look inactive (grayed)

> Inactive controls and links that look active (ungrayed)

In practice, many websites commit the first violation, and few commit the second. Therefore, the focus here is on examples of graying controls and links that are active.

Before a recent site upgrade, *Erlbaum.com* used gray on its navigation bar to indicate pages other than the current page. The current page's link in the navigation bar was solid black, and the links to all other pages were gray. The image shown is from the home page (Figure 8.28). The link colors falsely suggests that the home-page link is active, and the others are inactive. In fact, all the links are active. Ironically, the only link that looks active in this navigation bar is the one that *should* be inactive (see Chapter 3, Blooper 20: The Circle Game: Active Link to Here).

Erlbaum.com's convention for making the current page stand out might make sense in isolation. However, the Web doesn't exist in isolation. It exists in the context of personal computers and desktop software. By violating the GUI convention, *Erlbaum.com* violates users' expectations.

Travelocity.com uses color saturation to focus users' attention on buttons that continue the current transaction. Buttons that continue the transaction appear bright, and those that cancel or diverge from the transaction appear pale. The Flight Search page has two buttons: *Search All Airlines* and *Cancel* (Figure 8.29[A]). The *Cancel* button looks as if it is inactive, but it is just as active as the *Search All Airlines* button. It is pale to show that it doesn't continue the transaction. On the Search results page, the *Buy Now* and *Hold/Save* buttons are fully saturated, and the two buttons at the bottom of the list of flights are pale, making them look inactive (Figure 8.29[B]).

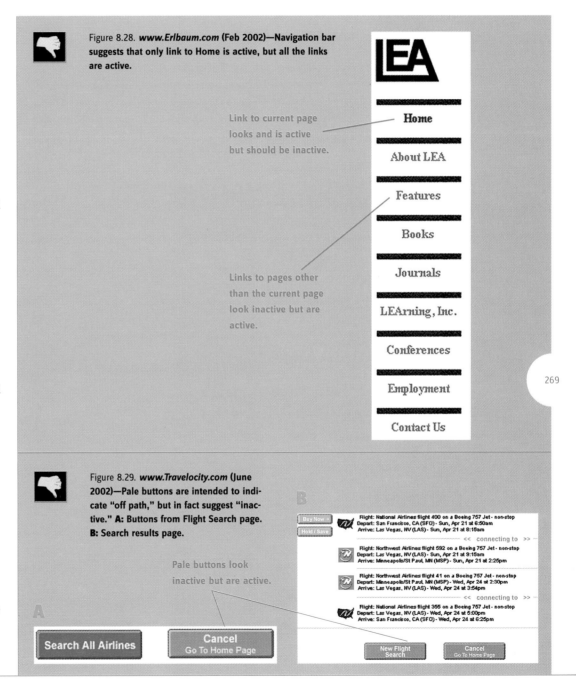

Figure 8.28. *www.Erlbaum.com* (Feb 2002)—Navigation bar suggests that only link to Home is active, but all the links are active.

Link to current page looks and is active but should be inactive.

Links to pages other than the current page look inactive but are active.

Figure 8.29. *www.Travelocity.com* (June 2002)—Pale buttons are intended to indicate "off path," but in fact suggest "inactive." A: Buttons from Flight Search page. B: Search results page.

Pale buttons look inactive but are active.

Again, Travelocity's convention wouldn't be bad, except that the pale buttons can easily be perceived as inactive.

Erlbaum and Travelocity at least have a clear rationale—albeit a misguided one—for graying links and buttons. In contrast, Radio Shack's website uses gray-looking buttons for reasons that to an outsider are obscure. *RadioShack.com's* home page has several navigation bars for different subsections of the site. In most of them, the buttons appear fully saturated (Figure 8.30[A]). However, in the Special Features navigation bar, the buttons appear grayed—inactive (Figure 8.30[B]).

Finally, we have an example of a site in which some buttons look inactive simply because of their color. *Monterey.com's* home page is festooned with buttons (Figure 8.31), most of which are bright and saturated. Two, however, are pale blue. A visitor to this site might assume they are inactive and not bother to try them. That visitor would be wrong, but when people are wrong about what something on your website means, it's not *their* problem, it's *yours*.

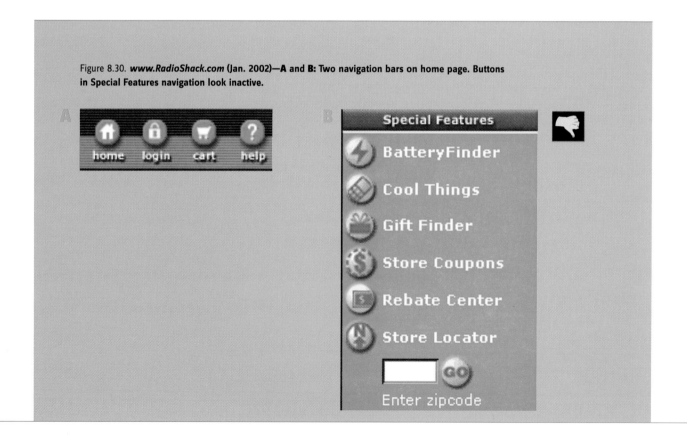

Figure 8.30. *www.RadioShack.com* (Jan. 2002)—**A** and **B**: Two navigation bars on home page. Buttons in Special Features navigation look inactive.

Figure 8.31. *www.Monterey.com* (Jan. 2002)—The last two buttons (lower right) are paler than the others and so could be misinterpreted as being inactive.

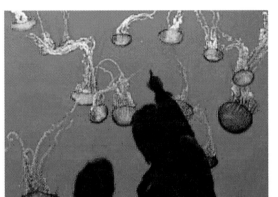

WELCOME TO THE MONTEREY PENINSULA

DESTINATIONS

CANNERY ROW

ATTRACTIONS

RECREATION

LODGING

ONLINE RESERVATIONS

DINING OUT

CALENDAR

SPAS

NIGHT LIFE

WINERIES

MEETINGS & CONVENTIONS

PENINSULA REAL ESTATE

SERVICE BUSINESSES

SEASONAL SPECIALS

AREA MAPS

TRANSPORTATION

SEARCH

FREE NEWSLETTER

WEATHER NEWSCHANNEL46.com

SAVE MONEY-CLICK FOR SPECIAL OFFERS FROM A VARIETY OF LOCAL BUSINESSES

Experience Monterey

These buttons could be mistaken for inactive because of their color.

271

Figure 8.32. Correction of blooper at *www.Erlbaum.com*—A: Before. B: After. Home-page link appears inactive because it is; this is the home page. All other links appear active and are.

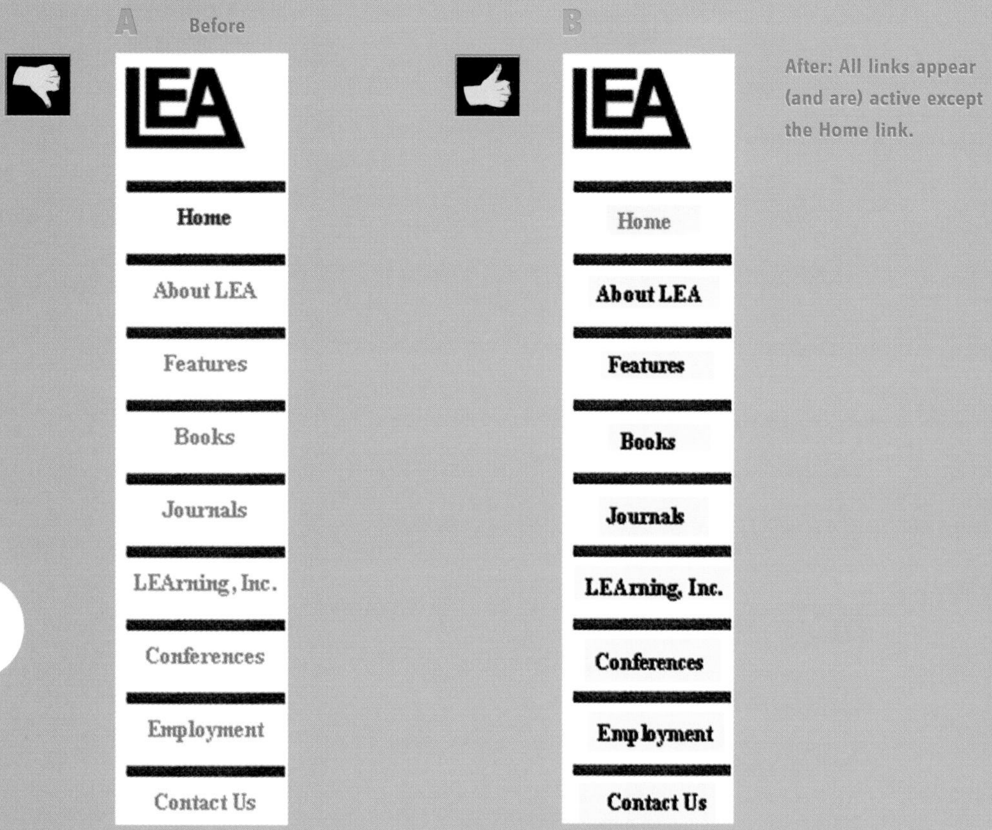

 A Before

 B

After: All links appear
(and are) active except
the Home link.

Figure 8.33. Correction of blooper at *www.Travelocity.com*—Both buttons are fully saturated and so appear active, but on-path button is highlighted in addition.

On-path button
is highlighted.

Off-path button
appears active.

AVOIDING THE BLOOPER

At least until PCs are replaced by Web appliances as the dominant vehicle for surfing the Web, designers need to recognize that most Web browsing occurs on a PC[32] surrounded by desktop applications. Therefore, GUI software convention that inactive controls are grayed should be followed—or at least not blatantly violated—on the Web.

As an example of how the convention can be applied to the Web, I modified the *Erlbaum.com* navigation bar (Figure 8.32[A]) to follow the convention. It still shows that we are on the home page, but its colors have been reversed: The link to the home page is gray; all the other links are black (Figure 8.32[B]). This works; because this is the navigation bar for the home page, the Home link *should* be inactive and all the others should be active.

Similarly, fixing the blooper at *Travelocity.com* requires making all active buttons look fully saturated, while marking on-path buttons in some way that doesn't make them look more saturated (Figure 8.33). I marked the Search button by giving it a thick black border. This is similar to how desktop GUI software marks "default" dialog box buttons—the ones that will be triggered if the user presses the Enter key on the keyboard (Microsoft 1999). That similarity is not an accident: Although Web pages can't have default buttons, on-path buttons are the ones most likely to be clicked.

[32] I am using "PC" here to mean any personal computer, regardless of whether it runs Windows, MacOS, Unix, Linux, or any other operating system.

Blooper 60: Terrible Tabs

In the mid-1980s, after GUIs had been invented but before they became dominant in desktop computer software, a clever designer got the idea of simulating tabbed pages on-screen, to let users easily switch between pages of information sharing the same screen space. Exactly who did this first is unclear, but certainly one of the first software products to use tabbed pages was Apple Computer's HyperCard, in its Help stack (Figure 8.34).

Tabbed panels are an on-screen simulation of tabbed cards such as those in a recipe box, or of tabbed pages in a notebook. Most computer users know how to use physical tabbed cards and pages. On-screen tabbed panels leverage that knowledge.

When a user clicks on a tab, the corresponding panel moves to the "front" of the stack, displaying whatever is on it. Tabbed panels allow a lot of information and controls to be organized into a compact space.

Web designers like tabbed panels for the same reasons that they are used in desktop software. However, tabbed panels—unlike radiobuttons, checkboxes, and pull-down menus—were not provided as a standard HTML control. Web designers had to "grow their own" tabbed panels. And so they did, some more successfully than others. Furthermore, tabs are often used on the Web in ways for which they are ill suited.

I'll be blunt: Many tabs on the Web are atrocious. Just because a designer creates a horizontal navigation bar and *calls* it "tabs" doesn't make it tabs. In order to be worthy of that name, it must *look* and *act* like tabs. Many so-called "tabs" on the Web do neither and so fail to tap into users' prior knowledge of how tabs work. The result is at least uncertainty and hesitation, sometimes even confusion, in users.

Three common flaws exhibited by tabs on the Web are as follows:

> Labeled tabs are not separated from each other.
> Labeled tabs do not appear contiguous with or connected to their corresponding panel.
> The tabs don't show which one is currently selected.

Let's look at examples of each of these flaws in actual websites.

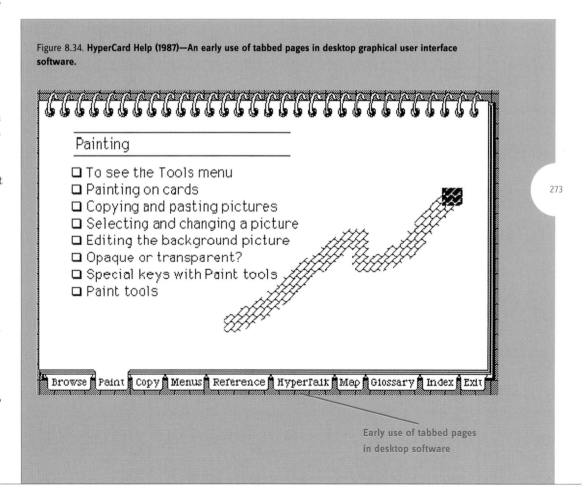

Figure 8.34. **HyperCard Help (1987)—An early use of tabbed pages in desktop graphical user interface software.**

Early use of tabbed pages in desktop software

273

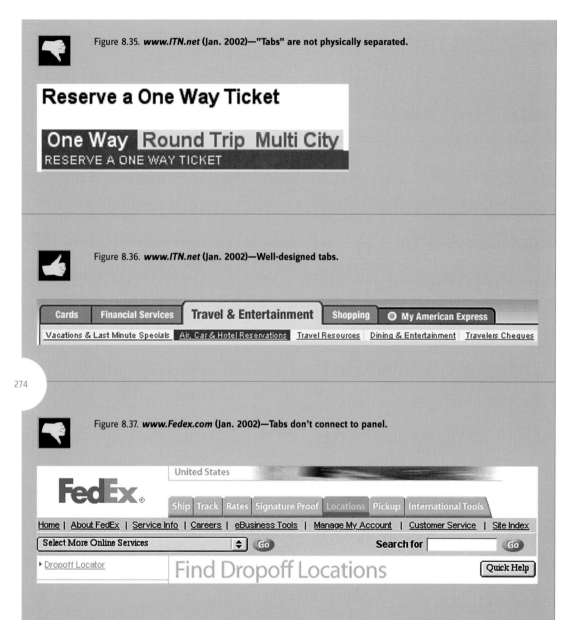

Figure 8.35. **www.ITN.net** (Jan. 2002)—"Tabs" are not physically separated.

Figure 8.36. **www.ITN.net** (Jan. 2002)—Well-designed tabs.

Figure 8.37. **www.Fedex.com** (Jan. 2002)—Tabs don't connect to panel.

Labels Not Separate

A good example of tabbed panels with poorly separated labeled tabs comes from *ITN.net*. The Airline Reservation page has tablike controls for switching between three different reservation forms, each specialized for one type of trip (Figure 8.35). These "tabbed panels" are primitive; that is, the labeled tabs are not separated. On the other hand, these tabbed panels do indicate the currently selected tab, and the label is fairly well connected to the panel.

The primitiveness of these tabs is difficult to understand, because at the top of the same page is another, better-designed set of tabs. They are for switching between various services of the parent company, American Express (Figure 8.36). They exhibit none of the three common flaws of tabbed panels on the Web. More coordination between designers could have improved ITN's poor tabs.

Label Not Connected to Panel

In the "nice try, but no cigar" category are tabs that visually separate different labels and mark the currently selected tab but have no visible connection to their corresponding panel. Their designers tried so hard to create nice tabs, but overlooked one important detail: When a tab is selected, it comes to the front and appears physically connected to—that is, contiguous with—its panel. If it doesn't do that, it may be a reasonable switching control, but it won't be recognized by users as tabs.

Fedex.com provides a good example. The site's main navigation bar appears as a set of orange tablike buttons near the top of the page (Figure 8.37). Though "tablike," these are not tabs, because there is no visible continuity between the selected tab and the corresponding content page.

WalMart.com shows what Web designers sometimes do to create a visual connection between the tabs and the corresponding content panels. Under the labeled tabs is a thin strip in the same color as the selected tab (Figure 8.38)—sorry, not good enough. The colored strip is too thin to give an impression that the tab connects to the panel below.

Current Tab Not Indicated

Possibly the worst tabs I have seen are those on the Acer America website, *AAC.Acer.com*. The main navigation bar is a set of "tabs" at the top of the content area of each page. The "tabs" commit *both* of the aforementioned flaws: The labeled "tabs" are all run together, and the selected tab does not appear connected to its corresponding panel. These "tabs" also commit the third flaw: The currently selected tab is not marked (Figure 8.39).

One could argue that Acer America doesn't have tabs—just a poorly designed horizontal navigation bar. However, the site is clearly designed to match the main Acer site, *Acer.com*. *Acer.com's* navigation bar, though initially looking similar to Acer America's, looks much more like tabs when an item is selected (Figure 8.40).

AVOIDING THE BLOOPER

A tabbed panel on the Web should look and act like tabs. Otherwise, it may be a horizontal navigation bar, but it isn't tabs and won't exploit people's experience with tabbed panels in desktop software and physical tabbed cards and pages.

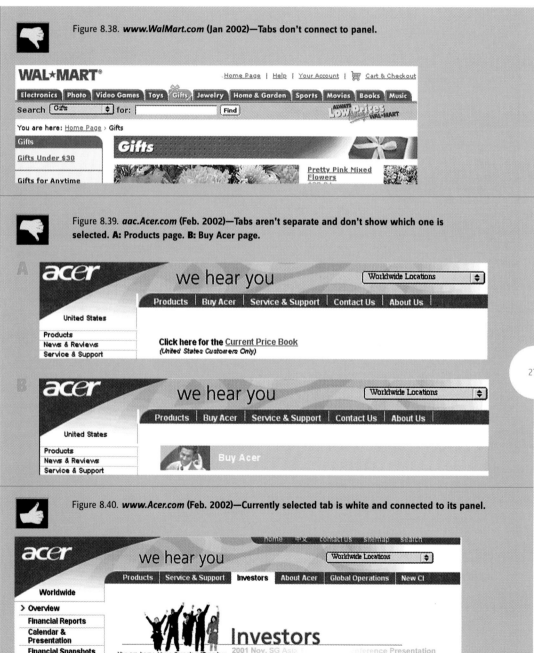

Figure 8.38. **www.WalMart.com (Jan 2002)—Tabs don't connect to panel.**

Figure 8.39. **aac.Acer.com (Feb. 2002)—Tabs aren't separate and don't show which one is selected. A: Products page. B: Buy Acer page.**

Figure 8.40. **www.Acer.com (Feb. 2002)—Currently selected tab is white and connected to its panel.**

275

Designing Tabs for the Web

Eventually, HTML or its successors should provide a standard tabbed panel component. It would be interpreted and presented by the browser, just as form controls such as radiobuttons are today. Until that day, Web designers will continue to have to "grow their own" tabbed panels.

Guidelines for designing tabbed panels that users will recognize as tabs can be devised simply by reversing the three flaws described earlier:

> *Separate labels.* Labeled tabs should be visibly separated from each other.

> *Connect tabs to panels.* Labeled tabs should appear contiguous with or connected to their corresponding panel. The best way to do this is to make the background of the panel the same color as the labeled tab and omit any visible line separating the tab from the panel.

> *Mark current tab.* The tabs should indicate the currently selected tab. If the tabs are well connected to their panels, that may be enough (as it is in desktop software). However, additional ways of marking the current tab can't hurt, for example, increased size, boldness of label, and color.

The Ideal: Desktop GUI Tabs

Consider tabbed panels in desktop GUI software to be the ideal. Tabs on the Web should look and act as much like GUI tabs as possible. The less like GUI tabs they are, the less likely Web users will be to recognize them as tabs (Figure 8.41).

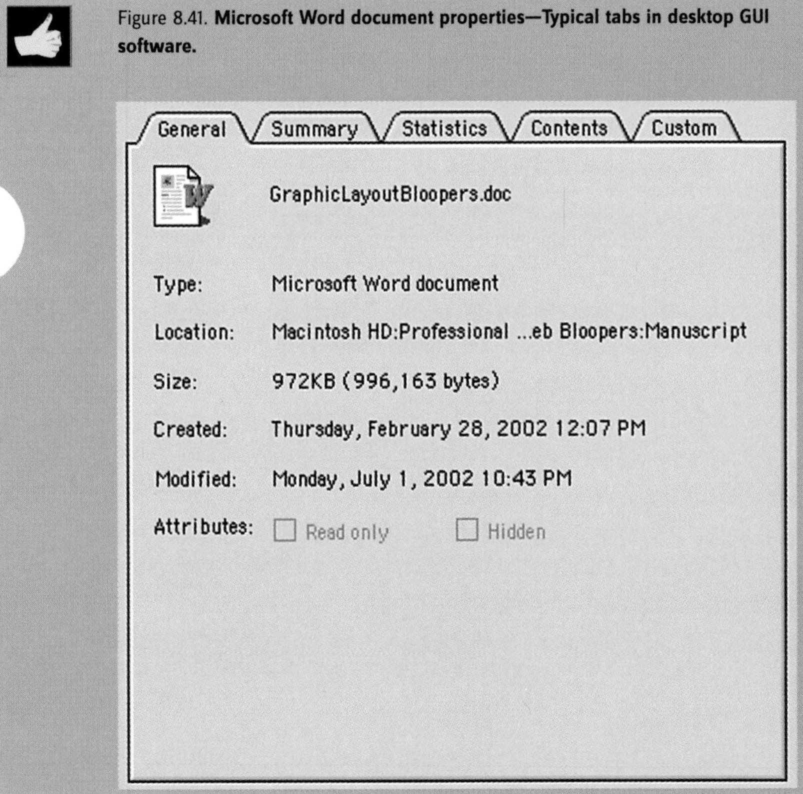

Good Web Tabs

The best tabs I have seen on the Web are at *AskJeeves.com* and *ESPN.com*. The tabs at these two sites follow all three design guidelines and as a result look very much like the tabs computer users know from desktop software (Figure 8.42).

A Band Is Better than Nothing

Remember the guideline that labeled tabs should appear connected to their respective panels. Sometimes it isn't feasible for the whole background of a tab's corresponding panel to be the same color as the labeled tab. A way to ap-

Figure 8.41. **Microsoft Word document properties—Typical tabs in desktop GUI software.**

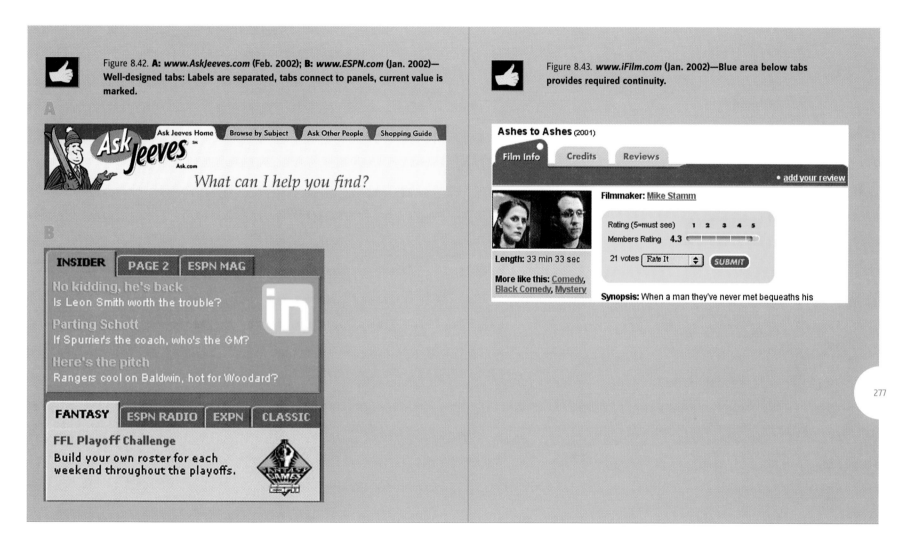

Figure 8.42. **A: *www.AskJeeves.com*** (Feb. 2002); **B: *www.ESPN.com*** (Jan. 2002)—Well-designed tabs: Labels are separated, tabs connect to panels, current value is marked.

Figure 8.43. ***www.iFilm.com*** (Jan. 2002)—Blue area below tabs provides required continuity.

proximate visual continuity is to have the tabs connect to a strip of the same color, hopefully with some data and controls on it. For the approximation to work, the strip must be at least 5 cm (¼ inch) wide. We saw in the *WalMart.com* example (see Figure 8.38) that a thin, colored line below the tabs doesn't create the effect of visual continuity between the tabs and the panels.

An example of a fairly successful approximation to tabs can be found at *iFilm.com* (Figure 8.43).

EPILOGUE

In the Introduction, I said that the Web has far to go before achieving the level of quality required for acceptance by the general population. What does "far to go" mean? It means we have our work cut out for us. Eliminating the common bloopers described in this book would be a good start.

Let's get to work.

APPENDICES

Appendix A   Memo to Managers

In producing websites, Web services, and Web applications, the decisions and practices of managers are at least as important as those of designers and implementers. Often, bloopers by developers are caused by bloopers by their managers.

This appendix summarizes the three biggest bloopers development managers make and how to avoid them. For more details see Johnson (2000, Chapter 8).

Assigning Jobs to the Wrong People

Imagine you're planning your dream house. you want state-of-the-art electrical wiring, so you hire a top-notch electrician to design that aspect of the house. But your budget is limited, so you also ask the electrician to design the house's plumbing, heating, insulation, frame, roof, and foundation. While you're at it, you ask the electrician to decorate the interior and paint the exterior.

Ridiculous as this scenario sounds, it's precisely what many organizations do with properties far more valuable than any dream house: their websites. People who are professionals at certain tasks are assigned additional tasks for which they are not. This amounts to entrusting the design of a site partly or mostly to amateurs.

One increasingly sees job announcements seeking a combination of programmer, graphic artist, interaction designer, usability tester, and technical writer all in one person. Take the following for example:

BankOfTheWeb seeks a Web designer with extensive experience in task analysis, interaction design, focus groups, user studies, DHTML, XML, JavaScript, Java, PhotoShop, Dreamweaver, and Flash. Excellent writing skills a plus.

Such people are extremely rare—perhaps nonexistent. Certainly, some people think they know everything. However, it is more common for people to know their limitations and welcome expert help in areas outside their competence. For example, Web programmers I have worked with are often grateful when a skilled writer relieves them of the responsibility for instructions and error messages. Job announcements such as the aforementioned one just represent wishful thinking by managers facing tight schedules and limited budgets.

If a person assigned to design part of a website lacks the relevant skills, experience, and guidelines, then part of the site is being designed by an amateur. The likely result will be some of the bloopers described in this book. Any such bloopers are the fault not of the people who commit them, but of their *managers.*

To avoid amateurish websites laden with bloopers, get the right people for the job:

> Task analysis, navigation, transactions, forms, and other interactive aspects of a site should be designed by experienced interaction or user-interface designers.

> Text in a site, especially link labels, instructions, and error messages, should be written—or at least reviewed or edited—by technical writers.

> Site color schemes, page templates, icons, and custom graphic elements should be designed by graphic designers.

> Sites, especially those with dynamic pages, should be implemented by skilled Web developers.

Trying to Slap a Usable User Interface On at the End

If a site's functionality and infrastructure are developed without concern for usability, the development team will have a hard time putting a user-friendly website on top of it all. Developing an easy-to-navigate, easy-to-use website requires designing for usability from start to finish, from top to bottom, from back to front.

Ensuring that this happens is the obvious responsibility of development managers and site architects. Other members of a Web development team must focus on their assigned portions or aspects of the project. If management doesn't maintain oversight of the big picture, no one will. The likely result will be a site that supports tasks poorly and has components that don't work well together, yielding a poor experience for users—that is, if the site has users.

283

Releasing without Testing on Users

As a website or Web application is developed, important design decisions and assumptions are made that affect its usability and usefulness. No matter how good the designers are, these design decisions should be validated through usability testing, long before the site is released. By the time a site is ready for release, many design decisions are deeply entrenched, either in the site architecture or in developers' egos, and can be revisited and changed only at great expense. Usability tests should be done when the design and architecture are incomplete and therefore still malleable. A website or application that is released without having first been usability tested is at high risk of having no appreciable audience.

Another point some development managers miss is that conducting a usability test should be accompanied by a commitment to spend time and effort fixing usability problems uncovered by the test. Amazingly, some development organizations conduct usability tests but don't allocate time or resources to do anything about the test findings before releasing their sites.

Appendix B   Websites Cited

This appendix lists all the websites that are cited as examples in the book. Sites cited as examples of bloopers are listed separately from those cited as examples of how to *avoid* bloopers.

For each website, the following information is provided:

> Web address (URL)

> Dates viewed for this book

> Brief description of site

> Chapters and bloopers in which it appears in the book

SITES USED AS EXAMPLES OF BLOOPERS (NEGATIVE EXAMPLES)

Anonymous Client Site and Internal Web Application (Nov. 2000, Apr. 2002, July 2002)
A fortune 100 company.

Chapter 2	Blooper 10: Pointless Choice
Chapter 4	Blooper 22: Making People Type
	Blooper 23: Intolerant Data Fields
Chapter 6	Blooper 42: Speaking Geek
Chapter 8	Blooper 57: Unobtrusive Error Messages

37Signals.com (Jan. 2002) A Web design firm.

Chapter 1	Blooper 1: Home Page Identity Crisis

AA.com (Sept. 2001, May 2002) American Airlines.

Chapter 2	Blooper 10: Pointless Choice
	Blooper 12: Clueless Back-end

AAC.Acer.com (Feb. 2002) Acer America Corporation, U.S. subsidiary of Acer Corporation.

Chapter 8	Blooper 60: Terrible Tabs

Acer.com (Dec. 2001, Feb. 2002) Acer Corporation, a manufacturer and vendor of computer equipment.

Chapter 1	Blooper 1: Home Page Identity Crisis
	Blooper 4: Conflicting Content
Chapter 3	Blooper 15: Site Reflects Organizational Chart
Chapter 7	Blooper 50: Bizarre Buttons: Click Target Smaller than It Seems

ACM.org (Mar. 2000, Jan. 2002, May 2002, Sept. 2002) The Association of Computing Machinery, a professional organization for computer professionals.

Chapter 5	Blooper 31: Baffling Search Controls
Chapter 6	Blooper 41: Too Much Text
	Blooper 46: Inconsistent Style

ACM.org/SIGCHI and **/CHI2002** (Apr. 2002) The Association of Computing Machinery's Special Interest Group on Computer-Human Interaction, a professional organization.

Chapter 6	Blooper 42: Speaking Geek

Agilent.com (Feb. 2001, Jan. 2002) Agilent, an instrument manufacturer spun off from Hewlett-Packard.

Chapter 2	Blooper 9: Requiring Unneeded Data
Chapter 4	Blooper 24: No Defaults
Chapter 7	Blooper 51: Wrapped Links: How Many?

Amazon.com (Feb. 2002, May 2002) E-commerce site that sells books and other products.

Chapter 3	Blooper 20: The Circle Game: Active Link to Here
Chapter 7	Blooper 48: Links Don't Look Like Links

AA.com (Oct. 2002) American Airlines.

Chapter 4	Blooper 26: Compulsory Clicking: No Default Input Focus

AmericanExpress.com (Jan. 2002) Travel agency and financial services.

Chapter 6	Blooper 46: Inconsistent Style

Andersen.com (Mar. 2002) Well-known accounting firm.

Chapter 7	Blooper 53: Been There, Done That? Can't Tell

Angelfire.com (Dec. 2001) Web portal and web-hosting service.

Chapter 8	Blooper 55: Camouflaged Text

Audi.com (Feb. 2002) Audi automobiles.

Chapter 6	Blooper 42: Speaking Geek

AYA.Yale.edu (June 2002) Yale University Alumni Association.

Introduction	
Chapter 7	Blooper 52: " Click <u>Here</u>": Burying Links in Text

BarnesAndNoble.com (Dec. 2001, Jan. 2002, Mar. 2002) Barnes and Noble, a bookseller.

Chapter 3	Blooper 18: Not Linking Directly
Chapter 5	Blooper 36: Needle in a Haystack: Piles of Irrelevant Hits
Chapter 6	Blooper 43: Calling Site Visitors "User"

285

BookPool.com (Jan. 2002). Online bookseller.

        Chapter 6   Blooper 43: Calling Site Visitors "User"

CalPerfs.Berkeley.edu (Mar. 2002) Concert-management affiliate of the University of California at Berkeley.

        Chapter 3   Blooper 17: Deceptive Duplicate Links

CalShakes.org (July 2002) California Shakespeare Festival.

        Chapter 2   Blooper 8: Redundant Requests

CharityFocus.org (Mar. 2001) Non-profit organization that develops websites for other non-profit organizations.

        Chapter 4   Blooper 28: Checkboxes or Radiobuttons

CheapTickets.com (Feb. 2002) Discount airline travel agency.

        Chapter 2   Blooper 11: Omitting Important Options

ChicagoFed.org (Nov. 2000, Feb. 2001, Sept. 2002) Federal Reserve Bank, Chicago branch.

        Chapter 8   Blooper 54: Tiny Text

                          Blooper 55: Camouflaged Text

                          Blooper 58: Shades of Beige: Color Differences Too Subtle

CIO-dpi.gc.ca (Dec. 2000) Treasury Board of Canada, Chief Information Office.

        Introduction

Citibank.com (Jan. 2002, July 2002) Online personal banking service of CitiBank.

        Chapter 2   Blooper 14: Agonizing Task Flow

        Chapter 8   Blooper 57: Unobtrusive Error Messages

Citibusiness.com (Mar. 2002) Online business banking service of CitiBank.

        Chapter 4   Blooper 30: Mysterious Controls

CL.UH.edu (May 2002) University of Houston at Clear Lake.

        Chapter 4   Blooper 29: Looks Editable but Isn't

CNN.com (Apr. 2002) Cable Network News broadcaster.

        Chapter 5   Blooper 32: Dueling Search Controls

Comdex.com (Sept. 2001) Information Technology conference and expo.

        Chapter 7   Blooper 49: Non-Links Look Like Links

ComputerWorld.com (Jan. 2002) Computer industry magazine.

        Chapter 3   Blooper 20: The Circle Game: Active Link to Here

Connectix.com (Jan. 2002, Feb. 2002) Connectix, Inc., a software company.

Chapter 3	Blooper 17: Deceptive Duplicate Links
Chapter 6	Blooper 44: Insider Jargon
	Blooper 47: Typos and Grammos: Sloppy Writing
Chapter 8	Blooper 58: Shades of Beige: Color Differences Too Subtle

Continental.com (Feb. 2001, May 2002) Continental Airlines.

Chapter 2	Blooper 8: Redundant Requests
	Blooper 10: Pointless Choice
	Blooper 12: Clueless Back-end
Chapter 4	Blooper 26: Compulsory Clicking: No Default Input Focus
Chapter 6	Blooper 43: Calling Site Visitors "User"
Chapter 7	Blooper 50: Bizarre Buttons: Click Target Smaller than It Seems

CPSR.org (Jan. 2002) Computer Professionals for Social Responsibility, an organization that examines the impact of computer technology on society.

Chapter 5	Blooper 32: Dueling Search Controls

CRLA.net (Dec. 2001, Feb. 2002) College Reading and Learning Association.

Chapter 7	Blooper 50: Bizarre Buttons: Click Target Smaller than It Seems
	Blooper 52: "Click Here": Burying Links in Text

CSMonitor.com (Jan. 2002) Christian Science Monitor newspaper.

Chapter 7	Blooper 50: Bizarre Buttons: Click Target Smaller than It Seems

DenPlan.co.uk (Feb. 2002) Dental insurance website in England.

Chapter 4	Blooper 30: Mysterious Controls

Dice.com (Jan. 2002) Online job-search service.

Chapter 5	Blooper 31: Baffling Search Controls
	Blooper 36: Needle in a Haystack: Piles of Irrelevant Hits
	Blooper 39: Search Terms Not Shown
Chapter 7	Blooper 49: Non-Links Look Like Links

DigiGuide.com (Feb. 2002, Apr. 2002) Online television program schedule.

Chapter 5	Blooper 33: Hits Look Alike
	Blooper 40: Number of Hits Not Revealed
Chapter 6	Blooper 45: Variable Vocabulary: Different Words for the Same Thing

DMV.CA.gov (Jan. 2002, Sept. 2002) California Department of Motor Vehicles.

Chapter 3	Blooper 19: Lost in Space: Current Page Not Indicated
Chapter 5	Blooper 31: Baffling Search Controls
Chapter 7	Blooper 53: Been There, Done That? Can't Tell

Earthlink.net (July 2001, Sept. 2001, Jan. 2002) Earthlink, an Internet service provider.

Chapter 2	Blooper 8: Redundant Requests
	Blooper 9: Requiring Unneeded Data
	Blooper 13: Dead-end Paths: *Now* You Tell Me!
Chapter 4	Blooper 30: Mysterious Controls
Chapter 6	Blooper 42: Speaking Geek

Earthwatch.org (Jan. 2002) The Earthwatch Institute, an organization that provides funding and volunteers for environmental research projects.

Chapter 1	Blooper 4: Conflicting Content

eBay.com (Jan. 2002) Online auction service.

Chapter 6	Blooper 43: Calling Site Visitors "User"

eDesignCorp.com (Dec. 2001) Design firm.

Chapter 2	Blooper 10: Pointless Choice

EDD.CA.gov (July 2002) California state government Employment Development Department, where—among other things—citizens can apply for unemployment benefits.

Chapter 4	Blooper 23: Intolerant Data Fields

Enron.com (Mar. 2002) Enron Corporation, an energy company that, in late 2001, declared bankruptcy after being exposed in a scandal involving price-manipulation and questionable accounting practices.

Chapter 1	Blooper 5: Outdated Content
Chapter 3	Blooper 20: The Circle Game: Active Link to Here
Chapter 5	Blooper 40: Number of Hits Not Revealed
Chapter 7	Blooper 49: Non-Links Look Like Links
	Blooper 53: Been There, Done That? Can't Tell

ERCB.com/DDJ (Sept. 2002) *Dr. Dobb's Journal,* a computer magazine.

Chapter 7	Blooper 49: Non-Links Look Like Links

Erlbaum.com (Feb. 2002) Lawrence Erlbaum Associates, a book publisher.

Chapter 4	Blooper 27: Lame Label Placement
Chapter 5	Blooper 38: Crazy Search Behavior
	Blooper 39: Search Terms Not Shown
Chapter 6	Blooper 45: Variable Vocabulary: Different Words for the Same Thing
Chapter 8	Blooper 59: Dead or Alive? Active Buttons Look Inactive

Eudora.com (July 2001) Customer service site for email software marketed by Qualcomm, a software and telecommunications company.

Chapter 3	Blooper 17: Deceptive Duplicate Links

Evite.com (Sept. 2002) Web-based invitation service.

Chapter 4	Blooper 25: Faulty Defaults

Fedex.com (Jan. 2002) Mailing and freight delivery service.

Chapter 8	Blooper 60: Terrible Tabs

FeldenkraisGuild.com (Oct. 2002) The Feldenkrais Guild, a professional organization of movement therapists.

Chapter 3	Blooper 21: Missing Links: It's *Back* or Nothing
Chapter 5	Blooper 37: Hits Sorted Uselessly
Chapter 6	Blooper 42: Speaking Geek

FinancialEngines.com (Sept. 2002) Investment portfolio advice service.

Chapter 6	Blooper 42: Speaking Geek
	Blooper 43: Calling Site Visitors "User"
	Blooper 46: Inconsistent Style
Chapter 8	Blooper 54: Tiny Text

FrontierAirlines.com (Sept. 2002) Frontier Airlines.

Chapter 8	Blooper 54: Tiny Text

Ford.com (Sept. 2002) Ford Motor Company, an automobile maker.

Chapter 4	Blooper 26: Compulsory Clicking: No Default Text Input Focus

Galor.com (Sept. 2002) Software company.

Chapter 7	Blooper 49: Non-Links Look Like Links

Greyhound.com (Jan. 2002) Greyhound Bus Company.

| Chapter 2 | Blooper 12: Clueless Back-end |
| Chapter 7 | Blooper 52: "Click Here": Burying Links in Text |

HauteAtHome.com (Jan. 2002) Online vendor of gourmet meals.

| Chapter 5 | Blooper 37: Hits Sorted Uselessly |
| Chapter 6 | Blooper 44: Insider Jargon |

House.gov (Nov. 2001) The U.S. Government House of Representatives.

| Chapter 2 | Blooper 9: Requiring Unneeded Data |

HP.com (July 2001) Hewlett-Packard, a computer, instrument, and electronics firm.

| Chapter 4 | Blooper 30: Mysterious Controls |

HotelDiscount.com (Mar. 2002) Online hotel-booking service.

| Chapter 7 | Blooper 48: Links Don't Look Like Links |

IEEE.org (Dec. 2001, Oct. 2002) The Institute of Electrical and Electronics Engineers, a professional organization for engineers.

| Chapter 3 | Blooper 18: Not Linking Directly |
| Chapter 4 | Blooper 26: Compulsory Clicking: No Default Text Input Focus |

iFilm.com (Jan. 2002) Online movie guide.

Chapter 3	Blooper 16: Numerous Navigation Schemes
	Blooper 20: The Circle Game: Active Link to Here
Chapter 5	Blooper 35: Search Myopia: Missing Relevant Items

IGC.org (May 2002) The Institute for Global Communication, an organization that promotes Internet communication among politically progressive groups.

| Chapter 3 | Blooper 18: Not Linking Directly |
| Chapter 5 | Blooper 31: Baffling Search Controls |

Intel.com (Mar. 2002) Intel Corporation, maker of computer microchips.

| Chapter 4 | Blooper 23: Intolerant Data Fields |
| Chapter 8 | Blooper 54: Tiny Text |

IOBA.org (Feb. 2002) Independent Online Booksellers Association.

| Chapter 4 | Blooper 27: Lame Label Placement |

ITN.net (Feb. 2002) Travel-booking website operated by American Express.

Chapter 4	Blooper 27: Lame Label Placement
	Blooper 30: Mysterious Controls
Chapter 6	Blooper 43: Calling Site Visitors "User"
Chapter 8	Blooper 58: Shades of Beige: Color Differences Too Subtle

JacksonAndPerkins.com (Sept. 2002) Online flower store.

| Chapter 4 | Blooper 25: Faulty Defaults |

Jeep.com (Sept. 2002) Maker of Jeep automobiles.

| Chapter 6 | Blooper 41: Too Much Text |

LATimes.com (Apr. 2002) Los Angeles Times newspaper.

| Chapter 5 | Blooper 32: Dueling Search Controls |
| | Blooper 34: Duplicate Hits |

Learn2.com (Jan. 2002) Educational resources.

| Chapter 6 | Blooper 43: Calling Site Visitors " User" |

LIU.edu (Mar. 2002) Long Island University.

| Chapter 4 | Blooper 27: Lame Label Placement |
| | Blooper 28: Checkboxes or Radiobuttons |

LLBean.com (Nov. 2000, Feb. 2002), E-commerce site of an outdoor equipment mail-order store.

| Chapter 4 | Blooper 24: No Defaults |
| | Blooper 27: Lame Label Placement |

Lycos.com (Feb. 1999) Web Search service.

| Chapter 5 | Blooper 33: Hits Look Alike |

Mailman Mailing-list management software, and all sites that use it.

| Chapter 4 | Blooper 30: Mysterious Controls |

Maps.Yahoo.com (Apr. 2002) Map service of online directory Yahoo.com.

| Chapter 6 | Blooper 43: Calling Site Visitors "User" |

Microsoft.com (Feb. 2001) Microsoft Corporation, a software company.

Chapter 2	Blooper 8: Redundant Requests
Chapter 3	Blooper 17: Deceptive Duplicate Links
Chapter 4	Blooper 23: Intolerant Data Fields
Chapter 8	Blooper 55: Camouflaged Text

MSDN.Microsoft.com (Feb. 2002) Microsoft Developers' Network website.

Chapter 3	Blooper 20: The Circle Game: Active Link to Here

MKP.com (Apr. 2002, June 2002) Morgan Kaufmann Publisher, a book publisher. Publisher of this book.

Chapter 1	Blooper 5: Outdated Content
Chapter 3	Blooper 21: Missing Links: It's *Back* or Nothing
Chapter 4	Blooper 25: Faulty Defaults

Monterey.com (Jan. 2002, Mar. 2002) Tourism-promotion website provided by the Chamber of Commerce of Monterey, California.

Chapter 3	Blooper 17: Deceptive Duplicate Links
	Blooper 18: Not Linking Directly
Chapter 4	Blooper 30: Mysterious Controls

NationalAcademies.org (Apr. 2002) Organization for the U.S. National Academy of Sciences and National Research Council.

Chapter 6	Blooper 47: Typos and Grammos: Sloppy Writing

Netscape.com (June 2002) Netscape, a software company that distributes a popular Web browser, and also a Web service provider.

Chapter 1	Blooper 3: Unhelpful Descriptions

NHASP.org (Jan. 2002) The New Hampshire Association of School Principals.

Chapter 1	Blooper 7: Unfinished Content
Chapter 8	Blooper 56: Centering Everything

NPR.org (Mar. 2000) National Public Radio (U.S.).

Chapter 5	Blooper 31: Baffling Search Controls

NSF.org (Sept. 2002) NSF International, a health and safety nonprofit organization (not the National Science Foundation).

Chapter 3	Blooper 20: The Circle Game: Active Link to Here

NWA.com (Sept. 2001, Feb. 2002) Northwest Airlines.

Chapter 1	Blooper 2: Confusing Classifications
Chapter 2	Blooper 12: Clueless Back-end

OfficeMax.com (Jan. 2002) Office equipment, furniture, and supply store.

Chapter 6	Blooper 42: Speaking Geek
Chapter 7	Blooper 49: Non-Links Look Like Links
	Blooper 53: Been There, Done That? Can't Tell

Pitsco-legodacta.com (Feb. 2002) Pitsco-LEGO Dacta, which sells LEGO kits and other educational toys.

Chapter 1	Blooper 3: Unhelpful Descriptions
Chapter 2	Blooper 11: Omitting Important Options
Chapter 4	Blooper 27: Lame Label Placement
Chapter 7	Blooper 52: "Click <u>Here</u>": Burying Links in Text

ProxyVote.com (Oct. 2001) Service that allows stockholders to vote online in corporate elections.

Chapter 2	Blooper 8: Redundant Requests
	Blooper 10: Pointless Choice

PWC.com (Jan. 2002) Seems to be an e-commerce search website, owned by UltimateSearch.com.

Chapter 1	Blooper 1: Home Page Identity Crisis

PWCGlobal.com (Jan. 2002) PriceWaterhouseCoopers, a large "professional services" (accounting) firm.

Chapter 1	Blooper 1: Home Page Identity Crisis

RadioShack.com (Jan. 2002) Electronics store.

Chapter 5	Blooper 38: Crazy Search Behavior
Chapter 7	Blooper 51: Wrapped Links: How Many?
Chapter 8	Blooper 59: Dead or Alive? Active Buttons Look Inactive

Rational.com (Feb. 2002) Developer of software for software development.

Chapter 3	Blooper 16: Numerous Navigation Schemes
	Blooper 17: Deceptive Duplicate Links

RealEstate.com (Sept. 2002) Online real-estate broker.

Chapter 3	Blooper 19: Lost in Space: Current Page Not Indicated
Chapter 7	Blooper 50: Bizarre Buttons: Click Target Smaller than It Seems

RCN.com (Nov. 2001) A site containing position papers on technology policy.

Chapter 3	Blooper 20: The Circle Game: Active Link to Here

RitzCamera.com (Apr. 2002) Ritz Camera stores.

Chapter 7	Blooper 50: Bizarre Buttons: Click Target Smaller than It Seems

RussellStover.com (Jan. 2002) Russell Stover, a candy company.

Chapter 1	Blooper 5: Outdated Content
Chapter 3	Blooper 21: Missing Links: It's *Back* or Nothing
Chapter 8	Blooper 55: Camouflaged Text
	Blooper 57: Unobtrusive Error Messages

SBC.com (Mar. 2000) Parent company of Pacific Bell, Southern Bell, and other telecommunications companies.

        Chapter 5   Blooper 31: Baffling Search Controls

Sciencenter.org (July 2002) Community science learning center in New York.

        Chapter 8   Blooper 55: Camouflaged Text

SDExpo.com (Feb. 2002) Software Development Conference and Expo.

        Chapter 7   Blooper 50: Bizarre Buttons: Click Target Smaller than It Seems

                                    Blooper 52: "Click <u>Here</u>": Burying Links in Text

SFGov.org/juryduty (Feb. 2002) Jury-duty website of the Superior Court of San Francisco.

        Chapter 3   Blooper 16: Numerous Navigation Schemes

SGI.com (Jan. 2002) Computer company.

        Chapter 3   Blooper 15: Site Reflects Organizational Chart

Sibelius.com (Jan. 2002) Sibelius, a music-software company.

        Chapter 2   Blooper 10: Pointless Choice

        Chapter 3   Blooper 21: Missing Links: It's *Back* or Nothing

SiliconValley.com (June 2002) Online news magazine.

        Chapter 5   Blooper 33: Hits Look Alike

        Chapter 8   Blooper 60: Terrible Tabs

SIwafer.com (Mar. 2002) International Wafer Service, a vendor of silicon wafers for electronics.

        Chapter 1   Blooper 7: Unfinished Content

Slims-SF.com (Oct. 2001) Slims, a music nightclub in San Francisco, California.

        Chapter 1   Blooper 6: Missing or Useless Content

Slip.net (July 2001) Internet service provider (now dissolved).

        Chapter 4   Blooper 24: No Defaults

Sony.com (Dec. 2001) Sony Corporation, a manufacturer of electronic appliances.

        Chapter 4   Blooper 23: Intolerant Data Fields

Southwest.com (Sept. 2002) Southwest Airlines.

        Chapter 2   Blooper 8: Redundant Requests

Stanford.edu (Sept. 2001, Jan. 2002) Stanford University.

Chapter 1	Blooper 7: Unfinished Content
Chapter 7	Blooper 48: Links Don't Look Like Links
	Blooper 52: "Click Here": Burying Links in Text

StanfordBookstore.com (Sept. 2002) Stanford University Bookstore.

Chapter 4	Blooper 24: No Defaults
	Blooper 25: Faulty Defaults
Chapter 6	Blooper 41: Too Much Text

TechReview.com (Jan. 2002) *Technology Review,* a publication of the Massachusetts Institute of Technology (M.I.T.).

Chapter 4	Blooper 27: Lame Label Placement

ThePattySite.com (Jan. 2002) Offers resources for Dreamweaver developers.

Chapter 1	Blooper 7: Unfinished Content

ThisDayInMusic.com (Mar. 2001) Web service based in the U.K. that looks up the number-one popular song for a specified date.

Chapter 4	Blooper 25: Faulty Defaults

TicketWeb.com (Jan. 2002) Online ticket-purchasing service.

Chapter 4	Blooper 28: Checkboxes or Radiobuttons

TowerRecords.com (Sept. 2002) Record store.

Chapter 4	Blooper 26: Compulsory Clicking: No Default Text Input Focus

TransitInfo.org (Jan. 2002) Public transit information website of the Santa Clara County (California) Transit Authority.

Chapter 6	Blooper 42: Speaking Geek

Travelocity.com (June 2002) Online travel agency.

Chapter 2	Blooper 11: Omitting Important Options
Chapter 8	Blooper 59: Dead or Alive? Active Buttons Look Inactive

UBid.com (Dec. 2001, Sept. 2002) Online service for bidding on new products.

Chapter 2	Blooper 8: Redundant Requests
Chapter 3	Blooper 17: Deceptive Duplicate Links
Chapter 4	Blooper 29: Looks Editable but Isn't

UNEX.UCLA.edu (Feb. 2002) University of California at Los Angeles.

Chapter 2	Blooper 11: Omitting Important Options

United.com (Feb. 2002, Mar. 2002) United Airlines.

Chapter 1	Blooper 4: Conflicting Content
	Blooper 6: Missing or Useless Content
Chapter 2	Blooper 7: Redundant Requests
Chapter 4	Blooper 23: Intolerant Data Fields
	Blooper 26: Compulsory Clicking: No Default Input Focus
Chapter 5	Blooper 36: Needle in a Haystack: Piles of Irrelevant Hits
Chapter 6	Blooper 42: Speaking Geek
Chapter 7	Blooper 51: Wrapped Links: How Many?

UPAssoc.org (Apr. 2002) Usability Professionals Association.

Chapter 7	Blooper 49: Non-Links Look Like Links

USPS.gov (June 2002) The United States Postal Service.

Chapter 1	Blooper 2: Confusing Classifications
Chapter 4	Blooper 22: Making People Type

ValcoElectronics.com (Jan. 2002) E-commerce website of Valco Electronics, an electronics store.

Chapter 1	Blooper 6: Missing or Useless Content
Chapter 3	Blooper 19: Lost in Space: Current Page Not Indicated
Chapter 6	Blooper 47: Typos and Grammos: Sloppy Writing
Chapter 8	Blooper 56: Centering Everything

VitaminShoppe.com (Jan. 2002, Feb. 2002) Online vitamin store.

Chapter 5	Blooper 34: Duplicate Hits
	Blooper 36: Needle in a Haystack: Piles of Irrelevant Hits
Chapter 6	Blooper 43: Calling Site Visitors "User"
Chapter 8	Blooper 56: Centering Everything

WalMart.com (Jan. 2002) E-commerce website of Wal-Mart, a large retail chain store.

Chapter 1	Blooper 2: Confusing Classifications
Chapter 8	Blooper 60: Terrible Tabs

Weather.com (May 2002) Online weather information service.

Chapter 2	Blooper 12: Clueless Back-end

Weather.Yahoo.com (May 2002) Weather service of online directory Yahoo.com.

Chapter 2	Blooper 12: Clueless Back-end

WebAdTech.com (Dec. 2000) E-Commerce site.

> Introduction

WiesnerBros.com (Feb. 2002) Gardening supply store.

> Chapter 7   Blooper 48: Links Don't Look Like Links

WisconSUN.org (Jan. 2002) Website that promotes solar energy in the U.S. state of Wisconsin.

> Chapter 3   Blooper 17: Deceptive Duplicate Links
> Chapter 7   Blooper 48: Links Don't Look Like Links

Yosemite.org (Feb. 2002) The Yosemite Association, an educational organization that supports Yosemite National Park.

> Chapter 7   Blooper 53: Been There, Done That? Can't Tell

ZBuyer.com (Feb. 2002) Online store that sells gadgets. A subsidiary of Amazon.com.

> Chapter 1   Blooper 2: Confusing Classifications
> Chapter 2   Blooper 10: Pointless Choice
> Chapter 3   Blooper 15: Site Reflects Organizational Chart
> Chapter 6   Blooper 44: Insider Jargon
>   Blooper 45: Variable Vocabulary: Different Words for the Same
>   Thing
>   Blooper 46: Inconsistent Style
> Chapter 8   Blooper 56: Centering Everything

SITES USED AS EXAMPLES OF HOW TO AVOID BLOOPERS (POSITIVE EXAMPLES)

37Signals.com (June 2002) A Web design firm.

> Chapter 1   Avoiding Blooper 1: Home Page Identity Crisis

AA.com (Feb. 2002) American Airlines.

> Chapter 6   Avoiding Blooper 43: Calling Site Visitors "User"

Acer.com (Feb. 2002) Acer Corporation, a manufacturer and vendor of computer equipment.

> Chapter 8   Avoiding Blooper 60: Terrible Tabs

ACM.org/SIGCHI (Nov. 2000) The Association of Computing Machinery's Special Interest Group on Computer-Human Interaction, a professional organization.

> Chapter 3   Avoiding Blooper 19: Lost in Space: Current Page Not Indicated
> Chapter 7   Avoiding Blooper 48: Links Don't Look Like Links

ACSCSN.org (Sept. 2002) The American Cancer Society's Cancer Survivors Network.

Albany.co.uk (Feb. 2002) Middleware software company.

AltaVista.com (Oct. 2002) Search engine.

Amazon.com (Feb. 2002, May 2002, Sept. 2002) E-commerce site that sells books and other products.

Amazoon.com (May 2002) Web store that gets business by having a name similar to *Amazon.com*.

AskJeeves.com (Feb. 2002) Information-search service.

BankOfAmerica.com (Mar. 2002) BankAmerica, a bank in the United States.

BarnesAndNoble.com (Dec. 2001, Mar. 2002) Barnes&Noble, a bookseller.

CA.gov (Sept. 2002) U.S. state of California.

CharityFocus.org (Mar. 2001, Sept. 2002) A nonprofit organization that develops websites for nonprofit organizations.

ChicagoFed.org (Nov. 2000, Jan. 2002) Federal Reserve Bank, Chicago branch.

Chapter 8   Avoiding Blooper 55: Camouflaged Text

                           Avoiding Blooper 58: Shades of Beige: Color Differences Too Subtle

Continental.com (June 2002) Continental Airlines.

Chapter 2   Avoiding Blooper 11: Omitting Important Options

CPSR.org (May 2002) Computer Professionals for Social Responsibility, an organization that examines the impact of computer technology on society.

Chapter 7   Avoiding Blooper 53: Been There, Done That? Can't Tell

Earthwatch.org (Jan. 2002) The Earthwatch Institute, an organization that provides funding and volunteers for environmental research projects.

Chapter 1   Avoiding Blooper 1: Home Page Identity Crisis

eng.UFL.edu (May 2002) Engineering department of the University of Florida.

Chapter 3   Avoiding Blooper 17: Deceptive Duplicate Links

Enron.com (Mar. 2002) Enron Corporation, an energy company that, in late 2001, declared bankruptcy after being exposed in a scandal involving price-manipulation and questionable accounting practices.

Chapter 1   Avoiding Blooper 5: Outdated Content

ESPN.com (Jan. 2002) A cable television network.

Chapter 8   Avoiding Blooper 60: Terrible Tabs

FeldenkraisGuild.com (Jan. 2002) The Feldenkrais Guild, a professional organization of movement therapists.

Chapter 5   Avoiding Blooper 37: Hits Sorted Uselessly

                           Avoiding Blooper 39: Search Terms Not Shown

Google.com (Sept. 2002) Popular search website.

Chapter 3   Avoiding Blooper 20: The Circle Game: Active Link to Here

Chapter 4   Avoiding Blooper 26: Compulsory Clicking: No Default Text Input Focus

                           Avoiding Blooper 27: Lame Label Placement

Chapter 5   Avoiding Blooper 31: Baffling Search Controls

Greyhound.com (Jan. 2002) Greyhound Bus Company.

Chapter 2   Avoiding Blooper 11: Omitting Important Options

HauteAtHome.com (Jan. 2002) Online vendor of gourmet meals.

Chapter 5   Avoiding Blooper 37: Hits Sorted Uselessly

IBM.com (Jan. 2002) Software, computer, and office equipment company.

    Chapter 7   Avoiding Blooper 51: Wrapped Links: How Many?

IEEE.org (Dec. 2001) The Institute of Electrical and Electronics Engineers, a professional organization for engineers.

    Chapter 7   Avoiding Blooper 50: Bizarre Buttons: Click Target Smaller than It Seems

iFilm.com (Jan. 2002) Online movie information service.

    Chapter 8   Avoiding Blooper 60: Terrible Tabs

IOBA.org (Feb. 2002) Independent Online Booksellers Association.

    Chapter 4   Avoiding Blooper 27: Lame Label Placement

IRS.gov (Sept. 2002) U.S. Internal Revenue Service, the income-tax agency.

    Chapter 7   Avoiding Blooper 50: Bizarre Buttons: Click Target Smaller than It Seems

Jeep.com (Sept. 2002) Maker of Jeep automobiles.

    Chapter 6   Avoiding Blooper 41: Too Much Text

LLBean.com (Feb. 2002), E-commerce site of an outdoor equipment mail-order store.

    Chapter 4   Avoiding Blooper 24: No Defaults

LIU.edu (Mar. 2002) Long Island University.

    Chapter 4   Avoiding Blooper 28: Checkboxes or Radiobuttons

Lycos.com (Mar. 2002) Web search service.

    Chapter 5   Avoiding Blooper 33: Hits Look Alike

Macromedia.com (June 2002) Software company known for Director and Flash products.

    Chapter 1   Avoiding Blooper 3: Unhelpful Descriptions

    Chapter 7   Avoiding Blooper 53: Been There, Done That? Can't Tell

Microsoft Word & Windows. Desktop software.

    Chapter 8   Avoiding Blooper 60: Terrible Tabs

Monterey.com (Jan. 2002, Sept. 2002) Tourism-promotion website provided by the Chamber of Commerce of Monterey, California.

    Chapter 3   Avoiding Blooper 16: Numerous Navigation Schemes

    Chapter 7   Avoiding Blooper 48: Links Don't Look Like Links

Netscape.com (June 2002) Netscape, a software company that distributes a popular Web browser, and also a Web service provider.

    Chapter 2   Avoiding Blooper 10: Pointless Choice

NetWorldMap.com (June 2002) Internet information service.

    Chapter 2   Avoiding Blooper 10: Pointless Choice

NPR.org (May 2002) National Public Radio (U.S.).

    Chapter 5   Avoiding Blooper 31: Baffling Search Controls

NWA.com (Mar. 2002) Northwest Airlines.

    Chapter 4   Avoiding Blooper 22: Making People Type

                        Avoiding Blooper 23: Intolerant Data Fields

                        Avoiding Blooper 30: Mysterious Controls

    Chapter 7   Avoiding Blooper 52: "Click Here": Burying Links in Text

OfficeMax.com (Jan. 2002) Office equipment, furniture, and supply store.

    Chapter 7   Avoiding Blooper 50: Bizarre Buttons: Click Target Smaller than It Seems

Pentagram.com (Oct. 2002) Design firm.

    Chapter 3   Avoiding Blooper 19: Lost in Space: Current Page Not Indicated

PLDstore.com (June 2002) Online store of Pitsco-LEGO Dacta, which sells LEGO kits and other educational toys.

    Chapter 2   Avoiding Blooper 11: Omitting Important Options

RealEstate.com (Sept. 2002) Online real-estate broker.

    Chapter 3   Avoiding Blooper 19: Lost in Space: Current Page Not Indicated

REI.com (Nov. 2000) Recreational Equipment, Inc., an outdoor clothing and equipment store.

    Chapter 4   Avoiding Blooper 24: No Defaults

    Chapter 8   Avoiding Blooper 57: Unobtrusive Error Messages

SBC.com (May 2002) Parent company of Pacific Bell, Southern Bell, and other telecommunications companies.

    Chapter 5   Avoiding Blooper 31: Baffling Search Controls

Sears.com (Nov. 2000, May 2002) Department store.

    Chapter 5   Avoiding Blooper 31: Baffling Search Controls

    Chapter 7   Avoiding Blooper 48: Links Don't Look Like Links

SeniorNet.org (Sept. 2002) Online resources and support for senior citizens.

    Chapter 8   Avoiding Blooper 54: Tiny Text

SharperImage.com (Nov. 2000) Store that sells gadgets.

  Chapter 1   Avoiding Blooper 3: Unhelpful Descriptions

  Chapter 5   Avoiding Blooper 31: Baffling Search Controls

Sibelius.com (Jan. 2002) Sibelius, a music-software company.

  Chapter 2   Avoiding Blooper 10: Pointless Choice

  Chapter 4   Avoiding Blooper 28: Checkboxes or Radiobuttons

Southwest.com (Sept. 2002) Southwest Airlines.

  Chapter 6   Avoiding Blooper 42: Speaking Geek

Stanford.edu (Jan. 2002) Stanford University.

  Chapter 5   Avoiding Blooper 39: Search Terms Not Shown

Sun.com (Sept. 2002) Sun Microsystems.

  Chapter 3   Avoiding Blooper 16: Numerous Navigation Schemes

United.com (Mar. 2002, June 2002, Sept. 2002) United Airlines.

  Chapter 2   Avoiding Blooper 12: Clueless Back-end

  Chapter 3   Avoiding Blooper 16: Numerous Navigation Schemes

  Chapter 4   Avoiding Blooper 22: Making People Type

UPAssoc.org (July 2001) Usability Professionals Association.

  Chapter 4   Avoiding Blooper 24: No Defaults

VitaminShoppe.com (Jan. 2002) Online vitamin store.

  Chapter 5   Avoiding Blooper 39: Search Terms Not Shown

WalMart.com (Jan. 2002) Wal-Mart, a large retail chain store.

  Chapter 6   Avoiding Blooper 43: Calling Site Visitors "User"

Weather.Yahoo.com (Apr. 2002) Weather service of online directory *Yahoo.com*.

  Chapter 6   Avoiding Blooper 43: Calling Site Visitors "User"

Yale.edu (June 2002, Sept. 2002) Yale University.

  Chapter 1   Avoiding Blooper 2: Confusing Classifications

  Chapter 3   Avoiding Blooper 16: Numerous Navigation Schemes

OTHER WEBSITES CITED (NEITHER POSITIVE NOR NEGATIVE)

SLACVM.SLAC.Stanford.edu (Dec. 1991) First U.S. website, hosted by the Stanford Linear Accelerator
Center (SLAC) of Stanford University.

> Introduction
>
> Chapter 5

UseIt.com (Sept. 2002) Jakob Nielsen's Web Usability site.

> Chapter 6

Appendix C   How This Book Was Usability Tested

This book recommends testing websites on representative users throughout development to inform design decisions and expose usability problems. The same argument can be made for this book. This book did in fact benefit from testing of two sorts.

Customer Feedback on "Release 1.0"

This book is a sequel to a similar book, and so can be considered "version 2.0." Its predecessor, *GUI Bloopers* (Johnson 2000), was published three years before. Readers of that book provided much feedback in comments posted at online bookstores, at *GUI-Bloopers.com*'s discussion area, and in email messages.

The positive feedback need not concern us here beyond noting that there was enough of it to justify a sequel. Of more interest here are readers complaints about *GUI Bloopers*. These were important input for *Web Bloopers*.

> *Verbosity.* Some readers complained that *GUI Bloopers* is more verbose than necessary. As a result, this book is much less so.

> *No figure captions.* Figures in *GUI Bloopers* were numbered and marked as good vs. bad examples, but they had no captions. Readers often had to read the surrounding text to understand the point of figures. In *Web Bloopers*, figures are captioned and annotated.

> *Made-up figures.* Many example screen images in *GUI Bloopers* were artificial, made up to illustrate particular bloopers well. In contrast, this book uses real websites as examples almost exclusively.

 > *No checklist.* Other than its Table of Contents, *GUI Bloopers* had no terse summary of all the bloopers for software developers to use as a quick-reference checklist. For *Web Bloopers*, a quick-reference list is available on the book's website: *Web-Bloopers.com*.

Pre-release Testing

In addition to feedback about its predecessor, this book benefited from usability testing of its own. Early drafts were reviewed by several experts including Web designers, interaction designers, and usability testers. These were intentionally not the academic human-computer interaction researchers who normally review books for the publisher, but rather practitioners who work on websites and Web applications. Their feedback helped:

> Focus the book on important issues

> Find good examples and choose the clearest ones

> Eliminate poor and unnecessary examples

> Eliminate unneeded text

> Organize the bloopers more coherently and usefully

In addition to pre-publication reviews, the almost-completed manuscript was given to a Web designer with instructions to try using it as a design tool and send us feedback. His main feedback was that the book needed a quick-reference blooper checklist, which, as mentioned above, we already planned based on feedback from *GUI Bloopers* readers.

Appendix D   Related Books and Websites

This book is not the first time someone has described common design mistakes. Several books and websites predate this book and deserve acknowledgment.

Previous Books that Describe and Discuss Common Web Design Mistakes

Brinck, T., Gergle, D., and Wood, S.D. *Usability for the Web: Designing Web Sites that Work.* San Francisco: Morgan-Kaufmann Publishers, 2001.

Flanders, V., and Willis, M. *Web Pages that Suck: Learn Good Design by Looking at Bad Design.* Indianapolis: Sybex, 1997. Describes common problems that plague websites, with some real examples.

Flanders, V. *Son of Web Pages that Suck: Learn Good Design by Looking at Bad Design.* Indianapolis: Sybex, 2001. The sequel.

Isaacs, E., and Walendowski, A. *Designing on Both Sides of the Screen.* Indianapolis: SAMS, 2001. Gives principles and practices for good user-interface design, from the point of view of both designers and programmers. Shows websites and other software that violates those principles.

Johnson, J. *GUI Bloopers: Don'ts and Dos for Software Developers and Web Designers.* San Francisco: Morgan-Kaufman, 2000. Describes common bloopers that make desktop software and websites difficult to use. Although most of the bloopers occur in both desktop software and on the Web, the examples are taken mainly from desktop software. Includes a short chapter devoted to Web-specific bloopers.

Krug, S. *Don't Make Me Think: A Common Sense Approach to Web Usability.* Indianapolis: New Riders, 2000. Explains in simple terms how websites should be designed, and why. Includes some examples of design flaws, with suggestions for improvement.

Nielsen, J. *Designing Web Usability: The Practice of Simplicity.* Indianapolis: New Riders, 1999. A very popular Web design book that includes real examples of Web design problems.

Nielsen, J., and Tahir, M. *Homepage Usability: Fifty Websites Deconstructed.* Indianapolis: New Riders, 2001. Points out problems in 50 real websites and describes how to fix them.

Spool, J., Schroeder, W., Snyder, C., and DeAngela, T. *Web Site Usability: A Designer's Guide.* San Francisco: Morgan-Kaufmann, 1999. Summarizes usability studies of several corporate websites. Includes examples of problems.

van Duyne, D., Landay, J., and Hong, J. *The Design of Sites: Principles, Processes, & Patterns for Crafting a Customer-Centered Web Experience.* Reading, Mass.: Addison-Wesley, 2001. Mainly about patterns to use (and reuse) in designing usable websites, but includes examples of mistakes to avoid.

Websites that Show and Discuss Common Web Design Mistakes

Web Pages That Suck *(www.webpagesthatsuck.com)*—Vincent Flanders' original site that pokes fun at bad websites and explains how to avoid following in their footsteps.

Fixing Your Website *(www.FixingYourWebsite.com)*—Vincent Flanders' business-oriented alternative to *Web Pages That Suck*. Much the same content as *Web Pages That Suck*, but more polished, less irreverent, more bottom-line focused.

UseIt.com—Jakob Nielsen's site, providing analysis, opinion, and design guidelines on Web usability. Includes Nielsen's periodic reassessment of the "top ten Web design mistakes."

UI Wizards, Inc. *(www.uiwizards.com)*—My consulting company website features a "Web Blooper of the Month."

Dey Alexander *(www.deyalexander.com)*—Usability consultant Dey Alexander's website includes a "Daily Blooper" column focusing on problems in websites.

Theo Mandel *(www.interface-design.net/Bloopers/bloopers.html)*—Usability author Theo Mandel's website includes a collection of user-interface bloopers, some of which are Web bloopers.

BIBLIOGRAPHY

Brinck, T., Gergle, D., and Wood, S.D. *Usability for the Web: Designing Web Sites that Work.* San Francisco: Morgan-Kaufmann Publishers, 2001.

Casaday, G. "Online Shopping: Or, How I Saved a Trip to the Store and Received My Items in Just 47 Fun-filled Days." *Interactions,* November-December 2001, 15–19.

Cooper, A. *The Inmates are Running the Asylum.* Indianapolis, Ind.: SAMS, 1999.

Flanders, V. *Son of Web Pages That Suck: Learn Good Design by Looking at Bad Design.* San Francisco: Sybex, 2001.

Flanders, V., and Willis, M. *Web Pages That Suck: Learn Good Design by Looking at Bad Design.* San Francisco: Sybex, 1997.

Grossman, J. *The Chicago Manual of Style: The Essential Guide for Writers, Editors, and Publishers.* Chicago: University of Chicago Press, 1993.

Isaacs, E., and Walendowski, A. *Designing from Both Sides of the Screen: How Designers and Engineers Can Collaborate to Build Cooperative Technology.* Indianapolis, Ind.: SAMS, 2001.

Johnson, J. "Modes in Non-Computer Devices." *International Journal of Man-Machine Studies,* 32: 1990, 423–438.

Johnson, J. *GUI Bloopers: Don'ts and Dos for Software Developers and Web Designers.* San Francisco: Morgan-Kaufmann Publishers, 2000.

Johnson, J., and Henderson, A. "Conceptual Models: Begin by Designing What to Design." *Interactions,* January-February 2002.

Krug, S. *Don't Make Me Think: A Common Sense Approach to Web Usability.* Indianapolis: New Riders, 2000.

Lynch, P., and Horton, S. *Web Style Guide: Basic Design Principles for Creating Web Sites.* New Haven, Conn.: Yale University Press, 2002. Available at: *info.med.yale.edu/caim/manual/index.html.*

Microsoft Corporation. *Microsoft Windows User Experience.* Redmond, Wash.: Microsoft Press, 1999.

Mullet, K., and Sano, D. *Designing Visual Interfaces: Communication Oriented Techniques.* Mountain View, Calif.: Sunsoft Press, 1995.

Nielsen, J. *Designing Web Usability: The Practice of Simplicity.* New Riders, 1999.

Nielsen, J. "User Interface Directions for the Web." *Communications of the ACM,* 42: 1999a, 65–71.

Nielsen, J., and Tahir, M. *Homepage Usability: Fifty Websites Deconstructed.* Indianapolis: New Riders, 2001.

NetCraft Web Survey. Available at *www.netcraft.com/survery/.* June 2002.

Paul, N. "Labels Slowly Build Trust in the Web." *Christian Science Monitor,* 13 May 2002, 18.

Raskin, J. *The Humane Interface: New Directions for Designing Interactive Systems.* Reading, Mass.: Addison Wesley, 2000.

Rosenfeld, L., and Morville, P. *Information Architecture for the World Wide Web.* 2nd ed. Sebastapol, Calif.: O'Reilly and Associates, 2002.

Rosson, M.B., and Carroll, J. *Usability Engineering: Scenario-Based Development of Human Computer Interaction.* San Francisco: Morgan-Kaufmann Publishers, 2001.

Rubin, J. "What Business Are You In? The Strategic Role of Usability Professionals in the 'New Economy' World." *Usability Interface,* winter 2002, 4–12.

Souza, R. "The X Internet Revives UI Design." *Forrester Tech Strategy Report,* April, 2002. Cambridge, MA: Forrester Research, Inc.

Spool, J., Scanlon, T., Schroeder, W., Snyder, C., and DeAngelo, T. *Web Site Usability: A Designer's Guide.* San Francisco: Morgan-Kaufmann Publishers, 1999.

Strunk, W., and White, E.B. *The Elements of Style.* New York: Macmillan Publishing, 1979.

van Duyne, D., Landay, J., and Hong, J. *The Design of Sites: Principles, Processes, & Patterns for Crafting a Customer-Centered Web Experience.* Reading, Mass.: Addison-Wesley, 2001.

Weinberger, E., editor. "The Analytical Language of John Wilkins." *Selected Non-Fictions by Jorge Luis Borges.* New York: Penguin Putnam, 1999.

INDEX

ABOUT THE AUTHOR

Jeff Johnson is President and Principal Consultant for UI Wizards, Inc., a product usability consulting firm based in San Francisco. He founded UI Wizards in 1996. Client companies of UI Wizards have included Advance Reality, Aspect Technologies, AT&T, Informix, InfoSpace, InXight, Oracle, Optical Microwave Networks, Inc., RightPoint Software, Silicon Graphics, Studio Archetype, Sun Microsystems, Tibco Financial Technologies, and Vitria. Prior to founding UI Wizards, Jeff worked as a user-interface designer and implementer, manager, usability tester, and researcher at Cromemco, Xerox, US West, Hewlett-Packard, and Sun Microsystems. He is the author of *GUI Bloopers: Don'ts and Do's for Software Developers and Web Designers* and has published numerous articles and book chapters on a variety of topics in human-computer interaction and technology policy (for details see his website at *www.uiwizards.com*). Jeff co-chaired the first U.S. conference on participatory design of computer systems: PDC'90. He has a B.A. degree from Yale University and a Ph.D. from Stanford University, both in experimental psychology, with additional studies in computer science.